THE PAPERS OF THE HOTHAMS, GOVERNORS OF HULL DURING THE CIVIL WAR

THE PAPERS OF THE HOTHAMS, GOVERNORS OF HULL DURING THE CIVIL WAR

edited by
ANDREW HOPPER

CAMDEN FIFTH SERIES
Volume 39

CAMBRIDGE
UNIVERSITY PRESS

FOR THE ROYAL HISTORICAL SOCIETY
University College London, Gower Street, London WC1 6BT
2011

Published by the Press Syndicate of the University of Cambridge
The Edinburgh Building, Cambridge CB2 8RU, United Kingdom
32 Avenue of the Americas, New York, NY 10013-2473, USA
477 Williamstown Road, Port Melbourne, VIC 3207, Australia
C/Orense, 4, Planta 13, 28020 Madrid, Spain
Lower Ground Floor, Nautica Building, The Water Club,
Beach Road, Granger Bay, 8005 Cape Town, South Africa

First published 2011

A catalogue record for this book is available from the British Library

ISBN 9781107016453 hardback

SUBSCRIPTIONS. The serial publications of the Royal Historical Society, *Royal Historical Society Transactions* (ISSN 0080–4401) and Camden Fifth Series (ISSN 0960–1163) volumes, may be purchased together on annual subscription. The 2011 subscription price, which includes print and electronic access (but not VAT), is £121 (US $203 in the USA, Canada, and Mexico) and includes Camden Fifth Series, volumes 38, 39, and 40 (published in April, July, and December) and Transactions Sixth Series, volume 21 (published in December). Japanese prices are available from Kinokuniya Company Ltd, P.O. Box 55, Chitose, Tokyo 156, Japan. EU subscribers (outside the UK) who are not registered for VAT should add VAT at their country's rate. VAT registered subscribers should provide their VAT registration number. Prices include delivery by air.

Subscription orders, which must be accompanied by payment, may be sent to a bookseller, subscription agent, or direct to the publisher: Cambridge University Press, The Edinburgh Building, Shaftesbury Road, Cambridge CB2 8RU, UK; or in the USA, Canada, and Mexico: Cambridge University Press, Journals Fulfillment Department, 100 Brook Hill Drive, West Nyack, New York, 10994–2133, USA.

SINGLE VOLUMES AND BACK VOLUMES. A list of Royal Historical Society volumes available from Cambridge University Press may be obtained from the Humanities Marketing Department at the address above.

Printed and bound in the United Kingdom at the University Press, Cambridge

CONTENTS

LIST OF ILLUSTRATIONS

Map

Figures

Figures 2–6 are reproduced by kind permission of the University of Leicester.

PREFACE

This volume grew out of my doctoral thesis examining parliamentarian allegiance in Yorkshire during the first civil war. The Hotham family archive proved to be a particularly rich primary source for this work, but the prominent role of the Hothams in empowering and then sabotaging the parliamentary war effort demands wider recognition. It is hoped that publishing their papers will restore the Hothams within their local context and secure their place in the national narrative of the outbreak of civil war. Highlighting the Hothams' kinship networks, their military resources, and their place within the parliamentarian coalition, this project combines all of their known papers, scattered across numerous archives, into one accessible volume. At the core of their family archive at Hull are the papers for Sir John Hotham's defence at his trial. Many of these are copies of the original letters, held by the Bodleian Library, that appear to have formed the papers for his prosecution. The neat handwriting of both Hothams has aided transcription but several of the trial papers in the family archive are frustratingly damaged and fragmented. Painstaking effort has been made with the palaeography but the full meaning of several items remains obscure.

I would like to thank Stephen Roberts for encouraging me in this project and for suggesting the Royal Historical Society as its publisher. I am also indebted to him and the History of Parliament Trust for copies of David Scott's entries on Sir John Hotham and John Hotham, which have proved very helpful. I would like to thank Ian Archer, the series editor, for his helpful advice, as well as Hester Higton and Gwenda Edwards. I am most grateful to Amanda Capern and Glenn Burgess of the University of Hull for their hospitality and encouragement, in addition to all their kind interest and support for this project. It was through Dr Capern's guidance when I was a postgraduate at the University of York that I first realized the potential of the Hothams for a collection of this nature. Barbara English, Helen Good, and Jason Peacey have all provided stimulating discussion of the Hothams. Professor English guided me on a visit to Scorborough and South Dalton, and Ms Good has been helpful with difficult parts of the palaeography. I am indebted to the archival staff at the British Library, the Bodleian Library, the Hull History Centre, and The National Archives, and for the permission of these institutions to publish transcriptions of their material relating to the Hothams. I am particularly grateful to Judy Burg and Kate Boyce, archivists of the University of Hull, who have been extremely helpful in arranging access to the family collection at the difficult time when the university archive was being transferred to the new Hull History Centre. I am thankful to Evelyn Cornell at the University of Leicester's library for access to the Fairclough Collection of portrait prints, and also to Harry Buglass of the University of Birmingham for illustrating the Hotham family tree and for the map of the East Riding. I would like to thank the University of Leicester's 'new blood' lectureship scheme for allowing me the relief from teaching and the travel expenses to complete this work. None of this would have been possible without the kind permission of Henry Durand Hotham, 8th Lord Hotham, and his son, the Hon. William Beaumont Hotham, the current owners of the Hotham papers.

Andrew Hopper
Marc Fitch House
Easter, 2010

ABBREVIATIONS

Add. MS	Additional Manuscripts
BL	British Library, London
Bodl.	Bodleian Library, University of Oxford
CJ	*Journals of the House of Commons*
CSPD	*Calendar of State Papers Domestic*
ERRO	East Riding Record Office, Treasure House, Beverley
Greaves and Zaller	R.L. Greaves and R. Zaller (eds), *Biographical Dictionary of British Radicals in the Seventeenth Century*, 3 vols (Brighton, 1984)
HHC: C	Hull History Centre: City of Hull Corporation Archives
HHC: U	Hull History Centre: Hull University Archives
HMC	Historical Manuscripts Commission
LJ	*Journals of the House of Lords*
ODNB	H.C.G. Matthew and Brian Harrison (eds), *The Oxford Dictionary of National Biography*, 60 vols (Oxford, 2004)
OED	J.A. Simpson and E.S.C. Weiner (eds), *The Oxford English Dictionary*, 20 vols (2nd edn, Oxford, 1989)
SP	State Papers
TERAS	*Transactions of the East Riding Antiquarian Society*
TNA	The National Archives, Kew, Surrey
TT	Thomason Tract
VCH	*Victoria County History*
YAJ	*Yorkshire Archaeological Journal*
YASRS	Yorkshire Archaeological Society, Record Series
YML, CWT	York Minster Library, Civil War Tract

INTRODUCTION

This volume publishes the papers and correspondence of the Hotham family during the civil wars and interregnum. The head of the family and first baronet, Sir John Hotham, is well known in the national narrative because of his critical role in denying the king entry to Hull on 23 April 1642. This episode ignited much contemporary controversy, raising the stakes in a pamphlet war between the king and his parliamentary opponents, and making armed conflict far more likely. It has attracted considerable attention from constitutional historians who have debated its legal ramifications, while political and military historians have recognized that the king's failure to seize the large arms magazine at Hull badly undermined the royalist war effort. Yet, despite their national importance in 1642, the Hotham family's papers have only rarely been utilized by academics. Late twentieth-century historians such as J.T. Cliffe, Barbara English, and Peter Roebuck drew upon the collection to inform their work on the wider theme of Yorkshire gentry landowners,[1] but few others have been to Hull to access the archive. This also reflects a relative neglect of northern England in civil war historiography. There has been no biography of either of the Hothams, and their most recent family histories date from as long ago as the First World War.[2] This is unfortunate, because Sir John Hotham and his eldest son were extremely colourful and enigmatic figures, whose letters reveal much about the cultural attitudes of the English gentry in the 1640s.

This volume seeks to redress this imbalance and restore the centrality of the Hotham family to the parliamentary cause. Reuniting the Hotham archive with surviving letters in other collections will deliver a comprehensive edition, making their papers fully accessible for the first time. The papers constitute an outstanding primary source for the build-up to war and the allegiance dilemmas faced

[1]J.T. Cliffe, *The Yorkshire Gentry from the Reformation to the Civil War* (London, 1969); B. English, *The Great Landowners of East Yorkshire, 1530–1910* (Hemel Hempstead, 1990); P. Roebuck, *Yorkshire Baronets 1640–1760: families, estates and fortunes* (Oxford, 1980), pp. 62–69.

[2]P. Saltmarshe, *History and Chartulary of the Hothams of Scorborough in the East Riding of Yorkshire, 1100–1700* (York, 1914); A.M.W. Stirling, *The Hothams: being the chronicles of the Hothams of Scorborough and South Dalton from their hitherto unpublished family papers*, 2 vols (London, 1918).

by Yorkshire's inhabitants before the king raised his standard at Nottingham on 22 August 1642. They detail the war's conduct in the north, illuminating the government of Hull and the parliamentarian administration of the East Riding. At the same time, they are useful for historians of allegiance because they richly demonstrate the family feud with the Fairfaxes of Denton, and an increasing dissatisfaction with the parliamentary cause.[3]

The present work includes transcriptions of all of the papers in the DDHO/1 classification of the Hotham family archives. These are supplemented with letters written by or to the Hothams that are now held in other archives, principally the British Library, the Bodleian Library, and the Hull city records. Most of the letters written by Sir John Hotham were penned in Hull and sought to protect the town and his estates to the north of it, either by pleading for reinforcements, pay, and supply from his Westminster contacts, or through clandestine negotiations with the enemy general, the earl of Newcastle, to spare the East Riding from a royalist occupation. His correspondents included William Lenthall, Speaker of the House of Commons, and such prominent MPs as John Pym and John Hampden. The other papers written by Sir John were connected to his trial in December 1644 for attempting to betray Hull to the royalists. He penned several drafts of a defence, interrogatories for the witnesses, and a general autobiographical account of his governorship of Hull.[4] These papers were retrospective, written during his imprisonment in the Tower of London. Their purpose was to save his life and their audience encompassed Sir William Waller and the members of the court martial who were judging him, as well as other members of parliament to whom Sir John might appeal.

The letters by Sir John Hotham's eldest son, John Hotham, were written from his military headquarters in Cawood and Beverley, and during his campaigning in Durham, Lincolnshire, Nottinghamshire, and the North Riding of Yorkshire. The majority of them were addressed to the earl of Newcastle and they constitute a nationally important source for the English gentry's politics of honour. These will prove of wider interest to literary scholars and cultural historians because they utilized a language of honour to court Newcastle's affections. They raised the prospect that the Hotham family would change sides as soon as they could do so without betraying their trust

[3]A. Hopper, 'The self-fashioning of gentry turncoats during the English civil wars', *Journal of British Studies*, 49 (2010), pp. 236–257; *idem*, '"Fitted for desperation": honour and treachery in parliament's Yorkshire command, 1642–1643', *History*, 86 (2001), pp. 138–154; *idem*, *'Black Tom': Sir Thomas Fairfax and the English Revolution* (Manchester, 2007), pp. 61, 163–165, 240.

[4]HHC: Hotham MS, U DDHO/1/31–46.

or impugning their reputations. There are several further letters and papers penned by Sir John's fifth son, Durand Hotham, who defended him during his trial, and his grandson John Hotham, his successor as second baronet. These were largely concerned with preserving the family estates after the executions of John and Sir John Hotham on 1 and 2 January 1645 respectively.

The Hotham family

As one of the leading county families in the East Riding of Yorkshire, the Hothams were a natural choice to head the parliamentarian war effort in the region, and their careers are ably summarized by David Scott's entries in the *Oxford Dictionary of National Biography*. Sir John Hotham was born in 1589, the son of John Hotham of Scorborough, esq. and Jane, the daughter of Richard Legard of Rysome. During the 1580s John Hotham had served as high sheriff of Yorkshire and MP for Scarborough and Hedon. In 1609 Sir John succeeded to his father's large estates and he was knighted on 11 April 1617. He gained brief military experience serving under Count Ernst von Mansfeldt in the Rhineland in 1619 and may have served at the Battle of the White Mountain in 1620. By 1621 he had returned to Yorkshire, where he was quickly appointed a justice of the peace, and he purchased a baronetcy in 1622. He soon became a patriarch, fathering many children, including his eldest son, John Hotham, the parliamentarian lieutenant-general, born in 1610.[5]

Sir John and his eldest son had married eight times between them before the outbreak of civil war. They may have enlarged the family estates through these marriage settlements to embrace a swathe of land across the Yorkshire Wolds stretching from Beverley to Driffield. Like most East Riding gentry, their wealth was rooted in agricultural rents. The gross annual rental of Sir John's estates on the eve of war reached an impressive £3,000, making him one of the richest men in Yorkshire. It included land in Allerston, Beswick, Fylingdales, Hutton Cranswick, Howsham, Lockington, Scorborough, Pickering, Risam, and Wilton.[6] Their virile loins, large family, and numerous offspring placed the two men at the head of a remarkably wide kinship network of northern parliamentarian gentry (see Figure 1), and their early activism for parliament influenced many of these gentry into falling in behind them. Sir John's administrative experience was vast. He

[5]D. Scott, 'Sir John Hotham (1589–1645)' and 'John Hotham (1610–1645)', *ODNB*; Stirling, *The Hothams*, I, pp. 25–26.

[6]Roebuck, *Yorkshire Baronets*, p. 64; English, *Great Landowners*, p. 102.

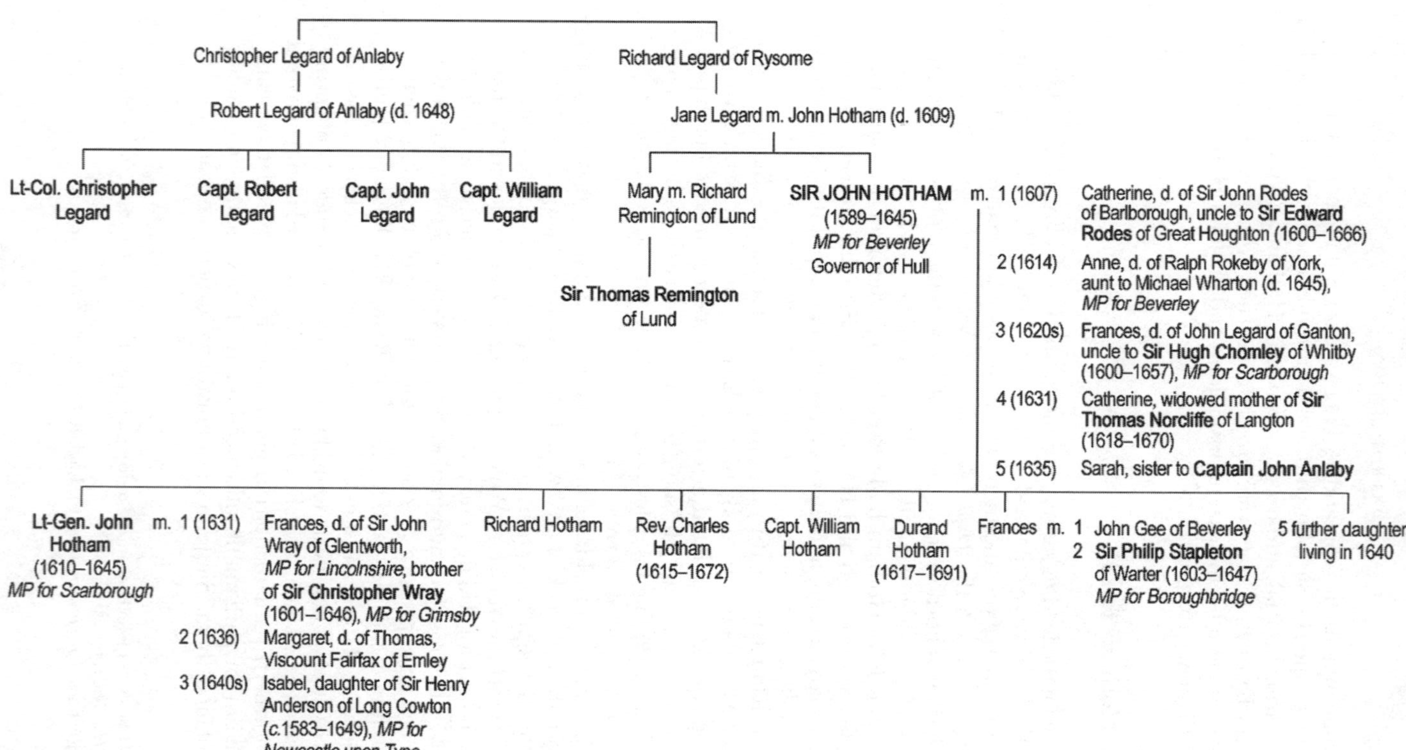

Fig. 1 The kinship network of the Hotham family, 1642–1643. Names in bold denote parliamentarian officers.

had served as MP for Beverley since 1625, and was governor of Hull during Charles I's wars in 1628. He was added to the North Riding bench in 1631,[7] and was high sheriff of Yorkshire in 1635, proving an energetic collector of ship money. He was colonel of a regiment of East Riding trained bands during the First Bishops' War in 1639.[8] He was also governor of Hull that year, but was personally affronted when the king entrusted the Hull magazine to Captain William Legge.[9]

Despite his support for the Caroline regime in the 1630s, Sir John Hotham had also crafted a reputation for himself as a champion of 'country' liberties. He was removed from the commission of the peace and imprisoned for refusing to pay the forced loan in 1627. He grew irritated by the king's increasing demands upon Yorkshire to raise, billet, and pay for the royal forces during the Bishops' Wars. By 1640 his opposition was vocal. Alongside Sir Hugh Cholmley, he led opposition to ship money in the East Riding. His speeches as MP for Beverley during the Short Parliament of April 1640 attracted the censure of the Privy Council and he was ejected from all his commissions and briefly imprisoned in the Fleet from 8 to 15 May.[10] During the Second Bishops' War that summer, he solicited petitions concerning Yorkshire grievances, provoking the king to warn that if Hotham did not desist he would hang him.[11]

Sir John remained MP for Beverley during the Long Parliament and became one of its most active members. David Scott has shown that he was named to over 100 committees between November 1640 and March 1642, often allying himself with John Pym and other leading opponents of the king.[12] During 1641 he participated in the dismantling of the Council of the North and other instruments of royal prerogative power, easing the burden on his locality when the royal army was finally disbanded and Hull's garrison and governor were discharged.[13] Despite his identification with opposition politics, several contemporaries noted his distaste for puritans. Sir Henry Slingsby commented that Hotham 'was manly for the defence of liberty of the subject and privilege of Parliament, but was not at all

[7]J. Broadway, R. Cust, and S.K. Roberts (eds), *A Calendar of the Docquets of Lord Keeper Coventry, 1625–1640*, List and Index Society, special series, 34 (2004), p. 65.

[8]*CSPD, 1638–1639*, p. 310.

[9]D. Scott, '"Hannibal at our gates": loyalists and fifth-columnists during the Bishops' Wars – the case of Yorkshire', *Historical Research*, 70 (1997), p. 280.

[10]Saltmarshe, *History and Chartulary of the Hothams*, p. 113.

[11]Scott, '"Hannibal at our gates"', pp. 277–281; J. Binns (ed.), *The Memoirs and Memorials of Sir Hugh Cholmley of Whitby 1600–1657*, YASRS, 153 (2000), pp. 102, 125n.

[12]Scott, 'Sir John Hotham'.

[13]The governor in 1640–1641 was Sir Thomas Glemham: Stirling, *The Hothams*, I, p. 38.

for their new opinions in Church government'.[14] Sir Hugh Cholmley noted Hotham's antipathy to puritan ministers and even Clarendon conceded that Hotham was 'not disturbed by any fancies in religion'.[15] Although he was no friend to the Godly, his virulent anti-Catholicism and hatred of the earl of Strafford could be counted upon by the opposition grandees. He gave evidence against Strafford and on 19 July 1641 supported a parliamentary proposal to geld priests and Jesuits.[16]

In addition to the context of Sir John's pre-war political activities, a familiarity with contemporary notions of honour is essential to a thorough understanding of the Hotham papers. By 1642, an increasing variety of notions of honour influenced gentry behaviour. Older, traditional conceptions stressed ancient lineage, blood, pedigree, outward display, and hunting. These ideas persisted alongside a more recent tradition that emphasized virtue, education, sobriety, restraint, magistracy, godliness, and public service.[17] Yet these traditions were not mutually exclusive and were often blended or appropriated for different purposes and audiences. Richard Cust has recently contended that, by the 1620s, Renaissance humanism, classical republicanism, and English Calvinism had melded to generate an image of the virtuous, incorruptible 'public man'. Drawing upon the writings of the Stoics, such as Plutarch, Seneca, and Cicero, this political culture stressed virtue and constancy, remaining steadfast to one's principles and conscience, as paramount determinants of nobility. In theory, the gentry were supposed to refrain from private interests and to prioritize their duty to serve the public.[18]

The Hotham letters suggest that by 1642 both father and son had dabbled in this fashion for neo-Stoic ideas. Their self-fashioning espoused restraint, duty, and constancy, but they could not eschew the traditional stress on blood, pedigree, and lineage. This is no surprise, because the Hothams boasted an unbroken lineage of direct succession from father to son stretching back to the twelfth century.

[14] D. Parsons (ed.), *The Diary of Sir Henry Slingsby of Scriven, Bart* (London, 1836), p. 92.

[15] Binns, *The Memoirs and Memorials of Sir Hugh Cholmley*, pp. 128–129; W.D. Macray (ed.), *The History of the Rebellion and Civil Wars in England Begun in the Year 1641 by Edward, Earl of Clarendon*, 6 vols (Oxford, 1888), III, 526.

[16] C. Russell, *The Fall of the British Monarchies, 1637–1642* (Oxford, 1991), p. 340.

[17] R. Cust, 'Honour and politics in early Stuart England: the case of Beaumont v. Hastings', *Past & Present*, 149 (1995), pp. 60, 91; M. James, *English Politics and the Concept of Honour, 1485–1642*, *Past & Present* supplement, 3 (1978), p. 92.

[18] R. Cust, 'The "public man" in late Tudor and early Stuart England', in P. Lake and S. Pincus (eds), *The Politics of the Public Sphere in Early Modern England* (Manchester, 2007), pp. 119, 126, 129.

Such continuity of lineage was held to prove a family's virtue, as longer, purer pedigrees concentrated levels of noble blood.[19] In part because of this, they were notoriously sensitive to perceived slights. When Sir John Hotham took offence to a change in the order of precedence of justices at the East Riding quarter sessions, he retired to write a hostile account of proceedings.[20] The earl of Strafford had cautioned the king against upsetting Sir John, considering him 'extreme sensible of honour, and discourtesies perhaps a little overmuch', while in 1642 the parliamentary leaders John Pym and John Hampden had to send placatory letters reassuring Sir John that his reputation remained unquestioned.[21] This temperament led Sir Hugh Cholmley to comment that, in later life, Sir John became 'so much wedded to his own humour, as his passion often overbalanced his judgment'.[22] This trait, so evident in the letters, did much to bring about his death. On the scaffold he was required to orate that for 'rash words, anger and such things, no man has been more guilty'.[23]

Hull and the East Riding in 1642

The East Riding was an overwhelmingly agricultural county. Anthony Fletcher characterized it as a 'basically centralized county', comparable to Essex.[24] With a population of up to 80,000 it was the smallest and least populated of Yorkshire's three Ridings.[25] It consisted of three geographical regions: the low-lying, fertile plains of Holderness east of the river Hull, the rich sheep pastures of the Yorkshire Wolds in the centre, and a lowland area of no predominant character to the west, bounded by the Ouse and Derwent rivers, the Howden marshes, and the limestone hills north-east of York.[26] The burden of taxation to maintain the Hothams' network of garrisons

[19] R. Cust, 'Catholicism, antiquarianism and gentry honour: the writings of Sir Thomas Shirley', *Midland History*, 23 (1998), p. 49; Stirling, *The Hothams*, I, p. 21.

[20] F. Heal and C. Holmes, *The Gentry in England and Wales, 1500–1700* (Basingstoke, 1994), p. 171.

[21] Saltmarshe, *History and Chartulary of the Hothams*, p. 112; HHC: Hotham MS, U DDHO/1/8.

[22] Binns, *The Memoirs and Memorials of Sir Hugh Cholmley*, p. 131.

[23] Stirling, *The Hothams*, I, pp. 96–97.

[24] A. Fletcher, *Reform in the Provinces: the government of Stuart England* (New Haven, 1986), p. 100.

[25] The North Riding numbered 120,000 and the West Riding 220,000: J.D. Purdy, *Yorkshire Hearth Tax Returns*, Studies in Regional and Local History, 7 (University of Hull, 1991), pp. 50, 69, 95, 123. Barbara English advanced the more conservative estimate of 53,000 as the population of the East Riding in 1600: English, *Great Landowners*, p. 3.

[26] English, *Great Landowners*, pp. 2–3.

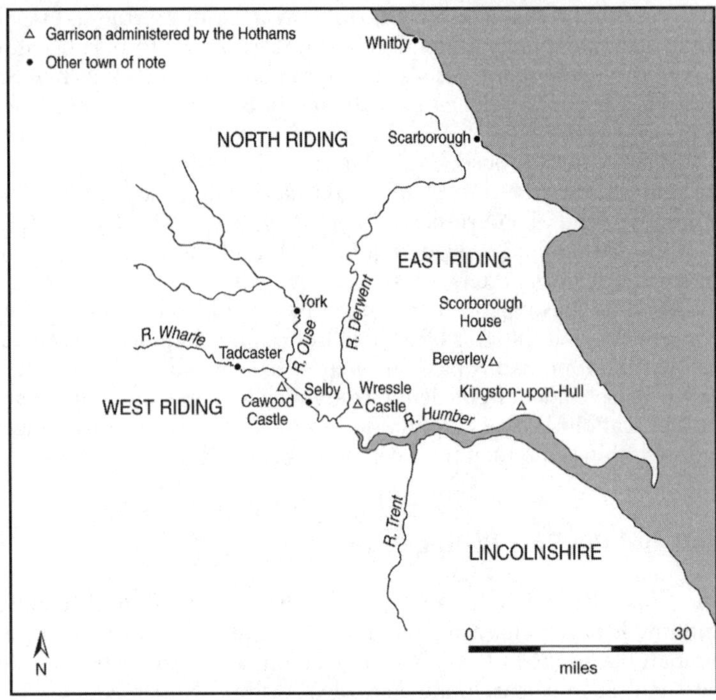

Map 1. The garrisons administered by the Hothams, 1642–1643.

fell most heavily upon Holderness and the Wolds. The wapentake of Holderness was separated into three divisions – north, middle, and south – while the Wolds were encompassed within the wapentake of Harthill, which was separated into four divisions: Holme Beacon, Hunsley Beacon, Bainton Beacon, and Wilton Beacon.[27] Each of these divisions in Holderness and Harthill was headed by a high constable responsible to the high sheriff for collection of ship money and to the deputy lieutenants for mustering the trained bands. Sir John Hotham had experience in dealing with such office-holders in both of these capacities, and the survey of all the foot arms in the East Riding was taken before him in 1636.[28]

[27] G.C.F. Forster, *The East Riding Justices of the Peace in the Seventeenth Century*, East Yorkshire Local History Society, 30 (1973), pp. 9–10.
[28] ERRO: DDRI 2,960, fo. 73.

Beverley, with its soaring minster and brick gatehouses, was the East Riding county town, with a population of just three thousand.[29] Its tiny electorate of twenty-six facilitated Sir John's long incumbency as one of Beverley's two MPs.[30] Although the Quarter Sessions occasionally still met at Pocklington, by the mid-seventeenth century the court usually met in the sessions' chamber in Beverley's Hallgarth.[31] No wall protected Beverley, but the medieval town ditch was broadened in 1642, with footbridges installed at the end of each lane into Westwood.[32] In October 1642 the corporation ordered the bars to be repaired, as well as locked and guarded each night.[33] Despite lacking fortifications, Beverley was important to the Hothams as a place to quarter their soldiers. It also played a critical role as a fund-raising centre, as discussed in Appendix II.

Six miles southward lay the independent borough of Kingston-upon-Hull, a separate county in its own right. Its population had reached seven thousand, making its size second only to York in all Yorkshire.[34] The extensive river networks of the Trent and Ouse formed a lucrative hinterland and facilitated the export of cloth from the West Riding through Hull into continental Europe.[35] The inhabitants took civic pride in Hull's walls, their municipal liberties, and the achievements of the corporation.[36] As a consequence of the Bishops' Wars, Hull was arguably the strongest fortress town in England. Its natural defensive situation at the confluence of the rivers Humber and Hull was enhanced by the possibility of exploiting the high Humber tides to flood besieging forces. Hull's medieval walls were protected by twenty-five towers and modern fortifications that included an outer ditch, the 'Bush Dyke', along with angled bastions, blockhouses, earthworks, forts, and half moons that were rare for England in 1642. A drawbridge had recently been constructed outside the Beverley Gate. Across the river Hull, the town's eastern side was protected by the castle, linked on either side to two blockhouses by a

[29] Purdy, *Yorkshire Hearth Tax Returns*, p. 129.

[30] J. Binns, *Yorkshire in the Civil Wars: origins, impact and outcome* (Pickering, North Yorks, 2004), p. 2.

[31] Forster, *The East Riding Justices of the Peace*, p. 30.

[32] K.J. Allison (ed.), *The Victoria History of the County of York, East Riding. Vol. VI: the borough and liberties of Beverley* (Oxford, 1989), pp. 178–179.

[33] ERRO, BC II 7/4/1: Beverley Minute Book 1597–1660, fo. 74v.

[34] Purdy, *Yorkshire Hearth Tax Returns*, p. 129.

[35] R. Davis, *The Trade and Shipping of Hull, 1500–1700*, East Yorkshire Local History Society, 17 (1964), p. 23.

[36] C. Cross, *Urban Magistrates and Ministers: religion in Hull and Leeds from the Reformation to the civil war*, University of York: Borthwick Papers, 67 (1985), p. 2.

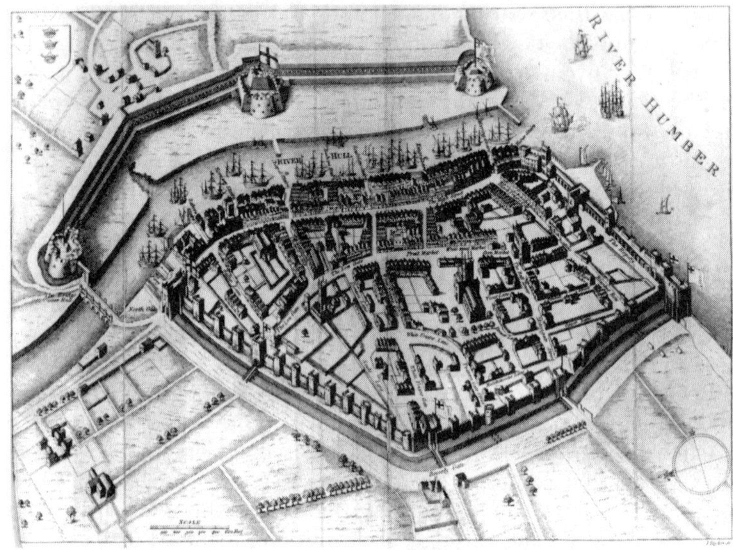

Fig. 2 Wenceslaus Hollar, engraving of Hull, 1640.

massive wall that was twenty-four feet high and fifteen feet thick.[37] The town could be supplied and reinforced by sea, while the crews and artillery of naval vessels could contribute to its defence. Furthermore, Hull housed England's second largest magazine, with arms for 20,000 men, 7,000 barrels of powder, and 120 pieces of artillery. Plans were originally formulated in February 1642 to send this magazine to equip government forces against the rebels in Ireland, but both parliament and king soon sought to acquire it for their forces in England.[38]

In contrast to the divided situation in the rest of Yorkshire, the MPs in the south of the East Riding all sided with parliament. Hull returned two MPs to Westminster, as did the East Riding boroughs of Beverley and Hedon. Sir John Hotham and Michael Wharton sat for Beverley, Sir Philip Stapleton and John Alured for the small town of Hedon, and Sir Henry Vane the younger and Peregrine Pelham

[37] A. Howes and M. Foreman, *Town and Gun: the 17th-century defences of Hull* (Hull, 1999), pp. 23–26; Binns, *Yorkshire in the Civil Wars*, p. 27.

[38] A. Fletcher, *The Outbreak of the English Civil War* (London, 1981), p. 185; R. Armstrong, 'The Long Parliament goes to war: the Irish campaigns, 1641–3', *Historical Research*, 80 (2007), pp. 88, 90.

for Hull.[39] Although Wharton changed sides and Hotham attempted to do so, the rest remained committed parliamentarians, with Alured and Pelham even becoming regicides.

The region also had a deep-rooted puritan presence. Godly Protestants were firmly established in Beverley, Hull, and adjacent villages such as Cottingham, Rowley, and Sculcoates. The ministers in Hull had persisted in nonconformity during the 1630s, and had frequently been called before the High Commission at York.[40] Yorkshire clergymen with similar reputations sought protection inside Hull after the outbreak of hostilities.[41] Many puritans in Rowley migrated with Reverend Ezekiel Rogers to Massachusetts in 1638,[42] while Samuel Winter's 'awakening and piercing' ministry at Cottingham was sponsored by Lord Fairfax.[43] J.T. Cliffe has pointed out that there was also considerable puritan strength in several parishes across the northern margins of the East Riding, in the wapentakes of Dickering and Buckrose.[44]

The Hothams at war

Contrary to popular accounts, it was not Sir John Hotham who seized Hull for parliament but his eldest son. He did so in opposition to the king's envoy, the earl of Newcastle, who had been refused entry on 15 January 1642. John Hotham arrived before Hull on 18 January with about three hundred men from his father's East Riding trained bands. When the corporation rebuffed him, he threatened to send to parliament a list of the names of refractory aldermen. Encouraging rumours that the Catholics of Holderness were arming themselves and that the Spanish intended to land, John Hotham utilized the politics of emergency to gain admittance and establish his government in Hull.[45]

[39] W.W. Bean, *The Parliamentary Representation of the Six Northern Counties of England* (Hull, 1890), pp. 740, 812, 844.

[40] Cross, *Urban Magistrates and Ministers*, p. 24.

[41] R.A. Marchant, *The Puritans and the Church Courts in the Diocese of York, 1560–1642* (London, 1960), pp. 102, 268, 275, 282, 293.

[42] English, *Great Landowners*, p. 132; W.J. Sheils, 'Provincial preaching on the eve of the civil war: some West Riding sermons', in A. Fletcher and P. Roberts (eds), *Religion, Culture and Society in Early Modern Britain: essays in honour of Patrick Collinson* (Cambridge, 1994), p. 291.

[43] BL, Birch MS 4,460, fos 34–35; J.C. Cox, 'Parliamentary survey of the benefices of the East Riding', *TERAS*, 2 (1894), p. 33.

[44] Cliffe, *The Yorkshire Gentry*, p. 262.

[45] I.E. Ryder, 'The seizure of Hull and its magazine, January 1642', *YAJ*, 61 (1989), pp. 141–142; T. Gent, *Gent's History of Hull Reprinted in Fac-simile of the Original of 1735* (Hull, 1869), p. 144; Fletcher, *The Outbreak of the English Civil War*, p. 314; B.N. Reckitt, *Charles the First and Hull, 1639–1645* (2nd edn, Howden, 1988), p. 23; English, *Great Landowners*, p. 135.

He was aided by kinsmen and local gentlemen such as Christopher Legard of Anlaby, William Goodricke of Skidby, John Anlaby of Etton, and Matthew Appleyard of East Halton, who soon held commissions in the garrison.[46]

Control of Hull became even more critical when the king, having fled London, established his court at York on 18 March. Sir John Hotham arrived in Hull during the same week, and on 22 March was ordered not to admit any forces into Hull without orders from both houses of parliament.[47] Attempting to seize the magazine before its contents could be shipped to London, Charles appeared before the Beverley Gate on 23 April. Sir John had notice of his approach and, fearing the king intended his execution, prepared to defend the town. Charles demanded entrance, but Hotham, standing on the low wall next to the gate, replied that he could not admit him without betraying his trust to parliament, and 'incurring to me and my posterity the odious name of villain and faith-breaker'. A brief discussion followed before the heralds proclaimed Hotham a traitor and the garrison were invited to throw him off the walls.[48]

This affair intensified the propaganda war. Sir Philip Warwick recalled that John Hotham brought the news of his father's stand to parliament with the inflammatory proclamation: 'Thus hath my father and myself served you; fall back, fall edge.'[49] Sir John was transformed into a national figure as parliament declared the king's treatment of him a breach of privilege. On 23 May he delivered a speech justifying his actions to a meeting in Hull. This was published as a pamphlet in London four days later, and parliamentarian sympathizers were soon referred to as 'Hothamites'.[50] Sir John's example invited seditious talk and polarized debate. On 10 June the Commons ordered that a scandalous picture of him that appeared to suggest he was the king's superior should be burned by the common hangman.[51] Fears for his life persisted, and on 30 April parliament ordered that John Hotham be appointed governor if his father should die.[52] On 7 May Margaret Eure

[46]For details of these gentlemen, see Appendix II.

[47]*LJ*, IV, p. 662.

[48]Gent, *Gent's History of Hull*, p. 145; Reckitt, *Charles the First and Hull*, pp. 27–34.

[49]Beinecke Rare Book and Manuscript Library, Yale University, Osborn Shelves, fb87, fo. 62r–v.

[50]BL, TT E200(45), *A learned speech made by the right worshipfull Sir John Hotham* (London, 27 May 1642); W.C. Trevelyan and C.E. Trevelyan (eds), *Trevelyan Papers, Part III*, Camden Society, first series, 105 (1872), p. 223.

[51]*CJ*, II, pp. 617, 622.

[52]*House of Lords MS*, HMC, 5th Report, Part I, Report and Appendix (London, 1876), p. 19; *CJ*, II, p. 551.

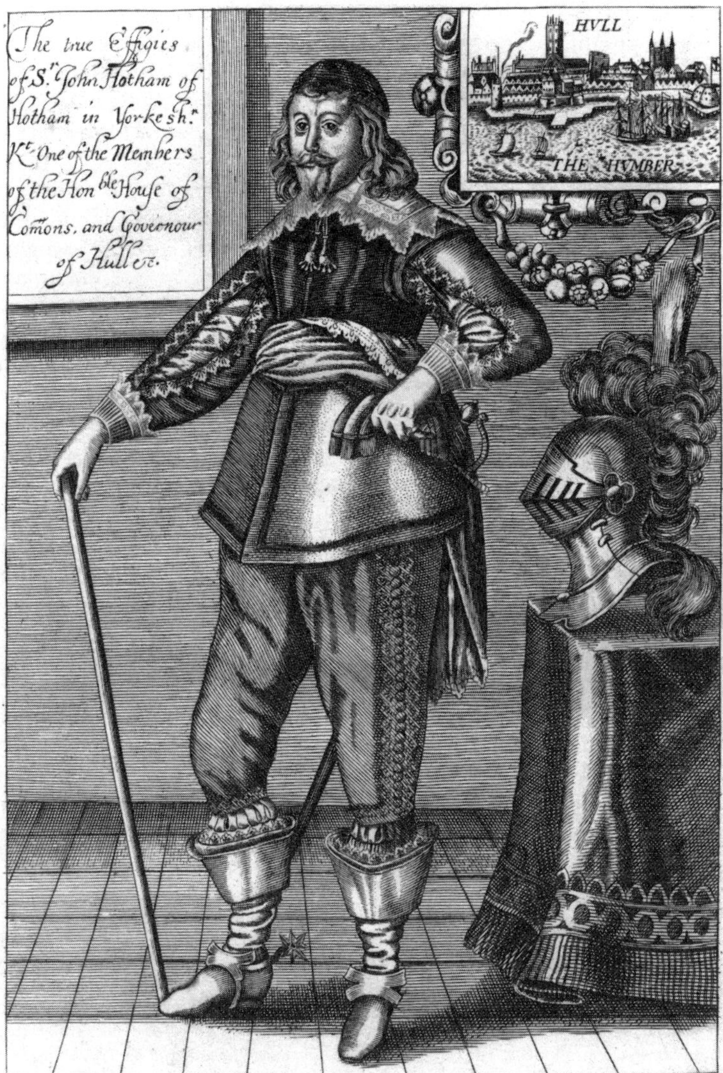

Fig. 3 Portrait print of Sir John Hotham.

called Sir John a 'poor wretch' who was 'affrighted if anything comes but near him'.[53] To prevent his garrison deserting, Sir John warned

[53] *Verney MS*, HMC, 7th Report, Part I, Report and Appendix (London, 1879), p. 438.

them that the king had authorized constables and justices to hang soldiers caught outside Hull.[54] He requested that parliament despatch a committee of MPs to share in his dangers and responsibilities. On 24 May parliament assented, sending John Hotham, Sir William Airmyn, Sir William Strickland, John Alured, Michael Wharton, Henry Darley, and Peregrine Pelham.[55]

During the summer of 1642 Sir John foiled several plots to deliver Hull to the king. The first, by Mr Beckwith of Beverley, intended to bribe two garrison officers, Lieutenant Fowkes and Captain Lowinger, into betraying the town.[56] Lord Digby, disguised as a Frenchman, also gained an audience with Hotham in early July. According to Clarendon, Digby persuaded Sir John to deliver Hull if the king appeared in force before it.[57] Despite lacking the military strength for a proper siege, the king appeared before Hull on 7 July with around 2,500 men.[58] In the meantime Hotham changed his mind, doubting his capacity to deliver a successful surrender. During the ensuing siege, he was reinforced by two powerful second rate warships, three companies of foot recruited in London, and the Scots commander, Sir John Meldrum, which swelled the garrison to 2,200 men.[59] Hotham flooded the approaches to Hull by cutting the sluices holding back the Humber and his soldiers vanquished the besiegers in numerous sallies until the king lifted the siege and withdrew.[60]

Despite Sir John's successful defence of Hull, and the king's departure from Yorkshire in August, a general parliamentary mobilization in the county did not follow. As late as September, parliamentarian military preparation elsewhere in Yorkshire was virtually non-existent. Although Ferdinando, Lord Fairfax was proclaimed leader of the West Riding parliamentarians at Leeds on

[54] Bodl. MS Clarendon XXI, fo. 79.

[55] *The Parliamentary or Constitutional History of England*, 24 vols (London, 1751–1761), XI, p. 61.

[56] Reckitt, *Charles the First and Hull*, p. 45; *CJ*, II, pp. 587–588; Saltmarshe, *History and Chartulary of the Hothams*, p. 124; J.J. Sheahan, *History of the Town and Port of Kingston-upon-Hull* (2nd edn, Beverley, 1866), p. 141; BL, TT E107(31), *Terrible news from Hull: concerning a great conspiracy which was intended against Sir John Hotham* (London, 20 July 1642).

[57] BL, TT E256(45), *A perfect diurnall of some passages in parliament*, 2–9 December 1644 (London, 1644), p. 560; BL, TT E67(22), *Certaine informations from severall parts of the kingdome*, 11–18 September 1643 (London, 1643), p. 268; Reckitt, *Charles the First and Hull*, pp. 49–52; HHC: Hotham MS, U DDHO/1/35; Macray, *The History of the Rebellion*, II, pp. 257–267.

[58] BL, TT E154(34), *Terrible and true newes from Beverley and the city of Yorke* (London, 1642), p. 1: *LJ*, V, p. 217.

[59] TNA, SP 28/138/4; J.R. Powell and E.K. Timings (eds), *Documents Relating to the Civil War, 1642–1648*, Navy Records Society, 105 (1963), p. 24.

[60] Reckitt, *Charles the First and Hull*, pp. 54–61; G. Duckett, 'Civil war proceedings in Yorkshire', *YAJ*, 7 (1882), p. 398; E. Broxap, 'The sieges of Hull during the great civil war', *English Historical Review*, 20 (1905), pp. 457–473.

19 September, he signed a truce with local royalists ten days later to keep Yorkshire out of the war. Understandably, the Hothams were outraged.[61] Anxious that they would be sacrificed if a premature peace was negotiated, they resented the treaty's conclusion – without their involvement – by those who had risked far less than they had. Both Hothams published vehement declarations against the treaty and John Hotham launched a military campaign to make it unworkable.[62] He captured Selby on 1 October and then Cawood castle three days later, tightening a stranglehold on the river network upon which York depended for its trade.[63] The royalists could not permit this to continue and the treaty was broken. On 21 October Fairfax was forced into armed conflict when his Bradford headquarters were attacked, and two days later John Hotham joined Fairfax's men in sweeping local royalists back towards York.[64] York was blockaded quickly, leaving Fairfax free to despatch Hotham on 9 November to rally the North Riding and defend the Tees crossings against Newcastle's large army gathering in Northumberland and Durham. Although Hotham assured Fairfax that he could prevent Newcastle from coming south that winter, on 1 December Newcastle's royalists routed Hotham's force at Piercebridge and poured south to relieve York. Fairfax withdrew to Tadcaster where Hotham rejoined him, by now mustering around 2,000 men. Newcastle attacked Tadcaster on 6 December, but Fairfax and Hotham held the town until nightfall before slipping away to establish new headquarters at Selby and Cawood respectively.[65]

Further west, a series of popular uprisings against the royalists was ignited at Bradford on 18 December, when a party of royalists tried to force their way into town. The Pennine clothing districts around Leeds, Bradford, and Halifax faced subsistence crisis as royalist troops

[61] BL, TT E240(20), *A perfect diurnall of the passages in parliament*, 26 September–3 October 1642 (London, 1642); BL, TT E119(29), *Fourteen articles of peace propounded to the king and parliament by the gentry and commonalty of the county of York* (London, 4 October 1642); A. Woolrych, 'Yorkshire's treaty of neutrality', *History Today*, 6 (1956), pp. 700–703.

[62] BL, TT E121(32), *The declaration of Captain Hotham sent to the parliament* (London, 1642); BL, TT E121(45), *A true & exact relation [. . .] also a protestation of Master Hotham, and divers other knights and gentlemen, against the 14. articles of pacification, and neutrality* (London, 12 October 1642), p. 14; BL, TT E240(30), *Reasons why Sir John Hotham, trusted by the parliament, cannot in honour agree to the treaty of pacification made by some gentlemen of York-shire at Rothwell, Sept. 29. 1642* (London, 1642), p. 3.

[63] *Sutherland MS*, HMC, 5th Report, Appendix, p. 191.

[64] Beinecke Rare Book and Manuscript Library, Yale University, Osborn Shelves b101, The commonplace book of Ralph Assheton of Kirkby Grange; Bodl. MS Fairfax XXXVI, fo. 5r; BL, TT E126(1), *Speciall passages*, 25 October–1 November 1642 (London, 1642), p. 102.

[65] YML, CWT, 42-12-20, *An exact and true relation of a bloody fight* (London, 1642); BL, Add. MS 18,979, fo. 129r–v; Parsons, *The Diary of Sir Henry Slingsby*, p. 86.

Fig. 4 Ferdinando, Lord Fairfax.

prevented them from transporting their cloth to Hull and receiving foodstuffs from the vale of York.[66] This populous region soon mustered

[66] Hopper, *'Black Tom'*, pp. 37–39.

double the numbers that Lord Fairfax had at Selby and began to dictate his strategy. Many recruits were cloth-workers armed with clubs and were so celebrated in London that one newsbook urged all England 'to rise and execute Bradford Club Law upon the Cavaliers'.[67] Gentry who had engaged for parliament principally to defend their estates from arbitrary power now feared whether victories for Fairfax's rabble were preferable. In the face of the 'club-law' uprisings and his disagreements with Fairfax, Sir John became inclined to a negotiated settlement with the king. On 10 January 1643, the House of Commons ordered that a letter from Sir John Hotham to Lenthall, dated 4 January, should 'be kept that no man might see it', implying that it had urged peace.[68] John Hotham experienced these doubts too, and sought to play upon them by establishing a remarkable correspondence with the earl of Newcastle from mid-December 1642 until his arrest at Nottingham in June 1643.

By January there was open hostility between the Fairfaxes and the Hothams. John Hotham continued to flout Lord Fairfax's authority, defying the orders of a parliamentary committee and Fairfax's commission as commander-in-chief of the northern counties.[69] On 12 January a letter from Lord Fairfax 'concerning some difference in the superiority of commands, between himself and Mr. Hotham' was read in the House of Commons. The House subsequently ordered that all forces drawn out of Hull should be under Fairfax's command and they desired the Lord General, the earl of Essex, to make a similar declaration.[70] Instead, Essex ordered the opposite. He instructed Fairfax that the Hothams could recall any of their forces to Hull and that John Hotham, who was commissioned lieutenant-general, would be permitted to continue with his troops as governor of Cawood castle.[71] Yet Sir Hugh Cholmley later reflected that Hotham was still unsatisfied with this rank, 'thinking himself not so absolute as before for his father keeping Hull, he commanded in chief in that field, and ranged the country without control'.[72]

This fractured command structure was permitted to continue, and Fairfax complained to parliament on 26 January that Sir John Hotham had hindered him raising money by way of loans upon the public

[67] BL, TT E86(5), *The kingdoms weekly intelligencer*, 17–24 January 1643 (London, 1643), p. 29; BL, TT E86(40), *The kingdoms weekly intelligencer*, 24–31 January 1643 (London, 1643).

[68] *CJ*, II, p. 920.

[69] J. Rushworth, *Historical Collections* (London, 1691), Part III, II, p. 64; BL, Add. MS 18,979, fo. 127r.

[70] *CJ*, II, p. 923.

[71] BL, Add. MS 18,979, fo. 131; BL, Add. MS 34,195, fo. 35.

[72] Binns, *The Memoirs and Memorials of Sir Hugh Cholmley*, p. 126.

Fig. 5 William Cavendish, earl of Newcastle.

faith.[73] The next day John Hotham joined Lord Fairfax's son, Sir Thomas Fairfax, at Wakefield, witnessing the clubmen army at first hand after their triumph at Leeds on 23 January. Hotham's presence provoked Sir Thomas to complain to Lord Fairfax: 'When he saw your lordship's order, he called for pen and ink to copy it out, it seemed by his peevish humour to have taken some advantage by it, but he did

[73] BL, Harleian MS 164, fo. 285r.

not. No order will be observed by him but what he please.'[74] Reports in London newsbooks that Fairfax and Hotham had reconciled their differences were wishful. The royalist newsbook, *Mercurius aulicus*, was more accurate, identifying the split on 17 January and reporting on 7 February that it was 'growing wider every day'.[75]

Lord Fairfax's status as leader of the West Riding Godly deepened this rift, as Sir John Hotham disapproved of puritans and ejected the Godly minister John Shaw from Hull.[76] Fairfax subsequently allowed Shaw to preach to his army at Selby that his outnumbered troops were 'the people of God', who had been 'scorned and nicknamed a long time for Waldenses, Hussites, Lollards, Lutherans, Huguenots, Precisians, Puritans (or all in one), Round-heads'.[77] The Hothams were further antagonized by Fairfax's promotion of the sectarian John Alured of Sculcoates to a colonelcy in the spring of 1643. Alured was a former captain in the Hull garrison, from where he had emerged as a vocal critic of Sir John Hotham.[78]

The queen's landing at Bridlington on 22 February further deteriorated the Fairfax–Hotham relationship. Instead of contesting her passage to York, John Hotham waited upon Newcastle at Bridlington under cover of exchanging prisoners, reportedly kissing the queen's hand.[79] On 9 March Sir John Hotham's son-in-law, Sir Philip Stapleton, reported that, if parliament directed Fairfax to send a thousand men to John Hotham at Beverley, Hotham would 'hazard a battle with the Earl of Newcastle' and prevent the queen's passage to York. The Commons subsequently ordered Fairfax to join Hotham in person or to send at least one thousand men.[80] Reluctant to divide his forces further, Fairfax disobeyed. Nevertheless, suspicions of Hotham grew in parliament that he had complained in a letter to Fairfax that

[74] R. Bell (ed.), *The Fairfax Correspondence: memorials of the civil war*, 2 vols (London, 1849), II, p. 36.

[75] BL, TT E85(15), *The kingdomes weekly intelligencer*, 10–17 January 1643 (London, 1643), p. 22; BL, TT E86(3), *Speciall passages*, 17–24 January 1643 (London, 1643), p. 198; BL, TT E86(7), *The kingdomes weekly intelligencer*, 17–24 January 1643 (London, 1643), pp. 301–302; P.W. Thomas (ed.), *The English Revolution III, Newsbooks I, Oxford Royalist*, 4 vols (London, 1971), II, pp. 21, 28; BL, TT E246(26), *Mercurius aulicus*, 5–11 February 1643 (Oxford, 1643).

[76] Macray, *The History of the Rebellion*, III, pp. 526–529.

[77] *CJ*, II, p. 40; J.R. Boyle (ed.), *Memoirs of Master John Shawe, Sometime Vicar of Rotherham, Minister of St Mary's, Lecturer at Holy Trinity Church, and Master of the Charterhouse, at Kingston-upon-Hull. Written by himself in the year 1663–1664* (Hull, 1882), p. 26; J. Shaw, 'The life of Master John Shaw', in C. Jackson (ed.), *Yorkshire Diaries and Autobiographies in the Seventeenth and Eighteenth Centuries*, Surtees Society, 65 (1875), Appendix, p. 369.

[78] Bodl. MS Fairfax XXXVI, fo. 7v.

[79] Binns, *The Memoirs and Memorials of Sir Hugh Cholmley*, pp. 126–127; J. Tickell, *History of the Town and County of Kingston-upon-Hull* (Hull, 1798), p. 465.

[80] BL, Harleian MS 164, fo. 318v; *CJ*, II, p. 995.

if he were not sent 'some succours he and Sir Hugh Cholmley must bee forced to take new counsels'.[81]

This threat proved prophetic, as Cholmley (John Hotham's cousin and parliament's governor of Scarborough) declared his change of sides on 25 March. Like the Hothams, Cholmley distanced himself from the Fairfaxes and had previously urged parliament to negotiate peace.[82] To prepare the ground for his defection, on 20 March Cholmley secretly met the queen at York, before returning to convert a majority of Scarborough's garrison. Sir John Hotham sent Captain Browne Bushell to regain the castle for parliament but was thwarted when Cholmley persuaded Bushell to join him.[83] The Hothams were angered that their close friend and kinsman had successfully changed sides without co-ordinating his plans with them, and John Hotham vented his disapproval in letters to Newcastle. On 2 April Sir John Hotham's report describing Cholmley's treachery was read in parliament, and Cholmley was impeached for high treason.[84]

Despite having spent months fortifying the place, Fairfax's army abandoned Selby on 30 March. This was partly in response to Cholmley's defection and to fears that the Hothams would follow. Fairfax marched to Leeds in order to join the clubmen in defending the clothing districts, thereby surrendering to Newcastle a passage southward. During the withdrawal, Sir Thomas Fairfax's rearguard was broken and captured on Seacroft Moor. Lord Fairfax blamed the 'Lincolnshire forces forsaking him' for his son's defeat.[85] Desperately short of cavalry, Fairfax was subsequently besieged in Leeds, and one royalist newsbook gloated that John Hotham was much blamed for not coming to his aid.[86]

According to Cholmley, in April John Hotham was invited into Lincolnshire 'by his alliance and friendship with the Wrays'.[87] He joined the local parliamentarians with five troops of horse and around two hundred foot, but was defeated at Ancaster Heath on 11 April.[88] Reporting the royalist victory, *Mercurius aulicus* alleged that some of

[81] BL, Harleian MS 164, fo. 337r.

[82] *Portland MS*, HMC, 29, 13th Report, Appendix, Part I, I, p. 90; YML, CWT, 43-01-18, *Newes from Yorke. Being a true relation of the proceedings of Sir Hugh Cholmley* (London, 1643).

[83] Binns, *The Memoirs and Memorials of Sir Hugh Cholmley*, pp. 143–146; *idem*, *'A Place of Great Importance': Scarborough in the civil wars, 1640–1660* (Preston, 1996), pp. 89–99; BL, TT E95(9), *A True and Exact Relation of All the Proceedings of Sir Hugh Cholmleys Revolt* (London, 7 April 1643).

[84] BL, Add. MS 31,116, fo. 40r.

[85] *Ibid.*, fo. 42v.

[86] BL, TT E100(18), *Mercurius aulicus*, 16–22 April 1643 (Oxford, 1643), p. 205.

[87] Sir Christopher Wray was Hotham's brother-in-law: Binns, *The Memoirs and Memorials of Sir Hugh Cholmley*, p. 127.

[88] The horse comprised the troops of John Hotham, Sir John Hotham (commanded by Major Lowinger), Sir Edward Rodes, Sir Matthew Boynton, and Captain Bethell. The foot

the Hothams' letters to John Pym had been intercepted. A godsend for royalist propaganda, these letters allegedly declared that, owing to Fairfax's secretary, 'Master Stockdale and his accomplices', all men of courage had left Fairfax's army 'but their own clan'.[89] On 13 April John Hotham's forces again failed to distinguish themselves, deployed alongside Cromwell at Belton. Hotham arrived in Lincoln soon after and wrote several letters to Newcastle about his negotiations with Lincolnshire parliamentarian leaders to lay down their arms. On 5 May Hotham, now styled 'Lieutenant General of the forces in Lincolnshire', complained to Speaker Lenthall that Ayscough, Wray, and he had been wrongly accused of failing to prosecute the war vigorously.[90] Anguish at their suffering reputations, blackened further by military defeats and allegations over the loyalty of their officers, invited these Lincolnshire gentlemen to reconsider their allegiance.[91] Hotham's reputation was further undermined when Lord Fairfax's report that he had disobeyed orders and deserted him was read in the House of Commons on 22 April.[92] Hotham was defeated once more, outside Grantham on 17 May, before he crossed into Nottinghamshire intending to delay the planned reinforcements for Fairfax.[93]

Arrest and trial

On 2 June John Hotham was at Nottingham, antagonizing the other parliamentarian commanders. Lucy Hutchinson recalled that, when her husband criticized the misbehaviour of Hotham's troops, Hotham replied 'he fought for liberty, and expected it in all things'. While Hutchinson and Cromwell wrote to warn parliament that they suspected him of treachery,[94] the disunity at Nottingham was so notorious in Oxford that Sir Edward Nicholas rejoiced 'that Hotham and Cromwell are ready to cut each other's throats'.[95] The Committee of Safety were informed that Hotham held private correspondence

were Hull greycoats under Captain Purefoy: TNA, SP 28/300/441; C. Holmes, *Seventeenth-century Lincolnshire* (Lincoln, 1980), p. 163.

[89] BL, TT E100(18), *Mercurius aulicus*, 16–22 April 1643 (Oxford, 1643), pp. 194–196.

[90] *Portland MS*, HMC, 29, 13th Report, Appendix, Part I, supplement, I, pp. 707–708.

[91] Holmes, *Seventeenth-century Lincolnshire*, pp. 164–166; C. Holmes, 'Colonel King and Lincolnshire politics, 1642–1646', *Historical Journal*, 16 (1973), p. 483.

[92] BL, Harleian MS 164, fos 378v–379r.

[93] BL, Add. MS 18,980, fo. 69r.

[94] BL, Add. MS 18,979, fos 141r–142v; N.H. Keeble (ed.), *Memoirs of the Life of Colonel Hutchinson* (London, 1995), pp. 108–109.

[95] F. Bickley (ed.), *A Report on the Manuscripts of the Late Reginald Rawdon Hastings Esq.*, HMC, 78, 4 vols (London, 1928–1947), II, p. 103.

with the royalists in Newark, plundered the well-affected, and offered to turn his artillery on Cromwell and give battle to Lord Grey over the latter's refusal to allow Hotham's troopers horse feed. The earl of Essex granted a warrant for Hotham's arrest.[96] On 22 June Hotham was dragged from his bed and incarcerated in Nottingham castle. There he penned a letter to the queen, delivered by his servant John Keys, inviting her to arrange his rescue. A troop of Lord Grey's horse was guarding him to Leicester, en route to London, when Hotham escaped, allegedly warning Captain Rossiter that 'we had better be subject to one than 300 tyrants', and 'you shall see in a short time that there will be never a Gentleman but will be gone to the King'. He rode to Lincoln, where he discoursed with Lord Willoughby, Captain Purefoy, and others, allegedly remarking that 'now he had got out of the protection of the Parliament he would keep out'.[97]

The queen, who had known of Hotham's correspondence with Newcastle since at least April, informed Newcastle on 27 June 'I hope now, that he will be prudent: better late than never.' The same day she wrote to the king that Hotham 'hath sent to me that he would cast himself into my arms, and that Hull and Lincoln shall be rendered'.[98] At Lincoln, Hotham wrote to his father of his escape and prepared the ground for his defection by writing a letter of protest to Speaker Lenthall on 24 June. It was read in the Commons three days later and noted by Sir Simonds D'Ewes. It complained that his arrest constituted an attack on his gentility that was doubly grievous because he had been the first man in arms for parliament.[99]

The House responded by ordering his fathers-in-law, Sir John Wray and Sir Henry Anderson, to write to Hotham to induce him to surrender his person at Westminster.[100] Instead he returned to Hull, where on 25 June Sir John had responded to his son's note: 'Your letter came joyful to me, both for the manner & the matter, that you have freed yourself from those false villains [. . .] They little think but that great Anabaptist hath you sure [. . .] I would see you here: we have a great game to play.'[101] Once reunited with his father, Hotham wrote to Newcastle on 28 June that he had been so maltreated by parliament

[96] *CJ*, III, p. 138.

[97] Stirling, *The Hothams*, I, pp. 79–80; Keeble, *Memoirs of the Life of Colonel Hutchinson*, p. 109; BL, TT E21(16), *Mercurius civicus: London's intelligencer*, 5–12 December 1644 (London, 1644), pp. 744–745, 749.

[98] M.A.E. Green (ed.), *The Letters of Queen Henrietta Maria* (London, 1857), pp. 191, 220–221; BL, TT E292(27), *The kings cabinet opened* (London, 1645), p. 33.

[99] BL, Harleian MS 164, fo. 234r–v.

[100] *CJ*, III, p. 146.

[101] By 'that Anabaptist', Sir John Hotham clearly meant Oliver Cromwell: BL, Harleian MS 165, fo. 107r; BL, Add. MS 44,848, fo. 287.

that 'no man can think my honour or honesty is further engaged to serve them'. He promised to attend Newcastle as soon as he could, but was unable to do so because his return to Hull had disastrous consequences for his father's government.[102]

Suspicion had already mounted upon Sir John Hotham for his refusal to let ships leave, and for his release of Browne Bushell to Cholmley for an inconsiderable exchange.[103] The testimony of the Hull gunner, Thomas Coatsforth, suggests that John Hotham's kissing of the queen's hand at Bridlington was known in Hull, while the fortification of the Hotham seat at Scorborough, and Sir John's redeployment of his heaviest artillery in the castle and south blockhouse to dominate the town and docks, had already excited rumour and suspicion. Despite this volatile atmosphere, Sir John prevailed upon Hull's council of war to sign an aggressive letter to parliament demanding justice against Cromwell for having arrested his son. Warning that they now reserved the right to reconsider their allegiance, the letter threatened 'we shall be excused both before God and man, to do the best we can for our own preservation'.[104] Captain Lawrence Moyer of the garrison warship *Hercules* was the only officer who refused to sign, so Sir John ordered his ship to depart. This confirmed Moyer's suspicion of Hotham, previously instilled by a letter from parliament.[105] He sent a letter to Mr Robert Ripley, asking him to acquaint the mayor of a plot against Hull. Ripley and Moyer organized the seamen and, from 5 a.m. on the morning of 29 June, they seized the Hothams' officers. Moyer's crew led companies of townsmen into the blockhouses to seize the soldiers' arms, where Lieutenant-Colonel Christopher Legard was taken after brief resistance. John Hotham was also quickly captured but his father fled towards the Beverley Gate, requisitioned a horse, and rode out. A musket and artillery piece fired after him 'made him set spurs and gallop as fast as he could'.

Sir John was unable to cross the tidal river Hull into Holderness, having tried at Stone Ferry and then at Wain Ferry, so a servant of Sir Matthew Boynton reached Beverley before him with a note to Boynton's son, Colonel Francis Boynton, to arrest Hotham. As Sir John rode into Beverley, he assumed command of the first company he met, but was soon faced with Colonel Boynton, who, according to one pamphlet account, 'took his horse by the reins and told him, Sir

[102]Stirling, *The Hothams*, I, p. 81.

[103]BL, TT E249(24), *A perfect diurnal of some passages in parliament*, 3–10 July 1643 (London, 1643), p. 10; BL, Egerton MS 2,647, fo. 9.

[104]Tickell, *History of Hull*, pp. 458–460.

[105]BL, TT E51(11), *Hull's managing of the kingdom's cause* (London, 1644), pp. 9–10; Stirling, *The Hothams*, I, p. 81.

John, you are my kinsman, and one whom I have much honoured but I must now waive all this & arrest you for a traitor to the kingdom'. Hotham allegedly replied 'Cousin I will be your true prisoner', before attempting to escape. He was clubbed from his horse by one of Boynton's musketeers and carried prisoner into Hull.[106] Later that day, Boynton's soldiers fought off a suspiciously timed attempt from Sir Hugh Cholmley to capture Beverley.[107] Around a week later, by order of Hull's committee for defence, both Hothams were conveyed on board the *Antelope* to London.[108]

The two Hothams had arrived in London by 24 July, accompanied by Sir William Fairfax and others who had come from Hull to testify against them.[109] On 21 August 1643, Gilbert Millington, the MP in charge of the evidences in the Hotham case, reported the examinations of John Hotham and then the witnesses against him, who included Fairfax's secretary at war, Thomas Stockdale, and two of John Hotham's own servants, John Keys and Thomas Hunter. D'Ewes noted that, to save his own neck, Keys accused his master of receiving intelligence from the queen in Yorkshire and at Newark, and that Sir John Hotham intended to deliver Hull to the earl of Newcastle. D'Ewes noted that, although 'Mr Hotham did answer with a great deal of subtlety and tergiversation', it nevertheless emerged that he had failed to prosecute the war against Newcastle's army and had frustrated Fairfax from doing so. Then one of John Hotham's letters to Stockdale was read out, in which 'he did express much spleen & indignation against him'. Another of his letters to Lord Fairfax was read out, stating that he would meet Newcastle at Ferrybridge to discuss a prisoner exchange and would not be bound by a council of war's vote to the contrary.[110] With the evidence growing against him, on 25 August John Hotham refused to answer further questions, arguing that, 'in his conscience, he ought not to answer any question that concerned his life, or might accuse himself'.[111]

On 6 September 1643 Sir John Hotham was moved from Alderman Bunce's house to the Tower, where none were to speak with him without his keeper's presence.[112] The next day he was brought to the bar of the House of Commons 'not kneeling', where he alleged

[106] BL, TT E59(2), *A true relation of the discovery of a most desperate and dangerous plot, for the delivering up, and surprising of the townes of Hull and Beverley* (London, 4 July 1643), pp. 3–5; Binns, *The Memoirs and Memorials of Sir Hugh Cholmley*, p. 129; Reckitt, *Charles the First and Hull*, p. 82.

[107] Reckitt, *Charles the First and Hull*, p. 85; Bodl., MS Tanner LXII, fo. 138.

[108] HHC: C BRS/7/67; Bodl., MS Tanner LXII, fo. 154.

[109] BL, TT E61(16) *Certain informations*, 17–24 July 1643 (London, 1643), pp. 209–210.

[110] BL, Harleian MS 165, fos 117v, 153v–154r.

[111] *CJ*, III, p. 218.

[112] *Ibid.*, p. 230.

his innocence and orated the services he had done parliament. He requested that his wife and papers might be returned to him and then, according to Sir Simonds D'Ewes, 'he fell a weeping like a woman & could scarce continue speaking'. Sir John appears to have made an enemy of Pym by suggesting that he had secretly transported money and plate overseas. At Pym's request, Lenthall asked Hotham if he knew anything concerning these rumours. Hotham allegedly replied in 'a fawning flattering way' that he knew nothing, and 'if I had said so I had told a famous lie'. According to D'Ewes, this shamed Hotham's own well-wishers. Millington then produced Sir John's unsigned examination, in which he confessed to a written correspondence with Lord Digby. This was enough for him to be ejected from the House and returned to the Tower.[113]

Detained 'by a real or pretended sickness' on 7 September, John Hotham was brought to the bar the following day. Like his father, he magnified his service, claiming to have been the first man in arms for parliament. He admitted disobeying Fairfax's orders but claimed that he held his commission directly from parliament. He denied holding correspondence with the queen and Newcastle but said that 'he wanted not temptations from the said Earl, who proffered him a free pardon & to command a third part of his army, and to be a baron if he would have joined with him'. He pleaded forgiveness for his errors and implored parliament to trust him again with further employment. Instead he was ejected from the House and returned to his imprisonment in a citizen's house before his transfer to the Tower was ordered on 3 October 1643.[114]

Initially it was thought that Essex delayed the Hothams' trials by refusing to grant a commission of lord president for the necessary council of war. When Essex suggested that John Hotham be tried by the earl's own colonels, some in the House of Commons feared that he intended an acquittal, and further debate was postponed on 12 October.[115] Essex set the date for the trials as 8 December 1643 but the Commons responded that this was too soon for all the witnesses to be ready.[116] The political struggle over the Hothams' fate grew violent when a key prosecution witness, Colonel Francis Boynton, who had arrested Sir John, was assaulted in New Palace Yard in February 1644 by three sons of Sir Christopher Wray.[117] The Hotham cases languished

[113]BL, Add. MS 31,116, fo. 77r; BL, Harleian MS 165, fos 170r–172r; BL, TT E67(22), *Certaine informations*, p. 268.

[114]BL, Harleian MS 165, fos 172r, 175r–176r; BL, Add. MS 31,116, fo. 77v; *CJ*, III, p. 262.

[115]BL, Add. MS 31,116, fo. 83r.

[116]*Ibid.*, fo. 95v.

[117]*CJ*, III, pp. 387–389; BL, Add. MS 31,116, fo. 114r.

until 4 June 1644, when Sir John Wray launched a motion for his son-in-law, John Hotham, to either stand trial or be released. After a long debate it was resolved to send him to Lord Fairfax in Hull, as many of the witnesses remained in the north.[118] Yet this order was never carried out and evidence against the Hothams mounted when three of their letters, allegedly offering to betray Hull, were taken from Newcastle's coach on Marston Moor and delivered to Gilbert Millington.[119]

A court martial under the chairmanship of Sir William Waller was eventually prepared to try the two Hothams. Thirty-three letters concerning Hull and the Hothams were delivered to the judge advocate on 19 October 1644 and nine more on 29 November.[120] On 2 November Sir Philip Stapleton procured parliamentary approval for Durand Hotham to help prepare the defences of his father and brother.[121] Durand was to act as Sir John's amanuensis throughout the trial and Sir John was permitted to call any MP as a defence witness. The charges laid against Sir John on 30 November were that he had betrayed his trust and adhered to the enemy. They incorporated refusing to supply Fairfax with powder, uttering scandalous words against parliament, and endeavouring to betray Hull. Sir John's incriminating letter to his son of 25 June 1643 was also included.[122] Among the prosecution's thirty witnesses were Thomas Stockdale, Colonels Francis and Matthew Boynton, the naval captains Lawrence Moyer and John Lawson, and the minister John Saltmarsh, as well as John Bernard, Maccabeus Hollis, and Thomas Coatsforth, a Hull alderman, merchant, and artillery officer respectively. They further included the servant John Keys and one Mr Rolston, secretary to the earl of Newcastle.[123] The defence's notes and interrogatories for witnesses survive among the family papers, although some of the notes are fragmented and in poor condition.[124]

Sir John crafted an elaborate defence. Conducted on 2, 3, and 4 December, several drafts and a polished version of this survive.[125] He denied that he intended to betray Hull, magnified his services to parliament, accused Lord Fairfax of backwardness, and argued that

[118] BL, Add. MS 31,116, fo. 142r–v; BL, TT E252(41), *A perfect diurnall of some passages in parliament*, 3–10 June 1644 (London, 1644), p. 355.

[119] *CJ*, III, p. 562; BL, TT E54(19), *A full relation of the late victory* (London, 11 July 1644), p. 13.

[120] HHC: Hotham MS, U DDHO/1/33.

[121] BL, Add. MS 31,116, fo. 171r.

[122] HHC: Hotham MS, U DDHO/1/42.

[123] *CJ*, III, p. 704; BL, TT E21(2), *Mercurius civicus: London's intelligencer*, 28 November–5 December 1644 (London, 1644), pp. 736–738; Stirling, *The Hothams*, I, p. 89; BL, TT E59(2), *A true relation of the discovery of a most desperate and dangerous plot*, pp. 5–6; Tickell, *History of Hull*, pp. 465–471.

[124] HHC: Hotham MS, U DDHO/1/40–41, 43.

[125] HHC: Hotham MS, U DDHO/1/34–38.

Thomas Stockdale and John Alured had been manipulated by the royalists into orchestrating a conspiracy against him. He explained that his correspondence with Newcastle was a strategy he had learned from Count Mansfeldt to deceive the enemy during the Thirty Years' War. His defence witnesses included his sons William and Charles Hotham, Commissary Lionel Copley, Sir Henry Anderson, Sir Thomas Remington, Lieutenant-Colonel Christopher Legard, Lieutenant Prestman, John Blackwell, Thomas Hunter, and several others. John Hotham's wife, Isabel, was prevented from testifying in her father-in-law's defence, as it was alleged that she had been involved in correspondence with Newcastle.[126] John Lambert warned Sir Thomas Fairfax that Hotham's defence had been so persuasive that he had 'left nothing unsaid or undone which may save his life'.[127] Nevertheless, Sir John was found guilty on 7 December and sentenced to be beheaded.[128] His wife's petition for his life was laid aside by the Commons four days later.[129]

The court martial began his son's trial on 9 December. John Hotham was charged with betraying his trust, adhering to the enemy, embezzling contributions, disobeying Lord Fairfax, and corresponding with Newcastle and the queen. Unlike the plentiful defence papers in the family collection for Sir John Hotham, none survive for his son, perhaps reflecting his untenable position and the greater certainty among contemporaries of his guilt. John Hotham's trial must therefore be pieced together from other sources. The twenty-seven prosecution witnesses were examined on 10 December and included one lord, one lieutenant-general, six colonels, a lieutenant-colonel, two majors, and four captains, namely Lord Grey of Groby, Oliver Cromwell, Edward Rossiter, Thomas Stockdale, Francis Boynton, Andrew Carter, and William White. There was also damning testimony from four family servants, including John Keys, and a statement from the late Sir William Fairfax that Hotham had attended the queen soon after she landed at Bridlington. John Hotham conducted his defence on 12 December, behaving submissively and seeking in vain to deflect blame onto his father. Of the twenty-six defence witnesses he called upon, all but six were his relatives, servants, or military subordinates. The judge advocate found against him on 21 December and he was sentenced to death on 24 December.[130]

[126]HHC: Hotham MS, U DDHO/1/34–35; BL, TT E21(2), *Mercurius civicus*, pp. 736–738.

[127]BL, Sloane MS 1,519, fo. 15.

[128]Stirling, *The Hothams*, I, p. 90.

[129]*CJ*, III, p. 721.

[130]BL, TT E21(16), *Mercurius civicus: London's intelligencer*, 5–12 December 1644 (London, 1644), pp. 744–750; BL, TT E22(8), *The weekly account*, 18–24 December 1644 (London, 1644);

Just before her stepson's sentence, Lady Hotham petitioned the Commons for her husband to have more time to settle his estate and prepare for death. Sir John also petitioned the Lords for a reprieve, 'seeing that his son's trial is not yet perfected, the doubtful issue of which hath much hindered the settlement of his affairs, and driven him to great anxiety of mind'. He was granted a reprieve of a week longer by eighty-five votes to sixty-five, with Cromwell as teller for those against it. On 28 December Sir John petitioned the Lords to spare his life or his son's, so that 'his whole family, that was the first that drew their swords in this Cause, may not be cut off root and branch'. The Lords recommended clemency but the Commons, by ninety-four votes to forty-six, refused to concur.[131] Sir Philip Warwick later believed that these eleventh-hour appeals were because both Hothams had been misguided into thinking that only one of them would be executed, and so 'the father endeavoured to sacrifice the son, & the son the father'.[132]

On 31 December the Lieutenant of the Tower brought Sir John Hotham out towards Tower Hill, when

> a man that had rid very hard came posting to him, with an order from the lords to stay his execution whereupon the throng of the people grew so violent and tumultuous, that all he could do was little enough to save his prisoner from being gotten away, he being got into the press a good distance from him.

The Lieutenant returned Sir John to the Tower, and by the time parliament had been sent word they had risen from sitting.[133] The next day, on 1 January 1645, John Hotham petitioned the Commons that he was prepared to pay £10,000 and undergo banishment if they would spare his life. This was rejected. Accompanied by his brothers he was taken to be beheaded on Tower Hill. He died unrepentant, refusing to acknowledge his offences, and in his last moments began to speak out against the council of war and parliament.[134]

With his son executed, on 2 January Sir John put another motion to the Commons to spare his life, '& it endured some debate in the House, many moving for it'. It failed, however, and Sir John was beheaded on Tower Hill at about 1 p.m.[135] His scaffold speech proclaimed that he

BL, TT E22(12), *Mercurius civicus: London's intelligencer*, 19–26 December 1644 (London, 1644), p. 760; Scott, 'John Hotham'.

[131] BL, Add. MS 31,116, fo. 182r–v; *The Parliamentary or Constitutional History of England*, XIII, pp. 357–359.

[132] Beinecke Rare Book and Manuscript Library, Yale University, Osborn Shelves, fb87, fo. 62r–v.

[133] BL, Add. MS 31,116, fo. 183r; Bodl., MS Tanner, LXI, fo. 212.

[134] BL, Add. MS 31,116, fo. 183r; Stirling, *The Hothams*, I, p. 93; BL, TT E23(9), *Mercurius civicus: London's intelligencer*, 26 December–2 January 1645 (London, 1645), p. 773.

[135] BL, Add. MS 31,116, fo. 183v.

had never betrayed parliament's trust, but that he deserved death for his sins, especially ingratitude and inclination to rash words and anger. In a calculated demolition of Hotham's notion of honour, Hugh Peter informed the crowd that Sir John wished to commend to them 'the vanity' of 'wit, parts, prowess, strength, friends, honour, or whatever else is merely of a terrestrial nature'.[136] Warwick's memoirs agreed with contemporary newsbooks that Sir John expected a reprieve on the scaffold 'but when he began to despair of that, he was desirous to have spoken somewhat more unto the people; but was not permitted: and therefore it might be easily judged, in what confusion of spirit he died'.[137] After the executions, some mercy was extended to the Hotham family. In May 1645 both Houses agreed to lift the sequestration on the Hotham estates, as it was settled that 'no attainder lay upon them to corrupt the blood of their heirs upon a judgment of martial law: as if they had been condemned by the Common Law'.[138]

The significance of the trial and execution of the Hothams has been overlooked by many civil war historians, hampered by a lack of concern to connect northern affairs with Westminster. This affair was highly political and conducted at a pivotal moment for the parliamentary cause. Simultaneous with the courts martial, on 11 December 1644 the Self-Denying Ordinance was brought before the House of Commons. Successful prosecution of the Hothams became a test of strength for those in favour of the new modelling of parliament's armies. In this way, the Fairfax interest became allies of Viscount Saye and Sele, Oliver St John, Oliver Cromwell, and the anti-Essex interest. This helped bring the many northern MPs connected with Lord Fairfax into sympathy with the war party and the Independents, who were prepared to take a tough stance on the Hothams. Conversely, those who urged clemency for the Hothams opposed the new army and Sir Thomas Fairfax as its commander, in particular the earl of Essex's supporters and emerging Presbyterian interest, who were often headed in the Commons by Sir John Hotham's son-in-law and the commander of Essex's lifeguard, Sir Philip Stapleton. When the Commons voted to reject clemency for Sir John, predictably Cromwell was teller for the anti-Hotham vote, with Stapleton opposing him.[139]

[136] Stirling, *The Hothams*, I, pp. 96–97.

[137] Beinecke Rare Book and Manuscript Library, Yale University, Osborn Shelves, fb87, fo. 62r–v; BL, TT E24(9), *Mercurius civicus: London's intelligencer*, 2–9 January 1645 (London, 1645), p. 776.

[138] BL, Add. MS 31,116, fo. 209v.

[139] D. Scott, 'The "Northern Gentlemen", the parliamentary Independents and Anglo-Scottish relations in the Long Parliament', *Historical Journal*, 42 (1999), pp. 347–375; Hopper, *'Black Tom'*, pp. 60–61.

In their victory over the Hothams, the Fairfaxes knew how to add insult to injury. Sir John Hotham's garrison regiment of foot was reorganized to become Lord Fairfax's own regiment of foot. Fairfax appointed Thomas Stockdale to inventory the Hothams' confiscated possessions, and, in a calculated affront, their rich apparel was sold to Fairfax's officers in lieu of their weekly allowance.[140] Isabel Hotham's will of 8 October 1651 complained that 'all mine and my husband's money, plate, jewels, goods, and personal estate, to the value of £7,000 at the least, was unjustly seized and taken away at Hull for satisfaction'.[141]

Sir John's government of Hull had been highly autocratic, and few outside his family mourned his passing. His confrontational temperament proved ill-suited to the testing demands of the parliamentary cause. In the face of siege, his co-operation with the corporation extended to pulling the mayor's gown over his head and setting a guard upon his house.[142] He accused Hull's MP, Peregrine Pelham, of uttering scandalous words against him and procured an order for Pelham's servant to be sent to parliament as a delinquent.[143] After Sir John's arrest, the corporation were quick to accuse him of tyrannical government and obliteration of their liberties.[144] One local minister lamented the 'harsh usage' that Sir John had meted out on the Godly, and declared that his arrest was an occasion of 'great joy' in the town.[145] Sir Hugh Cholmley later marvelled that, during the coup against him, Sir John could not find 'so much as one man to lift a hand in his behalf'. Cholmley attributed this to Hotham's notorious 'straight-handed' manner with his garrison's pay, when it was well known that he was 'rich in purse'. Bulstrode Whitelocke agreed that Hotham's 'rough carriage' towards his own soldiery alienated them. Sir John might have avoided this, considering that his personal estate in 1643 has been estimated at £10,000, of which at least £4,800 was in ready money. According to Cholmley, Sir John was 'of a rash and hasty nature', while Wentworth concurred that he was 'extreme sensible of honour, and discourtesies perhaps a little overmuch'.[146] The Hothams'

[140] HHC: C BRS/7/74, BRS/7/77.

[141] J.W. Clay (ed.), *Abstracts of Yorkshire Wills*, YASRS, 9 (1890), p. 42.

[142] BL, TT E107(32), *Exceeding good newes from Beverley, Yorke, Hull and Newcastle*, 20 July 1642 (London, 1642), pp. 3–5.

[143] BL, TT E244(15), *A perfect diurnall of the passages in parliament*, 12–19 December 1642 (London, 1642); *Portland MS*, HMC, 29, 13th Report, Appendix, Part I, I, p. 67; *CJ*, II, p. 863.

[144] Bodl., MS Tanner LXII, fo. 155.

[145] BL, Egerton MS 2,647, fo. 29.

[146] Binns, *The Memoirs and Memorials of Sir Hugh Cholmley*, pp. 128, 131; B. Whitelocke, *Memorials of English Affairs*, 4 vols (Oxford, 1853), I, p. 206; Cliffe, *The Yorkshire Gentry*, pp. 313, 382.

place among the most status-obsessed of gentry families was therefore a key factor in their ruin. Next was their realization that they had so disobliged the king that only by delivering him an exceptional advantage would their defection be satisfactorily accepted. Yet their procrastination indicates that a conspiracy to deliver Hull, Beverley, and Lincoln to the king was beyond even their impressive network.

The Hothams' unique position, as well as their temperament, was inclined to polarize factional conflict within the parliamentary cause. Both had been forced to choose their allegiance at a very early stage, when armed conflict still appeared unlikely. Sir John grew despondent as the destructive effects of war became apparent, and increasingly quick to take personal affront when parliament found paying his garrison difficult. Gardiner explained the falling away of the Hothams from parliament as happening because they had taken up arms 'from political rather than from religious motives', and that therefore they 'felt themselves ill at ease as the cause for which they fought showed itself as more distinctly Puritan'. The most prominent Yorkshire turncoats, such as Cholmley and the Hothams, certainly tended to be religious moderates.[147] Yet the seeds of their disaffection also lay in the fractured and contested parliamentary command structure in Yorkshire, their disdain for the Fairfaxes, and their suspicion of an army of clubmen mobilized in the West Riding clothing districts.

In response to mounting perceived slights, and prompted by fears for their persons and estates, the Hothams considered the ultimate sanction of changing sides. Clarendon remarked that Sir John was 'a man apt enough to fear his own safety',[148] and this is hardly surprising given the plethora of reported assassination attempts against him and his son.[149] There had been much talk among royalists of seeing him hanged, and from June 1642 he remained among the few

[147] S.R. Gardiner, *History of the Great Civil War, 1642–1649*, 4 vols (London, 1904), I, p. 105; Cliffe, *The Yorkshire Gentry*, p. 346.

[148] Macray, *The History of the Rebellion*, II, p. 258.

[149] BL, TT E239(6), *A soveraign antidote to prevent appease, and determine our unnaturall and destructive civill-wars and dissentions* (London, 18 August 1642), p. 23; BL, TT E122(24), *A declaration of the lords and commons assembled in parliament* (London, 17 October 1642); BL, TT E240(40), *A perfect diurnall of the passages in parliament*, 10–17 October 1642 (London, 1642), p. 8; BL, TT E242(19), *England's memorable accidents*, 14–21 November 1642 (London, 1642), p. 87; BL, TT E127(48), *The effect of all letters read in the House of Parliament*, 14–23 November 1642 (London, 1642); BL, TT E90(12), *Special passages*, 14–21 February 1643 (London, 1643), p. 232; BL, TT E90(16), *A continuation of certaine speciall and remarkable passages*, 16–23 February 1643 (London, 1643); BL, TT E246(30), *A perfect diurnall of the passages in parliament*, 20–27 February 1643 (London, 1643).

parliamentarians exempted from pardon.[150] There was little sympathy from royalists after his arrest; Sir Edward Nicholas declared that both Hothams deserved punishment, 'for falser men then he & his son live not upon the earth'. Likewise, hoping to portray his own trimming in a more positive light, Lord Savile echoed condemnations of Sir John: 'how infamous, how inconstant, how detestable a traitor that man was'. Whitelocke considered Hotham 'high and morose', while Clarendon recalled him as 'a rough and rude man; of great covetousness, of great pride, and great ambition; without any bowels of good nature, or the least sense or touch of generosity'.[151] This chorus of contemporary abuse from across the political spectrum indicates the full cost of miscarriage for failed turncoats. Sir John Hotham and his son paid for their change of heart not just with their lives but also with their posterity.

By 1643 the Hothams' notion of injured honour undermined their allegiance. This sense of honour militated them towards royalism after they had chosen to support parliament; their notions of self-worth and concept of honour were unable to adapt to the horrors of popular uprisings, yeomen captains, and sectarian officers. They also lacked restraint in dealing with subordinates. Sir John Hotham's refusal of the king at the Beverley Gate on 23 April 1642 was the parliamentarians' greatest strategic achievement that year. Yet, only the following year, had the Hothams' attempted defection been better co-ordinated, their conspiracy might have proved fatal to the entire parliamentary cause. They planned to surrender three thousand men, plus the towns of Hull, Beverley, and Lincoln, just when parliament's fortunes were on the verge of collapse. Having saved the parliamentary cause in 1642, in 1643 they might have destroyed it. Their examples demonstrate better than any the fluid nature of allegiance during the English Revolution.

Provenance

Since 2010, the Hotham papers have been held in the Hull History Centre as part of the archives of the University of Hull; further letters survive in the British Library and the Bodleian Library at the University of Oxford. The civil war letters, papers, and tracts that remained in the Hotham family were deposited by Henry Frederick

[150] BL, TT E154(34), *Terrible and true newes from Beverley and the city of Yorke* (London, July 1642), pp. 6–7; BL, TT E153(15), *True newes from Yorke. Consisting of severall matters of note, and high concernment, since the 13. of Iune* (London, 1642); BL, Harleian MS 164, fo. 278r–v.

[151] Bodl., MS Carte VI, fo. 11; Bodl., MS Clarendon XXIV, fo. 24v; Whitelocke, *Memorials of English Affairs*, I, p. 206; Macray, *The History of the Rebellion*, II, pp. 261–263.

Hotham, 7th Lord Hotham, in the East Riding Record Office in 1954. The collection was transferred to the Brynmor Jones Library and Archive at the University of Hull in 1974, before its recent transfer to the new Hull History Centre. The collection is primarily made up of manuscripts and pamphlets, with few larger printed books because Sir John Hotham's books were taken by Thomas Raikes, mayor of Hull, after his arrest and passed on to Lord Fairfax, who later donated them to York Minster Library as part of his failed attempt to establish a university in the north.[152] The large family collection of printed pamphlets in DDHO/2 is discussed and listed in Appendix I.

The part of the manuscript collection dealing with the civil wars and the interregnum encompasses eighty-six items dated between 1641 and 1660. There are letters addressed to Sir John Hotham from prominent parliamentarians such as John Pym, John Hampden, and Ferdinando, Lord Fairfax. There are also many papers relating to the trial of Sir John Hotham in December 1644, which together formed the materials used in his defence: these include an early draft of Sir John's defence[153] and an altered and rewritten version in his own hand for delivery during his trial,[154] as well as drafts of part of his defence[155] and two copies of the defence made in a later, eighteenth-century hand.[156] There are further papers handling the disposal and inheritance of his estates. Most of the collection is in good condition, although some of the defence notes relating to the trial are torn and fragmented. Of central interest is a series of sixteen copies of letters written by Sir John Hotham and John Hotham to the royalist general William Cavendish, earl of Newcastle. The dates on these copies range from 18 December 1642 to 26 April 1643, and historians have often confused father and son in attempts to ascribe authorship.[157] This uncertainty can be resolved by knowledge of the military narrative and attention to the place of writing. Letters signed at Hull were usually written by Sir John Hotham, while his son's letters were penned from his campaign headquarters at Cawood, Beverley, or Lincoln. The originals of many of these letters survive in the Nalson collection in the Bodleian Library, the purpose of the copies that survive in the family collection being to inform Sir John Hotham's defence. As the Hothams' papers were seized and confiscated at their arrests, Barbara English has suggested that these papers were copies that the

[152] *CJ*, III, p. 704; Hopper, *'Black Tom'*, p. 153.
[153] HHC: Hotham MS, U DDHO/1/34.
[154] HHC: Hotham MS, U DDHO/1/35.
[155] HHC: Hotham MS, U DDHO/1/37–38.
[156] HHC: Hotham MS, U DDHO/1/36.
[157] HHC: Hotham MS, U DDHO/1/14–29.

prosecution supplied to Sir John's defence, headed by his son Durand Hotham. This might explain the absence from the collection of the Hothams' more incriminating and less defensible letters written in May and June 1643, with Durand eschewing items that could not be accommodated in the defence or that might prove embarrassing for posterity.[158]

The Hotham letters that survive in the Nalson and Tanner collections of the Bodleian Library are primarily original letters written by John Hotham to the earl of Newcastle, and by Sir John Hotham to William Lenthall, Speaker of the House of Commons. The broken seals remain on many, along with evidence of numbering and heading by notes in another hand on their reverse sides, suggesting that they were subsequently used by the prosecution during Sir John Hotham's trial. On 29 August 1644 the House of Commons ordered that all papers concerning the Hothams were to be delivered to the judge advocate of their court martial;[159] thirty-three letters were accordingly delivered on 19 October and nine more on 29 November.[160] These included the three letters taken from the earl of Newcastle's captured coach after the battle of Marston Moor, which were read in parliament and used to press for the Hothams to be brought to trial.[161] Too late to have been used in the trial, a further letter from John Hotham to the earl of Newcastle dated 3 April 1643 was taken by Sir Peter Wentworth after the surrender of the royalist garrison in Pontefract castle on 21 July 1645.[162] Wentworth obtained this letter by 5 August and delivered it to the House of Commons on 1 October 1645, along with other letters from both Hothams addressed to Newcastle.[163]

After the trial and execution of the Hothams, these original letters were retained in the office of the Clerk of Parliament, prior to their removal by the royalist historian the Reverend John Nalson for his intended publication of *An Impartial Collection of the Great Affairs of State* (London, 1683). After Nalson's death in 1686, part of his collection eventually passed to Bishop Thomas Tanner, while the rest went to Nalson's grandson, Philip Williams, who by 1730 had arranged them into bound quarto volumes. Williams also transcribed copies of several of the Hotham letters now in MS Nalson XI. The letters then probably passed to the Reverend William Cole of Ely, son-in-law of Zachary

[158] B. English, 'Sir John Hotham and the English civil war', *Archives*, 20 (1992), pp. 220–221.
[159] *CJ*, III, p. 610.
[160] HHC: Hotham MS, U DDHO/1/33.
[161] Saltmarshe, *History and Chartulary of the Hothams*, p. 140.
[162] HHC: Hotham MS, U DDHO/1/12.
[163] *CJ*, IV, p. 295.

Grey, and then to his brother, Charles Nalson Cole. Their history thereafter remains obscure until Maxwell Lyte discovered them in a cupboard in the duke of Portland's library at Welbeck Abbey in 1885. They were calendared for the Historical Manuscripts Commission by 1891,[164] and were deposited at the Bodleian Library in 1945 before being donated to the Bodleian in 1987.

Editorial decisions and practice

The objective has been to provide a clear and readable version of these manuscripts, in order to render them accessible to a wide audience. Throughout the text and appendices, therefore, capitals, spelling, and punctuation have been modernized, with abbreviations silently expanded. Where the manuscript source is damaged and words partially obscured, I have endeavoured to supply the legible characters, as they appear. Footnotes have been used to point to other manuscript copies and published transcripts of the documents, and also to identify individuals and provide context for events discussed in the text. Words crossed out within the text are marked with angle brackets, <. . .>, and insertions with asterisks, *. . .*. Where the accuracy of transcription is uncertain the word(s) are embraced by question marks, ?. . .? . Dates are given in 'old style', but new years are taken to commence on 1 January.

For ease of reference, the archival shelf number for each document has been given in bold, followed by the author, recipient, and the place and date of its writing. Rather than reproducing the documents in order of their archival references, the transcriptions have been arranged in chronological order. It is hoped that this merging of the Hothams' papers from a range of archives will facilitate a deeper understanding of their position in the context of the rapidly changing events of 1642 and 1643. While this codification and arrangement has been possible for most documents, a number remain unidentified and undated. Some of these have been approximately dated by their content or by evidence from elsewhere, but, where it has not been possible to date documents beyond reasonable doubt, they have been grouped in a separate section at the end of the text.

[164] *Portland MS*, HMC, 29, 13th Report, Appendix, Part I, I.

THE LETTERS AND PAPERS
OF THE HOTHAMS

DATED LETTERS AND PAPERS

HHC: C BRL/251: Sir John Hotham to the mayor of Hull, Scorborough, 9 February 1635

Mr Mayor,

I received since our being at Hull a letter from the lords of the council signifying that if we desired it His Majesty would be graciously pleased to lend us a ship of his own but with this, that if we relied upon that favour, we must raise £1,635 more than the £4,980 already assessed. I have writ to my lord mayor of York who it seems hath writ something to you about it, whose letter I send you herewith. I pray consider well of it and let me have your answer. I think the sheriff and I meet at Barton upon the seventeenth of this month. Betwixt and then I pray write me your mind herein, for if you can take order amongst you to provide a ship, then we need assess no more. If not then we must proceed to the raising the whole sum. This is all I have for the present, but to write this truth that I will ever be found,

your very loving friend to serve you,
John Hotham.

[*On reverse*] To the right worshipful, my much respected friend Mr Denham, mayor of the town of Hull, these:

HHC: C BRL/252: Sir John Hotham and Walter Norton to the mayor of Hull, Barton-upon-Humber, 18 February 1635

Mr Mayor,

We having received a letter from the lords of the council bearing date 15 January for the speedy providing of such a ship as in a former writ is mentioned. And whereas, upon intimation from you and the rest of the mayors then present, we certified their lordships, that you had neither havens nor timber fitting for the preparing such a ship within the time limited. Whereupon their lordships have let us know that His Majesty is graciously pleased to let us have a ship of his own, so that the sum of £1,635 be added to £4,980 already assessed. The contents of which letters having made known to you, and receiving from you

answer that you can by no means tell how to provide a ship, we have thereupon proceeded to <an> the assessment of the said money and taking into consideration the state of your town and county, together with the abilities of the maritime towns betwixt Hull and York. We have assessed upon your town and county £66-13s, which is £150 less than according to the former proportion which we have taken from you and laid upon the maritime towns. We understand that it is by some conceived that there ought to be levied upon the lords' letter but £1,385. We have this day perused the lords' letter and are clearly of opinion that £1,635 is intended. Thereby thus desiring you to use all possible diligence for the speedy levying of this and the rest of the monies assessed upon you.
We bid you heartily farewell and rest,

your very loving friends,
John Hotham, Walter Norton.

[*On reverse*] To the right worshipful, our very loving friend the mayor of Kingston-upon-Hull. These for His Majesty's service:

HHC: C BRL/253: Sir John Hotham and Walter Norton to the mayor of Hull, Barton-upon-Humber, 3 March 1635

Mr Mayor,
We have this day met at Barton and have taken into consideration the lords' letters of 15 February sent us by the Lord Mayor of York, and though that we are still of opinion that the £250 in question will in the conclusion be required which makes the total £6,615, yet because the lords in their letters are pleased to write to us that there is required only £1,385 over and above the £4,980 already assessed, we have thought fit hereby to signify unto you that you may forbear the levying of £50 of that last assessment upon your town, and if the £250 be not required then so much is abated in your assessment. If it be required then you know your rate. We shall desire that there may be no delay for the speedy levying the monies because we do not know how soon it may be required at our hands. So commending us kindly to you, we rest,

your very loving friends,
John Hotham, Walter Norton.

[*On reverse*] To the right worshipful, our very loving friend the mayor of Kingston-upon-Hull. These:

HHC: C BRL/254: Sir John Hotham to the mayor of Hull, Scorborough, 16 March 1635

Mr Mayor,
I send you here enclosed a letter I received the other day from the lords of the council whereby you will perceive the difference decided for the £250 which you now see must assuredly be paid. And for the last £50 (which if the other had been spared) was taken of your assessment must now be paid and then your proportion will be upon the first £660, upon the second £66-13s, in all £726-13s, which I shall entreat you will not fail to pay into my lord mayor's hand at York sometime this week. And his acquittance with a letter to me for the receipt of it shall be to you a discharge. I pray sir do me the favour not to fail herein for I have private directions to make all possible haste therein. So commending me kindly to you, I will ever rest,

your affectionate friend,
John Hotham.

I pray return me the lords' letter by this bearer.

[*On reverse*] To the right worshipful, my very loving friend, the mayor of Kingston-upon-Hull. These for His Majesty's service:

HHC: C BRF/6/32: Memorandum of Sir John Hotham concerning ship money, Scorborough, 23 March 1635

Memorandum that Mr Denman, mayor of the town of Kingston super Hull, and Mr William Pecke sheriff of the same town, hath paid into the hands of Mr Thomas Hodson, lord mayor of York by my appointment £726-13s-od being the rate imposed upon that town and county for the providing and furnishing of a ship of 800 tons for His Majesty's service according to the writ directed to me and the sheriff of Lincolnshire. In witness whereof and for the discharge of the said mayor and sheriff I have hereto put my hand the day and year above written at Scorborough,

John Hotham.

In the presence of John Bourdenand,[1] Henry Dalton.

[1]For John Bourdenand of Scorborough, servant to Sir John Hotham, see HHC: C BRS/7/29; A. Hopper, 'A directory of parliamentarian allegiance in Yorkshire during the civil wars', *YAJ*, 73 (2001), p. 101.

HHC: Hotham MS, U DDHO/1/69: Order in Star Chamber concerning Sir John Hotham, Westminster, 16 October 1635

Whereas Sir John Hotham, knight and baronet, late high sheriff of the county of York, is called up by process of this court to answer an information intended to be exhibited against him by His Majesty's attorney general for letting his undersheriffwick to farm. The right honourable the Lord Keeper,[2] this day, upon the signification of His Majesty's pleasure, by Mr Secretary Cooke,[3] hath ordered according to his highness's good pleasure, in that behalf now signified unto him, that no information shall be exhibited against the said Sir John Hotham, for that matter, nor other prosecution had against him thereupon.

M. Goad.

HHC: Hotham MS, U DDHO/1/1: Sir Hugh Cholmley to Sir John Hotham, Whitby, early December 1635[4]

Here was lying above the bridge a Dunkirk ship, and the Hollander hath sent in his boat and <taken> beaten the Dunkirkers out and boarded their ship which they intend to if they can to come forth of the harbour. <Jo> I myself, by chance light of the captain with his pistol in his hand, [and] have him now in custody. <my> I desire your assistance with all speed and advice what is fit to be done. So in great haste I rest,

your assured cousin,
Hugh Cholmley.

HHC: C BRL/259: Sir John Hotham to the mayor of Hull, Fyling Hall, 10 May 1637

Sir,
We have received directions from the lords for muster [*MS damaged*] the forces of the county and I know 'tis [*MS damaged*] intention that

[2] R. Cust, 'Thomas Coventry, first Baron Coventry (1578–1640)', *ODNB*.

[3] Coke was one of the two principal secretaries of state to Charles I in the 1630s: M.B. Young, 'Sir John Coke (1563–1644)', *ODNB*.

[4] Although this letter is undated, Jack Binns has pointed out that this incident in Whitby harbour, described by Cholmley in his memoirs, took place in early December 1635: J. Binns (ed.), *The Memoirs and Memorials of Sir Hugh Cholmley of Whitby 1600–1657*, YASRS, 153 (2000), p. 96n.

those of your town and county [*MS damaged*] manner be dealt withal as the rest. I shall god [*MS damaged*] upon Thursday the eighteenth of this present [*MS damaged*] if you please that notice may be given that the old [*MS damaged*] be made good. Sir, I have no more for the present but my best respect to yourself and the rest of my good friends [*MS damaged*] you I will ever be found ready

to serve you wherein I may,
John Hotham.

[*On reverse*] To my much honoured friend, the mayor of the town of Kingston-upon-Hull. Present, these:

BL, Add. MS 28,082, fo. 80v: Sir John Hotham's regiment of trained bands, *c.*1639

Sir John Hotham, Lieutenant-Colonel of 1040 men (vizt) in Hunsley and Bainton Beacons, within the wapentake of Harthill, and in Beverley 451, in Wilton Beacon within the same wapentake 203, in Howdenshire 146, and in Hull and the county 240. His captains are: Sir Marmaduke Langdale, Sir John Lister, Sir Richard Remington, John Hotham his son, Robert Crompton, esq., William Goodrick, esq., Christopher Ledgerd, esq.

HHC: Hotham MS, U DDHO/1/83: Muster roll of infantry in royal army, 23 October [1640]

[*Column 1*]
Lord Marquess – 214
Lieutenant-Colonel Feilding – 163
Sergeant-Major Beray – 150
Captain Dawson – 110
Captain Monyngs – 109
Captain Smith – 108
Captain Paine – 106
Captain Langley – 106
Captain Walthall – 109
Captain Bozonne – 110
Captain Greene – 110
Captain St John – 110
Captain Watson – 109
[Total] 1,616 [*sic*]

Colonel Wentworth – 192
Lieutenant-Colonel Waite – 140
Sergeant-Major Brockett – 141
Captain Roberts – 106
Captain Parry – 105
Sir Christopher Aboy – 097
Captain Holman – 91
Captain Lloyd – 102
Captain Fotherby – 93
Captain Windebank – 95
[Total] 1,162

[*Column 2*]
Lord General – 178
Lieutenant-Colonel Ashburnham – 165
Sergeant-Major Latham – 102
Captain Lloyd – 104
Captain Croft – 75
Captain Washington – 95
Captain Atkins – 104
Captain Porter – 94
Captain Chudleigh – 104
Captain Dowse – 079
Captain Edwards – 109
Captain Heron – 99
[Total] 1,308

Colonel Glemham – 212
Lieutenant-Colonel Pawlett – 167
Sergeant-Major Beaumont – 128
Captain Mynn – 98
Captain Kirby – 89
Captain Kirton – 108
Captain Codrington – 104
Captain Perkins – 110
Captain Dimmock – 089
Captain Withers – 102
[Total] 1,207

[*Column 3*]
Lord Newport – 162
Lieutenant-Colonel Monke – 125
Sergeant-Major Warren – 116
Captain Sheldon – 100
Captain Kirton – 082
Captain Croft – 082

Captain Coope – 77
Captain Stradling – 77
Captain Burrowes – 96
Captain Vanpeece – 76
[Total] 993

Colonel Merrick – 185
Lieutenant-Colonel Carne – 157
Sergeant-Major Davies – 146
Captain Seymor – 106
Captain Herbert – 109
Captain Broughton – 108
Captain Button – 102
Captain Maxy 106
Captain Skrimshaw – 098
Captain Hide – 103
[Total] 1,220

[*Column 4*]
Sir Jacob Astley – 192
Lieutenant-Colonel Selwyn – 100
Sergeant-Major Astley – 106
Sir William Uvedall – 99
Captain Townshend – 95
Captain Russell – 100
Captain Baynton – 103
Captain Bellasis – 96
Captain St John – 93
Captain Astley – 91
[Total] 1,015 [*sic*]

Colonel Colepepper – 167
Lieutenant-Colonel Gibson – 100
Sergeant-Major Turvill – 095
Captain Owen – 082
Captain St Leger – 90
Captain Cooke – 082
Captain Lukenor – 077
Captain Thurland – 94
Captain Paten – 77
Captain Boyer – 90
[Total] 954

[*Column 5*]
Colonel Goring – 146
Lieutenant-Colonel Kirke – 154

Sergeant-Major Willis – 144
Captain Gray – 85
Captain Shelley – 71
Captain Gerrard – 78
Captain Daniell – 91
Captain Myns – 57
Captain Prediaux – 82
Captain Elliott – 79
[Total] 987

Sir Charles Vavasor – 207
Lieutenant-Colonel Howard – 155
Sergeant-Major Appleyard – 146
Captain Donnell – 108
Captain Wynde – 99
Captain Pate – 94
Captain Kingsmill – 92
Captain Thornton – 109
Captain Scudamore – 100
Captain Dimock – 77
[Total] 1,187

[*Column 6*]
Lord Grandison – 169
Lieutenant-Colonel Ballard – 72
Sergeant-Major Sibthorp – 108
Captain Pretty – 104
Captain Smith – 89
Captain Villiers – 97
Captain Ellis – 88
Captain Lisle – 96
Captain Vervay – 99
Captain Boyes – 91
[Total] 1,013

Colonel Vavasor – 103
Lieutenant-Colonel Mynn – 80
Sergeant-Major Pagett – 74
Captain Gilmore – 67
Captain Brett – 62
Captain Beningsfield – 60
Captain Holtby – 60
Captain Leighton 56
Captain Ferrers – 59

Captain Nicolls – 56
Captain Maxwell – 86
[Total] 763

[*Column 7*]
Colonel Aston – 212
Lieutenant-Colonel Bole – 160
Sergeant-Major Coningsby – 140
Captain Lukyn – 98
Captain Leighton – 96
Captain Keyes – 95
Captain Courtney – 97
Captain Thomas – 96
Captain Tompson – 100
Captain Bradshawe – 96
[Total] 1,190

Colonel Lunsford – 163
Lieutenant-Colonel Lunsford – 72
Sergeant-Major Powell – 70
Captain Edward Powell – 59
Captain Pomeroy – 84
Captain Lunsford – 86
Captain Martyn – 74
Captain Cooper – 67
Captain Hipsley – 72
Captain Dillon – 59
[Total] 806

[*Column 8*]
Lord Barrimore – 181
Lieutenant-Colonel Burrage – 162
Sergeant-Major Usher – 146
Captain Trafford – 104
Captain Brian – 101
Captain Gerrard – 106
Captain White – 105
Captain Power – 101
Captain Henise – 105
Captain Pursell – 104
[Total] 1,215

Colonel Ogle – 207
Lieutenant-Colonel Buck – 161

Sergeant-Major Lawdey – 118
Captain Ferrer – 77
Captain Drury – 80
Captain Andrews – 47
Captain Ventres – 66
Captain Sandys – 47
Captain Poore – 44
Captain Griffin – 70
[Total] 917
Sum total: 17,553 [*sic*]

By me, Ralph Errington
Deputy commissary

HHC: Hotham MS, U DDHO/1/6: Sir Arthur Ingram[5] to Sir John Hotham, York, 9 September 1641

Worthy sir,
Your kind letter I have received by this post, for which I heartily thank you. In your letter you are pleased to write that upon a letter my Lord General[6] sent unto the House which was that he intended to go forward in the discharging of the army before he would take any course in the discharging of the artillery; the which you did fear the House might take ill. I must confess I have spoken to my Lord about it and acquainted him with your care of him, which he taketh very kindly from you. But his answer was that his letter was mistaken, for he hath given order for the discharge of the train of artillery, and that some part of the horse belonging to them are already discharged, and all the rest shall totally be discharged forthwith. And I may say that if the £20,000 and the £30,000 that you moved the House for were come down with the money we shall receive from the several shires, I make no doubt but that the whole army, the train of artillery, the two garrison towns, and all other things that hath any manner of dependency upon the army will be wholly discharged. And that being done, all manner of doubts and feares will be taken away and that you will find in all things my Lord General hath carried himself like a noble, faithful, honest man. My desire is to cherish a firm good liking in my Lord of you, which is now very well settled, and I shall

[5]In the summer of 1642, the king established court at Ingram's house in York: S. Healy, 'Sir Arthur Ingram (b. before 1571, d.1642)', *ODNB*; W.M. Ormrod (ed.), *The Lord Lieutenants and High Sheriffs of Yorkshire, 1066–2000* (Barnsley, 2000), p. 133.

[6]Ingram refers to the earl of Holland, who was lord general of forces north of the Trent in 1641: R.M. Smuts, 'Henry Rich, first earl of Holland (bap. 1590, d. 1649)', *ODNB*.

endeavour with all the poor means I can to continue it between you. I do not find by your letter any certain time of the adjourning of the House, the which I pray you in your next letter to write me the certainty of it, that I may direct the course of my coming to London accordingly, and so I rest,

your most faithful friend to serve you,
Arthur Ingram.

HHC: Hotham MS, U DDHO/1/71: Resolution of both Houses of Parliament concerning Sir John Hotham, Westminster, 11 January 1642[7]

Resolved upon [*MS damaged*] by the Commons' House of Parliament [*MS damaged*] that the Lords [*MS damaged*] with this House, that [*MS damaged*] of the trained bands, next adjoining to Hull, be forthwith put into that town, for the safeguard of the town of Hull and magazine there, and to be under the command of Sir John Hotham. The Lords do consent and concur with the opinion of this House in this resolution.
Resolved upon the question: That Sir John Hotham or such person as he shall be responsible for, do instantly repair to Hull and put some of the trained bands of the parts next adjoining to that town, for the defence of that place and magazine there, according to the resolution of both Houses.
Henry Elsynge,[8] clerk of the House of Commons.

HHC: Hotham MS, U DDHO/1/72-73: Order of the House of Lords to Sir John Hotham, Westminster, 11 January 1642

To Sir John Hotham, knight, the elder:
It is this day ordered by the Lords in Parliament, that some of the trained bands of Yorkshire, nearest to Hull in the said county, under the command of Sir John Hotham, knight, shall with all speed be put into the said town of Hull, for the securing of the King's magazine there, and the said town, and hereof the said Sir John Hotham is by virtue of this order commanded to perform it accordingly.
John Browne,[9] clerk of the House of Lords.

[7] For the Hothams' involvement in the seizure of Hull for parliament, see I.E. Ryder, 'The seizure of Hull and its magazine, January 1642', *YAJ*, 61 (1989), pp. 139–148.

[8] J.C. Sainty, 'Henry Elsynge (bap. 1606, d. 1656)', *ODNB*.

[9] J.C. Sainty, 'John Browne (*c*.1608–1691)', *ODNB*.

Bodl. MS Tanner LXVI, fo. 256: John Hotham to William Lenthall, Hull, 4 February 1642

Sir,

I have in obedience to the orders of both Houses, drawn in 700 of the trained bands of the county of York into the town of Hull, for the securing of that place, and the magazine. What endeavours there were to hinder it, I know this House is well informed, and how I have made a shift to get through them. The reason that I drew in so many was, I *saw* the malignant party so averse to your order and so violent the other way, that less forces could neither secure that place, nor perform that trust which you have put upon them. For while we were at the gates the papists were freely admitted, but scarce any of ours, to buy their fellows necessary victuals. When we were got in, although we entreated them with all civility and respect to billet the soldiers, they would not admit a man but would have had them starve in the streets. So that I was put to this exigency either to disband my men to your disservice, and scorn, and the loss of the place, or <the> to billet them whither they would or no, yet with the greatest fairness that I could possibly. Their opposition was so violent by the encouragement of some ill affected people to your service, that some of the officers were very ill hurt by the townsmen, yet [we] did not reward them with the like. Sir Thomas Glemham's regiment were readily admitted,[10] and billeted, and then these good Commonwealthsmen said nothing of the liberty of the subject that was infringed, by which you may judge them. Sir, I hear they will complain, for their factors are gathering hands to justify themselves, and accuse me. I hope the House will suspend their judgement, until I be heard, and that is all I shall desire. If I have not done my duty as a faithful servant to the House, let *me* be punished. I desire you would be pleased that we may have some order for the billeting, and something to the gentlemen that they may see you take their readiness to serve you in good part. It will else weaken those hands that are affectionate to your service, and if this town and magazine slip out of your hands it will be harder to recover than the House may for the present conceive, for our papists storm much that it is where it is, and great riding and posting there is with them, but about what I cannot yet learn. I desire the House would be pleased to send me down an order, for ammunition out of the magazine by this post, for when we were kept out, they dealt it freely abroad, but *now we* can get none. Sir, I hope the wisdom <will> *of* the House will not stand upon the nice formalities of law and lawyers seeing that *salus*

[10]John Hotham was referring to the time when Sir Thomas Glemham was military governor of Hull, from 1640 to 1641: B.N. Reckitt, *Charles the First and Hull, 1639–1645* (2nd edn, Howden, East Yorks, 1988), pp. 13–14; A. Hopper, 'Sir Thomas Glemham (1595–1649)', *ODNB*.

populi is *suprema lex*. The monthly charge will be about £900.· If they please to lessen it they may, but yet it is scarce safe. Sir, if I may but know their command, they shall be readily obeyed by

your friend and servant,
John Hotham.

[*On reverse*] Sir John Hotham letter.[11] To his much honoured friend William Lenthall, esq., Speaker of the House of Commons, these present:

Bodl. MS Nalson II, fo. 373r: John Metcalfe to John Gifford,[12] Hamburg, 18 April 1642

From a merchant of Hamburg, one Mr John Metcalfe to Sergeant-Major Gifford at Hull.
Little news here in these parts; His Majesty of Denmark[13] hath his ships in a readiness and it is reported intending for Hull. But he is not over hasty since he hears of our navy being out at sea, besides we report you are very strong and if he come he will be bidden welcome. He is about rising over tolls at Gluckstadt as well as in the Sound but of that I refer you to the passengers.

Your approved friend,
John Metcalfe.

This is an extract of a letter written from Hamburg by Mr John Metcalfe to Sergeant-Major Gifford at Hull, compared with the original by us:
[The earl of] Stamford,[14] Edward Ayscough,[15] Christopher Wray,[16] Samuel Owfield,[17] Thomas Hatcher.[18]

[11]This letter was wrongly ascribed to Sir John Hotham, rather than his eldest son, John Hotham.

[12]For John Gifford, see Appendix II.

[13]Christian IV, king of Denmark 1588–1648, was uncle to Charles I.

[14]Stamford was the parliamentarian lord lieutenant of Leicestershire sent to Hull to confer with Sir John Hotham in April 1642: A. Hopper, 'Henry Grey, first earl of Stamford (*c.*1599–1673)', *ODNB*.

[15]Ayscough was a prominent parliamentarian and knight of the shire for Lincolnshire: D.R. Woolf, 'Sir Edward Ayscu (1596–1654)', *ODNB*.

[16]Wray was MP for Grimsby and joined John Hotham in Yorkshire with his troop of horse in October 1642: A. Hopper, 'Sir Christopher Wray (bap. 1601, d. 1646)', *ODNB*.

[17]Sir Samuel Owfield (*c.*1595–1643) of Elsham, Lincolnshire, was MP for Gatton in Surrey from 1640 to 1643. He served the parliamentary war effort as a committee man for Lincolnshire and died in Hull in May 1643: M.F. Keeler, *The Long Parliament, 1640–1641: a biographical study of its members* (Philadelphia, 1954), p. 291.

[18]Hatcher was MP for Stamford and joined John Hotham in Yorkshire with his troop of horse in October 1642: D. Scott, 'Thomas Hatcher (*c.*1589–1677)', *ODNB*. His troop mustered on 29 September 1642, numbering sixty troopers and officers, including its lieutenant, Lawrence Parsons: TNA, SP 28/253/b/part ii/350.

HHC: Hotham MS, U DDHO/1/74: Resolutions of both Houses of Parliament exonerating Sir John Hotham, Westminster, 26 April 1642

Resolved upon the question:
That Sir John Hotham according to this relation hath done nothing but in obedience to the command of the Houses of Parliament.
Resolved upon the question:
That the declaring of Sir John Hotham traitor, being a member of the House of Commons is a high breach of the privilege of Parliament.
Resolved upon the question:
That this declaring of Sir John Hotham traitor, without due process of law, is against the liberty of the subject and against the law of the land.
These resolves were agreed upon by both Houses.
John Browne, clerk to the House of Lords.
Henry Elsynge, clerk to the House of Commons.
It is this day ordered by the Commons House of Parliament that two thousand pounds shall be forthwith purposed to Sir John Hotham for the payment of the garrison at Hull.

[*On reverse*]
Order the 26 April 1642
Votes for your indemnity upon refusing the king entrance into Hull.
Henry Elsynge, clerk to the House of Commons.
These votes are agreed upon and thus passed by both Houses of Parliament.
Henry Elsynge, clerk to the House of Commons.

HHC: Hotham MS, U DDHO/1/2: John Hampden[19] to Sir John Hotham, Westminster, 17 May 1642

For my noble friend, Sir John Hotham. These:
I received your letter, which I take for a testimony of your favour to me, and I pray you, do believe that I shall not appear altogether unthankful for it, when you shall have occasion to make trial of me, in any particular service. I was present at the reading of your letters this morning, upon which that order was made, and those Committees chosen that I hope will give you full satisfaction. Sir Henry Vane is neither well nor in town. Sir William Strickland, absent too, but I think he will be sent away as soon as he comes. When we first heard that the captains suspended their obedience to the commands of the

[19] Sir John Hotham enjoyed contacts at the heart of the opposition junto: C. Russell, 'John Hampden (1595–1643)', *ODNB*.

Houses, it did something amuse us, but, when their own letter was read to my Lord Admiral, which was soon after yours, the House received very good satisfaction. I hope things are not in so ill a posture as you apprehend them to be, but that it is rather your vigilancy and tender care of the peace of the kingdom that makes you suspect the worst. And no doubt it is the part of a wise man to foresee and be prepared. Since your letter came so safely I wish you had been plain in two particulars. One, what that good means is to quench the fire by; the other, what is that right way that is now gone and never was before? For you that are where the scene of business lies can discern better how every part is or ought to be acted then we can at so great a distance, and your judgement of things either done or to be done would have been a great light to me. We are every day entertained with new messages or occurrences from York, which takes up all our time from all our other business. God put an end to these distractions in his own way and season, which are the best. The Lords and Commons go on unanimously, and the countries hereabouts are like to give a cheerful obedience to the Ordinance of the Militia, which is now putting in execution. <and> The late approach to Hull, with that purpose of adjourning the term to York, hath given little satisfaction to men's minds in the south parts, whatsoever it hath done to those in the north. I fear your messenger may be gone. Therefore no more now but my service to your son and Mr Pelham.[20] Let me hear from you as often as you can, and be assured, you shall ever find me

your faithful friend and servant,
[*Unsigned*]

We suspect opening of letters.

[*On reverse*] [*Seal*] 16. John Hampden.

HHC: Hotham MS, U DDHO/1/3: John Hampden to Sir John Hotham, Westminster, 28 May 1642

Sir,
I went from this town *into Buckinghamshire* on Monday morning last where I have been till now about the militia of that county. During

[20]Peregrine Pelham, MP for Hull, supported Sir John Hotham when the king was denied entrance and remained in the town during the siege of July 1642, but later clashed with Sir John over his government of the town: A. Hopper, 'Peregrine Pelham (bap. 1602, d. 1650)', *ODNB*.

this absence I find you have been pleased to favour me with two of your letters which my brother Pym[21] read when I was away, and the latter of them he imparted to the House as it was necessary he should, and is even now returning you the sense of the House in answer to it. I see God hath showed himself wonderful in his deliverance of you from treachery, and He that hath done it will still deliver. I know not what hath passed the House in my absence, having been here but about an hour. But I may tell you they seem confident and secure above what I could expect, considering how great a noise the withdrawing of the Lords made in the country, and the soldiers have performed their parts very well. Besides our trained bands, we have many volunteers that have armed themselves at their own charge and formed themselves into bands. I have no more to write of at this present being such a stranger here. But now you shall find me ready to serve you here, and certainly I have very great cause for by these your letters and confidence in me you have obliged me to make it my study how I may discharge that trust faithfully, which upon all occasions I shall endeavour, even with the best affections of

your most assured friend and humble servant,
John Hampden.

My service to your noble son and Mr Pelham.

HHC: Hotham MS, U DDHO/1/4: John Hampden to Sir John Hotham, [Westminster], 7 June 1642

For Sir John Hotham, Governor of Hull. These:
Sir,
According to your desire expressed in your letter of the 3rd of this present I obtained this enclosed order: the Houses were very careful to satisfy your desires, but it was not without fear that by the stay of those gentlemen in Hull, the service of Lincolnshire to which they were designed, might suffer prejudice, which it will be your wisdom to prevent in the making use of this order. The Houses received yesterday the information of the great meeting at York upon which no conclusion can be made, since nothing was required of the people nor anything declared by them. But the Houses are much affected with the carriage

[21] Pym was a central figure in the opposition junto at Westminster: C. Russell, 'John Pym (1584–1643)', *ODNB*.

of my Lord of Lindsey[22] and my Lord Savile[23] that so violently hindered the delivery of the Country's petition and not a little sensible of the rescuing of Mr Bethwick.[24] They are very apprehensive now of the danger the King, Kingdom and Parliament are in by reason of the dangerous counsels, and are in a way to provide the best they can for keeping of the peace, which I assure myself is their principal aim. You cannot but hear how resolutely the kingdom of Scotland have carried themselves at Edinburgh; therefore to take you up no more at this time I present my service to your noble son and Mr Pelham, and rest ever

your assured friend,
John Hampden.

[*Seal*].

HHC: Hotham MS, U DDHO/1/5: John Hampden to Sir John Hotham, [Westminster], 14 June 1642

For Sir John Hotham, Governor of Hull. These:
Sir,
I received yours of the 10th since I sent away mine this morning. I am very glad when I find you in life and cheerfulness, notwithstanding difficulties. The Lincolnshire blades have carried themselves with great resolution; and I verily believe there will be many as little daunted as they have been. Yet what discouragements do those *revolting* Lords endeavour to bring upon honest men. They vote as they do, execute the votes as favourably as any, then desert them, as if there were neither principle of conscience or honesty left among men, but I leave them to the comfort they will find in this way. Our Lord Lieutenant went away on Saturday night last and overlooked my Lord of Bristol at Sir Kenelm Digby's mother's.[25] But there be, God be thanked, of

[22]Lindsey was lord lieutenant of Lincolnshire and killed at Edgehill: P.R. Newman, *Royalist Officers in England and Wales, 1642–1660: a biographical dictionary* (London, 1981), p. 27; A. Thrush, 'Robert Bertie, first earl of Lindsey (1582–1642)', *ODNB.*

[23]Lord Savile was disabled from sitting in parliament on 6 June 1642 for having gone to the king at York and having obstructed the delivery of petitions from parliamentary sympathizers on Heworth Moor: A. Hopper, 'Thomas Savile, first earl of Sussex (bap. 1590, d. 1657×9)', *ODNB.*

[24]The puritan martyr Dr John Bastwick was imprisoned in York castle during the summer of 1642: F. Condick, 'John Bastwick, (1595?–1654)', *ODNB.*

[25]Hampden was referring to the defection of William, Lord Paget, lord lieutenant of Buckinghamshire. Paget had supported the Militia Ordinance but joined the king at York on 14 June 1642: G. Goodwin, rev. J. Sutton, 'William Paget, sixth Baron Paget (1609–1678)', *ODNB.*

those noble lords that will live and die in doing their duty to the utmost. The Commons also are more entire than ever. More of them than I could have imagined have declared themselves to assist in the last propositions which I am sure you have seen. The City likewise continues full of affection to the Parliament. They lent £100,000 very lately, and when these propositions of horse and plate were made to them in a great assembly at Guildhall, there were large testimonies of approbation. If there be the least stop of your money let me hear instantly. All diligence shall be used for your satisfaction, and there will be a great readiness in the House to perform it. The orders you mention could not be propounded this morning. Some doubt ariseth to me about that which should be for the malicious opposers of the Parliament, because it is in the nature of a warrant dormant. But send us up the names of some of such and their faults and you shall hear of us quickly. We believe the Danish fleet is to fetch salt. Let me hear of you often, and command freely

your servant,
John Hampden.

[*Seal*].

Bodl. MS Nalson II, no. 43: Sir John Hotham, John Hotham, John Alured,[26] and Peregrine Pelham to Sir Philip Stapleton, Hull, July 1642[27]

Since our last of the 3rd of June the Providence hath landed six great pieces of battery, whereof three are demi cannon of 24 pound bullet. You may see by the declaration that a speedy course of violence is intended against here. We have by our former advertised you how unable without present supply of more men *we are* to subsist. <wh> We have as we conceive certain intelligence that this ship hath within her 24 pieces of ordnance besides 14 of her own which if she cannot get of herself off the sands then they will have the addition of those. We believe they have at this instant together 300 horse and about 2,000 foot. They have arms, powder and other ammunition, and so take up all men that come. We believe that they will instantly, if not opposed, be a considerable body, yet of such men as if the Parliament take a quick course (but it must be) without delay as will not hazard much for them. We shall, God willing, do our best but our outwork

[26] For John Alured, see Appendix II, p. 249, n. 55.

[27] For summaries of this letter see *Portland MS*, HMC, 29, 13th Report, Appendix, Part I (London, 1891), I, p. 41.

being not yet tenable 'tis not much we can do without we suddenly have more men sent us by sallies to hinder their approaches. You have oft had it reiterated from hence the necessity of a good committee here. You have appointed some but we are no better. We are not at this instant four. We desire you will be pleased to send down *Sir William Strickland*,[28] <Sir Philip> Sir Hugh Cholmley,[29] Sir Philip Stapleton,[30] Sir Henry Cholmley.[31] They are gentlemen that in these times may do good with their credit in the country. If while you sit voting these other be doing you will soon find but a bad issue. Horse speedily sent down where [*sic*] of great use. We shall earnestly entreat you will take to heart this, as sent from them whose utmost endeavours if you will *enable* them *shall be* to serve you. So we rest,

your humble servants,
John Hotham, John Hotham, John Alured, Peregrine Pelham.

We have certain intelligence, they intend instantly if they can to make quick work with us here.

HHC: Hotham MS, U DDHO/1/7: John Hampden to Sir John Hotham, Westminster, 18 July 1642

For my much honoured friend, Sir John Hotham, Governor of Hull. These:
Sir,
Mr Hill hath brought your letters of the twelfth of July, arrived here yesterday morning. Sir Philip Stapleton was gone down to the King, so I opened your packet. This morning order is issued for money to pay your garrison and to provide you with necessaries, for six pieces of ordnance to be sent you, and for thanks to be presented

[28] Sir William Strickland was MP for Hedon and an active committee man at Westminster. His seat at Boynton Hall was plundered by the royalists in 1643: A. Hopper, 'Sir William Strickland (*c.*1596–1673)', *ODNB*.

[29] Sir Hugh Cholmley was a cousin of John Hotham and MP for Scarborough. He was appointed parliamentarian governor of Scarborough before defecting to the king in March 1643: Binns, *The Memoirs and Memorials of Sir Hugh Cholmley*.

[30] Sir Philip Stapleton, MP for Boroughbridge, had married Sir John Hotham's eldest daughter, Frances, in 1629. He became a protégé of the earl of Essex and captain of his lifeguard, furthering the Hothams' interests with the parliamentarians' commander-in-chief: A. Hopper, 'Sir Philip Stapleton (bap. 1603, d. 1647)', *ODNB*.

[31] Sir Henry Cholmley, MP for Malton, raised a regiment of foot for the earl of Essex's army in summer 1642: Hopper, 'A directory of parliamentarian allegiance in Yorkshire', p. 96; Keeler, *The Long Parliament*, p. 134.

to Captain Moyer and Captain Piggott,[32] and for the <pieces of ordnance> release of Captain Horner. The men that are to supply your garrison are many of them shipped and the rest will follow apace after. Your courage and constancy hath demonstrated that Hull is tenable for above five hours, which hath been opposed by diverse arguments. The General hath his ordinance passed both Houses. My Lord of Bedford is chosen General of the Horse.[33] We are of opinion the King's forces will not stay long before Hull, but that he will march southward, yet six pieces of ordnance shall be presently sent you *or at least some of them*. We should be glad to hear from you oftener. I hope this messenger will propound you a safe and speedy way for intelligence. If you find there be truth in the plot of firing the town, I pray let us know the particulars for it is very necessary we should have information of them. This enclosed message of the King's came from Beverley upon Monday and our petition went away upon Wednesday. There is no express answer returned, but we hear it will <not be very w> *be* such an one as will not be very welcome when it comes. They speak from court of great forces, and no less confidence, but we are not easily induced to believe it. Yet here are persons ill affected enough to Parliament working in every corner. But the Lord in heaven will plead for his poor servants, and either give us peace or preserve us from violence. There is a Committee of Lords and Commons chosen for the safety of the kingdom and if you direct of us [*MS damaged*] we shall take care of effecting your desires and returning you answer. You may do very well to send us up the names of your prisoners, of which I have taken care that none shall be released without the knowledge of the committee, who will be very careful that you sustain no prejudice therein. There shall be present order taken to send you meal, malt, cheese etc. I can think of nothing else. Mr Hill is to deliver your three thousand pounds, and you shall have more very shortly. It will be good to know whether you will not need a Colonel or Lieutenant-Colonel *to be sent to you* when you have so many men. Among the captains that now come to you, I recommend unto your care my

[32]Captain Lawrence Moyer commanded the fourth rate armed merchantman *Hercules*, with a crew of 150 men and 28 guns. Captain Joseph Piggott commanded the *Mayflower*, with a crew of 121 men and 28 guns. Both ships were attached to the Hull garrison in 1642–1643: J.R. Powell and E.K. Timings, *Documents Relating to the Civil War 1642–1648*, Navy Records Society, 105 (1963), pp. 9, 11, 25, 70.

[33]William Russell, earl of Bedford, dated his service as general of horse from 22 July 1642 to 12 February 1643. Thereafter, he resigned his commission and joined the king in Oxford: BL, Add. MS 28,721, fo. 14; V. Stater, 'William Russell, first duke of Bedford (1616–1700)', *ODNB*.

nephew Hammond,[34] in whom you may fully confide. The rest are strangers to me, but I hope they will acquit themselves like soldiers and men of honour. Mr Hill speaks of great outrages committed by the cavaliers, especially upon the families and goods of such as have come in to you to Hull. If it be possible let us have certain intelligence of the truth of this and as particularly as you can be informed. For if this be the beginning of their behaviour before they can be sure of the event, men may easily judge what the end will be if they should prevail. You shall receive herewith an order for thanks to be given to Captain Moyer and Captain Piggott for their good service. If there had been time it should have come with a particular letter but the committee is extremely full of business, and I hope this will satisfy them for the present who may justly expect a real reward hereafter.

Your faithful servant,
John Hampden.

[*On reverse*] [*Seal*]. 10. Sir John Meldrum.[35]

HHC: Hotham MS, U DDHO/1/9: Ferdinando, Lord Fairfax,[36] and others to Sir John Hotham, Denton, 7 September 1642

Sir,
We have considered at this meeting in what condition a great part of this Riding stands, and we find that though there be neither want of affection, nor resolution to serve our country, yet there is so great a defect of arms that for the present 'tis doubtful that our endeavours may not only prove fruitless but dangerous both to the service, and ourselves, unless we be supplied by you according to the declaration of Parliament, with such a number as we shall need, and you can spare. We conceive 500 foot arms will be useful, and 30 barrels of powder with match, answerable, and 100 horse arms if you have them. Then shall we be as well enabled, as resolved to perform all parliamentary commands both in preventing and suppressing of the

[34]Robert Hammond, later a colonel in the New Model Army and the king's gaoler on the Isle of Wight, began his civil war service in Hull's garrison: see Appendix II; Greaves and Zaller, II, p. 44; G.E. Aylmer, 'Robert Hammond (1620/21–1654)', *ODNB*.

[35]The Scots professional commander, Sir John Meldrum, led into Hull the reinforcements raised in London by early July 1642. He played an important role in the ensuing siege: C. Carlton, 'Sir John Meldrum (b. before 1584?, d. 1645)', *ODNB*.

[36]Ferdinando, Lord Fairfax, commissioned as general of parliament's forces in Yorkshire on 3 December 1642: A. Hopper, 'Ferdinando Fairfax, second Lord Fairfax of Cameron (1584–1648)', *ODNB*.

disturbance of the public peace and securing the safety of this county. The treaty though it [*MS damaged*] suspend action yet not preparation, your speedy [*MS damaged*] shall receive a ready account of the [*MS damaged*] and forwardness of

your affectionate friends to serve you,
Ferdinando Fairfax, Thomas Fairfax,[37] Edward Rodes,[38]
William Lister,[39]
Richard Hutton,[40] John Lambert,[41] William White,[42]
Thomas Lister.[43]

[*On reverse*] [*Seal*]. To our honourable friend, Sir John Hotham, knight and baronet at Hull. This:

Bodl. MS Nalson II, no. 82: Sir Edward Rodes and John Hotham to William Lenthall, Selby, 1 October 1642[44]

For our honourable friend William Lenthall, esq., Speaker of the House of Commons. These present:
Sir,
Since we received your letter of encouragement and directions to us and others, dated 27 September, diverse who were principally concerned in it have concluded a most disadvantageous agreement

[37] Sir Thomas Fairfax, eldest son of Ferdinando, and first commanding general of the New Model Army: A. Hopper, *'Black Tom': Sir Thomas Fairfax and the English Revolution* (Manchester, 2007).

[38] Sir Edward Rodes of Great Houghton became the only West Riding parliamentarian entrusted with a military command by Sir John Hotham, whose first wife, Katherine Rodes, had been Sir Edward's cousin: Hopper, 'A directory of parliamentarian allegiance in Yorkshire', p. 107.

[39] Sir William Lister of Thornton-in-Craven, or his son, Captain William Lister, who was killed at Tadcaster in December 1642: Hopper, 'A directory of parliamentarian allegiance in Yorkshire', p. 119.

[40] Richard Hutton of Poppleton, Co. York, esq., had married Dorothy, daughter of Ferdinando, Lord Fairfax: W. Dugdale, *The Visitation of the County of Yorke*, Surtees Society, 36 (1859), p. 173.

[41] For John Lambert of Calton, see D. Farr, *John Lambert: parliamentary soldier and Cromwellian major-general* (Woodbridge, 2003).

[42] William White of Bashall was later commissioned colonel by Lord Fairfax and was recruiter MP for Pontefract from 1645: Hopper, *'Black Tom'*, pp. 26, 34, 58, 77; *idem*, 'A directory of parliamentarian allegiance in Yorkshire', p. 115.

[43] For Thomas Lister of Westby, see BL, TT E128(28), *Speciall passages*, 22–29 November 1642 (London, 1642), and BL, TT E242(5), *A perfect diurnall of the passages in parliament*, 31 October–7 November 1642 (London, 1642).

[44] For summaries of this letter, see *CJ*, II, p. 792; *Portland MS*, HMC, 29, 13th Report, Appendix, Part I, I, p. 64.

both to the service of the kingdom and to the safety of this county, the copy whereof we herewith send you.[45] Whereby the House may *please to* observe in what condition we stand who are actually engaged and with God's blessing fully resolved to persist in our obedience to the commands of Parliament. Therefore we present it as our humble suit that instructions may be sent down for raising of horse, money and plate, and because 'tis so doubtful who now stands right amongst us, that blanks may be left for the names of commissioners. And that some timely monies may be supplied from thence because they cannot suddenly be raised here. But especially that they would move the Lord General that two regiments and four troops may march to us with all speed. We being now betwixt eight and nine hundred foot and one troop *of the Hull forces* at Selby, having left three hundred foot and another troop at Doncaster *of the country*. We further desire the pleasure of the House concerning such who assist with horse, money, or otherwise against the Parliament or shall shroud their disaffection in a pretended neutrality. Also, if they think fit that warrants may be sent for the apprehending of some of the most notorious delinquents by name, and that overtures of making their peace may be intimated to others, to which and to all other their instructions will be given the most ready and willing observance of

your friends and servants,
Edward Rodes, John Hotham.

HHC: Hotham MS, U DDHO/1/8: John Hampden to Sir John Hotham, 4 October 1642

To my much honoured friend Sir John Hotham, knight and baronet, governor of the town of Hull. These:
Noble sir,
I think myself very happy that I have been so rightly represented to you in the business concerning the two gentlemen of our House you mention in your letter. Which gives me occasion likewise to give you this assurance that the evidence you have given to all the world by your noble actions of that judgement and honesty which is in you, shall never be called in question by me upon slight grounds. And therefore let me desire this justice from you that you will not believe of me

[45]This was the peace treaty concluded by Lord Fairfax with local royalists at Rothwell on 29 September 1642: BL, TT E119(29), *Fourteen articles of peace propounded to the king and parliament by the gentry and commonalty of the county of York* (London, 4 October 1642). For a discussion of this failed treaty, see A. Woolrych, 'Yorkshire's treaty of neutrality', *History Today*, 6 (1956), pp. 696–704.

otherwise than what I now profess upon any misinformation until you do me the favour to let me answer for myself. I shall only desire *you* to manage the business concerning those persons with that tenderness that without absolute necessity no public discouragements <be put> may fall upon them who have ventured far in the public, and have incurred you know in a very high degree the displeasure of the court. But your wisdom I doubt not will so moderate these things as will give very good satisfaction to all objections. We are sending horse and foot to your noble son with all speed and think ourselves not well dealt with in the late pacification made by Yorkshire, as by our declaration will appear. I shall trouble you no farther at this time but shall ever be

your most faithful friend and servant,
John Hampden.

[*On reverse*] [*Seal*] 13.

Bodl. MS Nalson II, no. 153: Sir John Hotham to William Lenthall, Hull, late October 1642[46]

For my honourable friend, William Lenthall, esq., Speaker of the honourable House of Commons. These:
I am very sorry I must of necessity trouble you and the House once again upon this subject I am now to write to you upon. You may be pleased to remember I writ to you that it were best for your service to send up for Mr Pelham to attend the service of the House, which I thank you, you believed me in and accordingly did. If I could have had that order obeyed in any measure I should not have needed to have gone any further (being nothing was in my heart of sharpness towards the man), more than in relation to the safety of this town. I had then heard of mutinous words he had given out against the greycoats (which were those southern forces you sent down), as that the town must keep a guard against them. And since the occasion requires it give me leave to do the gentlemen that commands them that right that they are men of sober condition, and do endeavour their utmost to restrain their men from doing wrong. Some few faults their men commit in the country, which as far as our power gives leave not having *had* martial law, we have endeavoured to remedy. Six I have delivered to the justice of the law to be tried and suffer according to law. But for any hurt done in the town or towards the townsmen I believe in any garrison was never less cause of <Compl> complaint.

[46]For summaries of this letter, see *Portland MS*, HMC, 29, 13th Report, Appendix, Part I, I, p. 66.

Upon the receipt of your order I sent it to him and expected a long time obedience to it, and if he had not proceeded in a great measure to have disturbed the peace of the town, truly I had left him to himself to have made his own answer. But you will perceive by this testimony here enclosed, taken before Sir Hugh Cholmley and Mr Wharton,[47] to what height his anger had drawn *him* to accuse me in plain open English that I meant to plunder the town, with other words at his pleasure, and truly though I hope you all believe that that accusation deserves *no* answer. If I had such an intent surely I chose a most unfit time for myself being that I had at the same time 600 of my foot forces at Cawood castle, my son with his troop of horse, my major I had sent in one of the ships riding here to Scarborough with 120 men more to surprise a hoy that came from Holland with 2,000 arms (who were gone just half a day before we could get thither). And I had yielded to Sir John Gell[48] of Derbyshire to lend him 120 more of my men to give a beginning to settle the militia in Derbyshire. Which country right settled (as they have assured me with those men they quickly can) gives great security to Yorkshire, Derby being the *best* pass into Yorkshire should any forces be sent from the King's army. And at that time Mr Aldred's troop was wholly in town you will think not much amicable to me. But more than enough of that. You will see he was angry as he saith concerning one Mrs Watkinson not let into her house, that was that Mr Watkinson's wife that was wholly employed by Captain Legge.[49] In whose practices my Lord Newport totally relied that if the King came to the gates it would not be in my power to keep him out.[50] This man stayed at York with the King, [and] all the time he was at York sent for to consult with upon all occasions. In his absence my son and his wife billeted at his house. While my son was at Selby, Mr Watkinson sends his wife hither (a woman practise[51] enough), and tongue more than I desire to be troubled with, she comes

[47]Michael Wharton of Beverley Park, esq., was Sir John Hotham's fellow MP for Beverley and on the parliamentarian committee in Hull in the summer of 1642. He defected to the royalists and was killed by a cannon ball while standing next to Sir Hugh Cholmley during the siege of Scarborough castle in 1645: Hopper, 'A directory of parliamentarian allegiance in Yorkshire', p. 98; Keeler, *The Long Parliament*, p. 379; J. Binns, *Yorkshire in the Civil Wars: origins, impact and outcome* (Pickering, North Yorks, 2004), p. 118.

[48]Hotham sent Gell a company of London greycoats in Hull in October 1642 to serve as the beginning of his Derbyshire regiment: T. Brighton, 'Sir John Gell, first baronet (bap. 1593, d. 1671)', *ODNB*.

[49]The king appointed Captain William Legge master of the armoury at Hull during the Bishops' Wars: I. Roy, 'William Legge (1607/8–1670)', *ODNB*. The Mr Watkinson mentioned here may have been James Watkinson, merchant of Hull, who was serving as keeper of the royalist arms magazine in York by 1643: TNA, SP 23/177/716.

[50]Newport allegedly advised the king to appear before Hull in April 1642: D.L. Smith, 'Mountjoy Blount, first earl of Newport (*c.*1597–1666)', *ODNB*.

[51]'To influence or persuade (a person) into some course of action, especially an evil one; to corrupt': *OED*, online edition.

to me, desires to have her house. I told her my daughter was there in her husband's absence and was a woman that loved not to be troubled with wrangling and entreated her to forbear till my son should come home and I doubted not but she should have all just things she could desire. This was that keeping her out of her house. Indeed when the King did besiege us ?having so just cause? (as if ever it be my fortune to see you in that House I shall acquaint you with the affair being no way fit for a letter), to fear some false measure, I framed this note (which I send you here enclosed) and tendered it generally to the town to be signed, which generally was readily signed except some few. I believe some twenty that refused it. As I take it about some eight of those that I suspected had their hands or were likely to have their hands in some practice against us. I willed to forbear the town and till these distractions be a little passed (if you otherwise direct me not) shall still wish them to forbear the town. The first (and if I should examine my heart to the bottom), all the offence I gave Mr Pelham was this: one of these (that married his sister) desired to be suffered to come into the town again which by me was denied him. He comes in whither I would or no (I suppose bearing high upon his great brother-in-law). I sent for him and wished him to be gone. He made many allegations that he was a merchant, had many business[es] in the town and desired to stay for [a] small time. To that I had but one answer, that he was in his conscience privy to the ill attempts he had against the town trusted to me by Parliament, yet if he would yet sign the paper with us he should have whatever he desired. While this man and myself were in discourse comes in Mr Pelham and needs must have not only but all the rest let in though 'tis so notorious, as I think himself will not deny (a worse affected man to Parliament is not in town). Upon the refusal of this he grew into a great passion and told myself then that [*MS damaged*] must keep a guard against the greycoats. Yourselves shall judge whether I had reason to let this Toppin,[52] Mr Pelham's *brother* into the town, having then in my hand (which I now send you enclosed), an examination of a master of a ship, a very honest, able man that heard this Toppin confess he was consenting and privy to the betraying the north blockhouse (the key of the town), and the setting the town on fire. When this information was given me (which I send you under the party's *hand*) of Mr Pelham's saying I meant to plunder the town, I was in some doubt what to do. (The man truly being beneath my anger) I asked advice of Sir Hugh Cholmley and Mr Wharton what was fittest for me to do. They both concurred (that such language *might* breed dissention in the town) and that it was

[52]In 1646, Matthew Topham, merchant of Hull, compounded for his delinquency in leaving Hull for York when it was garrisoned for the King: M.A.E. Green (ed.), *Calendar of the Committee for Compounding (Domestic), 1643–1660* (London, 1889), II, p. 1037.

fit to sequester him presently, least he might do more harm to one of the <Hul> King's ships riding here and to send him to you, there to be proceeded with according as to you in your wisdoms should be thought just. This I did, yet in the hearing of these gentlemen and many of my chief officers, I offered him that if he would give his word as a gentleman that he would be ready (when called upon to go aboard and in the meantime forbear any practice with the townsmen to the prejudice of the Parliament he should <in the mean> have liberty to go home and dispatch his private affairs. This he refused in great scorn. If any one syllable of what I have writ in this letter be denied I then desire and shall expect your justice) to prove every particular punctually. For I never loved untruth, though to my own disadvantage. Sir now you have heard all this you shall well see how little I regard the man or his language more than may reflect to your service here. If I should have called a council of war (as against a public mutineer) none of you that are acquainted with those ways but must know how heavy the punishment must have been. I only refer this to your consideration whether to give the town satisfaction concerning their being plundered by me. It be not necessary he make some public recognition of his error in that point. In plain English: sir, you see I desire not to sit idle in your businesses but to employ those forces you have trusted me with abroad to your best advantage. And shall have every day I fear new occasions which to the best of my judgement I shall manage your advantage. But while I send my men abroad I had need have all occasions nipped in the head that shall mutiny the town against me at home, and truly I am confident that if this town *shall see* that this man have no abettors in the House of which I am most confident, they will remain in very good measure firm to your service. But too much of this. I am made believe to have so much money *lent upon the propositions* from my neighbours as will pay a troop of horse without any present charge to you and maintain them. I shall make a shift with some relics of arms in the magazine to arm them. If you think fit to send me a commission by this bearer. I send you enclosed an advertisement given from a very good hand by which you will see 'tis needful to make all the force we can. Sir, I have no more but desire when the House is full you will acquaint them with this letter. So, with my service presented I rest

your very humble servant,
John Hotham.

Postscript
Sir, I shall only propose to you my Lord of Essex now being at Worcester with his forces, if one of the aldermen of Worcester had said to the townsmen, my Lord of Essex intends to plunder you, 'tis fit

we stand upon our guard. If he had presently called a martial court and hanged that alderman, could you justly have blamed him?

One word of mirth. Upon Sunday night last (as the neighbours of Sherburn tells our men) they drew certain forces out of York to have set upon my son's men at Cawood. When they came in Sherburn, a village three miles from Cawood, belike espied a windmill, which they took for my son's colours marching to meet them and certain stooks[53] of beans which they took for his men in order. Whereupon they returned in some more haste than they came.

Sir, I send these enclosed informations of the proceedings of my Lord of Newcastle's and their associates that you may the more clearly see how our affairs stand here and the necessity there is of somewhat to be done. We have heard long of two regiments, Constable and Fairfax,[54] to come to our aid, but none yet appears. If they had come in any time I am confident your business had been done before this.

BL, Add. MS 11,692, fo. 23: Sir John Hotham to John Pym, Hull, 1 November 1642

I received yours of the 26 with the relation of our Sunday's work. We have here but 'tis upon great uncertainties of a new fight upon Monday and another upon Thursday. God almighty who is the God of battles I doubt *not* but will crown his own work. Our business of Yorkshire stands thus: my Lord Fairfax who (since the Parliament's declaration against that unfit pacification hath really performed the part of an honest man) caused [them] to retreat from Leeds with some more haste than they came, and in a manner he and my son upon the west side holds them besieged *in York*. Upon the other side I hope this night Sir Hugh Cholmley, with such forces as he hath massed will cut off their victuals, and if forces from the northern papists do not relieve them we hope to give a good account of the business. But we hear of very great endeavours my Lord Newcastle and the papists make in those parts, commissions now being granted to the papists publicly. Sure that is not as was made many believe. I am now to desire two things which I pray [you] dispatch with all speed. The first is in these parts where I am the country is very willing to contribute upon the public faith towards these extraordinary charges, and if I mistake not,

[53] *OED*, XV, p. 295 and XVI, p. 768.

[54] Although they had been pledged to Yorkshire, the foot regiments of Sir William Constable of Flamborough and Sir William Fairfax of Steeton remained with the earl of Essex's field army and fought at Edgehill on 23 October 1642: P. Young, *Edgehill 1642: the campaign and the battle* (Moreton-in-Marsh, Gloucs, 1998), pp. 246–248.

the paper of your propositions is that the money so contributed must be returned to London and from thence paid. Now if the country may see their money spent here for their own defence they will cheerfully do it, and though in some shires where no occasion is, it may seem not fitting, yet with us being as we are if we can be able to serve you with our own purses you may well allow us to dispend it ourselves, being also if the Parlia <must> ment stand we have delinquents well able to pay the score. The second is you know you sent down £4,000 which as this day fortnight (will be every penny gone), £1,000 is for the soldiers' clothes for which I have bought cloth. £3,000 will by then be gone and if before the Monday after we be not supplied I know not how to shift. For our rents we get not and money is not to be borrowed. I was in good hope now you can guess at our weekly charge you would always have taken order to have sent us a month charge beforehand. I have paid according as you writ to me for all charges for setting to sea the *Providence*. You cannot but see if this garrison had not marched out I believe the King's party had here levied an army against you, both for men and money. I have at this instant 160 men helping our neighbours in Derbyshire. I pray sir take such order as our monies may come in time. Every catch we send is 20 charge and this winter I dare not hazard by sea. Beside that way it may be so long in coming that we cannot subsist till it come. Thanks be to God, since Mr Pelham went from hence the town is in very good temper and better affected than ever since I came hither. In your own time I shall expect your justice. Sir I ever am most assuredly yours to serve you,

John Hotham.

HHC: Hotham MS, U DDHO/1/11: Lancashire committee to Sir John Hotham, Manchester, 4 November 1642

For the right worshipful Sir John Hotham, knight, governor of the town of Hull. These:
Noble sir,
We acknowledge with all thankfulness the credence this messenger and our letter received from you the last time and the courtesy to us in the 5 barrels of powder we had from you. We have since that time <had> sent us from the Lord General 8 barrels and other ammunition which was intercepted upon the way in Staffordshire, and 10 other barrels sent us down from London was also carried away and intercepted in Cheshire. The parts near unto us do much depend on our town for

supply herein and our provision is far spent by a garrison we are forced to keep for our own securities. And therefore we are constrained to take the boldness again to desire by this bearer what quantity you can conveniently spare us (if it may be 1,200 or 1,000 weight) and we shall be ready (according to your own appointment) to give full satisfaction for it and the former and acknowledge it your special favour to us. We are necessitated to seek to you herein, not having the like hopes elsewhere as from yourself, nor other place whence we can with safety procure it and so we take leave to remain

your friends and servants,
T. Hanley, Richard Holland, John Booth, Peter Egerton,
Thomas Birch.[55]

[*On reverse*] [*Seal*].

Bodl. MS Nalson II, no. 95: Sir Christopher Wray, John Hotham, and Thomas Hatcher to the Committee of Safety, Northallerton, 12 November 1642[56]

My lords,
We have thought fit to give you an account how the public affairs stand here, upon Wednesday being the 9th we with our three troops and 3 companies of foot marched from Tadcaster, with intention to hinder the relief that York could expect both of men and victuals, because we were certainly informed that divers Yorkshire gentlemen were gone to my Lord Newcastle to solicit him to march with what power he could raise to York, and after he had cleared the country, as they made themselves believe he would do, <some> then to march into Lincolnshire, and so to the King. The desire of preventing this growing danger, so many troops being certainly raised and under convict recusants, made us resolve to try if a sudden venture upon them might either dissipate or dissolve this their so hopeful a project. And therefore leaving all our foot at Topcliffe,[57] 18 miles from Darnton[58] where their horse lay, we with our 3 troops and 20 dragoons marched

[55]For Booth, Egerton, and Holland see J.M. Gratton, *The Parliamentarian and Royalist War Effort in Lancashire 1642–1651*, Chetham Society, third series, 48 (2010). Birch was a parliamentarian captain during the siege of Manchester in October 1642. He was later commissioned colonel by Lord Fairfax, and returned as recruiter MP for Liverpool in 1649: D. Whitehead, 'Thomas Birch (bap. 1608, d. 1678)', *ODNB*.

[56]This letter was probably written by Hotham himself as Wray and Hatcher signed with different ink. A summary appears in *Portland MS*, HMC, 29, 13th Report, Appendix, Part I, I, pp. 68–69.

[57]Topcliffe, four miles south-west of Thirsk.

[58]Darlington.

night and day directly <upon> *towards* them and upon Friday morning by daylight came to Darnton, where Captain Pudsey's[59] troop was drawn up at this end of the town with intention to relieve my Lord Dunbar[60] from our troops. But meeting us at the town end and thinking we had *been* Captain Sare, another of his fellows, he came up directly to us until he found his error by our shooting bullets which made him run too fast for an honourable retreat. We followed with what speed we could but they were a great deal better horsemen. Yet we got 10 *prisoners* with their horses and pistols, and but for a large fir bush that hid him had got the captain too. 4 or 5 troops that lay thereabouts ran all presently into Durham thinking the plain country too hot for them. Upon which we marched to Yarm,[61] there to meet the gentlemen of the North Riding and to give them encouragement, which we hope hath done a great deal of good in those parts as they informed us, and that by the countenance of our forces they should be able to raise a considerable strength. From thence we came to Northallerton to countenance the well affected gentlemen of Richmondshire. And they tell us that our dispersing the papists and being near to cherish the good and awe the bad will bring in all that side of the country, so that we intend to hover up and down in these parts a while, and if it be possible to hinder this pestilent growing mischief, which if it increase, then we shall join all our forces together, and I hope make them run with a rattle. For I believe we shall be able to draw together 4,000 horse and foot. We send you here enclosed some intercepted letters which lay open their intentions, and certainly it would benefit the public much if you would please they might be printed. At our first coming to Northallerton, we met with a Danish Ambassador that landed at Newcastle some 3 days before, and was going to the King. We durst not venture to stay *him*, although we thought it was *not fairly* <honourably> done of him to bring 6,000 arms for the King and Colonel Cockran, the Scottish man that had been soliciting there to bring over strangers, as appeared by his *papers*. The colonel we have put in safe custody and desire to know what we shall do with him. We are certainly informed that the highland men in Northumberland that are tenants to my

[59]Ralph Pudsey of Stapleton was a Roman Catholic royalist officer, later commissioned as a lieutenant-colonel under the earl of Newcastle: Newman, *Royalist Officers*, p. 308; R.P. Cust and A.J. Hopper (eds), *Cases in the High Court of Chivalry, 1634–1640*, Publications of the Harleian Society, new series, 18 (2006), pp. xxx, 105, 175, 184, 231–233, 307–308.

[60]Henry Constable, Viscount Dunbar was a Roman Catholic active in raising troops for the king in 1642 and was later commissioned as a lieutenant-colonel under the earl of Newcastle: Newman, *Royalist Officers*, p. 81; J. Binns, 'Henry Constable, first Viscount Dunbar (1588–1645)', *ODNB*.

[61]Yarm, five miles south-west of Stockton-on-Tees.

Lord Northumberland and my Lord Grey, begin to get together and refuse to obey any commands from my Lord Newcastle. And divers well affected gentlemen of that county join with them, to prevent which Sir William Widdrington[62] is marched <from Newcastle> from Newcastle with some drake[s] to bring them to obedience, but we hope the strength of the country and their good cause will protect them. Some report these honest men have possessed themselves of Alnwick castle, and that my Lord of Newcastle is drawing some battering pieces thither. Thus with the tender of our humble respects to your lordships we shall take our leave and remain

your most humble servants,
Christopher Wray, John Hotham, Thomas Hatcher.

HHC: Hotham MS, U DDHO/1/13: John Hotham, Sir Christopher Wray, and Thomas Hatcher to Ferdinando, Lord Fairfax, Darlington, 23 November 1642

My Lord,
We have forborne to give your lordship an account of our proceedings in these parts till we had achieved something worthy your lordship's knowledge. We shall now acquaint your lordship that having understood that there lay sundry troops of horse and dragoons at the town of Darlington, which four times made inroads into Yorkshire to plunder and spoil the houses of such honest well affected persons as lived near the river of Tees and to commit other outrages. Thereupon we took resolution to march up with our horse and foot to try if we could force them out of their quarter at Darlington and the adjacent villages, which we accordingly performed and came this morning to this town. But they had provided better for themselves and upon notice of our intention were departed early this morning towards the sanctuary of Durham, whither we believe their fears hath accompanied them and will easily infect all the fair ladies there with the same disease. Here we intend to quarter this night at least but have not considered of yet how to dispose of ourselves for the future, by which next your lordship shall understand what course we resolve next to pursue. My lord we conceive we have effected this good by this attempt: that the earl of Newcastle, who had designed his march southwards at this very time will now not be in condition to begin it so

[62]From December 1642, Widdrington was president of the earl of Newcastle's council of war: M. Bennett, 'William Widdrington, first Baron Widdrington (1610–1651)', *ODNB*; Newman, *Royalist Officers*, p. 411.

soon and perhaps may be retarded this winter, for the ways now grow so ill as will be soon unpassable. And besides we have by this retreat of theirs gained the opportunity to beat down Piercebridge[63] which hitherto they have defended and begun to make works and fortify for the better maintaining of it. The trained bands of Richmondshire get up very slowly, neither are they in Cleveland very considerable. We had not used the assistance of either of them in this action, although we had cause to suspect that if the hearts of the Bishopric forces had been equal to their number they might have proved too hard for us. My lord, we shall trouble your lordship no further than with our hearty profession to remain

your honour's most faithful servants,
John Hotham, Christopher Wray, Thomas Hatcher.

Bodl. MS Tanner LXIV, fo. 119: Sir John Hotham to William Lenthall, Hull, November 1642[64]

By this you may see by Monday next we shall be out two thousand pound at least, our weekly charge being towards seven hundred pound every week, which if you think too much I shall disband as many of the companies as you think fit. You may believe I husband your money to the utmost, but so many unavoidable charges fall out every day besides the pay of the soldiers, that cause money go fast away. You had need send us down no less then six thousand pound, being that a great part of it will be spent before it come hither. I shall entreat you will make a quick dispatch in this business for money. *As* for my own rents, I now receive none. I have used my credit almost as far as it will go. I know not in all the world how to shift, for without money the soldier will slip away, do the best I can. Thus nothing doubting of your good help herein, I humbly take leave and will ever remain

your very humble servant,
John Hotham.

Postscript
I shall humbly beg at this House not to be misinterpreted as if I did conceive any part of this relation of Mr Pelham's man to proceed from any sense that he might justly ?alter? any act or opinion of the House, but merely upon the vanity or folly of the man or master. For I must acknowledge that I have had such ample testimony of their favours and the good interpretation they have made of all my actions here,

[63] Piercebridge, four miles west of Darlington.
[64] Read in the House of Commons, 25 November 1642.

performed in their service that such a thought cannot find the least place in me.

Sir,

Here is sent to me to Hull taken by my son, one Colonel Cockerin, he that brought over the arms from Denmark. He was taken in company with the Danish Ambassador. I pray you write what you would have done with him. We have ill accommodations for the safe keeping of such persons, but I shall look to him as well as I can till I hear from you.

Bodl. MS Nalson II, no. 100: Sir John Hotham to William Lenthall, Hull, 25 November 1642[65]

For my honourable and very good friend, William Lenthall, esq., Speaker to the House of Commons. These:

Sir,

There arrived the other day a great ship upon the coast of Lincolnshire, loaden with ammunition, who, having lost her mast was driven by stress of weather thither. The country and men of Boston finding her to be loaden with ammunition, apprehended five of their seamen, and presently dispatched a messenger away to me desiring my advice what was fittest to be done. These men did it out of their earnest and good affections to the Parliament, it being not apparent unto them but the ammunition might be carried a wrong way. Since this, the ship being got off the coast of Lincolnshire is come into the river of Humber, who, though her master hath given me some good satisfaction that the ship was going for London, yet in a business of so great consequence as the carrying of so much ammunition to a wrong place might prove, I thought it fit to stay him here for some few days till I might receive advertisement from you. <the maist[e]r> I have sent you here enclosed the examination of one of the men. I shall humbly make these propositions following to you. The magazine at Hull *wherein* we had but left at first 300 barrels of powder, is now in a good part lessened, both by reason of our <exp> just occasion of expense of powder we have had here, also by reason of *good quantities of* powder we have [sent] abroad by virtue of orders sent from the House of [*MS damaged*] (to help our neighbo[u]rs). For without your orders, I [have sent] none except to the town of Manchester, who when [they] were in that extremity with my Lord Strange [*MS damaged*] with me for five barrels of powder, which I hope [you] will not think ill spent. I shall therefore desire that [*MS damaged*] agree with the merchant at London for 200 barrels [*MS damaged*] powder to be kept here for your

[65] A summary of this letter appears in *Portland MS*, HMC, 29, 13th Report, Appendix, Part I, I, p. 74.

use. As also for [*MS damaged*] quality of match which he hath, aboard which [*MS damaged*] get here for money, it is in such continual exp [*MS damaged*] here as we shall soon have great want of it. 'Tis true I have sent for powder at Hambrough, but it is so small a quantity as will not be considerable. The second is this that you will agree with the merchant, to send down what he can afford his muskets for, and I shall send into the country that wants arms, that if they will give ready money for them here they may be served. If they will not he may come to London within six or seven days. Sir, I have no more but ever am

your affectionate friend and servant,
John Hotham.

Postscript
If you dare not take some speedy course to send down money to pay this garrison and that in a good measure, all your affairs in the north are like to break a pieces. £6,000 for £3,000 will be gone before it can arrive here.

Bodl. MS Nalson II, no. 114: John Hotham to William Cavendish, earl of Newcastle, Cawood, 18 December 1642[66]

Right honourable,
I am under your favour of the same opinion that I was before, that there is a difference betwixt prisoners taken in their houses and taken in arms. I did not make the difference whether they took arms on your side or ours. The event will tell us who was in the right, for I am sure whosoever gets the better, will judge the other to have been in the wrong. If I may know what prisoners of ours you have released that were not released by exchange, I will instantly set as many of yours at liberty. My lord, I take it as a great favour that these differences, that I hope God in his good time will make up again, cause you not to forget ancient friendship. I wish I could always light upon such friends. However, this nobleness of yours will I am sure engage to serve you.

Your most humble servant,
John Hotham

[*On reverse*] [*Seal*]. 2. To the right honourable the earl of Newcastle. These present:

[66]A draft of this letter is in HHC: Hotham MS, U DDHO/1/14, marked on its reverse as exhibit 2 among the defence papers. See also *Portland MS*, HMC, 29, 13th Report, Appendix, Part I, I, p. 80.

Bodl. MS Nalson II, no. 116: John Hotham to William Cavendish, earl of Newcastle, Cawood, 19 December 1642[67]

My noble lord,
Whatsoever I am engaged to do, in reference to the trust reposed in me I know you are so full of honour you will not blame me for. Otherwise to your particular I have ever been a servant. As to that worth I have <ever> observed in all your actions you are pleased by your kind respective letter to double the obligation, and I hope you shall not bestow your favours upon an unthankful man. And so much confidence have I in your word, that I shall with <confidence> *assurance* rely upon it, and wait upon your lordship in any place, <tha> or in any fashion that you in your judgement shall think fit. As to the condition we now stand in, and not to bring suspicion upon it, I should humbly offer it thus: that if you please to appoint some gentleman of quality to meet and treat for the prisoners, I shall use the matter so, as I will be the man on our side. And then either your lordship may privately be there, or appoint some other place, for I have some odd people to please here <and>. This I shall wholly refer to your better judgement and desire you to believe that you shall never be prejudiced by anything you communicate to

your humble faithful servant,
John Hotham.

Bodl. MS Nalson II, no. 119: John Hotham to William Cavendish, earl of Newcastle, Cawood, 27 December 1642[68]

Right honourable:
Your free and noble expressions of doing me so many great and real favours shall make me endeavour either to requite them, or be extremely thankful for them. The gentleman I writ to is very sensible of those good offices you were pleased to promise, and will not I hope be wanting in anything that befits an honest man or a good subject.[69] But the business being of so high concernment, as his good name, and very being. He desires to have some time to consider with himself,

[67] A copy of this letter is in HHC: Hotham MS, U DDHO/1/15, marked on the reverse as exhibit 3. See also *Portland MS*, HMC, 29, 13th Report, Appendix, Part I, I, p. 80.

[68] A copy of this letter is in HHC: Hotham MS, U DDHO/1/16, marked on the reverse as exhibit 4. See also *Portland MS*, HMC, 29, 13th Report, Appendix, Part I, I, pp. 81–82.

[69] John Hotham refers here to his father, Sir John Hotham.

before he can give a full and perfect answer. And it shall be with all the convenient speed that is possible. In the *mean* time he wished me to assure your lordship, that whatsoever others shall whisper to His Majesty, it shall be found that he hath none more real and firm unto his person and service, than he and his family will be, and that he hopes His Majesty conceives that what he hath done was only to discharge the public trust imposed upon him, and not any disaffection to his service. He likewise returns your lordship many thanks for your nobleness in not forgetting your old friend, as too many in these troublesome times take occasion to do. I hope a little delay can be no great prejudice to the business, *and* that you will be pleased not to think that there is anything intended but reality to His Majesty and the commonwealth by your lordship's

most [humble and faithful servant,
John Hotham].[70]

[*On reverse*] 4. Sir John Hotham to the earl of Newcastle.

Bodl. MS Nalson II, no. 126: John Hotham to William Cavendish, earl of Newcastle, Cawood, 2 January 1643[71]

My noble lord,
Since I could not be so happy as to attend you myself without a whole country's talking, a fitter means could not have been found than by this noble gentleman, whom you will find to deal really and plainly and not like a pedant. And my lord it shall not need <for> to do otherwise, for with faith and honour to serve the King and the commonwealth is all our ambition, and to leave that to posterity which our ancestors left us, an untainted name. We have Caesars and Solomons as highly deceived as yours, although our Secretary Stockdale[72] thinks he knows all as he directs all to our general. I shall not need to trouble your lordship but leave all to the bearer, but only bewail the unhappiness of these distractions that hinders from attending upon your lordship

your most faithful, humble servant,
John Hotham.

[*On reverse*] [*Seal*] 6. Sir John Hotham's letter.

[70] The corner with the signature is torn off.

[71] A copy of this letter is in HHC: Hotham MS, U DDHO/1/17, marked on the reverse as exhibit 6. See also *Portland MS*, HMC, 29, 13th Report, Appendix, Part I, I, pp. 83–84.

[72] Thomas Stockdale of Bilton Park, Knaresborough, esq. (1594–1653), was secretary at war to Lord Fairfax and recruiter MP for Knaresborough, 1645–1653: Hopper, 'A directory of parliamentarian allegiance in Yorkshire', p. 113; B. Jennings (ed.), *A History of Harrogate and Knaresborough* (Huddersfield, 1970), pp. 140–152.

Bodl. MS Nalson II, no. 131: John Hotham to William Cavendish, earl of Newcastle, Cawood, 9 January 1643[73]

My noble lord,
You may if you please peruse this enclosed copy, and by it perceive what is already done. Another to that purpose went from another place. I hope no just nor honest man can dislike it, for he that desires not a good peace deserves ill of this poor country that hath given him his subsistence. My lord there is no man that hath any reasonable share in the commonwealth can desire that either side should be absolute conquerors, for it will be then as it was betwixt Caesar and Pompey. Whosoever had the better, the Roman liberty was sure to have the worse. I honour the King as much as any and love the Parliament, but do not desire to see either absolute conquerors. It is too great a temptation to courses of will and violence. My lord, there is one thing more, which I fear much. That if the honourable endeavours of such powerful men as yourself do not take place for a happy peace, the necessitous people of the whole kingdom will presently rise in mighty numbers. And whosoever they pretend for at first, within a while they will set up for themselves, to the utter ruin of all the nobility and gentry of the kingdom. I speak not this merely at random. The west part of this county affords mighty numbers of them, which I am very confident you will *see* necessitated and urged to rise in far greater bodies than thrice the armies that are already gathered here.[74] My lord, necessity teaches to seek a subsistence, and if this unruly rout have once cast the rider, it will *run* like wildfire in the example through all the counties of England. My lord, I shall humbly desire your pardon for this great digression, and for my overweening to propose these things to a judgement so much greater than mine, but your lordship's favours as they have obliged, so they have emboldened

your most faithful affectionate servant,
John Hotham.

[*On reverse*] 7. Sir John Hotham. For your lordship:

[73] For a copy of this letter, see HHC: Hotham MS, U DDHO/1/18, marked on the reverse as exhibit 9. For a later copy that incorrectly identifies Sir John Hotham as the author, see BL, Add. MS 32,096, fo. 248r–v. See also *Portland MS*, HMC, 29, 13th Report, Appendix, Part I, I, p. 87.

[74] Here John Hotham refers to the recent anti-royalist uprisings in the West Riding's populous clothing districts, beginning at Bradford on 18 December 1642: A. Hopper, 'The clubmen of the West Riding of Yorkshire during the first civil war: "Bradford club-law"', *Northern History*, 36 (2000), pp. 59–72.

Bodl. MS Nalson II, no. 140: John Hotham to the earl of Newcastle, Cawood, 15 January 1643[75]

My noble lord,

I have not yet heard from London since the letter went, but expect it every hour. I doubt not but there may come very good fruits of it and the continued endeavours of such men as desire peace with the King's honour and the public security. And that I hope to see effected through all opposition. My lord, you are now great in power with His Majesty, and your advice will sway much. Which if you please to make use of to him incline to peace, the whole kingdom would be obliged to you. And for the greatness of the work, it is the more honour if it be effected. And he that begins well hath half done. Nothing is so hard as it seems at first. The propositions for peace go on fast, and I hope the jugglers will be deceived, although I believe cunning enough on all sides. For my part, if I can serve the King and the commonwealth as a gentleman should do, and be esteemed worthy your lordship's friendship, it is all I expect, and I shall think it honour enough. I hear of 2 converts in the Parliament, Holles and Pierrepont.[76] Our general here thinks you raise men as the sand,[77] and the king of Denmark in a string. It was not like your business at Sheriff Hutton should thrive better, being conducted by 3 such cavaliers. You will find more such among my countrymen. Our senators *here* think of saving themselves, as you may well see, we are so quiet. For the wishes of these gentlemen to me, I thank God, I never thought them valuable. If I had, I could have had them cheap enough. My lord, you are he that I set my rest on, as my noble friend, and you shall command me. For I know nothing will come from you, but of honour, and you shall never find more truth and gratitude in any that you have obliged than in your most affectionate, humble servant,

John Hotham.

[*On reverse*] Mr Holles and Mr Pierrepont named in this letter. Sir John Hotham to the earl of Newcastle.

[75] A copy in a later hand is in BL, Add. MS 32,096, fos 248v–249r. Both versions incorrectly name Sir John Hotham as author.

[76] Denzil Holles, MP for Dorchester, was one of the 'five members' whom the king failed to arrest in January 1642. After his regiment was decimated at Brentford on 11 November 1642, he led those MPs intent on negotiating a settlement with the king. William Pierrepont was MP for Much Wenlock and a member of the Committee of Safety who temporarily became inclined towards Holles and the peace party in January 1643: J. Morrill, 'Denzil Holles, first Baron Holles (1598–1680)', *ODNB*; G. Yerby, 'William Pierrepont (1607/8–1678)', *ODNB*.

[77] This was a disparaging reference to Ferdinando, Lord Fairfax, whose headquarters at Selby were just four miles south-east of John Hotham's at Cawood castle.

BL, Add. MS 18,979, fo. 131r–v: Robert Devereux, earl of Essex, to Ferdinando, Lord Fairfax, Sir John Hotham, and John Hotham, 31 January 1643[78]

Instructions to be observed by the right honourable Ferdinando, Lord Fairfax, Sir John Hotham, baronet, and Captain John Hotham, for the better managing of the present war in the northern parts.

1. First; That you nor any of you shall at any time hereafter during the war raise any money or forces of horse or foot upon any part of the county of York without consent of the council of war to be established there, or by the major part of them, & such money or forces raised or to be raised shall from time to time during the war be disposed of & employed as you and the said council of war shall order.
2. Secondly; You shall permit and suffer the castle of Cawood to continue under the command of Captain Hotham as governor, which with all the forces therein & those which came out of the garrison of Hull you shall keep, & employ for the service of the state. And that all the officers & soldiers there shall be commanded as by you & the said council of war shall be thought fit and ordered, or by the major part thereof.
3. That you nor any of you shall assess or levy, or cause to be assessed or levied upon any part of the county of York any sum of money or anything whatsoever or cause any tax to be made, or taken upon the River of Ouse, or elsewhere but by the express order of you and the said council of war, or the major part thereof. And that as well all such money so to be assessed or taken, as all other monies assigned for the service of the war in those parts be paid into the hands of a treasurer who may be appointed by the Lord Fairfax if he will be responsible for him, otherwise to be chosen by you and the said council of war, or the major part thereof.
4. Fourthly; That in case Sir John Hotham shall hereafter send out any forces from his garrison at Hull for the service of the war in those parts, that he have liberty upon danger threatening the garrison to recall them notwithstanding any order of the council of war in that case.
5. Fifthly; You shall frequently sit in your council of war for the ordering and disposing of all affairs tending to the war; & you shall carefully put in execution such designs as shall from time to time

[78] Note on reverse: 'purchased at Sothebys 28 June 1852, lot 185'.

be ordered by you and the said council of war, or the major part thereof.

Essex.

Bodl. MS Nalson II, no. 156: John Hotham to William Cavendish, earl of Newcastle, Cawood, 11 February 1643[79]

My noble lord,

I am very sorry you should have the least occasion to think that I am not mindful of that friendship which I shall ever so value. I make no question, but you will still honour me with your good opinion, until you find I do some act unworthy of it, which I know you never shall. I should think it happiness enough to me and my posterity that any act of mine might prove an advantage to His Majesty and a settlement to this distracted kingdom. And whatsoever ill hap, I have had to be scandalled with His Majesty, I hope to make it appear that his honour and safety are as dear and precious to me, as to those that have made far greater brags. For Sir Ralph Hopton's miracles,[80] or Sir Hugh Chomley's defeat,[81] they are no motives to me. I should as soon do what I think is fit for an honest man to do after my Lord of Essex had got a victory as before. I confess I pin my faith upon no man's sleeve, nor will I follow any man's courses, if I be not satisfied on that they suit with honour and justice. I hope to see the endeavours of honest men prevail so far now that the propositions are gone to the King, that we shall once again see truth and peace in our days. And I wish with all my heart that which side soever will not condescend to waive trifles for the settlement of church and state, that his own side may leave him. For my own part rather than be a slave to either, I would live of bread and water in another kingdom. I am of your opinion, if we agree not we shall trouble one another to little purpose. But that I

[79]A copy of this letter is in HHC: Hotham MS, U DDHO/1/19, marked on the reverse as exhibit 10. A later transcript is in BL, Add. MS 32,096, fo. 249r–v. See also *Portland MS*, HMC, 29, 13th Report, Appendix, Part I, supplement, I, p. 699.

[80]This was Sir Ralph Hopton's defeat of the Devon parliamentarians at Braddock Down on 18 January 1643: C.E.H. Chadwyck Healey (ed.), *Bellum Civile: Hopton's narrative of his campaign in the west, 1642–1644*, Somerset Record Society, 18 (1902), p. 30.

[81]A detachment of Sir Hugh Cholmley's Scarborough garrison sent out to prevent Sir George Goring crossing the River Tees was destroyed at Yarm on 8 February 1643: J. Binns, *'A Place of Great Importance': Scarborough in the civil wars, 1640–1660* (Preston, 1996), p. 89; BL, TT E246(26), *Mercurius aulicus*, 5–11 February 1643 (Oxford, 1643).

was tur*n*ed the wandering Jew you had heard before this from, my lord,

your most faithful, real servant,
John Hotham.

[*On reverse*] [*Seal*]. <10.> Sir John Hotham to the earl of Newcastle. To your lordship:

Bodl. MS Nalson II, no. 158: John Hotham to William Cavendish, earl of Newcastle, Cawood, 12 February 1643[82]

My noble lord,
You are pleased still to increase the obligation of him that was before as much a servant to your person and worth as ever any friend you had in the world. And truly it is a great comfort to me in the midst of these mighty disturbances, which every private and the public groans under, that I have so noble a friend to rely on in those great exigencies of the commonwealth. I know your lordship's quality, estate and good affection in the country where *you* have lived may make you more happy than anything at court can, although I well know your lordship's great interest there. The cause is plain why those Caesars would fall into the East Riding more than into the west, because they think <pillage> there will be fewer blows than in the west, for there you shall constantly have their advice to fall on. I know them of old. Your lordship's respects to me is no less for that. But I would I could meet with a knot of them single to make sport. You may remember Leeds and the commander in chief.[83] I will say no more but that I shall inviolably remain

your most faithful servant,
John Hotham.

[*On reverse*] <11> Sir [*sic*] John Hotham's letter to the earl of Newcastle. For your lordship:

[82] A copy of this letter is in HHC: Hotham MS, U DDHO/1/20, marked on the reverse as exhibit 11. A later transcript is in BL, Add. MS 32,096, fo. 249v. See also *Portland MS*, HMC, 29, 13th Report, Appendix, Part I, supplement, I, p. 699.

[83] It appears that John Hotham may have been teasing the earl about the West Riding royalists. When Sir Thomas Fairfax captured Leeds on 23 January 1643, the commander of the royalist garrison, Sir William Savile of Thornhill, only managed to escape by swimming across the River Aire: J. Kirby, 'Savile family (per. *c.*1480–1644)', *ODNB*; Newman, *Royalist Officers*, p. 332.

Bodl. MS Nalson II, no. 157: John Hotham to William Cavendish, earl of Newcastle, Cawood, 12 February 1643[84]

Right honourable,
I am glad for the prisoners' sake that the time is so near. I make no question but every man will contribute his endeavours to a work of so great charity. All things promised shall be really performed by

your humble servant,
John Hotham.

[*On reverse*] [*Seal*] 13. For the right honourable the earl of Newcastle.

HHC: Hotham MS, U DDHO/1/10: John Pym to Sir John Hotham, [Westminster], 20 February 1643

For my very noble friend, Sir John Hotham, governor of <Portsmouth> Hull in Yorkshire.
Noble sir,
I presented your short letter of this week to the House. I am very heartily sorry you are in such straits. I assure you it wanted no remembrance and solicitation, neither in the House nor at the committee, but truly we have had so little money come in of late that the whole army was even ready to disband and the <other> garrisons of Portsmouth, Conyer Point, Dover, Plymouth, Chatham and others are much longer behind than you. But now the City is fallen into a vein of giving money and I hope we are in a way of providing a certain proportion answerable to the certainty of the charge. The House was very sensible of your wants and have taken into consideration to write to the town to receive soldiers upon billet for a fortnight or thereabouts within which time I doubt not but we shall send you a considerable money. But this was not fully resolved, only the House commanded a letter to be written to you acknowledging the great service you have done and the estimation they have of your merit and desire to give you content. Which was first committed yesterday to Sir Philip Stapleton to deliver, but he being gone to the army before it was done it is now left to be done by the Committee of Safety. From whom I believe you will very shortly receive it and I hope the certain direction for a good sum of money. I am very glad to hear of the success which

[84] A copy of this letter is in HHC: Hotham MS, U DDHO/1/21, marked on the reverse as exhibit 13. See also *Portland MS*, HMC, 29, 13th Report, Appendix, Part I, supplement, I, p. 699.

your son hath had of his campaign, and his special deliverance. Above all, I rejoice to hear that you and my Lord Fairfax do concur so well in this common service. I am one of the committee of 6 lords and commoners who are to go to my Lord General *early tomorrow* to consult with him and the council of war about some conditions of a cessation of arms which though I hope we may contrive to as without any great inconvenience it may be assented *to*, yet truly we shall find may entreat <prolations> doubts and objections. As soon as it is resolved we will take care to give you notice, but till you hear from us I pray be careful not to slack the industry of the army there, for your success and forwardness will much advantage us in the treaty. We have it in our care to send you some men [and] ordnance. I pray rest assured of my readiness to serve you with the affectionate respects and endeavours of

your faithful and humble servant,
John Pym.

Just now a messenger who came to me out of Holland doth assure me that he saw the Queen embarked upon Thursday last so that I believe she will be at Newcastle before this letter can come to you. She brings with her 150 thousand pound in money and store of arms and munition. What opportunity of service this will afford you before this supply can pass from Newcastle to York, you being masters of the field can best judge.

[*On reverse*] [*Seal*]. 20. Mr Pym a letter thanking me for my good service, and rejoicing at the agreement.

Bodl. MS Nalson II, no. 163: John Hotham to William Cavendish, earl of Newcastle, Beverley, 2 March 1643[85]

My noble lord,
There shall [be] nothing that may any way accommodate the Queen, receive the least impediment from me. If you please that any may be sent to Hull, the cellars shall all be open to them. And for the way of conveying it, if I may know how you intend it, I shall give it all the furtherance I can. For Sir William Fairfax,[86] although there be some

[85] For the defence's copy of this letter, see HHC: Hotham MS, U DDHO/1/22, marked on the reverse as exhibit 15. A later copy is at BL, Add. MS 32,096, fos 249v–250r, with a printed transcript at *Portland MS*, HMC, 29, 13th Report, Appendix, Part I, I, p. 99.

[86] A nephew of Lord Fairfax, Sir William Fairfax delivered his uncle's offer of protection to the queen when she landed at Bridlington on 22 February 1643: A. Hopper, 'Sir William Fairfax (bap. 1610, d. 1644)', *ODNB*.

truth in wine, yet it is not all truth. There was something in your last letter that something troubled me, which was some doubt that promise would not be kept upon the cessation. If you mean it of me, then am I very unhappy to suffer so much in your opinion which I so much value. For I confess I value my word above all side<r>s. I am very sorry to hear that your lordship hath any intention to make this poor country the seat of war. I am sure the clamours of all our friends and <neih> neighbours undone by it will make us ashamed to be seen with those that are the actors in it. My lord those counsels may get your soldiers pillage, yourself neither friends nor strength. I know well the fountain of these violent counsels, and am sure all his friends that trusted to it, sank under the burden. For myself and friends, nothing can be of that bad consequence to us, as the utter ruin of all our friends, tenants and neighbours. We can then be no worse. We are fitted for desperation. This is all submitted to your deep judgement by

your most faithful, affectionate servant,
John Hotham.

[*On reverse*] [*Seal*]. For the right honourable the earl of Newcastle. <Sir William Fairfax> Sir John Hotham to the earl of Newcastle.

Bodl. MS Nalson II, no. 169: Sir John Hotham to William Lenthall, Hull, 9 March 1643[87]

For my honourable friend William Lenthall, esq., Speaker of the honourable House of Commons. These:
Sir,
I have divers times writ to you of the urgent and pressing need we have of money for this garrison and the forces that I have sent abroad for your service. I hear you have voted me £6,000. I must return you my most humble thanks for it <must> *but* must withal entreat you to consider that unless I have it and that quickly I am no whit the better. I received advice by this post that there is received of it but one thousand pound, which how little good it will do yourselves may judge. Tomorrow, being Saturday, I shall make some shift to pay. Then either I must billet upon the town or the soldier must not eat. I desire your directions what in this strait I must do, and I pray believe me in very good earnest there is no other way left. I hope by the next post to receive your directions in this. For our affairs here, the Queen is at

[87]See also BL, Add. MS 32,096, fo. 250r; *CJ*, II, p. 1000; *Portland MS*, HMC, 29, 13th Report, Appendix, Part I, I, p. 102.

York. The enemy keeps still the passes at Stamford Bridge and Malton to pass into this East Riding at their pleasure. We have at Beverley about 900 horse and foot, much too weak if the enemy fall on to make good that town. They have plundered all where they come. But above all Sir William Strickland, and two near kinsmen of his. Sir William hath lost above £4,000 in his goods and all his evidence[s] seized upon. Sir, I will not trouble your great affairs any longer. I ever am

your affectionate friend and servant,
John Hotham.

Bodl. MS Nalson II, no. 170: Sir John Hotham to William Lenthall, Hull, 11 March 1643[88]

For my honourable good friend, William Lenthall, esq., Speaker to the honourable House of Commons. These:
Sir,
I send you here enclosed a packet of letters that came from the Low Countries to be delivered to Mr Jermyn.[89] I opened them because I conceived something they might contain that concerned the safety of this place or your affairs here. There is in some of them matter <worth> if I be not mistaken worth your knowledge. However you will accept of his goodwill that intends you a service in it. You will pardon one observation of mine in that passage of Mr Strickland's (who it seems serves you with faith and diligence), when he complains of the Prince of Orange[90] about the Dunkirk frigates. It is (though truth) judged a scandal. I observe either those states ill affected to you or extremely in slavery to the Prince of Orange. 'Tis a business to my seeing in its consequences of great concernment, and may trench upon your affairs farther than at first sight may be thought upon. Sir, these things I leave to your own wisdom. I writ to you by a Londoner about monies for us. It may be this will come first. Our need is so great as I am ashamed to write you must pay this post for here is none for necessary business. My credit you have broke by not paying those small sums my necessity has forced me for your service to take up. You have made me orders at two several times for £6,000 a time but of them I had small fruit. Of the last but £1,000. So as rumours of great sums sent hither stir abroad and nothing so I must acknowledge

[88] See also BL, Add. MS 32,096, fo. 250r; *Portland MS*, HMC, 29, 13th Report, Appendix, Part I, I, p. 102.

[89] Henry Jermyn, a favourite of the queen, was with her when she landed at Bridlington and became colonel of her lifeguards: A.R.J.S. Adolph, 'Henry Jermyn, earl of St Albans (bap. 1605, d. 1684)', *ODNB*.

[90] Frederick Henry, Prince of Orange (1584–1647) had married his son, the future William II of Orange, to Mary, daughter of Charles I.

the great favour of the House is readily and cheerfully granting all just things I have desired. But when you have made your orders upon honest and just reasons to have them made frustrate, I dare not say by private practices (but something there must needs be in it), is to yourselves prejudicial when we that serve you faithfully abroad shall see your orders secretly made nothing worth. Pardon this freedom. Necessity for your service on the one side forceth me to it and on the other side your interest. If you send hither the remainder of the £6,000 <you> you will give us a subsistence and in my opinion vindicate your own rights. I hear of many jealousies and scandals cast upon us here. I shall in due time demand *your* justice upon the authors. But first I hope by my actions to make themselves ashamed. I writ to you in my last that having now made known to you in such a fashion my wants I *hope you will relieve them*. This and that, I know not which may come later. I pray I may know your pleasures and commands herein. For you shall ever find me with my best endeavours ready to serve you. Sir, I am

your most humble servant,
John Hotham.

Bodl. MS Nalson II, no. 173: Sir John Hotham to William Lenthall, Hull, 17 March 1643[91]

For my honourable friend William Lenthall, esq., Speaker of the honourable House of Commons. These:
Sir,
I received yours of the 28 February, the 14 March, and shall with [*MS damaged*] do my best for the relief of Dr. Bastwick and Captain Ludlow. I shall s[end today] a trumpeter to offer any two officers we have in exchange for the [*MS damaged*] or sergeant majors. I have heretofore sent to them about the same business [*MS damaged*] found them stiffly to insist upon the release of Commissary Windam for [*MS damaged*] in my judgement I can no way yield to, being he is a man as I conceive of those abilities and affections to their cause, that they have very few such. But I shall shortly give you a better account how that affair stands. I have sent you here enclosed an extract of two letters written to two merchants in this town of good quality from Hamburg. If there be any danger from the Dane it will be needful, we should be well

91 Parts on right-hand side are torn and lost – conjectural reconstructions are given in square brackets. See BL, Add. MS 32,096, fo. 250r; *CJ*, III, p. 10; *Portland MS*, HMC, 29, 13th Report, Appendix, Part I, I, pp. 103–104.

provided here. I have writ divers times for some ordinance, as many members of the House can inform you, but yet can get none. I writ this the rather, because a member of your House told a shipmaster of this town, that if they had not ordinance it was the governor's fault, for it was denied to no towns in England. I hope yourself and divers of the House will witness it was not my fault, and indeed we stand [in] great need of them. I writ to you concerning the billeting the soldiers here, but diverted by Mr Pelham, which I cannot believe. We think if the soldiers have no money to buy meat, he must eat somewhere, and that this town that now enjoys so much safety and trade may very well not think much for the billeting of so few soldiers for some time, till the House shall find fit to satisfy for it. [The] poor town of Beverley upon a single motion from myself and my [son] yielded to billet almost as many of our forces there till we can repay [them out] of an assessment which we have laid in the East Riding for the subsistence [of the] forces we have abroad. The other day divers papists as I hear made [*MS damaged*] suit to my Lord of Newcastle to be employed to pillage a little house and [*MS damaged*] of mine, which accordingly they did, and took away all my breed of horses, and [everything] that I had there. But in their return, Sir Hugh Cholmley, with his troop of horse and dragoneers, charged them very gallantly, broke their horse all to pieces, killed divers, took prisoners Sergeant Major Huddleston, a captain, 2 cornets, and divers other officers, who are now coming by water *from* Scarborough to Hull as prisoners. What I have lost in this business I know not, but I shall do my best, that upon these papists I light, they shall neither carry it to heaven nor hell. Sir, I have ever found the good respect and favour of the House, and shall endeavour upon all occasions to deserve their good opinion, and shall desire to approve myself

your affectionate friend and humble servant,
[John Hotham].

Bodl. MS Nalson II, no. 178: John Hotham to William Cavendish, earl of Newcastle, Hull, 22 March 1643[92]

Right honourable,

I shall desire you to excuse me that I cannot grant a safe conduct to Sir Marmaduke Langdale,[93] for I am sure his last coming to Malton set

[92] For further copies of this letter, see HHC: Hotham MS, U, DDHO/1/23, marked on the reverse as exhibit 18; BL, Add. MS 32,096, fo. 251r; *Portland MS*, HMC, 29, 13th Report, Appendix, Part I, I, p. 105.

[93] Sir Marmaduke Langdale was a friend, neighbour, and kinsman of the Hothams and a prominent royalist commander under the earl of Newcastle: Newman, *Royalist Officers*,

people's tongues too much at liberty. Besides if he <should be> should be admitted hither, all the country hereabouts that think he hath been the cause of their suffering, would all say that their suspicions are now grown certainties, seeing Sir Marmaduke Langdale admitted but within the walls of Hull. My lord, I hope you will pardon [me] for *not* doing a thing of no advantage and much prejudice.

Your humble servant,
John Hotham.

And for the business, it will be better done without such a meeting.

[*Seal*]

Bodl. MS Nalson II, no. 177: John Hotham to William Cavendish, earl of Newcastle, Hull, 22 March 1643[94]

My noble lord,
I have sent this other letter to excuse me for not granting Sir Marmaduke Langdale a safe conduct, and to deal freely with your lordship, he shall never have one from me. Nor do I care to treat with him, I know him too well. My lord, for a letter to the Queen that I will certainly come <itt>*in*, and at such a time, I cannot do it. This enclosed you may show her if you please or else burn. For your lordship knows that I ever said unto you that I would do anything which *might* further His Majesty's service in the peace of the kingdom, and that if the Parliament did stand upon unreasonable terms with him, I would then declare myself against them, and for him. But otherwise to leave my party that I had set up with, and no real cause given that an honest man may justify himself for so doing before God and the world, I never would do it although I endured all the extremities in the world. For I well know no man of honour or worth will ever think such a man worthy of friendship or trust. For the prejudice you undergo for not spoiling the East Riding, truly you have put an obligation upon me by sparing it this long. But rather than your lordship shall suffer anything of prejudice either in your honour or affairs, I shall not desire the thing any longer, but you may take what course you please and we shall do so for our defence. For Sir Hugh Cholmley and his manner of coming in, every man must satisfy his

pp. 221–223; A. Hopper, 'Marmaduke, first Baron Langdale (bap. 1598, d. 1661)', *ODNB*; F.H. Sunderland, *Marmaduke, Lord Langdale of Holme-on-Spalding-Moor, Yorkshire* (London, 1926).

[94] For another copy of this letter, see HHC: Hotham MS, U DDHO/1/24, marked on the reverse as exhibit 17. A transcription in a later hand is in BL, Add. MS 32,096, fos 250r–251r. See also *Portland MS*, HMC, 29, 13th Report, Appendix, Part I, I, p. 105.

own conscience and then all is well. All are not of one mind. My lord, if it please God that we once join and that I be thought worthy your friendship, it shall be seen you have got a friend that will not leave you for every wind or hope or fear. My lord, we shall now soon see whether the King will be refused just things. Which if he be, I shall take no long time to resolve. If the Parliament offer all fairness and it be obstinately refused, truly I will not forsake them, come the worst that can come. For this I conceive is just and honest, and from that ground it is not fit for him that values his honour to secede. For my Lord Fairfax, I do not think <you> *Nevill* will speed, for he cannot offer him to be so well as he is and sure fear will never do it. My lord, I know your worth [is] so great that you will not value less for his plain dealing

your most humble, affectionate servant,
John Hotham.

For my Lord of Dunbar's son, he is delivered as a prisoner to the mayor's prison for entertaining a priest, and so I cannot yet release him.

[*On reverse*] Sir John Hotham to earl of Newcastle. For your lordship:

HHC: Hotham MS, U DDHO/1/25: John Hotham to William Cavendish, earl of Newcastle, Hull, 22 March 1643[95]

For your lordship,
My noble lord,
I should take it for a great happiness to me that any act of mine might be of advantage to His Majesty's affairs. For whatsoever hath been represented to him or to Her Majesty of my disaffection, I hope it shall be found that nothing but sense of honour to perform the public trust I have undertaken hath held me in these ways. I shall and do intend to serve His Majesty, but I cannot do it so unseasonably as to make my so doing of no advanta*ge* to him, and a dishonour to myself. I know the King desires to be served with honest men and not with knaves. For he that forsakes his party without cause or colour, or for base ends, well may he as the Spaniard says, have some honour

[95] Part of this letter is published in P. Saltmarshe, *History and Chartulary of the Hothams of Scorborough in the East Riding of Yorkshire, 1100–1700* (York, 1914), p. 135.

but never any trust. My lord, I hope you will yet have a little patience, and not think ill for a little delaying of

your most affectionate friend to serve you,
John Hotham.

I wish the endeavours of those that are powerful men [be] employed to procure a happy peace. It would bring immortal honour to the actors in it.

[*On reverse*] 19.

Bodl. MS Nalson III, no. 6: John Hotham to William Cavendish, earl of Newcastle, Beverley, 30 March 1643[96]

My noble lord,
I received your 2 letters and cannot enough express my thankfulness unto you for them, in that you are pleased so favourably to interpret the actions of your servant. And if your lordship knew my real intentions you would be far from blaming me. I confess I am very tender of my honour, for I know it is like a woman's honesty, not to be repaired, if once touched. And to forsake my party when I can say nothing for it but to please my ambition or lightness is to me a terrible thing. I know you would not desire to see it in any man you esteemed worthy your friendship, although for the present it may disadvantage your affairs. You have gotten by Sir Hugh Cholmley's turning when he could give no reason for it, but an old castle which will cost you more keeping than it is worth.[97] His captains and soldiers are all here and have left him naked enough, we say not 60 men. We made bold to stay 2 ships of his at Hull, the one 6 piece of ordinance, the *other* bringing him good store of provisions from the Parliament. We talk confidently of peace. And now I shall entreat your lordship to laugh as heartily at our valiant captains of the west that have quit all their strong quarters without a shot as ever they did at others. High talking and strong drinking is not *that* that kills Sconderbag.[98] I confess when I heard

[96] A copy of this letter is in HHC: Hotham MS, U DDHO/1/26, marked on the reverse as exhibit 21. See also *Portland MS*, HMC, 29, 13th Report, Appendix, Part I, I, p. 109.

[97] John Hotham's cousin, Cholmley, the parliamentary governor of Scarborough, changed sides on 25 March 1643, taking most of his garrison with him: J. Binns, 'Sir Hugh Cholmley, first baronet (1600–1657)', *ODNB*.

[98] Hotham makes use of a contemporary term of abuse employed by playwrights, perhaps also in mocking reference to an earlier newsbook that had proclaimed that 'Scanderberg, like the Lord Fairefax, wasts little by little that Popish power': BL, TT E86(3), *Speciall passages*, 17–24 January 1643 (London, 1643), p. 196; *OED*, XIV, p. 575.

it first I did not much marvel at it as some did, well knowing that if *it* had not been for some they had never shot shot at Tadcaster when you came first, but I shamed them <into> into it. But no man is valianter then he should be, nor no woman honester, so says the proverb. For the business you writ of Portington,[99] it was thus: Sir William Savile[100] and Rockby met him, and bade him tell Sir John that they were infinitely his friends and wished the peace of the kingdom. His answer was he was theirs, and if he understood from *them* any propositions that were honest and honourable, conducing to that end he should be glad to hear them and do any office he could for the public good. This was all, and indeed, he did this to see what would come of it, and so let you know as soon as it was worth it. I had sent you notice of this before, but that I must send you a little more for I have had an instrument from Sir Marmaduke *with* long persuasions of his good will and what great things I should have. I gave him many thanks, but told [him] I was in such a condition as needed nothing, and so there is an end I think. I could write some of our southern news. First peace, next Sir William *Waller* hath got a great victory, and my Lord Northampton[101] slain and Colonel Hastings[102] prisoner at Stafford. But I am grown to believe nothing because I think our masters of both sides feed us with such meat as they think fittest for us. My lord, I shall crave your pardon that I have detained you so long from your more weighty affairs, but a little mirth doth well sometimes, and that hath emboldened to venture upon your patience,

your most humble, affectionate servant,
John Hotham.

This enclosed is the particular description of Mr Portington's business as you desired.

[*On reverse*] 21. Tadcaster. Mr Hotham to earl of Newcastle.

[99] This was Michael Portington of Eastrington, a major in Sir Thomas Metham's regiment of East Riding trained bands: Newman, *Royalist Officers*, p. 301.

[100] Savile was appointed governor of York in November 1643: Newman, *Royalist Officers*, p. 332; Kirby, 'Savile family'.

[101] Spencer Compton, earl of Northampton, was slain at the battle of Hopton Heath on 19 March 1643: Newman, *Royalist Officers*, p. 80; M. Bennett, 'Spencer Compton, second earl of Northampton (1601–1643)', *ODNB*.

[102] This was Henry Hastings, royalist colonel-general of Leicestershire, Derbyshire, Nottinghamshire, and Rutland. Hotham was correct to doubt the rumour that Hastings had been captured: Newman, *Royalist Officers*, p. 179; M. Bennett, 'Henry Hastings, baron Loughborough (1610–1667)', *ODNB*.

Bodl. MS Nalson XI, no. 208: Sir John Hotham to William Lenthall, Hull, 1 April 1643[103]

Sir,
By Sir Matthew Boynton and Mr Philip Nye[104] some days since, I writ to you the state of our affairs here, with the relation of Sir Hugh Cholmley's unfortunate deserting us. I have now this to add. That since, by the industry, faith and courage of Captain Bushell,[105] that castle and town is regained. I sent him thither from here upon such assurance of his faith as gave me full satisfaction. I am this morning sending him some supply of men, money and ammunition. The place is strong and a good harbour and very considerable to keep all that quarter in obedience to you. But you know if a garrison be there, something must be said. If you enable me and refer it to one, I shall, God willing, to the best of my understanding do it for your most advantage. And if you so think fit to refer it likewise to me the naming of a commander for that place, I intend it him that hath so gallantly performed his faith, both to you and me. But I conceive it far better for your affairs that he have his dependence from hence and orders from me than otherwise. Sir, this is all I have for the present, but his due respects whoever is

your most humble servant,
John Hotham.

HHC: Hotham MS, U DDHO/1/27: John Hotham to William Cavendish, earl of Newcastle, Beverley, 1 April 1643[106]

For the right honourable the earl of Newcastle.
My <lord> noble lord,
I am very sorry you should ever harbour such an opinion of me as to think that any motive whatsoever could ever move me to betray the

[103]This letter is a copy transcribed from the original by John Nalson's grandson, Philip Williams, rector of Doddington, *c.*1730. See also *CJ*, III, p. 27; *Portland MS*, HMC, 29, 13th Report, Appendix, Part I, supplement, I, p. 701.

[104]Note in margin: 'a stickling Independent Preacher'. See B. Donagan, 'Philip Nye (bap. 1595, d. 1672)', *ODNB*.

[105]Unknown to Hotham, Bushell had already changed sides on 29 March and joined Sir Hugh Cholmley. Bushell was executed exactly eight years later, on 29 March 1651, for having betrayed Scarborough: J. Binns, 'Browne Bushell (bap. 1609, d. 1651)', *ODNB*; *idem*, 'Captain Browne Bushell: North Sea adventurer and pirate', *Northern History*, 27 (1991), pp. 90–105.

[106]A later transcript of this letter by the Revd Philip Williams appears in Bodl. MS Nalson XI, no. 209. Part of the letter is also published in *Portland MS*, HMC, 29, 13th Report, Appendix, Part I, supplement, I, p. 701.

public trust I have undertaken. Unless they had unquestionably fallen from principles of honour and honesty, I could never have satisfied myself, but I should have been the scorn and byword of every boy in the street. My lord, my particular affection to your person was a motive to me to be glad to serve you if a way might be found to do it as befitted a gentleman. Otherwise I would not serve the greatest emperor although reward and punishment were proposed in the highest measure. And therefore for an end of the treaty, as you please, I shall speak no more of it at all. But now to give you a taste that all is not as you think at court, I shall freely tell you this. That within this four days some very near Her Majesty spoke such words of contempt and disgrace of you as truly for my part I could not hear them repeated with patience. And you will plainly see if they dare venture it, you will have a successor. This my lord is no fiction and further such offers of grace and favour and honour have been made within this very few <da> days to your servants here, with a very great undervaluing of you, as it may be you will not believe. But it shall not be said that an answer shall be returned to any of them. My lord, I speak not this of myself. I can shift in any fortune, but for the great esteem I have of your worth that you be not abused and ungratefully used by the malice of your enemies that envy your virtues. And this my lord is all the end of

your most faithful servant,
John Hotham.

For the Lincolnshire business you know my near relations there, and I confess at the instance of such friends as I could not deny and with such great importunity, made me seem content they should use my name which they persuaded themselves would do their business good standing but then in a reasonable condition.

[*On reverse*] 22.

HHC: Hotham MS, U DDHO/1/12: John Hotham to William Cavendish, earl of Newcastle, Beverley, 3 April 1643[107]

My noble lord,
I received your 2 letters, and for my promise that you write of I believe that I might write some such thing. And I am in the same mind still that

[107] A later transcript of this letter by the Revd Philip Williams, with omissions, appears in Bodl. MS Nalson XI, no. 210. Part of it is printed in *Portland MS*, HMC, 29, 13th Report, Appendix, Part I, supplement, I, pp. 701–702.

I should be glad of an opportunity to serve His Majesty, but it must be such a one as not to bring upon me the odious name of knavery. But now for the particular you write of, upon your engagement, which I confess I trust above all, that it shall be made use of as to your private, I shall give you all the particulars. The words were these: that you were a sweet general, lay in bed until eleven a clock and com'd till 12, then came to see the Queen, and so the work was done, and that General King[108] did all the business. They were spoken by my Lady Cornwallis in the hearing of Mr. Portington, a fellow cunning enough. And this to my father and another gentleman with many other words of undervaluing, which he said were spoken by others. For the great offers that were made, they were from my Lord Goring,[109] the instrument, Mr George Butler. And it was offered that he should meet my father in any place upon his word and strong things really performed. My lord, the great esteem I have of your private friendship leads me to do this and not anything of the public. And if you think the friendship of a gentleman worth your acceptance, you shall have it with as much affection and integrity to your particular as you can expect. And I shall be faithful to you whatsoever become of the public, and for their court tricks I value them not, as never intending to be within the reach of them, God saying Amen. For I have taken such course as if the times be bad to me, my wife and children have to put meat in their mouths, and if I live I shall shark for meat and drink. And if I be knock'd in the head the care is taken, I need not winter jerkin. For attending you I doubt I cannot. Sir Hugh Cholmley's business hath drawn such a jealousy upon me and our people talk at large. My lord, you can expect nothing at court but tricks. The women rule all, and what certainly can be hoped for from them, he that knows them may easily guess. Strengthen yourself with such friends as will not forsake you upon every frown of the court. The papists will for their dependence is merely that way. My lord, although I am not worthy to advise you, this course always you have taken. You have now done great service that will be forgot when they think they can shift without you. None hath fortune in a string and amongst those many that are now beholden to you, you may choose out some that will be yours

[108] James King, Lord Eythin was an experienced Scots professional soldier and lieutenant-general of Newcastle's infantry: S. Murdoch and T. Wales, 'James King, Lord Eythin (1589–1652)', *ODNB*.

[109] Lord Goring was a favourite of the queen who had accompanied her from the continent when she landed at Bridlington on 22 February 1643: B. Donagan, 'George Goring, first earl of Norwich (1585–1663)', *ODNB*.

in despite of your enemies. I hope you will be pleased to pardon this boldness in

your most affectionate, humble servant,
John Hotham.

My lord, if I or any friend of mine fail you private, say we are knaves. For the public a man cannot do but as to his engagements unless he be highly neglected and then he must shift as he can.

[*On reverse*] Sir John Hotham's letters taken at Pontefract, 3rd parcel numbered in by Sir Peter Wentworth, 5 August 1645.

Bodl. MS Nalson XI, no. 220: John Hotham to William Cavendish, earl of Newcastle, Lincoln, 14 April 1643[110]

My noble lord,
It is a part of my unhappiness that I am necessitated by my employment to be so far distant from you, and not to hear of your well being by a line or two. I have not been idle since you writ last to do His Majesty and your lordship the best service I could, although to bring that about I was glad to go seemingly the contrary. I have since I came into this country[111] dealt with some of my friends that they would not be so violent against His Majesty's service, and was bold to promise them a pardon if they would retire and give way that this country might be wholly at his devotion. The gentlemen are so considerable, that of my knowledge if they desist there shall not be a man here to hold up his hand against His Majesty. I was so earnest with them that I am confident it will be done if your lordship will be pleased to return me an assurance that they shall have His Majesty's favour and pardon. The gentlemen are Sir Christopher Wray and Sir Edward Ayscough, men as considerable as any in the north. And for myself, your interest in me must wholly guide me. I shall submit to such a course as you shall think fit for him that you were pleased to name your friend. And my lord when this is done, I hope it will well appear that none hath done that great considerable service as you have done. And I doubt not but His Majesty's grace and favour will

[110]This letter is a copy transcribed from the original by Nalson's grandson, Philip Williams, *c.*1730. See also *Portland MS*, HMC, 29, 13th Report, Appendix, Part I, supplement, I, pp. 702–703.
[111]Lincolnshire.

be on you accordingly. And I hope you will not be worse for having totally yours

your most humble, affectionate servant,
John Hotham.

HHC: Hotham MS, U DDHO/1/28: John Hotham to William Cavendish, earl of Newcastle, Lincoln, 18 April 1643[112]

My <Lord> noble lord,
I received your letter and the safe conduct of my trumpet, but with them a message that I must either come this day to you or not at all, and indeed the safe conduct is only until Wednesday night. I was very sorry to see myself put upon an impossibility, for it was 12 a clock before the boy came, and then I had to acquaint those gentlemen with it, and ride 26 miles after, which could not be done in that time. My lord, if your occasions do at this time call you northward then I cannot for the present attend you. Yet I doubt not but to make it appear when I have the honour to wait upon you that His Majesty's service here hath all that time by your means made a very large progress. For I hope to gain my Lord Willoughby,[113] and all those that have either power or reputation. One thing yesterday disadvantaged me much. A letter that I received from some gentlemen at Newark about the exchange of prisoners, so full of pride, folly, and what is not in a gentleman, that these men of quality here said nothing in the whole business troubled them so much as joining with men of so great folly and little worth. The letter I have sent you. They had an answer sharp enough, and they will never be treated with again, by any that understands himself. My lord, command what you please and it shall be observed by

your humble, affectionate servant,
John Hotham.

[*On reverse*] Lord Willoughby. 24.

[112] On the reverse of this letter is written 'Lord Willoughby 8° Aprilis 1643'. A later transcript of this letter by the Revd Philip Williams appears in Bodl. MS Nalson XI, no. 223. Part of it is published in *Portland MS*, HMC, 29, 13th Report, Appendix, Part I, supplement, I, p. 704.

[113] Willoughby may have wavered in his allegiance in 1643, but he did not change sides until 1648: M.A. LaCombe, 'Francis Willoughby, fifth baron Willoughby of Parham (bap. 1614, d. 1666)', *ODNB*.

Bodl. MS Tanner LXII, fo. 71: John Hotham to William Cavendish, earl of Newcastle, Lincoln, 20 April 1643

My noble lord,
Just as I was taking my horse to attend you our scouts brought in word that the Newark forces were upon [a] march to Gainsborough so that I was forced to stay my journey to look upon the enemy. For if I should have come to Welbeck upon a treaty and they in tow, all the world would exclaim of me. I shall therefore desire your lordship will excuse my not coming upon so just an excuse, and as soon as this business is over, I shall then not fail to attend you, and in the mean time remain

your most humble, affectionate servant,
John Hotham.

HHC: Hotham MS, U DDHO/1/29: John Hotham to William Cavendish, earl of Newcastle, Lincoln, 26 April 1643[114]

For your lordship:
My noble lord,
I am very glad you sent Sir Marmaduke Langdale over, rather than that I should have waited upon you myself. *For* although I little regard what people talk, yet something is to be yielded unto in that respect in these unhappy times. My lord, I make no doubt he comes instructed from you to treat in such a way as is fit for gentlemen that value their honour above anything, for he is a knave that desires to outlive it. I make no question but that well stated good fruit may come of his journey for His Majesty's honour and your satisfaction. For what concerns myself, I thank God, I have neither hopes nor fears that can remove me from what befits a gentleman and your obliged servant. For it was the honourable opinion I had of your worth that ever moved me to put pen to paper on this subject, and if any unhappiness break this, I will come in with the generality, or let all go. And this is the perfect resolution of

your most humble, affectionate servant,
John Hotham.

[*On reverse*] Sir Charles Thompson's papers. 29.

[114] A copy of this letter is in Bodl. MS Tanner LXII, fo. 83.

Bodl. MS Tanner LXII, fo. 88: Sir John Hotham to William Cavendish, earl of Newcastle, Hull, 30 April 1643

Right honourable,

I received yours of 29 April and this I shall and must profess that in your particular no man shall serve you in anything within my power with more faith and affection than myself. And if I do not, let this paper be a witness against me. I hope this will come safe to you, being I suppose this is a messenger of your own. Therefore, I shall write my mind the more freely. If those of the very Cabinet Council had advised His Majesty to have offered reason to the Parliament, I should with my life and fortunes more willingly have served him than ever I did [*MS faded*] in my life. But I must ingraciously confess to you whom I dare trust with my life that this last message wherein 'tis stood upon that ships, forts, magazines, militia should be put into his hands, all ordinances of Parliament declared illegal, the Parliament adjourned 20 miles from London, and taking arms unlawful: these I doubt hath more disadvantaged his cause as I conceive than any action done since these troubles. I must confess at and other times when for just causes of distrust were not. The first soever of these it were not reason to deny him. And I am persuaded if peace were one year settled would be cheerfully granted him. But certainly if they should now before power might be put into those hands that would do their best to advise His Majesty to make wrong use of it. My lord, be not displeased with me to tell you that as I conceive make not you nor any person of so much honour privy to some of their secret designs. They know you are not for their purpose. And if you heard what is in every man's mouth here *and at York* you would believe me. I dare write no more. I shall God willing with your very first opportunity send your letters to my son who I make no questions will write suddenly to you. Some of your forces are come over they say to besiege Wressle castle, I believe as formerly you writ in case of Pomfret[115] to wash a Blackmoor. But those forces if they remain in the East Riding must make us here the more active which else we desire not. My lord, I shall ever profess that I earnestly and really desire to remain

your honourable, most faithful and humble servant,
John Hotham.

[115]Pontefract.

WRESSEL CASTLE, *in* YORKSHIRE.

Bodl. MS Tanner LXII, fo. 90: John Hotham to William Cavendish, earl of Newcastle, Lincoln, 31 April 1643 [*sic*]

My noble lord,
I make no question that Sir Marmaduke Langdale acquainted you with what was spoken of here. I have acquainted my father with the same, and find him inclinable to serve His Majesty and your lordship in any just, and honourable way. For this that was propounded, he likes it well, only desires to know what limitations it must have both in respect of persons and places, and in what measure of good service it shall be reckoned to those that really perform it. For upon your assurance herein, order will be taken to prepare the business for it, and to hinder Colonel Cromwell's marching hither that is now far on his way. For that, if necessity force not, you would be pleased not to advance too fast *into* this *country* that things may be done in a handsomer way. I hope you will excuse me, if these things run not so fast as could be wished, being it is to pass many hands, and every

man, must be pleased in his humour, and have his word about. But a little delay may be borne with when there is hope of working a real effect, and violent hasting to a business not ripe doth put it into distraction. My lord, I hope you think that His Majesty's affairs may be more advanced by drawing to his service some number of men of quality although it cost some time, than by coming single. My lord, your unwearied good opinion much emboldens to trouble you.

Your most affectionate, real servant,
John Hotham.

Bodl. MS Nalson XI, no. 248: John Hotham to William Cavendish, earl of Newcastle, Lincoln, 4 May 1643[116]

My noble lord,
I am something ashamed that I should make you believe more certainly than I doubt you will find in some gentlemen here. The truth is they are divided. Some upon the business of the south going high are off again, others still the same men. I should desire your opinion what to do in it, for my Lord Willoughby hangs most off. I think you are mistaken in my father. For the reason of his standing a little aloof is that he so infinitely wishes the peace of the kingdom, which he thinks the King's last answer tends not to, that I know it hath staggered him much, and my not having opportunity to speak with him since, and some other that do very ill offices in that place. But I hope to remedy all. There have been those ladies treating that you write of, and they were as well fitted with an answer of nothing. But there is another manner of treater there than they, and it was said from a good hand, that the Queen thought much, you did not enough communicate with her and take her directions, but you were not yet to be displeased. My lord, for my self I am as much your servant as ever, and twenty such businesses as Reading[117] shall make no alteration. But these fickle people put me to my wits' end, yet there is hope to overcome the difficulty with a little patience. If His Majesty's affairs suffer not too much by it, it may do well yet. Our lying still and not hasting Cromwell to join, is I am sure some advantage. For he is still kept to eat up the fat clergy at Peterborough, although my Lord

[116]This letter is a copy transcribed from the original by Nalson's grandson, the Revd Philip Williams, *c.*1730. See also *Portland MS*, HMC, 29, 13th Report, Appendix, Part I, supplement, I, p. 707.

[117]Cholmley later remarked that the Hothams delayed defecting because they were awaiting the result of the earl of Essex's siege of Reading. The town fell on 27 April and John Hotham indicates here that he was conscious of such rumours about him: Binns, *The Memoirs and Memorials of Sir Hugh Cholmley*, p. 128.

of Essex hath writ often to the contrary to him. For what Sir Hugh Cholmley says it is no matter, it is not the first time he hath scandalled his friends and then denied it. I confess I am in a very great strait in these businesses. Your lordship's wisdom can best give directions in it to

your most humble, affectionate servant,
John Hotham.

I wish I could do you any service worthy the least of those honours your nobleness is pleased to think me fit for. I shall never desire anything more than to keep my old place in your good opinion.

Bodl. MS Nalson XI, no. 253: John Hotham, Sir Edward Ayscough, and Sir Christopher Wray to William Lenthall, Lincoln, 5 May 1643[118]

Noble sir,

We cannot but hear that some to colour their own fears, others, that the blame should rather light upon others than themselves, have reported that we have not been so diligent to promote the public service in these parts as we ought to have been. To vindicate ourselves from these imputations, we have thought fit to give you a narrative of some particulars. There hath not any time this three weeks passed one day that we have not writ both to Colonel Cromwell, the Norfolk gentlemen, and my Lord Grey[119] to appoint a place of meeting, and we would march to them wheresoever it were. Their answer always was they would meet, but something of importance was first to be done in those countries they then were in, which hitherto hath been the cause that little is done, only the particular countries where we quarter put to a very great charge without benefit to the public. Sir, we have sent you here enclosed the last letter that came from Colonel Cromwell, that you may see we are in no fault. The committee here is grown to two, all else at London or Hull, and so they may with great ease sit safe and talk of what they please of those actions and particulars they take up at second hand. Sir, we shall desire this justice, that those of this county may be sent down to rectify what is amiss, and if you please some soldiers of knowledge with them, and they shall have all here

[118] This letter is a copy transcribed from the original by Nalson's grandson, the Revd Philip Williams, *c.*1730. See also *CJ*, III, p. 75; *Portland MS*, HMC, 29, 13th Report, Appendix, Part I, supplement, I, pp. 707–708.

[119] Thomas, Lord Grey of Groby: E.T. Bradley, rev. S. Kelsey, 'Thomas Grey, Baron Grey of Groby (1622–1657)', *ODNB*; J. Richards, *Aristocrat and Regicide: the life and times of Thomas, Lord Grey of Groby* (London, 2000).

surrendered into their hands to manage.[120] And it shall be delivered them in as good or better condition than it was yet in Lincolnshire. Sir, if the House please to do us this justice, it will encourage us to serve them hereafter, and we shall ever remain

your humble servants,
John Hotham, Edward Ayscough, Christopher Wray.

Bodl. MS Nalson III, no. 12: John Hotham to William Lenthall, Lincoln, 12 May 1643[121]

Sir,
Though there is nothing at this time more common than to see men's actions censured by the weekly pamphlets, yet when persons of honour are scandalized by their falsehoods there is nothing so necessary as speedy reparation. Sir, you may therefore please to know that there is lately come to our view a printed paper here enclosed, wherein such a formal relation is made of the jealousies and suspicions of Major Purefoy, governor of this city of Lincoln, that we who are best judges of his actions could not do less than vindicate the honour of so noble a gentleman, both by causing such books as came hither to be publicly burnt, and to desire your justice against the printer of them.[122] So that what possibly may be repaid of due to his merit, who we assure you hath ever since his coming hither served the commonwealth with as much fidelity and affection as can be expected from a man of honour in which assurance we leave him to expect your favour whilst we remain

your most humble servants,
John Hotham, Edward Ayscough, John Broxolme,[123]
Christopher Wray.

[*Seal*] For our much honoured friend, William Lenthall, esq., Speaker of the House of Commons. These:

[*On reverse*] Letter from Lincoln concerning Mr Purefoy.

[120] For the breakdown in the parliamentarian administration of Lincolnshire in the summer of 1643, see C. Holmes, 'Colonel King and Lincolnshire politics, 1642–1646', *Historical Journal*, 16 (1973), pp. 451–452.

[121] See also *CJ*, III, p. 86; *Portland MS*, HMC, 29, 13th Report, Appendix, Part I, I, p. 116.

[122] The newsbook against which Hotham complained was BL, TT E249(2), *A perfect diurnall of the passages in parliament*, 1–8 May 1643 (London, 1643). This scandal was referred to the Committee for Examinations on 15 May 1643. Purefoy was eventually arrested by the Lincoln committee, upon information received from the mayor of Hull, on 2 July 1643. He was to be tried by the earl of Essex's council of war in November 1643 but his fate is unknown: BL, Harleian MS 165, fo. 107r; *CJ*, III, pp. 86, 202, 303, 309.

[123] John Broxholme was MP for Lincoln and, despite being largely inactive at Westminster, he contributed money to the parliamentary cause and was on the committee for securing the militia in Lincolnshire in 1642: C. Holmes, *Seventeenth-century Lincolnshire* (Lincoln, 1980), pp. 140, 143, 180.

R. Bell (ed.), *The Fairfax Correspondence: memorials of the civil war*, 2 vols (London, 1849), I, p. 45: John Hotham to Ferdinando, Lord Fairfax, Nottingham, 24 May 1643

For the right honourable Ferdinando Lord Fairfax, general of the northern forces, these present.
May it please your lordship,
I received your letter, and do intend to fulfil your commands with all expedition. I am now marched up to Nottingham, and Colonel Cromwell's forces with me; here is Lord Gray come too, and this day we expect Sir John Gell; Sir William Brereton hath order to draw down to us, then we shall be strong. The Manchester forces have orders to draw down to you, and furnish you with what you want. I shall endeavour all I can to join with you, or otherwise to distress the enemy. Our misery is, we know not where his force lies, nor in what condition he is. I shall desire to have some information from you on that point, and I shall not fail to endeavour that which may be best for the public service, and will ever remain,

Your lordship's humble servant,
John Hotham.

BL, Add. MS 18,979, fo. 141: John Hotham, Sir John Gell, Oliver Cromwell, Sir Miles Hobart, and Thomas, Lord Grey of Groby, to Ferdinando, Lord Fairfax, Nottingham, 2 June 1643[124]

May it please your lordship,
We were even ready to march with all the forces here to attend you when we had certain intelligence of the state of my Lord Newcastle's army, so weak and in such a distraction that we conceive it far unfit to force your lordship in your quarters. We had certain notice likewise that a good strength of horse and foot were marched from him to Newark to face and attend the moving of the forces that are here. Upon Tuesday last there was towards 40 troops of horse and dragooners appeared in a body some 4 miles from this place, and we hear behind them stood their foot. We drew out to fight them but they had chosen such a ground as we could not come to them without great disadvantage. At night they drew away and are still within 6 or 7 miles. However up and down the country, until we see what these

[124]The letter is written in John Hotham's hand. There is a note on the reverse, probably referring to the letter's purchase at Sotheby's: '15 June 1852, lot 245'.

people intend or which way my Lord Newcastle will move we think it best to stay here and *not* to draw down into Yorkshire to eat up what small remainder of provisions that is left and by that means do your lordship more prejudice than the enemy can do. This we thought fit to offer to your consideration and if notwithstanding all this you shall *think* it fitter for us to move towards you, it shall be readily done by

your lordship's humble servants,
John Gell, Oliver Cromwell, Thomas Grey,
John Hotham, Miles Hobart.[125]

[*On reverse*] For the right honourable Ferdinando, Lord Fairfax, general of the northern forces, these present at Leeds: [*Seal*]
[*Also on reverse, unsigned, in a different hand, probably by Lord Fairfax himself*]: After I had concluded this letter, I received yours dated 2 June and do notwithstanding all the objections and difficulties herein represented, desire that as you tender the public faith you draw down this way with all the forces you have and join with me to suppress this popish army here, which else *whatsoever report gives it out to you* is of power without God's miraculous deliverance to destroy our forces and so by degrees to ruin the kingdom.

BL, Add. MS 44,848, fo. 287v: Sir John Hotham to John Hotham, Hull, 25 June 1643[126]

Your letter came joyful to me, both for the manner and the matter, that you have freed yourself from those false villains. Some must be privy to it that have no reason upon the first notice of your taking, I despatch't away to the House, Nye and Saltondish,[127] with a formal letter to the Lords and Commons, but with this instruction, to tell them in plain English, if they instantly sent you not hither to me, I would (if please God) right myself. They little think but that the great Anabaptist[128] hath you sure. If it be possible I would see you here. We have a great game to play. The great God of heaven direct us to his glory. How you can come safe I know not (for assure yourself the king's party will lay strong watch and I would not have you in their

[125] Sir Miles Hobart was the colonel of a regiment in the Eastern Association in 1643–1644.

[126] This is a copy: see also HHC: Hotham MS, U DDHO/1/42.

[127] John Saltmarsh, the Godly minister of Heslerton and kinsman of Sir John Hotham, took shelter in Hull in 1642. He was entrusted by Sir John to protest at Westminster about John Hotham's arrest at Nottingham in June 1643 and later became an important prosecution witness during Sir John's trial: R. Pooley, 'John Saltmarsh (d. 1647)', *ODNB*.

[128] Sir John refers to Oliver Cromwell, whom he held responsible for his son's arrest at Nottingham.

hands that way). Du Moulin's man will be with me within 8 days. I have not leisure to write fully, but if without danger I never would so gladly see you. And, God willing you shall see the difference between a false friend and a father, for I will live and die with you and your honour. The fool Cholmley, I cannot get quiet for 10 days, that I fear I must ?&it?: he is a fool beyond measure. If you can come to Hull, but not with hazard, gladly would I speak with you, yet loath you should miscarry in the haven. The great merciful God, to whom if you give your heart you cannot miscarry, bless, direct and perfect you.

Your loving father,
John Hotham.

HHC: C BRS/7/66: Note of the Committee of Hull, 3 July 1643

It is desired by Sir John Hotham that Sir John Hotham may have out of his money £200, that his horses may be kept by his men in his own stable with his own provision of beans and oats. That a carbine, a case of pistols with holsters may be delivered to Richard Frank, being Mr Frank's own goods.

HHC: C BRL/308: Sir John Hotham to the Mayor and Committee of Hull, Hull, 4 July 1643[129]

Sirs,
This unfortunate business which I doubt but you have done of your good affections to the parliament, I hope God in his mercy will turn to the good of all. My going up is so sudden that I can hardly think how to compose my requests. The first is that my wife may have notice with my children and some servants to hire a ship and follow me to London with my two sons William and Charles. The second that you will please to let me have the use of £500 of my money. I have a wife [and] 8 children to maintain and you know at London how money spends and not now to be got. The third is that my wife may have liberty to bring up her household stuff, hangings, linen and bedding and such things. The fourth that Mr Mayor may take into his custody such papers as he thinks fitting, the rest being the evidences of my land may be secured. I hear you have dealt like gentlemen with my

[129]Another transcription of this letter is in T. Tindall Wildridge (ed.), *The Hull Letters: documents from the Hull Records, 1625–1646* (Hull, 1886), pp. 32–33.

wife in sparing her her own money for which I may live to thank you. The fifth that one of my servants may go in the ship with me for I am not able to help myself at all. The sixth my trunk of wearing clothes may be sent me for I am clean out of them.

Your humble servant,
John Hotham.

HHC: C BRL/310: Sir John Hotham to the Mayor and Committee of Hull, Hull, 4 July 1643[130]

Gentlemen,
I thought good to signify unto you, that I did borrow of Mr John Barnard of Hull, alderman, for the payment of the garrison, the sum of £400, for which I did give him my bills exchange, expecting the Parliament would punctually have paid it there; but *did* promise if they refused, the money to remain in my hands to keep for him, if in case it would not be paid at London. Therefore this is to request you all, that you will let him have his own monies again, which I did but only keep for him, and for a truth I have set to my hand.

Your servant,
John Hotham.

There was likewise £100 in the same kind of Sir Christopher Wray's money: and £120 of a tradesman of London. If you please to let me have so much sent me hither, for I stand likewise *charged* with those sums.

your servant,
John Hotham.

HHC: C BRS/7/67: The Committee of Hull's answer to Sir John Hotham's demands, Hull, 5 July 1643

The Lady Hotham shall have notice of Sir John Hotham's going to London in the ship the *Antelope*. And she, her children and maidservants are permitted to go to London <also in any other ship> by shipping at some convenient time hereafter which the committee will appoint. Also, Mr Charles and Mr William Hotham may go along with them if they please. It is thought fit that Sir John Hotham shall have delivered unto him for his better maintenance <of himself, his

[130] Another transcription of this letter is in *ibid.*, pp. 33–34.

wife, children and servants> *as he desires* forth of the monies in Mr Mayor's custody, which was brought from his house the sum of one hundred pounds, which is delivered to Captain Moyer. It is <thought fit> *agreed that* the Lady Hotham shall have liberty to carry up with her *at her going* to London such necessary *and convenient* household stuff, as shall be thought fit by the Committee. It is thought fit that all Sir John Hotham's evidences shall be secured in such places of the town as he shall appoint, at his own adventure and hazard. It is thought fit that Sir John Hotham may have his trunk of wearing clothes sent him aboard of the *Antelope*, which is now delivered to his man Alexander Richardson. That care be taken for a man to go up with Sir John Hotham in the *Antelope* for his better help in waiting & attending upon him.
<Sir, these things are thought fit to>
<Sir, we shall take order that these things are carefully observed>
Sir, we shall take as much care in these particulars as we can, that we may <be able> show ourselves your friends and servants.

HHC: C BRS/7/68: Order to indemnify the Committee of Hull for arresting the Hothams, 10 July 1643

Whereas Thomas Raikes, mayor of Hull, Sir Matthew Boynton, knight and baronet, Sir William St Quintin, baronet, Sir Richard Darley, knight, Sir John Bourchier and Sir William Allenson, knights, Lancelot Roper, Nicholas Denman, John Barnard, and William Popple, aldermen, John Penrose, gent, Robert Johnson, clerk, having received information that there was a design for the betraying of the town of Hull, in their opinions could not be prevented but by a speedy seizing of the blockhouses and other places of strength in the town, as also of the persons of Sir John Hotham, Sir Edward Rodes and Captain Hotham. And whereas accordingly they with others seized on the said places of strength for the preservation of the said town, and also of the persons of the said Sir John Hotham and Sir Edward Rodes, and of the treasure, plate, trunks, and writings, and other things of the said Sir John Hotham's and Captain Hotham's, and to be in safe custody till further directions from the Parliament. And whereas the said mayor of Hull, Sir Matthew Boynton, and the rest of the persons first above named did issue out their warrants and directions commanding Captain Scarth to march from Scorborough with his soldiers, arms and ammunition he had there, to Beverley for the defence of that place, and with the goods there of consequence to be preserved in Beverley till further directions from the Parliament. And whereas they did issue out their warrants and directions unto divers other captains for to march with their soldiers from Hull to Beverley for the defence of that place. The Lords and Commons do declare that it was an acceptable [service] to the King and Parliament in that which the said mayor of Hull, Sir Matthew Boynton, and the rest of the gentlemen abovenamed and all others have done therein, and that the Lords and Commons will keep them and all others that have assisted them therein indemnified and saved harmless.

HHC: Hotham MS, U DDHO/1/47: The Committee of Hull's answer to the demands of Lady Hotham, Hull, no date, July 1643

An answer to the Lady Hotham's demands:
1. It is desired that the Lady Hotham forbear her going up to London for some time, until the Parliament shall send down some directions touching Sir John Hotham's business in respect she desires not only her personal liberty but also liberty to transport her goods, which is not yet thought convenient.
3. To the third proposition concerning the evidences, such of them as shall run to the committee's hands shall rest in the town until Sir John Hotham shall appoint some place for keeping them there at his own adventure and hazard, according to his own request, or that the Parliament shall give further directions.
5. To the fifth proposition concerning the arms, they will be enquired after, and care taken that such of them as shall come to their hands shall be put into safe custody until the Parliament's directions be <given> signified to the committee. And the horses are *already* ordered to be kept by Sir John Hotham's own servants as is desired.
The second, fourth and sixth propositions are answered in the answer given to the first.

[*On reverse*] Desires of my wife to the committee at Hull.[131]

HHC: C BRS/7/31: Unsigned fragment, probably in the words of John Hotham, undated but July 1643

My troop that hath served you eleven months & had not money to buy them bread are likewise, by this committee stripped of all they have, and their horses and arms taken from them and my captain a prisoner in Captain Moyer's ship.

[131] This is Sir John Hotham's later copy. The original answer of the committee, dated 11 July 1643, is HHC: C BRS/7/70.

HHC: Hotham MS, U DDHO/1/76: Orders of the House of Commons, July 1643

Ordered by the Commons:
That the committee at Hull, or the major part, shall open the trunks and boxes of Sir John Hotham and Captain Hotham, and take an inventory of what is contained in them, and certify to the House what monies and plate or other goods there are, and out of the said monies shall take and borrow £1,000 upon account and employ it for the pay of the garrisons of Hull and Beverley. And that they shall likewise take out £500 of the said monies and deliver it upon account to Captain Moyer, Captain of the *Hercules*, a part of the £800 received by Sir John Hotham of the customs etc. 'Tis left to the said committee to consider of the charge and expenses of Sir William Allanson's[132] in his journey up and down and to satisfy out of the said monies.
Second order by the Commons:
Ordered that all monies, plate and goods seized at Hull which were formerly in the custody of Sir John Hotham or Captain Hotham or any other for their use (except such as shall appear upon <the> examination before the committee to belong to other persons, members of this House, and except the £1,500 assigned for the garrison and Captain Moyer), shall be forthwith delivered unto my Lord Fairfax upon account for the pay of the forces under his command.
Sir, these are the full answer to your question.

[*On reverse*] Order for giving away my monies.

Bodl. MS Tanner LXII, fo. 250: Petition of John Hotham to the House of Commons, Westminster, 12 August 1643

The humble petition of Captain John Hotham to the Honourable House of Commons.
Humbly showeth,
That he hath served you long in peace and war, and with as much faith and industry as any other, whatsoever is pretended by his adversaries. That he well hopes in favour to him and example of justice to your own proceedings, you will not now create a new precedent (as he humbly conceives) not known to former ages. That he hath now this 8 weeks endured a most close and hard imprisonment, all the comforts

[132] Allanson was MP for the city of York and present in Hull during the summer of 1643: Hopper, 'A directory of parliamentarian allegiance in Yorkshire', p. 90; Keeler, *The Long Parliament*, pp. 83–84; Tindall Wildridge, *The Hull Letters*, pp. 39, 44, 47, 84, 152.

of life and ways of clearing his innocency utterly debarred him, and all things else that may either preserve body or soul. His estate not gotten in your service, seized and given away before hearing or trial and thereby his wife and small children utterly ruined and beggared contrary to law and your continual practice. That himself hath been examined with an 100 several sorts of interrogatories, and the words and actions of his whole life called in question, if it were possible out of them to create a crime. That his wife, friends, alliance, servants have been all ?trocassed? and torn with several sorts of examinations to betray him. Them that would, promised rewards, and proffered them that would not, cast into the gaol. This usage and a great deal worse hath he felt already, and by those that he will prove have been so far from doing you good service as they have done you very ill. He humbly desires in consideration of the premises that you will imitate the great God, that wills not the destruction of a sinner, much less of his servant. That you will give order that his estate be not wasted, but sequestered, that as his enemies have all means and encouragements to accuse him, so he may have for his justification. That your weighty affairs not admitting his present hearing, he may be admitted bail, and not rot and languish in close imprisonment. These he hopes you will not deny, being granted to the 12 bishops by yourselves accused of high treason, and lately to the 2 lords imprisoned for the same in the Tower. He humbly conceives that by this course you will much vindicate your own honour to show as much favour and justice to one of your own members that hath long served you, as the Lords and you have done to others. And you will besides avoid the example of making an ill precedent. All this he humbly submits to your better judgement and will ever remain

your humble petitioner and servant,
John Hotham.

HHC: Hotham MS, U DDHO/1/77: Order of the House of Commons for the Corporation of Hull to deliver the military government of Hull to Lord Fairfax, 19 August 1643

Whereas the mayor and aldermen of Kingston-upon-Hull with others who since the apprehension of Sir John Hotham their late governor and his son Captain John Hotham, the 29 June last have faithfully negotiated the affairs of the said town and diligently applied themselves for the well government thereof, are by a late ordinance of the Lords and Commons assembled in Parliament, dated 22 July 1643, ordered to deliver up the military government of the said town and forces therein into the hands of the right honourable Ferdinando, Lord Fairfax. It is ordered by the House of Commons that the said mayor, aldermen and others, assistants, whose care and diligence in the vacancy of a new governor is well approved of shall be hereby authorized to deliver up into the hands of the said Lord Fairfax, the military government of the said town of Kingston-upon-Hull, and magazine therein, and blockhouses, as also the possession of the remainder of such monies, plate, and other goods by them formerly seized at Hull which were in the custody of Sir John Hotham or his son, Captain Hotham aforesaid, by an inventory to be taken of all the particulars now in their custody.

Henry Elsynge, clerk of the House of Commons.
This is a true copy of the original order of Parliament examined by Thomas Raikes, Henry Barnard, Nicholas Denman, William Popple.[133]

HHC: Hotham MS, U DDHO/1/30: Order of the House of Commons, Westminster, 7 September 1643

Sir John Hotham was again called in and his examination taken by a committee concerning correspondence he held with the Lord Digby [which] was read unto him. And being demanded [by] Mr Speaker whether it was true [what] he had there expressed, answered: I [*MS damaged*] only concerning that of Sir Hugh Cholmley and Keys his son's servant, some ?instance? which he desired to have read accordingly. Then he said that when Keys came to him at Hull (he wondering to see him), said how the devil comes thou hither? How couldst thou come through the Queen's army? And that was all he said unto him. He said further, it was true that my Lord Digby did send a declaration unto him to present unto the world of the reason of his turning in allegiance to the King, but he tore it in pieces, and told him he would not serve the King [till] he had sent just propositions to the Parliament. And being pressed [*MS damaged*] to answer to some further questions concerning the Lord Digby, he said to the committee he was not bound to accuse himself, and so made no farther answer. And confesseth that he did refuse to set his hand to that examination. Resolved etc.
That Sir John Hotham shall be discharged of <any> being any longer a member of this House during this Parliament. Ordered that Sir John Hotham be delivered over to the Sergeant, who is hereby required

[133] These men were the mayor and aldermen of Hull: Hopper, 'A directory of parliamentarian allegiance in Yorkshire', pp. 90–91.

to carry Sir John Hotham to the Tower, to be there kept in safe custody close prisoner and none permitted to speak with him but in the presence and hearing of his keeper.

Henry Elsynge, clerk of the House of Commons.

[*On reverse*] Sir John Hotham order of examination.

HHC: Hotham MS, U DDHO/1/31: Sir John Hotham's draft petition to the House of Commons, Westminster, undated, *c.*7 September 1643

The humble desires of Sir John Hotham to be represented to the House:
1. First that he may come to his trial for that for which he is restrained. Follies he confesseth he may [have] committed many and something presuming upon the favour of the House which else he would not. But if guilt be found in him to have betrayed his trust by rendering up the town of Hull, then he desires no favour, or that he had any intention so to do.
2nd. That whereas he hath certain money, plate and household stuff seized at Hull, that according to the law of England as he conceiveth, he may have the possession of his own goods, at least that they be not disposed of.
3rd. That whereas all the evidences of my land are seized upon, that they may be delivered to whom I shall appoint.
4th. That my servants' goods and their clothes which are seized upon, may be restored, and likewise that the clothes of my two younger sons may be delivered them, having no money nor means to buy other.
5th. To take into consideration that they impose oaths upon my servants in Hull to discover my goods.
6th. That till the House shall have leisure to hear my accusation and defence, my friends may have liberty to come to me or that I may be bailed.
He shall entreat the House to consider that these monies are his only subsistence, all his rents being seized upon by the king's party. That he hath out of them a wife and twelve children to maintain, which if this be taken cannot put meat in their mouths. That three thousand pounds of this money is the portion of my last wife's former husband's children as shall be plainly made appear upon oath. Their brother[134] and divers other that are privy to it being now in town. That he will hope they will give order that my wife may have liberty to dispose of

[134] Sir Thomas Norcliffe of Langton was the son of Sir John Hotham's fourth wife by her first husband. See Dugdale, *The Visitation of the County of Yorke*, p. 341.

herself or to come up with her household stuff, and that she may have such monies of mine delivered to her as will keep us from extreme want, at least so much as the children's portions, being three thousand pounds. All these and himself he humbly refers to the House from whom his soul is so far from any ill intention to them, he cannot but hope for all justice with favour.

[*On reverse*] My desires to the House.

HHC: Hotham MS, U DDHO/1/32: Proceedings of the House of Commons, Westminster, 7 September 1643

Sir John Hotham according to an order of yesterday was brought to the bar, and being acquainted by Mr Speaker that he had liberty to speak to the House if he did desire it. He had (he said) some petitions to present to the House which was that his lady might come up with her coach and horses, children, servants and evidences and some goods and plate, which she hath for her maintenance and the maintenance of her children. He desired he might continue where he is till his trial, and did protest his own innocency, and did not doubt but if he might know his charge, but to make his innocency appear as clear as the sun. Ordered that Sir John Hotham's lady shall have liberty and a pass to come from Hull with her coach and horses, children, servants and evidences.
Sir John Hotham was again called in, and being commanded whether he knew of any members of this House, or of the Lords that have conveyed any treasure beyond seas. He answered he knew of none if he were to die tomorrow. Being demanded whether he knew that Mr Pym had conveyed any treasure beyond sea, with some astonishment <answered> asked if this question were asked him in earnest, did protest he knew nothing of it. And being asked if he had reported any such thing, answered no.

Henry Elsynge, clerk of the House of Commons.

[*On reverse*] Petition the House for a charge.

HHC: Hotham MS, U DDHO/1/61: Durand Hotham[135] to unknown recipient, undated but *c.*1643–1644

Sir,
Having found so much favour from you during your being here as to promise an engagement of your endeavours for the freedom and

[135]Durand was the fifth son of Sir John Hotham and his second wife, Anne Rokeby: G. Goodwin, rev. B.J. Gibbons, 'Durant Hotham (1616/17–1691)', *ODNB*.

accommodation of my mother in her coming from Hull, which being now prevented by my Lord Fairfax his kindness, I am yet very loath that any offer of respect from you to me should fall to ground for want of usage. So that I am bold to trouble you to present these respects to my lord and I am confident that from your mouth they will not seem unreasonable. Sir, the business is this: my lord was pleased (after the receipt of the Parliament's order for my mother and her necessaries' transportation hither) to refer the proportioning of them to the committee there, who amongst other things ordered her £100 worth of plate. Now upon what grounds I am not informed, my lord thought fit to contract the allowance to £20, which considering our great necessity and numerous family amounts to a weak and short help to our subsistence. Sir, I should desire you to move my lord <in it> to confirm their favour and though the necessity of his garrison be great, the request is but a small pittance of what was seized and put into his dispose by the Commons. And I am confident that their justice and mercy is so much that they cannot find fault with such a charitable relief. My other request is this. My mother came away when the town was besieged, for [*MS damaged*] my lord would not suffer her to carry away her coals, of which was about 10 cauldron sea coal and other, not knowing to what distress the town might be brought. Now seeing by God's mercy you are eased of that difficulty,[136] I desire you would be a means to my lord that she may now have them. I am sure you know how precious they are here, one year's fuel exhausting a poor man's estate to which condition we are brought.[137] Sir, I shall trouble you no further, only to take notice that my father's real estate is I hear seized by my Lord Fairfax under what notion I know not. I am sure till conviction no name nor notion of delinquency can be justly fixed on any man by the law of England. I know you are so prudent as not to manage business of this nature at their full bent. You were gone out of the town before Sir Philip Stapleton's return from the army, else he had desired to have spoke with you about this particular.

Sir, I am your servant,
Durand Hotham.

The bearer hereof Joseph Person will wait upon you for my lord's pleasure.

[*In margin*] A copy of a letter [*a draft copy enclosed*].

[136] The earl of Newcastle raised the siege of Hull on 11 October 1643.

[137] The royalist occupation of Newcastle and the north-east denied coal to London and other parliamentarian areas, causing extreme hardship. Some towns and cities raised subscriptions to regain Newcastle for parliament: F.R. Beecheno, 'The Norwich subscription for the regaining of Newcastle', *Norfolk Archaeology*, 18 (1914), pp. 149–160.

Bodl. MS Nalson XXII, no. 144: John Hotham to the House of Commons, London, 11 January 1644[138]

The humble petition of Captain John Hotham to the honourable House of Commons.
Humbly showeth,
That the sense of your displeasure hath been a very great affliction to him, that he hath endured 28 weeks' imprisonment with the loss of all that he had. He hath submitted to your pleasure and <all> answered to all examinations, and will in all things else obey your commands, for no misery shall ever estrange him from being *your* servant. He most humbly desires that he may not longer live under infamy, but that you will suffer him to come to a speedy trial. And if it there appear that he be guilty of that unworthy crime of falsifying his faith and honour, let him suffer <the death of a traitor> *any punishment*. If your great affairs will not give leisure to this, he humbly desires you will admit him bail and that he your old servant may not rot in prison under infamy, when so many everyday enjoy your clemency and mercy for greater faults than his can prove. This he humbly submits to your wisdom and justice and will remain

your humble petitioner and servant,
John Hotham.

He most humbly desires some relief of money for he is like to starve for money and clothes.

[*On reverse*] Captain Hotham's petition, read 13 January.

HHC: C BRS/7/74: Inventory of money and possessions seized from Sir John Hotham and paid to Lord Fairfax, Hull, 30 March 1644[139]

Item one library of books particularly mentioned in an inventory or catalogue thereof in paper signed with his lordship's hand.[140]

[138] See also *CJ*, III, p. 366; *Portland MS*, HMC, 29, 13th Report, Appendix, Part I, I, p. 166.

[139] A partial copy of this appears at HHC: Hotham MS, U DDHO/1/77. There is a similar, undated list of trunks and their contents at HHC: C BRS/7/77, ending with this appended note by Lord Fairfax's treasurer, William Harrison: 'Divers parcels of these goods with all the best apparel were delivered to Mrs Hotham at my Lord General's command, some sold to the officers for the payment of their weekly allowance, the rest remaining in my hand, all which I desire may be appraised as the other were and then I shall be responsible for the sum in gross.'

[140] The books were not listed here, but the corporation tried in vain to avoid relinquishing them to Lord Fairfax: Tindall Wildridge, *The Hull Letters*, p. 163.

An inventory indented and made 30 March 1644 of all the monies, plate, and other goods late being in the custody of Sir John Hotham, or his son Captain Hotham, and which upon their apprehension were seized by Thomas Raikes, mayor of Kingston-upon-Hull, and were afterwards directed by several ordinances of Parliament in that behalf made to be delivered by inventory to the right honourable Ferdinando, Lord Fairfax. And which money, plate and goods have been accordingly paid and delivered to his lordship, vizt:
Monies paid to his lordship as followeth:

Item, paid his lordship in monies	July 17th 1643	500-00-00
	July 24th 1643	700-00-00
	August first	1000-00-00
	August 5th	1000-00-00
	August 7th	500-00-00
	August 12th	500-00-00
	August 18th	400-00-00
	August 23rd	200-00-00
Item, paid his lordship the 25th of August in part of the £1,400 in gold claimed by the Lady Anderson[141] }		1000-00-00
Item, paid his lordship the 25th of September in full of the said £1,400 in gold claimed by the Lady Anderson}		400-00-00
		6200-00-00
Item, delivered over to his lordship in silver and gold which was in Sir Richard Hawksworth's trunk:[142]		677-03-08
	Total	6877-03-08

Plate delivered to his lordship as followeth:
Item, there was delivered over to his lordship in plate which were in Sir Richard Hawkesworth's trunk: 0391 1/4.
Item, there was delivered over to his lordship in white plate for his private use before he had any order from the Parliament to receive the same: 0293 1/4 ounces.
Item, there was delivered over to his lordship at another time in plate: 6869 3/4.

[141] This was John Hotham's mother-in-law, the wife of Sir Henry Anderson of Long Cowton. For her examination by the committee at Hull in July 1643, see HHC: C BRS/7/76; Tindall Wildridge, *The Hull Letters*, pp. 45, 158, 162.

[142] Sir Richard Hawksworth of Hawksworth in the parish of Otley was a friend and neighbour of the Fairfax family who had been arrested by royalists in October 1642 and imprisoned in York: J.T. Cliffe, *Puritans in Conflict: the Puritan gentry during and after the civil wars* (London, 1988), p. 92; Hopper, 'A directory of parliamentarian allegiance in Yorkshire', p. 116.

Total: 7554 ¼ ounces
Goods delivered over to his lordship <which Mr Harrison received> as followeth, vizt:
3: Item, one great trunk marked I.R: <supposed to belong> belonging to Sir Richard Hawkesworth, and therein (over and above <the> *his said* money and *plate*) <plate) two watches and gold ring before mentioned those particulars vizt> *two silver watches, one fair gold ring*, one little red leather box or trunk with a lock on it, one little black leather trunk or box with lock on it, one other little red leather trunk with lock on it, <and therein> one four square cabinet *with* lock<ed> and bound with silver and set with pearl, <also therein> one little box or cabinet trunk fashion covered with red plush, <also therein> one other little box covered with cloth of silver & silk tafts <in gold, also therein> one white bone box with two little stones in it, one table book, one bible with strings, one merchant's purse made of coloured silk with certain other purses, an indenture of feoffment and some other writings not inventoried.
4: Item, one large trunk marked G. S. and therein one large turkey quilt, two bed testernes of red taffety, one part of valance for the same, three red cloth curtains with valance suitable, one suite of red taffety curtains branched, with valance suitable, one suit of green taffety curtains with bullion valance. A counterpart or covering for a bed of tawny covered velvet, laid with three silver laces, one pink coloured cradle cloth of silk damask lined with taffety, and laid with three silver laces, one shag[143] cradle cloth, four bed pommels covered with red cloth, red cloth coverings for the posts of a bed, and one little piece of new red cloth.
5. Item one little seal skin trunk, unmarked & therein one little morter & pestle of alabaster, one little ivory salt, one ivory box with counters, a loadstone, three little jeat[144] boxes, one gold hoop ring, one stone bullet and one can of harts horn, tipped with silver and with a silver lid.
6. Item one trunk marked H.A. challenged by the Lady Anderson, & therein one double testament, two stomachers of silk, and one of cloth of gold, three pieces of new Holland, one parcel of Scotch cloth,[145] two pieces of course lynne[146] and one pair of stockings with some thread and tape.

[143] 'A cloth having a velvet nap on one side, usually of worsted but sometimes of silk': *OED*, XV, p. 137.

[144] I.e. 'jet', a glossy black piece of marble or lignite, from which ornaments were fashioned, in this case probably originating from the Upper Lias shale in the Whitby area: *ibid.*, VIII, p. 223.

[145] 'A textile fabric resembling lawn, but cheaper; said to have been made of nettle fibre': *ibid.*, XIV, p. 689.

[146] 'Flax spun or woven; linen thread or cloth': *ibid.*, VIII, p. 973.

7. Item one trunk marked H.A. 1631 and therein five pieces of new coloured buckram,[147] a silk quilt, two old & one new turkey carpets, one piece of new red cloth and one other carpet.
8. Item one sword with a gilded hilt and one other sword hilt gilded.
9. Item one trunk laid with wooden edges marked J.H. and therein two parcels of silver lace, and two parcels of silver and gold lace weighing in all thirty-seven ounces and an half Troy weight, seven pair of worsted stockings, eight boards of silk edging lace, one gross of dozen green silk lace, eleven pair of plain cordevant[148] gloves, two knots of tape, three pair more of gloves, three dozen of white gloves, six dozen and eleven pair more of white gloves, nine pair of stirrup silk stockings[149] half-legged, five pound of black and grey thread, one ell of dimity,[150] one parcel of Scotch cloth cont 8 yards, eight yards of dimity, half a pound of raw silk, and one silk waistcoat.
10. Item one trunk with a hat case marked 1637, and herein one *old* scarlet cloak <of old scarlet> lined with green velvet and a clow[151] of lace ripped off the same, one cloak of black branched satin lined though with plush and a suit of the same satin, one suit of black plush, one green must colour cloak of cloth lined through with satin, one black satin suit; one silver grogram[152] doublet, three satin doublets, one pair of scarlet britches, one pair of pink colour cloth breeches and two books of annals in folio.
11. Item one gilded cabinet, and herein certain mathematical instruments, thirty-two points edged with gold and silver lace, ten silk loops with buttons, one pair of rich beaver gloves, one pair of red velvet mittens, nine pair of white gloves, five pair of cordevant gloves, two instruments called sectars,[153] half a dozen washing balls, one little bracelet of amber beads and ten gross[154] of new silk buttons.
12. Item one altar cloth, and a bag embroidered with gold and silver, an embroidered trencher, an embroidered handkercher with gold & a doublet collar.
13. Item one rich embroidered handkercher which was supposed to have been the Queen's and her picture.

[147] 'A kind of fine linen or cotton fabric': *ibid.*, II, p. 616.

[148] Made of leather manufactured in Cordoba: *ibid.*, III, p. 928.

[149] 'A kind of footless stocking having a strap which passes underneath the foot': *ibid.*, XVI, p. 724.

[150] 'A stout cotton fabric, woven with raised stripes or fancy figures; usually employed undyed for beds and bedroom hangings, and sometimes for garments': *ibid.*, IV, p. 676.

[151] I.e. 'clew': 'a ball formed by winding thread; a ball of thread or yarn': *ibid.*, III, p. 317.

[152] A coarse fabric of silk, of mohair and wool, or of these mixed with silk; often stiffened with gum: *ibid.*, vi. 863.

[153] I.e. 'sectors', mathematical instruments for the mechanical solution of various problems: *ibid*, XIV, p. 847.

[154] A gross was equal to twelve dozen: *ibid.*, VI, p. 870.

14. Item one trunk marked with nails 1634, and therein, one piece of new fewgered[155] satin cont about 16 yards, two Latin bibles, the Annals of Queen Elizabeth, Latin, six other small books, a piece of new red Padua serge, and about eight yards more, one red curtain, two priest copes, one altar cloth, three strings of great gawdy beads, & one new string of coral beads.
15. Item one trunk marked G.S. without lock, and therein two black velvet doublets, a silk grogram suit, an old chamlet[156] cassock lined with fur, a buff coat, the sleeves all laid with silver lace, another buff coat lined with satin, a shammoy[157] waistcoat, a black cloth cloak lined with velvet, a silk grogram cloak lined with plush, a pair of grogram boot hose tops, a pair of black plush breeches and a piece of black velvet.
16. Item one desk of wainscot and herein one nest of boxes made of ivory with a silver lock, and divers letters and papers in the desk.
17. Item one other wainscot desk with lockers and some writings and papers in the desk.
18. Item one cabinet of wood with letters and papers in it.
19. Item one old trunk bound with iron and divers old books and papers supposed to belong to Mr Stapleton.
20. Item one wainscot press or chest of drawers wherein was Sir John Hotham's evidences and other writings which was by my lord's order perused by Mr Stockdale and Mr Wastell,[158] and by them delivered over to Robert Stockdale, Sir John Hotham's servant.

Bodl. MS Nalson XXII, no. 137: Sir John Hotham to the House of Commons, London, [28 October 1644][159]

The petition of Sir John Hotham, knight and baronet, late governor of Hull and member of the House of Commons.
To the honourable the House of Commons.
Humbly showeth,
That your petitioner having been one of the most early in your service and in pursuance of your commands borne the burden and heat of the day, he is notwithstanding to his great grief and damage fallen

[155] I.e. 'figured'.
[156] An expensive eastern fabric, supposedly made from silk and camel or goat hair: *ibid.*, II, p. 807.
[157] I.e. 'chamois'.
[158] John Wastell of Scorton, MP for Northallerton: see Hopper, 'A directory of parliamentarian allegiance in Yorkshire', p. 93; Keeler, *The Long Parliament*, p. 380.
[159] See also *CJ*, III, p. 679; *Portland MS*, HMC, 29, 13th Report, Appendix, Part I, I, p. 189.

under your displeasure, as he well feels. Though he takes God to witness he has not heard from you the least accusation or crime this whole fourteen months of his restraint, to which he might frame his much desired defence, only now of late heard a summons from the honourable the court martial at Weavers' Hall, which occasioned him to represent some few things to your consideration, as he conceives particular to his case.

That he received his commission from this House in these words annexed to the petition, and had from you no other law, direction or rule to square his actions by but this particular commission.

That he never received from this House or any other any signification or commands concerning martial law, nor was it ever published in his garrison or the Association of Yorkshire, Lancashire, Durham etc. And that your petitioner finding some unruliness in his garrison did by a letter to you solicit you to send him some commands concerning martial law, but was by you denied it by an order in these words: That such persons under Sir John Hotham as shall offend against any law shall be punished by the law, but for such as offend against the safety of the town and peace of the army as mutinies and such like, them he shall commit to prison till upon information to this House further course may be taken.

That the ordinance of martial law, whereby he received his summons and the instructions thereof are a law made fourteen months after his <crime was> pretended crime was committed, and therefore humbly conceives it cannot be extended to the trial of it.

That he had his commission and instructions only from you. By you he was trusted and conceives himself bound solely to answer it to you. That he returned all his addresses to you, and was always your immediate agent. Therefore *craves* leave not to submit, nor to be put upon any trial, but immediate by you. That to you and to your judgements he submits his estate, life, and honour. He confesses many errors, and lays himself down at the feet of your justice. And anything else that can be against him, he will willing*ly* embrace a trial by any law extant or known to him when they were committed. For where no law is, there is no transgression.

All this he humbly presents to your just thoughts, with a full and true relation of his whole government of Hull, which he craves it as a favour from you that you would read. Which he doubts not but you will grant him, considering he has laid now fifteen months prisoner in silence and has not interrupted your <leisure> *business* with the least word of petition for his private advantage.

And your petitioner shall pray,
John Hotham.

HHC: Hotham MS, U DDHO/1/34: Account by Sir John Hotham relating his government of Hull, London, undated but *c.*November 1644[160]

I have often thought that seeing my restraint debars me from converse of my friends to have given them some short satisfaction in writing concerning the whole management of my government at Hull, by reason I perceived that all my actions and intentions are made intricate and suspicious with multitudes of calumnies cast on them by printed papers, but have deferred it hitherto, conceiving all wise men whom I solely have the leisure to please would reserve an ear to hear my defences. Yet perceiving that now at last things of seeming importance against me have been divulged, whereby discreet men's mouths are become full of questions, and these seeming evidences valued at that rate as to rake up, in them reading, some part of time from the public affairs of state. I esteemed it my duty to all my friends to give them a sincere narrative of my whole employment, not aiming it as particular confutation of any fault famed against me, yet I doubt not but it will prove such as will make all appearance of crime to vanish and settle me in the just merit of my actions.

You well remember the state of affairs when I first took the government, at what time it was doubted by the wisest whether love to a man's country and the being of parliaments could engage a man to such an eminent hazard without some mixture of foolhardiness. Nor was I so void of understanding as not to see the dangers I undertook. My commission for the execution of my place was very general, commanding me to keep the town and magazine then secure, neither to deliver up either of them till I had the King's authority signified by both Houses of Parliament's command. In this latitude of my trust I went down, and till I was seized on continued so without the least restriction from the Parliament or general.[161] By this you see how vastly I resigned to the justice of the Parliament's good interpretation of my choice of means for the effecting their commands having no other than this large instruction to authorize me to each particular action.

Lord how secure was I in my honest thoughts towards them, how regardless of representing the difficulties I went through in their service, how sparing in relating my many merits to their true proportion, as accounting the deed the reward, and myself as nearly obliged in prosecuting their just ends as if all my own interests had been at the

[160] This may have been an earlier draft of Sir John Hotham's defence, as it includes some identical and many similar sentences. However, there is other content not found in his defence.

[161] The parliamentarian commander-in-chief, Robert Devereux, earl of Essex: J. Morrill, 'Robert Devereux, third earl of Essex (1591–1646)', *ODNB*.

stake. And whosoever was there present must confess the measure of diligence I used could be taught in no other than the school of love.

[*page break*]

I shall always acknowledge it was the goodness of God that I selected such means for the safety of my trust as I received the Houses' thanks and approbation in the first and second scenes of my employment. But though with as real intent on my part to their service and as sincere a heart to the safety of my charge, all the rest miscarried. Distance created misinterpretations and those jealousies both which made known to my enemies in the town made my power to serve the state less and encouraged those whom in and for its service I had disobliged to manage all these misfortunes to my ruin.

At my first acceptance of my charge, I sent my son down to draw some companies into Hull, but as it happened in many of the Parliament's affairs it proved the difficult play of an after game, for my Lord of Newcastle by the King's commission was come into the town and wanted solely the drawing in of Sir Thomas Metham's[162] regiment to have made good his authority. Which, had it succeeded, those that employed me must have been really what they used in former times to term themselves, we, the poor Commons of England. But I may justly say God's providence upon my son's vigilance and courage and in the strength of my interest with the gentry thereabouts defeated this first and most dangerous design. For without any delay he drew a regiment of trained bands to the gates and placed his ensign upon the bridge, and by the well management of threats and treaties brought the whole town in subjection to his garrison.[163] But the King retaining by much the stronger party in the town, entertained daily treaties and courtships among them, making in short time the government too hot for a deputy. So at the earnest desire of Mr Pym, who sent me intelligence of some dangers threatening the town, one night late I took the immediate charge upon me and next morning went down resolving to stand all shocks.[164]

When I got thither I found the town five parts of seven affected to the King, animated against my authority by continual arguments from court of security and success. Nay our own party so timorous that scarce any durst avow to speak publicly with my son, all my soldiers plain countrymen, heartless and heedless of all the duties of soldiers, myself as far to seek as having a part to play unprecedented by any.

[162] Sir Thomas Metham of Metham (1575–1644), a prominent local Roman Catholic who commanded a regiment of East Riding trained bands in 1642: Newman, *Royalist Officers*, p. 253.

[163] John Hotham seized control of Hull on 23 January 1642.

[164] Sir John Hotham did not arrive in Hull until mid-March 1642.

I had quick advertisement that the King would come to the town and try the presence of a sovereign's command in this kingdom in man's memory, especially among country people who never had seen the image of it but in his coin which is current everywhere.

[*page break*]

I saw all the dangers in the worst vizards,[165] other men's cunning, fear or love could represent them to me, and what I did when I came to try the worst of these effects, I need not relate it was in sum that by God's good hand myself and soldiers overcame unpassable difficulties and all things succeeded by His assistance beyond belief. And in confidence that in this action I had served the commonwealth, I sat down with joy under the name and hazard of a traitor.[166]

After this though I was thus in public branded by His Majesty yet I was daily in private assaulted with offers from court larger than my thoughts, honour, and wealth, I contemned in a large proportion. The King's solemn oath of ruining me taken before the town gates, I valued at as little, though I well feel he hath too well kept it from my good reasons I have to believe that my prosecutors have had from time to time their intelligence, evidence and instructions from court. One particular which will in some measure give you satisfaction I shall crave pardon to relate, though it be digression.

I had upon some discontent with the Lord Fairfax written a sharp letter *to the House* against Mr Stockdale,[167] by whom he was guided, and who I thought usurped more authority than either his estate or understanding in war could challenge. This letter the enemy intercepts and sends to my Lord Fairfax that he would dispatch one over and they would communicate to him things worth his knowledge. Whereupon he sends one Captain Alured, to whom they show these letters, assuring him besides that I and my son treated with them. This captain being before sufficiently disaffected to me, comes up through the enemy's quarters with conduct from them to the Parliament and was the first man that durst speak ill of me publicly.

This I relate that you may see from whence my crime first came and how little use or hope of advantage the enemy could create out of my many treaties other than this: their subtlety framed out of unwary simplicity and aptness to be jealous of our friends. But I return to the business of my denial of the King's entrance into the town and shall desire you to consider some passages worth your notice.

[165] Vizard: 'to conceal or disguise (something) under a false outward show or appearance; to represent falsely or speciously; to mask; or a mask': *OED*, XIX, p. 718.

[166] Sir John Hotham was declared a traitor by the heralds for refusing to allow the king through Hull's Beverley Gate on 23 April 1642.

[167] See p. 75, n. 72.

The King coming to the town gates, and I by virtue of my commission I then had and still have without any addition or diminution treated with His Majesty concerning the delivery of the town, and our not agreement upon articles proved the sole stay of his entrance, which treaty was approved by both Houses and I by solemn vote declared not to have exceeded my commission. Yet my treaty with my Lord of Newcastle, which on my soul would have proved more to their advantage altogether, as much within the verge of my commission and the ordinary power of every governor, is called treason, myself branded with infamous names, and my posterity ruined

[*page break*]

before any legal trial, process, examination or accusation in any place where there was a possibility in me to give answer. Notwithstanding that in my own case it was declared a breach of privilege so much as to proclaim me traitor without due process of law, and in the case of the 5 members it was voted such a *piaculum* as all the kingdom was summoned to take that the King by that transgression touched them in the apple of their eye. Yet I, a member of their House, a governor constituted by them, and in some near relation of good service to them, suffered to be seized upon, that appeared as good service, then showed to the world as an object of shame, and last of all a committee appointed to examine what crime I had committed.

I come now to my second treaty with one of the most notorious papists in those parts, one Beckwith, to whom I made some of my officers promise at such a time he should be let in and the possession of one of the gates given to him and 500 men he should bring with him.[168] All this treaty went on till I saw fit time to reveal it to my advantage, which when I did I had the thanks and approbation of the House for my well management of it.

In this broad way I walked long afterward without the least check or suspicion to their great advantage and my own preservation. For by this means I constantly knew who of the town or soldiery kept correspondence with the enemy, and so little did His Majesty gain from me in those private negotiations that in despair of prevailing, he rose from the town and chose rather to assault some weaker enemy.[169]

By this time was there an army raised in the south and the King moves from us, compassing the kingdom to gather up his dispersed

[168]This was the first of several plots to betray Hull to the royalists. Thomas Beckwith of Beverley, esq., conspired with his son-in-law, Lieutenant Fowkes, and Captain Lowinger, officers in the Hull garrison, who informed Sir John Hotham of the plot: Saltmarshe, *History and Chartulary of the Hothams of Scorborough*, p. 124; Reckitt, *Charles the First and Hull*, pp. 44–45.

[169]The king attempted to besiege Hull from 7 July until the end of the month, soon after which he marched south to raise his standard at Nottingham on 22 August 1642.

party, yet leaves so many in the north as should defend those that had furnished him with stock to set up with against those of [which] the garrison at Hull was the sole armed party. Out of which I drew as many as I could spare under the command of my son, who with 500 foot and one troop of horse protected the well affected of the western parts till they could arm themselves under the command of the Lord Fairfax. And when through ill management, they relapsed into that bankrupt treaty at Rothwell,[170] obliging the whole country to a neutrality, he again set on foot the Parliament's interests, relieved my Lord Fairfax besieged in Bradford,[171] and did many other special services which not appertaining to my business I omit.

HHC: Hotham MS, U DDHO/1/35: Legal defence of Sir John Hotham, London, undated but *c.*November 1644[172]

When this Parliament was pleased first to honour me with their commands to execute the government of Hull, you all know the state of affairs was such as it was disputed by the wisest whether love to man's country and the being of parliaments could engage a man of so flourishing a fortune to such a hazard without some mixture of foolhardiness. I saw the danger I undertook, yet well knew my duty and how little respect or consideration my private sufferings or ruin could claim when the whole interest, parliaments and liberties of England were in most men's judgements at stake.

The commission <you> *the Parliament* gave me for the execution of my place was very general, and in truth more left to my discretion and judgement upon the particular result of occasions than I had confidence to believe I could well go through with. The words you have <in my petition> *heard read*. In that latitude I went down and continued till I was seized on without the least restriction, instruction, or limitation.

[170] A treaty to keep Yorkshire out of the civil war was signed at Rothwell, near Leeds, on 29 September 1642, by the West Riding parliamentarians, led by Ferdinando, Lord Fairfax, and by the local royalists, headed by Henry Clifford, earl of Cumberland: Woolrych, 'Yorkshire's treaty of neutrality'; BL, TT E119(29), *Fourteen articles of peace propounded to the king and parliament by the gentry and commonalty of the county of York*, 4 October 1642 (London, 1642); BL, TT E240(30), *Reasons why Sir John Hotham, trusted by the parliament, cannot in honour agree to the treaty of pacification made by some gentlemen of York-shire at Rothwell, Sept. 29* (London, 1642).

[171] Lord Fairfax's forces repelled a royalist attack on their Bradford headquarters on 21 October 1642: BL, TT E126(5), *A true and perfect relation of a victorious battell obtained against the earl of Cumberland and his cavaliers, by the Lo: Fairfax and Capt: Hotham*, 2 November 1642 (London, 1642).

[172] This defence was initially written for an audience of MPs, but was later altered to address his court martial. There are two further copies in a later, eighteenth-century hand, at HHC: Hotham MS, U DDHO/1/36.

By which you see how vastly I resigned myself to the justice of <your> *the Parliament's* good interpretation of my choice means to the effecting <your> *their* commands, having no other than this large instruction to authorize me in each particular action.

Lord, how secure was I in my honest thoughts towards <you> *them*, how regardless in representing the many difficulties I went through in <your> *their* service, how sparing in relating my many merits in their true proportion, as esteeming the deed the reward and

[*page break*]

and myself as nearly obliged in prosecuting of <your> *their* ends and commands as if all my own interest had been at stake. And whoever was there present must confess, the diligence I used could be taught nowhere but in the school of love.

I shall always acknowledge it the goodness of God that I selected such means for the safety of my trust, as I received <your> *their* thanks and approbation in the first and second parts of my employment. But (though with as real an intent on my part, and as sincere a heart to the safety of my charge) all the rest miscarried. Distance created misinterpretations, and those jealousies which made known to my enemies in the town made my power to serve <you> *them* less and encouraged those whom in and for <your> *their* service I had disobliged to manage all misfortunes to my ruin.

At my first acceptance of my charge I sent my son down to draw in some companies according to <your> *their* order into Hull. But it proved the difficult play of an after game for the Lord of Newcastle, by the King's commission was come into the town, and wanted solely the drawing in of Sir Thomas Metham's regiment to have made good his authority. But I may justly say God's providence on my son's vigilance and courage with the strength of my interest with the gentry thereabouts defeated this first and most dangerous design. For without any delay, he drew a regiment of trained bands to the gates and by the well management of threats and treaties brought the whole town in subjection to his garrison.

But the King retaining by much the stronger party in the town made the government too hot for a deputy, so I went down and took the immediate government, myself resolving to stand all shots.

When I got thither I found the town five parts of seven affected to the King, animated against my authority by continual arguments from court of security and success. Nay our own party so timorous that scarce any of them durst <my sonn> *avow* to speak publicly with me, all my soldiers plain

[*page break*]

plain countrymen, heartless and heedless of all the duties of soldiers, and myself as far to seek as having a part to play unprecedented by any.

I saw all the dangers in the worst visors, other men's fear, cunning or love towards me could present them to me and what I did when I came to try the worst of their effects I need not relate. And in confidence, that in the action I had served the commonwealth, I sat down with joy under the name and hazard of a traitor.

After this, though I was thus in public branded by His Majesty, yet I was daily in private assaulted with offers larger than my thought. Honour and wealth I contemned in a large proportion. The King's protestation of ruining me taken before the gates of Hull, I valued it as little, though I well feel he hath too truly kept it, having good reason to believe that some of my persecutors have their intelligence and evidence from court. A particular concerning this I shall crave pardon to relate, though it be a digression.

I had, upon some discontent with the Lord Fairfax, written a sharp letter against one Mr Stockdale by whom I conceive he was guided and who I thought usurped more authority than either his estate or understanding in war could challenge. This letter the enemy at York intercepts, and sends to my Lord Fairfax that he would dispatch one over to them and they would communicate to him things worth his knowledge. Whereupon he sends Captain Alured, to whom they show these letters, assuring him besides that I and my son treated with them, and by acquainting the House with it Mr Stockdale might be sufficiently revenged. This captain being before sufficiently disaffectionate to us, comes up to the Parliament through the enemy's quarters with safe conduct from them and was the first that durst speak ill of me publicly.

[*page break*]

This I relate to you that you may see from whence my ruin first came, and how little use or hope of advantage the enemy could create out of my many treaties other than this subtlety framed out of our own too much wariness, whereby we are apt to be jealous of our friends.

But I return to my business and shall make bold to give to this House an ample and honest view of all my treaties in their ends and circumstances as being the whole matter of my pretended crime from first to last.

When I was by the honourable House sent down, and had by intimation from <you> *them* an assurance that the King had a set purpose of coming in person to Hull and trying the effects of his presence in command uncontrolled in this kingdom in man's memory. I writ earnestly to His Majesty to divert him from any such attempt, and when he sent divers to me to persuade to some very plausible terms, he received always a constant denial, which he called undutiful carriages, yet by several ways of love and fear he still prosecuted his end. Till after much treaty finding me inexorable, he came in a public attempt to enter the town.

When he came to the town gates by virtue of my commission I then had and still have without the least addition or diminution, I treated with His Majesty concerning his entrance into the town, and our not agreement upon articles proved the sole stay of his entrance. All which treaty was approved of by both Houses, and I by solemn vote declared not to have exceeded my commission.

My next treaty was with one Beckwith, a most notorious papist as was in any of those parts. This man when His Majesty was at Beverley, attempted some of my under officers who acquainted me with it. I instructed them what they should do, authorizing them to promise Beckwith to deliver

[*page break*]

deliver him the north gate, which he should enter and possess with 500 men. All this treaty was carried with as great punctuality and secrecy as could be, rewards agreed on by all sides, all the materials prepared. But when fire was to be given, I conceived it too dangerous to manage to the last pinch, least some blood might have been shed in which we were all justly tender in the beginning of these sad times. So I revealed it to <you> *the House* and had <your> *their* thanks and approbation for my well managing of it. I beseech you consider if in the midst of this treaty before my discovery of it to <you> *the Parliament* some of the town had found it out and seized upon me. Might they not with the same justice have called this also treachery? Nay far more for this complot was plain and particular, all the other treaties only in general words. So much bait put on as would singly cover my hook, and I shall always conceive I had as much authority for the rest of my treaties as for this.

In this broad way I walked long after to your advantage and mine own preservation. For by this means I constantly knew who of the town or soldiers kept correspondence with the enemy, and so little did His Majesty gain from me in these private negotiations, that in despair of prevailing he rose from the town and chose rather to assault some weaker adversary.

My third treaty or intelligence was with a Frenchman which since proved to be the Lord Digby,[173] the particulars of which are these.

[173] Digby had been impeached by the House of Commons in February 1642 and had fled to the Dutch Netherlands: R. Hutton, 'George Digby, second earl of Bristol (1612–1677)', *ODNB*.

When the ship called the Providence struck in upon Humber coasts, I sent some ships abroad to try what might be done against her. Who, finding an assault too

[*page break*]

too difficult, left the enterprise, and roving a little further found a small vessel hiding herself in a creek with passengers and letters, all which they brought into the committee of Lords and Commons residing at Hull and myself. Amongst whom was one in the habit and garb of a Frenchman, who sent me word by Colonel Ayscough that he had something of consequence to reveal to me. I slighted his message and sent him word that if he had anything of consequence, the person was of as much consequence that would bring it. But at his much instance, I sent for him, who told me that he was a soldier of fortune, promising me mountains of intelligence and if I would lend his liberty for such a purpose he would be my constant spy, that he was a stranger to both parties. But the obligation I should put upon him in this should make him eminent in service to us and if I would trust the word of a soldier, he would show me what advantage in intelligence he could bring and return within 6 days, which he performed punctually. Thus much I remember I certified some members of the House, and no other was understood by the committee of Lords and Commons at Hull who had as near a prospect of him as myself.

This man I made use of, and had as I told you passing good intelligence with which he returned once or twice publicly. And you all know he hath so much wit that had he suspected he was or could be known to be the Lord Digby, he would not have trusted himself in such a hazard, especially coming openly where all men's eyes were judges who he was. After that he came no more but by a letter to me discovered himself to be the Lord Digby and solicited

[*page break*]

and solicited me (as he termed it) to return to my allegiance. To whom I returned that when the King offered such propositions as the Parliament thought good to accept I should be extreme glad with the rest of his subjects to enjoy the good fruits of them and be His Majesty's servant, wherein I was able. And this was all the advantage he received at my hands.

For a great while I heard no more of this business, but a party of my lord general's horse going towards Winchester comes upon the Lord Digby's quarters at Wantage, from whence he flying in some haste left a cabinet and some letters, which Colonel Hurrey[174] taking, gave them to some of the Lords' House or Commons. Amongst them were some of mine, but it seems he to whom he delivered them acquainted neither of the Houses with the business, nor ever gave me the least notice or check whereby I might have demonstrated to this House the reason why I did it in mine own justification. But as it appears, whispered it abroad privately, whereby to beget a jealousy of me and cast me under the lingering consumption of a dangerous misconceit. I confess I had presently notice of it, yet not so public as I could take a lawful occasion to represent to <you> *the House* the whole ground of the business. But yet in my next letter to <you> *them* I complained of jealousies and misconstructions, in which complaint I knew I was understood by the most, (care having been taken to disrepute me privately). And in the same letter I assured <you> *them* of my faith to <you> *them*. Upon which to give me satisfaction of the good opinion <you> *they* had of me, and future trust <you> *they* would repose in me, <you> *they* ordered in these words: that Sir John Hotham hath performed his duty with all fidelity and trust to the commonwealth, both in his proceedings in his government of Hull, and in his other proceedings for the safety of the county of York.

This order

[*page break*]

This order gave me full satisfaction of the good esteem <you> *they* had of me, and assured me that <you> *they* approved all the ways I had taken for the advancement of <your> *their* ends and service, and were in a great measure underhand treaties. And by this I received encouragement when I saw it for <your> *their* advantage to begin anew which I am now about to show you, and I shall always stand confidently upon it that for anything done by me, good or bad, that order is to the date of it a full discharge.

I well know I need not take this way of justification of myself, but might and do avow that by all the orders of law-martial, foreign and domestic, a governor of a town may treat and is tied to no manner of words or circumstances at what times and in what exigencies he must do it, but is left in his full liberty in creating of his own advantage, and that I was placed in that town in as great an absoluteness as ever any was. None assigned me to consult with, no counsel of war to assist me, nor did I ever consult with any till my last treaty which I am now about to show you.

[174]Colonel Urry was the civil war's most notorious multiple turncoat: E.M. Furgol, 'Sir John Urry (d. 1650)', *ODNB*.

But I must be forced to begin afar off and recount to you the necessity that forced me into that course.

When monies fell short, I was driven as the rest of the kingdom to seek many necessitous shifts, which wheresoever I used proved as so many fatal disobligations to me, having the countenance of some in power substracted from all my actions which from thenceforth were read through a mist of groundless jealousies.

I had in 20 weeks received but £1,000 from you. Those that expected pay from me were 6 troops of horse and dragoons and 2,500 foot, all which out of my single endeavours and affection I had raised in the country. You will easily conceive it was no small sum nor of

[*page break*]

nor of easy invention that would satisfy all those mouths, and whatever person I fixed on for relief in this extremity, I knew I might add him to the catalogue of mine enemies.

These straits I acknowledge troubled me sore, yet no way moved me from the foundation of trust or honesty. I built my first action upon £1,600 at that time I borrowed of the town, and afterward by the consent of the aldermen framed an excise, the consequence of which a small foresight would reason a man into, and by those two ways I was compelled to take I disobliged poor and rich, and truly weighed ran a greater hazard than denying the King entrance into the town. But before these my last exigencies, I levied an assessment upon the East Riding, the particulars whereof being the substance of my last treaty and much towards the vindication of the ruin I suffer under by common fame. I shall give you an ample view of my whole affair therein, which I doubt not but will administer great light to discover the imposture of my accusers.

When the Queen returned out of Holland with the purchase of the whole year's endeavours, and hovered at sea upon our eastern coast, the Lord of Newcastle who had of late much increased his army, commanded the whole body of horse and foot towards the seaside to a town called Burlington 2 leagues from which he understood the Queen lay at anchor, who immediately upon his coming landed herself and provisions. I profess sincerely, the stage being the East Riding, I had a violent desire to have fought them at their landing, hoping to find them as indeed they were in an unsoldierlike posture, and to this end sent message upon message to the Lord Fairfax to desire his whole assistance. And if his lordship thought that too much that he would send us 1,000 foot and I would have undertaken to have

[*page break*]

to have rendered a sober man's account.

But upon what grounds I could never comprehend, my desire took no place so I acquainted you with the design, whereupon you sent immediate command to the Lord Fairfax to march to our assistance but the hopeful opportunity was lost. The Lord of Newcastle retired to York and we in the East Riding left to bewail the loss of a promising advantage. I was at that time vehemently forward to have embraced it, and should I call to your remembrance the concurrent state of affairs throughout the whole kingdom, you would judge that our victory would have brought the end of these hateful tr*o*ubles within view which now alas are at such a distance.

I cannot but passionately relate this misadventure that came attended with so many mischiefs, for all the while Newcastle stayed, he miserably oppressed and plundered the country and when he dislodged left in some places little else but bare walls and empty houses. But I should have told you that while he stayed there he began to make cruel inroads into the heart of the East Riding from whence I received subsistence for the forces I had raised, and who justly expected my protection. My desires of doing it by force were, as I showed you, made ineffectual by others' backwardness. So I was necessitated by some cast of cunning to compass this, my just end, and upon these and no other reasons made fair general promises if Newcastle would abstain from violence to that part of the country under my wing, I would do this and that for his service, and in time make him a fair account how much I was his. And under these pretences of affection to him I then and long after served <you> *the Parliament and* my employment at the enemy's cost, for they had that power in the country that they might without contradiction have marched to the gates of Hull.

Neither did I this in a corner, but <finding> *selected* men of eminent note and seeming rigid affection to the Parliament as Mr Nye

[*page break*]

Nye and Mr Saltmarsh, to whom I communicated the purpose of my actions. And several times when I saw Newcastle greedy upon the country which I kept flourishing, I renewed my engine, making my offers probable with passionate relations of my discontents, least my treaties should seem groundless and render the whole management suspicious.

This craft I learnt of Count Mansfeld[175] when I served under him, who when the Spanish General Buckquoy was upon him ere he

[175] As the Protestant general defending the Palatinate in 1621–1622, Mansfeld had negotiated with several Habsburg commanders about changing sides: R. Asch, '(Peter) Ernst (II) von Mansfeld, count von Mansfeld (*c.*1580–1626)', *ODNB*.

was aware and he in an unfortified town, he 10 days kept him in treaty, urging how himself had been abused by the Palsgrave.[176] In the meantime, while he was amused with these offers he fortified the town and then sends him word that he could not proceed in the first treaty with the honour of a soldier.

But you see these are dangerous shifts for subsistence. Yet all furnished me not with so much money as to satisfy my hungry soldiers, but that several times they made desperate mutinies, driving some of their officers to fly for refuge to my chamber. Twice they attempted my life but were by God's providence prevented.

I show this honourable <House> *court* the shifts in short, but had any of you been upon the place and felt the pressure and straits they compelled me unto, you would judge that there is little reason to call what I did treason, or to receive it with other affectation and reward than were those my many treaties in the beginning of my service. But so it happened that the intercourse about those businesses produced several letters betwixt us of all which I have most truly related to you my utmost ends and thoughts. Yet that is my treason, and these letters the evidence. [I] truly hope you have all of them that you may evidently see by their date and my actions at the same time compared, how far distant

[*page break*]

distant they were from those things I offered, and how little preparatory to the end I am accused of and Newcastle hoped for.

These things I observe to you that you may see that my actions and my endeavours were the same from first to last, yet fell under this misfortune that love interpreted my first and jealousy the last.

Thus you have seen some of the hard difficulties I passed for my particular services, which I was no way obliged to do either by my place or commands, urged only by my affections to the cause and its progress, but all these and all others be silent. I desire not to balance the real good I did with the ruin pretended. Nor shall I crave privilege of doing you the least disservice upon the stock of my forepurchased merits. But desire out of these considerations to be admitted to the place of a true man in all honest and wise men's thoughts.

I come now to the last part when all difficulties were heightened by time and jealousies grown greater. At which time my son was seized upon at Nottingham, I must acknowledge I was much amazed at it and in confidence of his innocence, passionately expressive of my mind, as conceiving it the act of some private men's malice who had incensed those in authority against him.

[176] R. Asch, 'Frederick V, Count Palatine of the Rhine (1596–1632)', *ODNB*.

Whereupon, I immediately dispatched <unto you> *to the Parliament* with my humble desires concerning his business. In the meantime, out of the integrity of my heart I was so little mistrustful of any ill intention towards me that I no way provided for the safety of my person, endeavoured to possess no man of my innocency, nor seek any security to myself other than I enjoyed under the shelter of <your> *their* party.

In this case I stood when others whose names I yet forbear by their depth of wit saw what never once entered into my thoughts

[*page break*]

thoughts. And when I was fast asleep found me betraying the town of which (by a letter feigned to be from some knowing man), they possessed the multitude and dispersed a sudden mutiny through the town, doing many things that to this day it is hard to give reasons for.

After I was in custody, all my actions were by them ript up and torn asunder to try if any of them could bear the name or face of treason. My officers were examined, some of them kept prisoners half a year to try if misery would ripen a confession, my servants pumped with offer of rewards. They searched underground and above ground where the train was laid. Yet I am sure they found not the least satisfaction to represent to <you> *the House* towards what they sought for, no tract of endeavour or complot to betray the least inch of it. No soldier or commander prepared, no blockhouse victualled beyond one day's necessity and I myself all the while in the weakest part of my trust. And I know really that concerning that business nothing can be alleged but a bulk of passionate and incoherent words where within my discontent I beat the air and no material action, complot or preparatory passage to the end I am accused of.

And now that this honourable <House> *court* hath seen a true account of my actions, I hope they will have a compassionate regard of my sufferings, which are thus in short.

I had when I took <your> *the Parliament* service an estate of £3,000 per annum. From my first denial of the King till I was seized upon I received not from it all much above £1,000. When I fell into <your> *the Houses'* disfavour I had £6,000 in monies which was my whole subsistence for me and my numerous family. That all, and £3,000

[*page break*]

£3,000 worth of goods was by a pretence of an order from <you> *the Parliament* given to the garrison of Hull. Though I conceive that by the words of that order <you> *they* intended no such thing.

My whole estate in lands is by the committee of sequestrations in Yorkshire sequestered, neither can I get one farthing from it.

My chief mansion house with the land about it given to my former wife's children upon an unjust pretence of portions presently due and use for them. I confess it is my own fault that these things were done, being extreme tender of troubling <you> *the Parliament* with petitions to plead my right.

And now at this present time though I lately enjoyed *all* this estate, I have not in all the world subsistence for livelihood for myself and 12 children. But in short *time* must all depend for bread upon the charity of others. Let people think of my riches what they will.

I refer my condition to your honourable judgments. I know my actions have been made intricate and suspicious by multiplicity of printed papers full of calumnies whereby discreet men's mouths have been full of questions and some seeming evidences against me valued at that rate as to take up some portion of time from <your> *the Houses'* public affairs.

But now I doubt not but this sincere narrative will make all appearance of treachery to vanish and settle me in the just merits of my actions, and if my further sufferings will be in any measure of advantage to the public good, I shall not refuse to be as eminent in my passive obedience as I have been in my active.

HHC: Hotham MS, U DDHO/1/37: Draft of part of Sir John Hotham's defence, London, undated but *c.*November 1644

May it please this honourable House:
Having undertaken all my employments of yours in [*MS damaged*] I confess I have much omitted my duty in giving you [*MS damaged*] time; of those things you committed to my charge your much [*MS damaged*] of the public's concernment has hitherto restrained me from begg [*MS damaged*] minute of your time to hear a private name vindicated, but having [*MS damaged*] a <paper> of summons from some at Guildhall, sitting as I am informed in [*MS damaged*] of a council of war, to appear before them for trial of something [*MS damaged*] my life; I could <not> in justice to this House and myself whose [*MS damaged*] and under whose protection and and [*sic*] authority I did all what I dy [*MS damaged*] remonstrate *to you* <to gent what> in the just way of appeal <ho> what authority [*MS damaged*] had; how large, and how to your sole judgements I <would> *and now myself I must* stand or fall.

When this House was pleased first to honour me with their commands to execute the government of Hull, you all know the state of affairs *was such* as it was disputed by the wisest whether love to a man's country and the being of parliaments could have engaged a man of *so* flourishing *a* fortune to such a hazard without some mixture of foolhardiness. I saw the danger I undertook, yet I well know my duty and how little respect or consideration my private suffering or ruin could claim when the whole interest and the parliaments and liberties of England were in all men's judgements at stake.

The commission you gave me for the execution of my place was very general and in truth more left to my discretion, judgement upon the particular result of occasions <that> than I was either willing should be or had confidence to believe I could well go through with. The words these:

Ordered that some of the trained bands of Yorkshire nearest to Hull in the said county under the command of Sir John Hotham shall with all speed be put into the said town of Hull for securing the King's magazine there and the said town. And hereof the said Sir John Hotham is (by virtue of this order) commanded to perform it accordingly, and the said Sir John Hotham is to command the town and forces therein, and all parties whom it shall concern shall give their obedience unto the said Sir John Hotham and his ministers. And lastly that Sir John Hotham or who else he shall appoint under him shall not deliver up the town of Hull or magazine there, or any part thereof without the King's authority signified to him by the Lords and Commons now assembled in Parliament.

In this latitude of my commission I went down and continued till I was seized without the least restriction from you or signification from the general that I was under his command or orders *no law martial did he ever send to me* he should publish, nor did ever conjecture other than that I stood in <the> *as* immediate relation of subjection to your command as the first day I undertook. I always made my addresses to you.

By all this you see how vastly I resigned myself to the justice of your good interpretation of my choice of means for the effecting your command, having

[*page break*]

[*MS damaged*] large instruction to authorize me in each particular action. Lord [*MS damaged*] was I in my honest thoughts towards *you*. How I regardless of [*MS damaged*] difficulties I went though in your service, how sparing [*MS damaged*] my many merits in their true proportion as accounting [*MS damaged*] myself as nearly obliged in prosecuting your just [*MS damaged*] commands <and> as if all my own interest had been [*MS damaged*] stake, and whoever was then present must confess that the [*MS damaged*] I used could be taught nowhere but in the school of love.

I shall always acknowledge it the goodness of God to me that I select [*MS damaged*] means for the safety of my trust as I received your thanks and [*MS damaged*] ation in the first and second part of my employ, but with as real intent on my part to your service and as sincere a heart to the safety of my charge, all the rest miscarried. Distance created misinterpretations and those jealousies, which made known to my enemies in the town, encouraged those (whom in and for your service I had disobliged) to manage all misfortunes to my ruin.

At my first acceptance of my charge, I sent my son down to draw some companies according to your order into Hull but it proved the difficult play of an after game, for the Lord of Newcastle by the King's commission was come into the town, and wanted solely the drawing in of Sir Thomas Metham's regiment to have made good his authority. But I may justly say God's providence on my son's vigilance and courage, with the strength of my interest with the gentry thereabouts defeated this first and most dangerous design. For without any delay, he drew a regiment of trained bands to the gates and by the good management of threats and treaties brought the whole town in subjection to his garrison.

But the King retaining by much the stronger party in the town entertained daily treaties and courtship among them and made the government in short time too hot for a deputy, so I went down and took the immediate government myself resolving to stand all shocks.

When I got there I found the town five parts of seven affected to the King, animated against my authority by continual arguments from court of security and success, nay our own party so timorous that scarce any of them durst avow to speak publicly with my son, all my soldiers plain countrymen, heartless and heedless of all their duties, myself as far to seek as having a part to play unprecedented by any.

I saw all the dangers in the worst vizards, other men's fear, cunning or love could represent them to me, and what I did when I came to try the worst, their effect I need not relate. 'Twas in sum that by God's good hand, myself and soldiers overcame unpassable difficulties, all things succeeding beyond belief and in confidence that in this action I had served the commonwealth, I sat down with content under the name and hazard of a traitor.

[*page break*]

After this, though I was thus in public branded by His Majesty, yet I was daily in private assaulted with offers larger than my thought, honour and wealth, I contemned in a large proportion. The King's protestation of ruining taken before the gates I valued at as little, though I well feel he has too truly kept it, having very good reason to believe

[*page break*]

that this honourable has seen a past relation of all my treaties and the reasons of them. More things there are, which though I am very sensible they would be much to my vindication, I purposely *omit* least I should offend. I know you are sensible that when time and place was the service I did was not contemned that if ?truly? I had done much ill, I might with some justice claim a balance. I am very sorry to find it that my most real enemies I now find are men [I] did disoblige in doing you service. *The King has some influence in this.* And now you have truly seen what I have done, I know this honourable House will have a compassionate regard to what of my sufferings I shall.

I had when I took your service an estate of £3,000 per annum. From my first denial of the King till it was seized on I received not £600 from it all. When I fell into your disfavour, £6,000, which was my whole subsistence for me and my numerous family, you ordered to be given to the garrison at Hull. My whole estate in lands is by the committee in Yorkshire sequestered, though I was never called to answer whether I had committed any crime within your ordinance, my chief mansion house with the land about it given to my former wife's children upon an unjust pretence portions due and use for them. I confess it is my own fault that these things were done, I being extreme tender of troubling you with petitions to plead my right.

And now at this present time, though I lately had all that estate, I protest before the eternal God let people think of my estate and riches what they will. I have in all the world subsistence for livelihood for myself, 12 children for twelve months to come, but after that we must all be forced to depend for bread on the charity of others. <My case refer to you and doubt not of your redress> And I have no other riches *or ?treasure?* to leave my sons than this: that when this kingdom become flourishing and religion pure though they be poor and contemned, yet they will see their father's name engraven upon one of the corner stones of the <foundation>.

I refer my condition to your honourable judgment. I know it has been made intricate and suspicious by multiplicity of calumnies cast on it by printed paper, whereby discreet men's mouths were become full of questions, and some seeming evidences against me valued at that rate as to take up some time from your affairs of state. But I doubt not but this sincere narrative will prove such as will make all appearance of treachery to vanish and settle me in the just merit of my actions.

HHC: Hotham MS, U DDHO/1/38: Draft of part of Sir John Hotham's defence, London, undated but *c.*November 1644

Now concerning those testimonies which you have heard that concern the betraying the town, you <I> have what is said. It is declared by these two gentlemen, my lieutenant-colonel and my sec*r*etary,[177] who were in reality rather governors of the town than myself. They declare that without their assistance I could not have done it, that I never spoke to them to assist me in any course or way to such an end, nor gave them a look intimating such a change. They tell you likewise, that myself alone, I could not have compassed such an end. They tell you that I never endeavoured to make a party in the town amongst officers, soldiers or townsmen to such an end or purpose, and being so near the business, yet <by> they can make no rational conjectures, out of which they can create a belief in themselves or evidence it by reasons to others that I have had any such intent. They likewise tell you that I had so bottomed all my officers and servants against breach of trust, so possessed them with the odiousness of the crime that they believe no officer or soldier would have joined with me, that I consulted always with the rigidest party, that I knew they would never be assistant to me to such an end, that I could not have betrayed the town except I had gained the blockhouses, that I never went in any way of preparation to the gaining of them. And last of all you have delivered unto you the state of the affection of the town with the true ends why I was seized on, which are thus laid down, that the malignant party were the most numerous and active in it; the heads of them wittier men that they did it that they might ruin me by the same authority I had scourged them. And that of those that were of the Parliament's party, more were moved out of hate to my person by reason of the excise and assessments than out of any knowledge they had of my disaffection to the Parliament. And they have heard many words to that effect, and they have heard many of the most active say that when they seized on me they had no evidence against me. You have heard it has been said that if I had not joined with that party which was for religion, but those for liberty, I had stood till this day. It hath been declared that not ten hours before I was apprehended, how diligent I was in sending away forces to resist and oppose the enemy, and how when my son came to me

[*page break*]

to Hull I assured him of my constant intention [*MS damaged*] ment.

[177] Lieutenant-Colonel Christopher Legard and Robert Stockdale. For Legard, see Appendix II.

You hear what Mr Conyers says and he is my friend a [*MS damaged*] I never hid my bosom from. He told me my words we [*MS damaged*] but he knew me too well to believe them, but desired satisfaction from my own mouth that he might give it to others. With his own and my authority you hear what he says of the ends of my speech. You hear how I imprisoned Nicholas Conyers,[178] chief servant to Sir Hugh Cholmley, seized his trunks and monies, and so kept him till I was sure upon [*unfinished*].

Now for my treaties with the earl of Newcastle y [*MS damaged*] in the ends, occasions and effects, you hear it delive [*MS damaged*] how I acquainted Lieutenant-Colonel Legard, Mr [Salt]marsh, and how passionate I was that such service should be hindered with such groundless jealousies [*MS damaged*] hear that the earl of Newcastle had forces sufficient [*MS damaged*] wasted the East Riding and marched within sight of ?Hull? [*MS damaged*] and had he come thither, besides his plundering the country [*MS damaged*] shortly have made the town unserviceable to your [*MS damaged*] and my safety, for our wants of money and the mutin [*MS damaged*] ritts of the soldiers, egged by town's malignity would [*MS damaged*] time made the town his. You see our necessity for money [*MS damaged*] £1,000 in 20 weeks for 3,000 men and more. You see how little force I had to resist him by force, and you see how I remedied all these inconveniences by a treaty. I kept him out of the country. I kept it safe, assessed towards £10,000 for our maintenance. And that in that treaty, I was not real. You see how by my kinsman, Michael Portington, esq., I had set the Queen and him together by the ears and you see with what diligence I prosecuted that, and how I was swallowed up with the hopeful effects of it. Then you see [*MS damaged*] came from the King to treat with me. Him I [*MS damaged*] speak with, others came to me from the Queen [*MS damaged*] I scorn and though the messages were loaden with [*MS damaged*] and wealth as to myself as by Mr Conyers you hear [*MS damaged*] and embraced none, but that wherein I sought and

[*page break*]

your advantage. And for the words that I used in those treaties, you know no man fisheth with a bare hook. I must some way make my offers probable and possible, either with passionate relations of my discontent, or high protestations, or solemn promises, or narrations of my preparations, which you see were false, else my treaty would have seemed groundless and rendered the whole management suspicious.

[178]Nicholas Conyers of Boulby had been cornet to Sir Hugh Cholmley but was later promoted to lieutenant and then captain in Ferdinando, Lord Fairfax's regiment of horse: TNA, E121/5/5, no. 1.

You see how far further I ventured in Beckwith's treaty. I promised a gate of the town, and set the time and rewards, and yet had thanks from the House, which I took as an acknowledgment of my power <of> to do it and an approbation of the way I took. <you see Mr Ny[e]s opinion of it then; though> Now my adversity has made it my fault, and deterred a safe walking man from acknowledging any cognizance of it.
[*Note in margin*] I must avow [*MS damaged*] Mr Nie more [*MS damaged*] once hath [*MS damaged*] me that he [*MS damaged*] out avow it [*MS damaged*] the world [*MS damaged*] my treatiz [*MS damaged*] Newcastle was [*MS damaged*] Parliament [*MS damaged*] age.

[*page break*]

For my deserting of my trust and adhering [*MS damaged*] I confess they are general words, and <not> whether [*MS damaged*] with the enemy *unfortunately* may not in time be called adhering [*MS damaged*] I know not. I could wish it were at large declared what it is. But to my own business you see it delivered unto you by my officers in town and abroad, that they know not nor could ever observe any such thing, not in the omission of the least opportunity. They deliver it into you, that I was so far from adhering to the enemy that I never so much as favoured the malignant party, but [*MS damaged*] to them all effects of severity in the town and country [*MS damaged*] how to the utmost of my power I did oppose, fight [*MS damaged*] resist the enemy, not only when he made incursions [*MS damaged*] place under my charge, hot extended my [*MS damaged*] to such places as needed my help. You hear how [*MS damaged*] in public and private I professed my faithfulness, instruc[ted] my agent, possessed my officers and friends concerning the odiousness of the Queen's and Newcastle's ways [*MS damaged*]. What satisfaction I gave publicly to the [*MS damaged*] must conceive me guilty of desperatest apos [*MS damaged*] all these professions and instructions I could [*MS damaged*] vices and courses which all by the ways and means I [*MS damaged*] had rendered so abominable. You see how eminent I was both in encouragement [*MS damaged*] satisfaction to our party, what forces I raised, [*MS damaged*] gaged all my kind.

HHC: Hotham MS, U DDHO/1/62: Durand Hotham, esq., to John Saltmarsh, London, 12 November 1644

Cousin,
I send you here enclosed a summons from my father to be at his trial. I do not doubt but you will come, and I hope your testimony *in those things* of which we shall interrogate you will add much to the

vindication from those aspersions he lies under. Sir, the nearer I look unto his business, the more I find his pretended crimes to be shadows, and empty names without reality or proof. I am fully confident you know as much, and that your seeming to speak against him hitherto has been your safe wisdom in which you have been much practised not to strive against a stream. But now that it hath pleased the Parliament to give way to a public trial and I hope as much countenance to those that shall appear for him as against him, as desiring I believe to clear the *innocent* rather than condemn the guilty. I do in justice expect you *should* give them that satisfaction in public that you gave me in private when I conjured you before God almighty, and in the sincerity of a friend to give me *an* account of what you thought was his real intent. You may perhaps have forgot some of it, but I hope you will give me leave to help your memory. Cousin, you know that you were the nearest in his counsels. You had freer access to his bosom than any, amended what you thought was amiss, and in truth were the only man with him. And you know what use you made of that freedom, whether to his safety or to your own ends. You know he employed you hither to London to negotiate several businesses for him, and your conscience cannot but tell you that you made him always rather worse than better. You know that in this last business concerning my *brother*, in which he trusted you, how *you* grossly failed and laid the plot to seize him, sending the paper to Moyer[179] to raise the mutiny at Hull against him, whereby his blood and the blood of his family lays at your door, crying we took sweet counsel together etc. And remember what I told you in my chamber and the agony [you] were in when I charged you with so much truth. And though perhaps you may have framed some sophisms to yourself to hinder the continual barking of your conscience, yet be sure when you are in the least adversity or sickness, or entered into any of the approaches to death, the true law of honesty and truth will revive and make these vain notions of public good which you pretend to disappear. You cannot but confess that I convinced you of the impossibility of what you give out you suspected. I demonstrated to you that no such groundwork was laid, that he conversed with none but yourself, nor sought any security but in the strength of the rigid party. For those words of passion, you are convinced of how little value they are. Sir, we now expect real truth, and know God almighty is above, who says that He abhors the bloodthirsty and deceitful man. I wonder you would avoid me so as

[179] Lawrence Moyer, captain of the *Hercules*, docked at Hull, instigated the arrest of the Hothams and their field officers in Hull on 29 June 1643.

you did the last time you were in the town. Sir, it will be as much your trial as my father's, therefore speak truth.

I rest your loving friend,
Durand Hotham.

[*The quote below from Proverbs 24:8 is crossed out in the left margin*]

<He that devise or do evil shall be called a mischievous person. Proverbs 24:8. Those diggeth a pit, he shall fall therein, and he shall rolleth a stone it shall return upon him.>

HHC: Hotham MS, U DDHO/1/33: Certificate of William Huntte, clerk of the House of Commons, Westminster, 3 December 1644

I delivered to John Milles, esq., Judge Advocate, on the 19th of October 1644 thirty-three letters in a bundle all concerning Sir John Hotham, Captain Hotham and Hull, as may appear by a note under the Judge Advocate's hand. And since that time (vizt) the 29th of November last I delivered to Mr William Haslope for the use of the Judge Advocate 9 letters and papers concerning the aforesaid business.

William Huntte: one of the clerks of Henry Elsynge, esq., clerk of the House of Commons.

HHC: Hotham MS, U DDHO/1/39: Petition of Sir John Hotham to the council of war, London, undated but December 1644

To the honourable the council of war, the humble petition of Sir John Hotham, knight and baronet, late governor of Hull.
Showeth to this honourable court,
That having received some informations of the management of the late trial of Sir Alexander Cary,[180] whereby he is extremely much encouraged that he shall have fair and free audience for himself and witnesses towards <the clearing> his vindication from those foul crimes he lies under, and desiring that the whole process of it may

[180] Carew was a harbinger of the fate that awaited the Hothams. He was governor of the fort on St Nicholas Island in Plymouth harbour and arrested on 19 August 1643 for attempting to change sides. He was tried by a council of war chaired by John Corbet at the Guildhall on 19 November 1644 and beheaded on Tower Hill on 23 December following: S. Wright, 'Sir Alexander Carew, second baronet (1608–1644)', *ODNB*.

be orderly and uninterrupted and all things on both sides <may be> clearly heard and understood. Therefore your petitioner prays that the two spaces on each side of the Bar may be reserved for the witnesses and a place on each side made for them to ascend into the court without disturbance of your petitioner at the Bar. And seeing your petitioner is lame and not able to stand long at the Bar, and that the place as he is informed is extreme inconvenient for your petitioner's easeful and quiet attendance to his defence that there may be some provision made <that made> of a seat behind the bar and a *the* a [*sic*] space railed in *for your petitioner* that he may not be pressed by the bystanders, but himself and those that assist him with his papers may have free room <to the business they are employed> quietly to hear what is spoken. And he is confident to give this honourable court satisfaction beseeming an honest and just man.

[*On reverse*] Brabbles betwixt my Lord General and Sir William Waller[181]
My Lord of Denbigh[182] and ?Porphing?
Committee of Kent and Sir William Waller and each or one part must needs transgress the positive law of war. All our contest were in the beginning when things were not settled.

HHC: Hotham MS, U DDHO/1/42: The charges against Sir John Hotham, London, undated but December 1644[183]

His general misgovernment and oppression of the town and county manifested, divers particulars tending to the overthrow of the cause and abusing of his trust in:
1. In countenancing the deserting of Lord Fairfax by his son and Sir Edward Rodes with their forces consisting of horse and foot.
2. In neglecting to send him ammunition when he desired.
3. His appointing at several times single troops of dragooners to be quartered in such places of danger as they became a prey unto the enemy, to the great advantage of the enemy, the loss of the est [*sic*] county.

[181] Sir John Hotham was well connected with the Earl of Essex and would have been well aware of Essex's ongoing quarrel with Sir William Waller, president of the council of war that was to try Hotham: B. Donagan, 'Sir William Waller (bap. 1598?, d. 1668)', *ODNB*.

[182] In late 1644, Denbigh was an ally of parliamentarian moderates such as the earls of Essex and Manchester: A. Hughes, 'Basil Feilding, second earl of Denbigh (*c.*1608–1675)', *ODNB*.

[183] These charges are summarized in Reckitt, *Charles the First and Hull*, p. 103.

4. His deep sessments in the county excise begun in the town, sessing men's persons for monies whereby great sums of [money] were raised, never the less soldiers unpaid, pretending want of money in so much [as] he borrowed £300 of John Barnard[184] the week before his mutation [*sic*]. Whereby it appears his purpose was to deceive the kingdom and country of their monies and to covert [*sic*] it to his own use, to the undoing of his trust reposed in him.
5. His often intelligence and messengers from the Queen and others of the enemy upon pretence of frivolous business.
6. His giving them such persons in exchange as were most pernicious to Parliament and advantageous to them, for inconsiderable persons.
7. His letter to his son at Lincoln upon his escape from Nottingham, testifying his joy therein, intimating a notable passage about fool Cholmley. [*A copy of this letter is transcribed in the manuscript below this list.*]
8. A letter sent to the Parliament by Nye and Saltmarsh requiring the vindication of his son's honour for his imprisonment at Nottingham.
9. Henry Jermyn intimating a desire to be with all expedition to be put in execution.
10. His flying forth of Hull to Beverley where he endeavoured to escape when he took notice they would apprehend him.
11. His son's message to the Queen at Newark assuring of his fidelity and service with his regiment of horse, with an engagement to his father at Hull on that behalf.

Letter[185]

Son, your letter came to me most joyfully both for the manner and matter you have freed yourself from those false villains. Some must be privy to it that little reason upon that nose [*sic*]. I dispatched away to the Parliament both Nye and Saltmarsh with a formal letter to the Lords and Commons, but with these instructions: to tell them in plain English, if they instantly send you not away to me, I would if please God right myself. They little think but that their great Anabaptist hath you sure. If it be possible I would see you here: we have a great game to play. The great God of heaven direct us to his glory. How you can come safe I know not, for assure yourself the Queen's party will lay strong watch for you. I would not have you to fall into their hands that way. Du Moulin's man will be with me within 8 days. I [have] not leisure to write fully, but if without danger I would never so gladly see you that God willing you shall see the difference betwixt a friend and

[184] John Barnard, alderman of Hull: Hopper, 'A directory of parliamentarian allegiance in Yorkshire', p. 90.

[185] A copy of this letter written by Sir John Hotham from Hull on 25 June 1643 is in BL, Add. MS 44,848, fo. 287v. It is briefly summarized in Reckitt, *Charles the First and Hull*, p. 104.

father, for I will live and die with your honour. The fool Cholmley, I cannot get him quiet for 10 days, that I fear I must. He is a fool beyond measure. If you can come to Hull, but [not] with hazard, gladly would I *speak with* you, yet loath you should miscarry in the haven. That great God, to whom if you [give] your heart, you cannot miscarry.

[*On reverse*] Abstract of accusation. My further accusations.

HHC: Hotham MS, U DDHO/1/40: Interrogatories for the witnesses, with notes for Sir John Hotham's defence, London, undated but December 1644

I cannot pass by to mention what I have once represented concerning this trial of me by martial law.
1. That I was employed by the Houses before there was any martial law, nay when it was declared against as destructive to the law of the land as in Sir Thomas Danby's case.[186]
2. That upon some necessities I had desired martial law from the House and it was denied me by the House by an order in these words.
3. That the ordinance of war which are called my Lord General were never published amongst us nor any signification came from him of any such rule he did command us to observe.
4. I showed you a precedent of a heinous crime committed by some soldiers of Colonel Langham's regiment and a council of war set and not promulgation of the law held for a sufficient plea and the council of war rise.
5. If anything what you urge as my crime be of date before the 25 of November [16]42 I shall not answer to it a guilt only to satisfaction; by reason that the House of Commons took notice of my good will in trusting my action to their after constructions and therefore gave me a discharge in these words.
And it being an order of the Commons and a favour I received from *them* I must and shall plead it confidently as esteeming it my duty for their honours' sake to stand as closely to a privilege that they shall grant me as ever I did to their commands.
[Interrogatories]:
Do you know or have you heard of any treaty Sir John Hotham had with the earl of Newcastle?
From whom had you it, or what do you conceive or have heard was the end of it?

[186] Sir Thomas Danby was a Straffordian captured by the parliamentarians and imprisoned in Manchester in 1643. He compounded for his estate in 1646: J.T. Cliffe, 'Sir Thomas Danby (1610–1660)', *ODNB*; Newman, *Royalist Officers*, pp. 101–102.

Whether had not the earl of Newcastle strength sufficient at that time to have wasted all the East Riding, and marched within sight of Hull?
Whether was not the garrison of Hull in necessity for want of money at that time, and whether had Sir John Hotham at that time received any monies from London?
Which way did Sir John Hotham maintain his garrison of Hull and other his forces in Yorkshire?
Whether had Sir John Hotham forces sufficient to have by force resisted the earl of Newcastle from the plundering of the East Riding?
Have you not observed drums come several times from the Lord of Newcastle to Sir John Hotham, and how were they conveyed to him?
Not that I would avoid your judgments or authority for I would not for all the world continue longer in suspense betwixt *crime and innocence*, hope and fear, be the effect life [or] death. But that 'tis my earnest desire that upon these reasons you would consider your threefold power granted you by that ordinance. That is first you have power to judge according to the nature of the offence, secondly as appertains to justice, third according [*MS damaged*] ensuing. Now for the two first which is the great enlargement of your power, to all cases in Chancery. Now will you be pleased to consider that power of judgment according to the nature of an offence, authorizes you to a survey of it in its essence and circumstances. Now concerning offences they are of two sorts, moral or civil. That which we speak of is civil, which is nothing else in its nature, but a thing prohibited. Now when you have it manifested before that there is no rule commanding or forbidding such or such actions, or assigning punishments to them, you know better what you have to do than I can tell you. But it may [be] worth your saddest thoughts, whether to punish a crime by a law of war published after be not to shed the blood of war in peace.
I speak not these things that I value them as part of my defence, for should not my actions in point of treachery or breach of trust (which are in reality moral faults *though not punishable as such by known laws*) be proof to the best of the rigidest letter of any law of war extant, I would myself have answered guilty and not have dared to have backed so horrid a crime with such a confidence as could spring from nothing but atheism.

HHC: Hotham MS, U DDHO/1/41: Interrogatories for the witnesses on behalf of Sir John Hotham's defence, London, undated but December 1644

1. Whether do you know Sir John Hotham or not, or how long have you known him and what relation had you to him?

1. [*Struck out*] <Whether do you bear any particular hatred to him or has he injured you in his management of the public or his private affairs>?

2. Whether have you not been offered or received rewards, or employment or favourable countenance if you would testify or appear against him?

<2>. Whether have you not been disrespected, abused or miscalled because you would not testify against Sir John Hotham, things contrary to your knowledge?

3. Whether have you not heard Sir John Hotham in his passion speak many words that you know in your conscience to be far from his heart and things he never intended to execute?

4. Whether do you know that Sir John Hotham hath deserted his trust and adhered to the enemy, either in his counsels or actions, or in any course of his government of Hull, or in the affairs of Yorkshire?

5. Do not you know and are persuaded in your conscience, that he hath not deserted his trust nor adhered to the enemy, but has as far as you can conceive endeavoured the advancement of the Parliament's ends and party, in his government of Hull and other his proceedings in Yorkshire?

6. Do not you know that he was so far from deserting his trust and adhering to the enemy, that he never so much as favoured or adhered to the malignant party in the town or county of York, but in both places they constantly felt many effects of severity from him?

7. Do not you know that he hath been so far from deserting his trust and adhering to the enemy, that he hath upon all occasions endeavoured to the utmost of the power and strength he had, to resist, oppose, and fight with the enemy, not only when he made any inroads and incursions to the places under his command, but also gave great assistance and encouragement to set the Parliament's interest afoot in the western parts of Yorkshire, setting up the Lord Fairfax, afterwards breaking the treaty of neutrality, raising Colonel Boynton a regiment of foot and a troop of horse, Lieutenant-Colonel Boynton a troop of horse, furnishing Sir Matthew Boynton[187] with a troop of dragoons to go with him into the North Riding and money to pay them, relieving of Manchester with powder, setting the militia on foot in Derbyshire,

[187] Sir Matthew Boynton of Barmston, baronet, and his two sons, Colonel Francis Boynton and Lieutenant-Colonel Matthew Boynton, were later instrumental in defending Beverley and arresting Sir John Hotham: Hopper, 'A directory of parliamentarian allegiance in Yorkshire', pp. 96–97; C.V. Collier, *An Account of the Boynton Family and the Family Seat at Burton Agnes* (Middlesbrough, 1914).

and giving great assistance to Lincolnshire. Do you not know all those and every particular of them, or what do you know concerning them?
8. Whether have you not in private and public heard him profess his faithfulness to the Parliament, and obliged or disobliged to continue constant to them and their party?
9. Whether were you present at a meeting Sir John Hotham had with the townsmen, and what did you hear him say to them?
10. Who did you observe to be Sir John Hotham's counsellors?
11. Whether upon the receipt of letters and all dispatches, did you not observe that he called Mr Nye, or Mr Saltmarsh, *and Sir Matthew Boynton,* or one of them?
12. Have you not known him to give encouragement to those of the Parliament's party, and real satisfaction to them that desired it, concerning the justness of the cause, and the reality of the Parliament's intentions?
13. Do you not know that very night he was apprehended, having a letter from Sir Edward Rodes of the approach of the enemy, he did use his utmost in his care, and diligence to resist and oppose him? And what do you know concerning it?
14. Whether having that nearness of relation to him that you had, and that trust in your hand, do you conceive he could have delivered up the town without your assistance?
15. Whether did Sir John Hotham ever speak to you to assist him in any course, way, or endeavour to betray the town, or to join with him to betray it?
16. Whether do you conceive or can believe that single, himself, alone, he could have betrayed the town without acquainting any of his servants or officers with it?
17. Whether did you ever hear or, do you know that he ever acquainted any of his servants or officers with any such intent, or do you not know on the contrary that he always made public and private professions and protestations against breach of trust?
18. Whether by anything you can rationally gather do you conceive or can you believe that he had any endeavour or intent to betray the town?
19. Whether having professed so publicly against the breach of trust, what a hateful crime it was, and how it rendered all a man's business unsuccessful?
20. Do you conceive or can you believe that any officers would have joined with him to betray the town, or do you conceive he could believe so?
21. Have you not heard some of the townsmen of Hull, and of the most active in seizing of Sir John Hotham, say that they had no evidence that he had an intention to betray the town?

22. Whether have you observed that he ever endeavoured to make a party in the town of Hull amongst the malignants there, or have you not observed that he never did any such thing nor consult, join or associate himself with them or any of them in any of his affairs?
23. What party did he ever consult with?
24. Do you conceive, know, or believe if that party that he did join with would have been assistant to him in betraying the town, or in any endeavours that way, and do you not conceive that he likewise knew as much?
25. Whether could he without making a party for the King in the town amongst both officers and soldiers have betrayed the town? Whether he could have betrayed the town except he had gained the blockhouses and castle?
26. Whether do you know of any letters from the duchess of Buckingham[188] to Sir John Hotham, and at what time was it?
27. To whom did he show it, and what said he at that time to those he showed it, and who were present?
28. Do you know of any treaty Sir John Hotham had with Sir Hugh Cholmley? What have you heard him say concerning him and his deserting the Parliament?
29. Whether do you conceive that the townsmen and others that rose against Sir John Hotham and seized upon him, did it out of affection to the Parliament or out of disaffection to his person, by reason of the excise and assessment he had laid upon them? And have not you heard many words to that effect?
30. Whether were not the malignant party as forwards and violent against him as any and these men employed in seizing his person?
31. What do you know concerning one Sir Francis Cobb[189] coming to Sir John Hotham, and the pretence of it, and the intent of it, and what answer he had?
32. What do you know concerning the releasement of any of the malignant party? Who were the movers to it and upon what reasons denied, and what the effects of the denial, and when granted, was not Trew released at Mr Nye's entreaty giving £200 bond and Mr Toppin denied.

[188] The duchess of Buckingham had remarried the royalist schemer, Randall MacDonnell, marquis of Antrim: J. Ohlmeyer, 'Katherine MacDonnell, duchess of Buckingham and marchioness of Antrim (*c.*1603–1649)', *ODNB*.

[189] Sir Francis Cobb of Ottringham in Holderness was a royalist commissioner of array who became colonel of foot in York's garrison and commander of Clifford's Tower: Newman, *Royalist Officers*, p. 75; Ormrod, *The Lord Lieutenants and High Sheriffs of Yorkshire*, p. 144.

HHC: Hotham MS, U DDHO/1/43: Notes of evidence from witnesses, London, undated but December 1644[190]

Words actions	Several Commands	2nd Com.
2 heads	My Com.	3 Chosen.

Lord Fairfax made general
Cap Hotham, lieutenant-general
Corr: Enemy
Non cor with friends
Preparation to his design
Intelligence Q. N. D. Ch.
Intercourse frequent continued
Treaty with Newcastle should have continued
Digby admitted to go and
Bland Portinton to the Q Chamber
From the Enemy notice secure myself
great rewards.
Return complying answers how to leave the Parliament accusable. Stay the Scots. Digby sends a declaration [*MS damaged*] agreed upon. Burning letters. Command his son [*MS damaged*] ate with Fairfax & prisoner. Send the Queen word [*MS damaged*] at her command.
[*MS damaged*] and die with him and his honour. Cholmley's money
[*MS damaged*] coat
[*MS damaged*] now with his own party
[*MS damaged*] -astances not with powder etc.
[*MS damaged*] not suffering to raise men. Sir Hugh Bethell[191] not to raise money set L with horse.
Disparaging the Lord Fairfax little forces. dissuade
lending money. Invalidates the ordinance
Waller
False upon the committees of Parliament
stand the Parliament
Contests threatens the Parliament right himself
Parliament ships
Preparations neither raised [*MS damaged*] nor men
platform run
Endeavoured to lessen [*MS damaged*] Legard
Capt Moyer plot to [*MS damaged*]
Discharge the garrison a [*MS damaged*]

[190] These notes for the defence are torn, fragmented, and in two columns, but have been transcribed according to the original line structure to aid comprehension.

[191] Sir Hugh Bethell of Ellerton, Co. York (d. 1662): Dugdale, *The Visitation of the County of Yorke*, p. 155.

[*page break*]

Bernard
Ship good 5 for Amsterdam about Challenor's business and oath that if the Protestations came to H he could not tell
Colonel Aldred doubted all would be betrayed for honour and money, spoken out of malice, his actions would justify him
The night before ye returned to send money
That he might send his trunks for ?beam?
Made no answer indebted to him
Advise to get his estate out of Hull
John Rogers and Somerfeild the said counsel to know his receiving a potent enemy command that command the country. He can not tell who told him so
Boynton.
At supper that the Parliament aimed at provoking the Parliament ship
Waller's oath
Is that the liberty we fight that
Boynton says the same
The Wednesday came to Beverley
To draw Sir Edward Rodes ?total?
give him account;
took advice how to manage themselves
to desire him to apprehend Sir John
Hotham
came back with him
his prisoner, disarmed him passed
his word but upon the letting go
rid away, knock of his horse, near morning

Matt
[*MS damaged for 5 lines*]
harsh expression left out
prayed to procure resolution
provide for himself
told him his thoughts
what if Parliament will not
leave my family and friend should ?bale?
I will be faithful 5,000 left with him
22 June Captain Moyer to go off to Scar-
brough
Went down to the south end stayed the ship
Mr Saltmarshe said all and undone
Brooke the business to Captain Moyer
Forbear till he received an answer

Sir John would attempt something
Came to London acquainted some members
Let them not think I am so far
cast of but I can; to do something
but I scorn to be so base

Barrat Wattson
2 letters one from the Lord [*MS damaged*]
To Mr Hotham, Mr Raikes [*MS damaged*]
them open
Barrett in company let [*MS damaged*]
Jermyn letters

Styles[192]
That Easter last the Lady Bland
came to the town provided her a lodging
what occasion, ans: about weighty
business, desired to speak with Sir John
Hotham, desired Sir John Hotham terms
of peace mediator to the Queen for
peace; an army of Papists; not to engage
herself, continued, set down in
writing; *conference* at 2 several times; and had
letter from the duchess of Buckingham
He was present when a messenger
came in, the Lady Hotham trouble

[*page break*]

Then discontented, expose
Hazard, ?told? sent a bay of Gold
Acquaint the Parliament exchange
Bushell; Betwixt person & cause

Mr Bourdenand
This deponent; that the said French was
call Du Moulin

Stockdale[193]
Understanding the Parliament had given
charge

[192] William Styles was vicar of Holy Trinity, Hull. He resisted the persuasions of the queen's lady-in-waiting Lady Bland to turn royalist: Rekitt, *Charles the First and Hull*, p. 75; T. Gent, *Gent's History of Hull: reprinted in facsimile of the original of 1735* (Hull, 1869), p. 151; J. Tickell, *History of the Town and County of Kingston-upon-Hull* (Hull, 1798), p. 454.

[193] Thomas Stockdale was a witness for the prosecution.

could get no powder; so forced to
quit Tadcaster
Seen the letter where the House of Parliament should take money
sent from Lords for force and powder
refused to send powder nor suffer
the Lord Fairfax to raise forces
but imprisoned Bethell
Desired forces and denied forces to
Tadcaster and Selby
[*MS damaged*] business countermanded
[*MS damaged*] told him he hoped to
[*MS damaged*] be in the ?___? of 10000 li
[*MS damaged*] sums of money
[*MS damaged*] he swears too
[*MS damaged*] to furnish powder

28 June 1643 my son came home
[*MS damaged*] got him out of hands of those
Anabaptists: he would keep
the Parliament would do no wrong
The Parliament
Robert Stockdale[194] came to give him
an account that he had given an account
a great many
showed a letter from the Lord Fairfax
you may as easily bring poules,
Sikes & he to send
None sent till written and received an answer
that if he or any man else did without
acquainting him
the walls ruined, he could do it
at any times
16 June 42

[*page break*]

Sir, 42 June 16
shall not I be strong when I have
a bank for you
observed he was attended with

[194]Not to be confused with Thomas Stockdale, Robert Stockdale was secretary to Sir John Hotham in Hull. See HHC: C BRS/7/74, C BRS/7/79, C BRS/7/81; Hopper, 'A directory of parliamentarian allegiance in Yorkshire', p. 91.

a guard of red coats
common fame that they intended
to betray the town
any mutinies in the town
deferred public faith but put
?time no fill?
monies found not know

Sikes[195]
before whom, intimate with Sir
John Hotham, send the powder
Found him in rage calling him
an Anabaptis[t]; send the powder to Wressle
castle means might have
use 'twas ridiculous
I will require justice from Cromwell
and the rascals the close committee
fetch him if they would have him
Pelham with ships to Hull
Sir John advised to lend no more
He would go on
Strange carriage made jealousy
ship arms for Boston;
that Mr Sikes should sent arms; to Boston
a letter to the Lord Fairfax
Captain Harrison
General of the north; that they are
rascals and I hope to see my son
revenged of them

Levitt
About Howden business
Sent and given order to fight with them
Let the fault lie where it is presence
of his lady
[*MS damaged for 4 lines*]

[*page break*]

When Mr John Hotham imprisoned
passionate
Not knowing how it came; letter from

[195]William Sykes was a merchant of Leeds and Hull who did much to supply the northern parliamentarians with arms: Hopper, 'A directory of parliamentarian allegiance in Yorkshire', p. 113.

Digby; ?attending? Du Mouline
He let fall expressions of turning out
Ministers
His faithful friend offered him
money; refused
when he read he commended, least of proffers
Charta blank;
speak bitterly against the Parliament let
fall words of security to himself
The collection from all these some actu-
all design upon the town
Met Mr Nye imputed fears to Captain
Moyer; contrived the business, Mr Saltma-
rsh should seem to go his way
dispatched them; he would right him
acquaint the
concerning Lady Bland's supping

Mr Nye
That about April, consulted with
Bow secured, declared that Sir John
Hotham held correspondence
Been with the Queen
Sir Mat and your deponent resolved to
send for their families
Mr Saltmarsh what Sir John Hotham
said you shall have send for their
families and return to Hull
Believed a treaty: He can justify it
I could not have kept my Lord
Advantage of a treaty,
extremity of sickness a letter, from
the Queen; called for it out of their
hands; rewards promised
his coming to London; to help about Hull
Moyer removed; pinnaces provided
Came to him & in passion [*MS damaged*]
From the House would ser [*MS damaged*]
[*MS damaged 2 lines*]

[*page break*]

Barrett's coming }
Watson's letter } Jermyn's letter

Pink[196] from Nye and Saltmarshe
Lawson[197] went to Sir John Hotham
Sir John had said to him
concerning traitor to King and Parliament
concerning going aboard of her
concerning his barks
Lawson said he could and gave Moyer
In writing
Ordinance to be carried to the blockhouses
Writ to Mr Ripley, written unto
?withchcotes? Goods
concerning Digby
Capt Staring a man of good quality
knew Digby
concerning the Pink; and sending money
Capt
Appeared against the Commission of [*MS damaged*]
Newcastle prevailed [*MS damaged*]
?Q valation? towards the Lord [*MS damaged*]
Jealous that he was not rig [*MS damaged*]
communicated with Sir Mat [*MS damaged*]
Nye
The Queen landed, while he [*MS damaged*]
False
Entreat to raise forces; he did [*MS damaged*]
stand these
Sir Marmaduke Langdale's increase
pass to raise forces
after the Queen's landing showed him letters
of exchange of prisoners son not
told him they might be of dangerous
consequence, beware of subtlety
showed him one letter, many expressions
full of compliance that he intended
left him to his own way, acquainted Sir
Mathew Boynton

[196] A small sailing vessel, usually having a narrow stern, or a boat with a flat bottom and bulging sides, used for coasting and fishing: *OED*, XI, p. 869.

[197] The sea captain John Lawson later claimed that he had played a part in discovering and preventing Sir John Hotham's intended treachery against Hull: J. Binns, 'Sir John Lawson (*c.*1615–1665)', *ODNB*; *idem*, 'Sir John Lawson: Scarborough's Admiral of the Red', *Northern History*, 32 (1996), pp. 90–110.

A discourse about Pompey; that he was meant by Pompey[198]
The Lady Bland came to Hull
[*Last line damaged*]

HHC: Hotham MS, U DDHO/1/44: Memorandum of documents of Durand Hotham, London, undated, 1644

An abstract of my father's accusation
A list of the Protestant officers
My father's desires to the House
Desires to the Committee at Hull
A bill for regulating apparel
A survey of Bainton Beacon
What law courts are in Yorkshire
Mr Milner's nota for my cousin Gee's goods
Sir Robert Cotton[199] concerning the power of the Commons
A letter from the council
A copy of a warrant
Receipt for ink
Receipt to take out copies
Receipt for the new ?wall?

HHC: Hotham MS, U DDHO/1/45: Petition of Sir John Hotham to the House of Lords for a reprieve, London, undated but December 1644

The humble petition of Sir John Hotham, knight and baronet.
Showeth,
That your petitioner being exceedingly sensible that he lies under your just displeasure, besides many other grievous burdens which have discomposed his mind from that just temper in which he is desirous to depart this life. And seeing that his son's trial is not yet perfected, the doubtful issue of which hath much hindered the settlement of all his affairs, and driven him into great anxiety of mind, whereby your honourable favour of his ten days last reprieve was rendered in

[198] See Bodl. MS Nalson II, no. 131: John Hotham to William Cavendish, earl of Newcastle, Cawood, 9 January 1643.

[199] Cotton was a prominent antiquary and MP who had written a treatise on the powers of parliament in the 1620s that was published in 1640: BL, TT E160(32), *A briefe discourse, concerning the power of the Peeres, and Commons of Parliament, in point of judicature. Written by a learned antiquerie, at the request of a peere, of this realme* (London, 1640); S. Handley, 'Sir Robert Bruce Cotton, first baronet (1571–1631)', *ODNB*.

some measure less fruitful to him. He humbly therefore prays that this honourable House would grant him such further time as in their wisdoms shall seem expedient.

And your petitioner shall pray etc.,
John Hotham.

Henry Elsynge, clerk of the House of Commons.

HHC: Hotham MS, U DDHO/1/63: Pass for Durand Hotham to leave for York, Westminster, 16 January 1645

These are to will and require you to permit the bearer hereof, Mr Durant Hotham and his servant Arthur Stringer,[200] with the horses on which they ride quietly to pass from London unto York without any your lets (they not carrying any letters nor doing any other thing prejudicial to the state) for which this shall be your warrant.

William Lenthall, Speaker.
To all courts of guard, officers and others whom it concerns.

HHC: Hotham MS, U DDHO/1/46: Order of both Houses removing the sequestration from Sir John Hotham's estate, Westminster, 12 May 1645

It is ordained and declared by the Lords and Commons in Parliament assembled that the estate, as well real as personal, of Sir John Hotham, knight, deceased, is hereby taken off, and discharged from sequestration, from the day of the date hereof. And all committees and other officers are required to take notice hereof. And to suffer the Lady Sarah Hotham, late wife of the said Sir John Hotham, and the children of them, and either of them, quietly and peaceably to receive and enjoy all the profits of the said Sir John Hotham's estate respectively, in every county and place within this kingdom, where any sequestration hath been made. And that the full possession thereof is hereby restored to the said Lady Hotham, and the said children, to be enjoyed by her and them as aforesaid, in as full and ample manner as at any time formerly hath been by the said Sir John Hotham, or should, or of right ought to have been, in case no sequestration

[200]Cornet Arthur Stringer was in Captain Robert Legard's troop that brought Sir John Hotham back to Hull on 29 June 1643. When the troop returned to Beverley, Stringer was arrested, imprisoned, and later interrogated. See HHC: C BRS/7/79; Tindall Wildridge, *The Hull Letters*, pp. 154, 158.

had been of the said estate. And former orders or ordinances to the contrary in any wise notwithstanding,

John Browne, clerk of the House of Lords.
Henry Elsynge, clerk of the House of Commons.

[*On reverse*] The ordinance for taking off the sequestration from the whole estate.

HHC: Hotham MS, U DDHO/1/64: Copy of a letter from Durand Hotham to William Fiennes, Viscount Saye and Sele, Scorborough, 31 May 1645

Letter from Durand Hotham esq., to the Lord Viscount Saye and Sele. Copied verbatim from the original in his own handwriting, by me, John Hotham.
My lord,
May it please your lordship to pardon my boldness in this way of address, the days of mourning for my father and brother being not yet expired, that I could myself wait upon your honour, with my humble suit, and the tender of that service which I shall always acknowledge I owe to your lordship, for the purchase of my liberty, and your many other noble favours and countenance. I understood lately by letters from London that your lordship has been pleased to grant the wardship of a son of my father's by the Lady Norcliffe,[201] (my brother Francis Hotham) to Sir Thomas Norcliffe, and his brother. I shall lay the true state of the business before your lordship, and submit it to your honourable justice. Sir John Bambrough had 3 sisters and no issue. One of these sisters was married to Sir Thomas Norcliffe, father to this Sir Thomas. He dying, left his widow the Lady Norcliffe, whom my father married. Sir John Bambrough dying without issue, his estate fell to his 3 sisters, of whom my Lady Norcliffe whom my father had married being one, she conveys her interest by a good conveyance in law to my father, and herself, for their lives, after their decease, to my father's issue by her, which is Francis Hotham, an infant under age, and for default of such issue to her right heirs, which are Sir Thomas Norcliffe and his brothers. After the Lady Norcliffe was dead, some of Sir Thomas Norcliffe's friends endeavoured to possess Sir Thomas of this very estate, as heir to his mother, notwithstanding the deed to my father and their joint issue, and an office was found as after the decease

[201] Katherine Norcliffe (d. 1634) was the fourth wife of Sir John Hotham. Her son from a previous marriage, Sir Thomas Norcliffe, had been a colonel under the Fairfaxes and claimed the wardship of Sir John Hotham's sixth son, Francis Hotham (d. 1653): J. Foster (ed.), *Pedigrees of the County Families of Yorkshire*, 3 vols (London, 1874), III, unpaginated; Hopper, 'A directory of parliamentarian allegiance in Yorkshire', p. 100.

of the Lady Norcliffe, wherein notwithstanding their endeavours that deed was allowed. Now when my father died (though the burden was wholly against my mind), he commanded me to endeavour to protect the child's estate from the Norcliffes, and by a deed declarative of his mind, willed me to take care of him and his estate till he came at age, as not conceiving him to be ward, the child being not heir but coming in by purchase. And truly I was made believe so too by my counsel, and therefore abstained from troubling your honour about it, an office having been already found and as I esteemed the whole duties to the crown discharged. By this I have informed you, your lordship may perceive that Sir Thomas Norcliffe beside that he claims a right to the estate as his own, is the next heir to whom if Frank die it must descend, and so not usually capable of that trust. My lord, I do not in this information any way seek my own benefit, but the security of the child's estate, and whether your lordship be pleased to dispose him according to his father's desire, or as shall seem otherwise meet to your lordship's wisdom. The profits will not be much, there having not £40 in 3 year last past been gotten out of the estate. Hitherto since my father died I have maintained the child, taken of the sequestration and bore the whole charge of it, and as yet received not from it £25. My lord I shall not be further troublesome to your lordship, but remain your lordship's freeman and most humble servant,

Durand Hotham.

HHC: Hotham MS, U DDHO/1/80: Report of the Committee of Yorkshire to parliament concerning the sequestered estates of the late Sir John Hotham, 1645

Sir John Hotham in December last made several deeds of some parts of his estate not formerly settled, by one of which he conveys a mansion house and some lands in Fyling to the use of himself and of his lady for their lives, the remainder to other uses, and by five other deeds he settles the immediate inheritance of some other lands upon his daughters and younger sons respectively, and by another deed assigns over his term for years which he had in the rectory of Beswick unto his son, Charles Hotham.

The Committee of Yorkshire certify these deeds and make doubt in respect the same were made after Sir John's delinquency, sequestration and imprisonment, whether they may give allowance to the same.

There have been also two other deeds produced and proved, *videlicet*: one dated 9 April 1639 whereby Sir John Hotham makes a former grant of the rectory of Beswick to his son, Charles Hotham, and the other dated 13 December 1644, by which Sir John Hotham settles the reversion of the manor of Fyling dale and some other lands there upon his son Durand Hotham and his heirs.

Upon the whole matter as to these lands thus conveyed and settled after the sequestration, Sir John Hotham being afterward adjudged and executed by martial law, which judgment as to corruption of blood or forfeiture (is alleged) not to work or disable as attainders at Common Law do. The Lady Hotham and younger children become petitioners to the Committee of Lords and Commons for Sequestrations to obtain discharge of the said sequestration. Wherein for clearing all scruples the said Committee have thought fit that the case should be presented to the consideration of the two Houses for their resolution therein, expressing their own sense to be that the lady and children should have justice with favour.

[*On reverse*] Report ?Bardshaw?

HHC: Hotham MS, U DDHO/1/78: Order of the Committee of Yorkshire discharging Durand Hotham's estate at Fyling from sequestration, 6 March 1645

By the standing committee for the county of York.
Upon perusal and proof of an indenture, dated 9 April [*MS damaged*] whereby Sir John Hotham conveys the [*MS damaged*] of John Stevenson [*MS damaged*] close in the occupation [*MS damaged*] the farm in the [*MS damaged*] and one close [*MS damaged*] occupation of John Wilkes late Marshalls [*MS damaged*] one farm in the occupation of John Gilleson and one farm in the occupation of James Browne, all situated and being in Fyling, to the use of himself for life and after to the use of his son, Durand Hotham, and his heirs as thereby appears. Which premises are now under sequestration for the delinquency of Sir John Hotham. And by virtue of an order from the right honourable the Committee of Lords and Commons for Sequestrations to this committee directed and dated 2 February last. This committee declares that the said conveyed premises ought to be and are hereby discharged of any further sequestration for the delinquency of the said Sir John Hotham.

Nicholas Forlush, clerk.

HHC: Hotham MS, U DDHO/1/84: Anonymous report on the arrears of pay of Hull garrison, *c.*1647

Sir,
By the report to have been made above three months since by Sir Henry Vane senior[202] or Colonel White.

[202] The elder Vane, father of the MP for Hull, served on the Committee of Both Kingdoms: R.M. Smuts, 'Sir Henry Vane (1589–1655)', *ODNB*.

The officers of the garrison of Hull are 30 weeks in arrears and the private soldiers 19 since the 12 August 1645 that the order for an establishment was. Since which time there is contrary to the intent of the ordinance of the 16 February 1644, £2,047-10s drawn from the garrison by the commissioners of the Customs.
That since January 1646 to the 19 February 1647 the Customs are in arrears £5,223-17s-5d as by the said report doth appear for that lead and cloth vends not from thence as formerly.
That the pay of the officers in pursuance of the former establishment is according to the late votes (except some very few) and that the late ordinance for pay is determined above two months since.
That the new establishment is to be agreed on by the Committee at Derby House, which in regard of so many weighty affairs may be long before it pass both Houses, and in the meantime the soldiers have nothing to subsist on.
The deputy governor[203] hath for four months past been constrained to borrow monies upon his own engagement from several hands, and of late one week's pay in the Excise Office in an unusual way, all which amounteth to £1,254-12s (to keep the soldiers alive and from mutinous insolencies), as by the particulars enclosed in a letter to the honourable the Speaker it doth appear.
That the soldiers have of late had no credit in their quarters (as in other garrisons whereby their necessities cry aloud, they having nothing but their penny to live on and all manner of victual extreme dear.
It is humbly desired that the Houses will be pleased to order the *paym[en]t* of the two forementioned sums amounting to £7[*MS damaged*]-7s-5d, being but only part of the garrison's late arrears, for which the said governor is so deeply engaged as abovesaid, and for their former quarters, so that most part thereof will go to several persons that are impatient for the same.
The garrison also is in great want of pikes and bandoliers.
[*Several numbers noted in margin*]

[*page break*]

[203]Lieutenant-Colonel John Mauleverer commanded a regiment in Hull from 1644 and, when Sir Thomas Fairfax was appointed governor in 1645, he substituted Mauleverer, well approved by the Hull corporation, to serve in his place. Mauleverer was replaced as deputy governor by Robert Overton in late 1647: A. Hopper, 'John Mauleverer (*c.*1610–1650)', *ODNB*; D. Scott, '"Particular businesses in the Long Parliament": the Hull letters, 1644–1648', in C.R. Kyle (ed.), *Parliament, Politics and Elections 1604–1648*, Camden Society, fifth series, 17 (Cambridge, 2001), pp. 282, 292–293, 339.

[*In a different, poor hand*]

for a pair of silk stockings	1-2-0
for 2 pair of buckskin gloves	0-9-0
for 2 pair of ?bidskin? gloves	0-3-0
for a pair of bukcum tops	0-5-0
for a pair of slippers	0-2-6
for bringing things fr*o*m Cambridge	0-1-8
Sum total:	2-3-2
for Mr John's diet	1-0-0
for ?purlar? and bullets	0-1-6
for a letter	0-0-6
for a letter	0-0-2
for ?holon? for Mistress Gee	8-18-6
for silver ribbon	0-2-8
for gloves for Mistress Gee	0-7- :
for ?tamma?	0-12-9
for lace	0-6-3
for 2 books	0-1- :
for making 2 handkerchiefs	0-2- :

HHC: Hotham MS, U DDHO/1/58: Draft response by Durand Hotham[204] to twenty religious queries of 'Georg' (probably George Fox),[205] no date but probably *c.*1651

Georg,

According to my engagement I have sent my present thoughts of these queries you sent (though truly with much reluctancy being very loath to enter a contest with any sort of men that pretend religion, <and> a command and notion above the reach of man's material frame to comprehend. And therefore would have what I here write, accepted with love as a declaration how these queries or rather affirmations of yours appear to me that stand below and examine them with the weights and lay them in the balance of a man. And give my poor opinion how they may suit either with the foregoing relations of God's appearances hitherto recorded in Scriptures; or have concordance with the natural rules of a just creature in fellowship. And if there by any fault in thus doing, be it upon you that desired it, myself being

[204]Durand was probably the justice of the peace whom George Fox met in late 1651 (and whom Fox described as 'a well wisher' to the Quakers) when he was travelling in Yorkshire.

[205]H.L. Ingle, 'George Fox (1624–1691)', *ODNB*.

very tender of standing in the way or interrupting [the] proceedings of any manifestation that assumes upon itself to reform the world by immediate designment from the great God. Though I be not satisfied it is such or should it prove from some other spirit, good, or bad, I should be slow to give provocation till it manifestly endeavoured to make itself master of that which being a creature I have assured right unto, and of which never any person or nation was divested unless he or they had by evident transgression of the plain law of natural communion, degenerated from walking justly in their kind, as is throughout evident in the story of the children of Israel's title to the land of Canaan and God's justification of Himself in his proceedings to the reason and comprehension of man. In all the stories of his converse with him extant among us, I shall confine myself to those queries I had from you, being far more warily drawn than those I received from others to which I have hitherto not answered anything nor intend it.

The general aim of the person querying is to entitle the deiform man or as he is in the paper styled, one grown to be head with the almighty power to be the person that hath the sole right, to give laws and decisions to others concerning their mutual converse, properties and personal disputes, and designments of what is offence with the limitation of the punishment of it, and that the person thus perfected hath a right to pass through all the nations of the earth wherever God's creature of mankind is and gather persons into his su [*MS damaged*] tion. And that those who do own him are thereby exempt from the tie of any law made by their consent and contract, or that is imposed upon them by any prince. And that neither national councils, nor any King hath original power of making laws and annexing punishment to crimes, but that every crime must take its weight and name from him. And that laws made by men are those spoken against in Scripture as inventions. Further that the people thus gathered are really Israel, obliged to the covenants Israel made: though no such demonstration of a presence of God with the creature be given.
This is no new question

[*page break*]

This is no new question, but that which is the foundation of the Papacy, who, as the vicar of Christ and great father, hath ever since the destruction of the Eastern Empire claimed that very power over all Europe, and exercised it over every prince and nation when he hath not by strong hand been debarred, deposing their kings, absolving natural born subjects from obedience, giving their kingdoms to neighbour princes, and controlling all laws made in diminution of his power and exempting (the clergy especially) and all the people from any civil obedience to them. And if we grant there is such a power as this in any, we may perhaps unwarily lay ourselves open to manifold concussions by the multitude of pretenders to the exaltation of soul, and when God hath visibly left enacting and inspiring some man or men as he hath done the Jew, and it may be a great part of that called the Christian world, yet people having once submitted themselves and laid by their reason to be directed in this authoritative way, yet will, hath, and is the disposition of their estates, power of life, and lawmaking claimed by the pretended successors, or imitators of former appearances, and the noble reason kept in perpetual infancy under these several usurpers of the throne of God. This, as to the inconvenience of such a submission, I proceed to the question where the right of such a person is asserted.

The first whether the seed of God was ever to bow down to any law but that from God only. The answer to this will I believe to a rational spirit give satisfaction to the remainder. First it would be known what seed of God you mean, for that the whole natural man is a creature or issue from God is plain, and to that I answer that no man as a natural man is <other> the coordinate state <and> hath <nott> *any* right by a law or power to subject any person to his will or power law.

In the subordinate state which is among parents and children till the age of ripeness of management, there is a natural right of the parent to give law to his wife and children in the circuit and proper affairs of the family.

In the co-ordinate estate of several families, covenants and submissions to rule and to be ruled are both as to the matter and manner the true and only lawful foundation of the lawmaking power governing every family, under such rules as are convenient for the whole body entered into covenant.

If by the seed of God be meant the man that is brought into the good principle, to do good for the love of it, I answer that he hath not thereby any more right to the creatures or the disposition of them than before, nor any more or further power over those that are not such, nor can thereby plead any exemption of obedience to the former covenants to the government under which he was born, or family wherein he was educated, but must submit his natural man in all its comprehensions thereunto. And in things that do not concern direct precise, and certainly assigned worship of God by his own special command (it lying not in the sphere of the best of natural *men* to limit, appoint or order it), his diligence and active obedience is required in the best of truth and uprightness.

If by the seed of God be meant Christ; himself saith my kingdom is not of this world, if it were my servants would fight for me, and could I not pray my father and He would

[*page break*]

He would give me legions of angels. And who made me a divider or judge over you, both which powers I am suspicious you claim. I would have you remember it was a temptation to Christ in which he was conqueror, he showed Him the kingdoms of the world and the glory of them and said all these will I give thee. Take heed you be not fallen into temptation. For the same you claim under pretence of being the seed of God. Further the Scripture saith he took upon him the form of a servant, and in that form we see him actively obedient to the law, and the Jews and Pilate's fault was not that they slew him, but that they did it without his fault and ground of law, he not claiming the kingdom or setting himself up, nor suffering the people to make him king. For it seems to me that when communities have made laws, either in affirmation of that righteousness that is connatural to the frame of man, or for the present interest and well being of a nation, the magistrate to whom they have committed the execution of them will be justified therein against all pretences of exemption whatever. As for example, if a parent will slay his own child in the zeal of whatever specious pretext. Or upon the second ground, it having been made felony of death to cut powdike,[206] if any man upon an opinion of a command from God or as reasoning with himself that God sets bounds to the sea and rivers, and man ought not to straighten or limit them, it being a human invention, <and> shall upon these motives cut the same. In either of these two cases the magistrate's infliction of the law appears to me to be just. For certainly if men will leave clear, natural, improved reason for *a* guide in acting in communion with their fellow creatures, and submit themselves and the government of their affairs to persons giving forth themselves to have familiarity with and commands from a spirit (without uncontrollable evidence that the same is by designation from the great God our creator), the world will never be rid of fanatic impostors nor mankind ever brought up higher than credence. And truly it is evident throughout all ages that particular spirits have assumed upon themselves the title of the supreme God and usurped his worship. What do yourselves think of those multitude of Gods in the Indies and that spirit that appeared to Mahomet and dictated his law?

As for Moses, from whom you assume this imitation of lawmaking, and seizing into your hands the civil and the spiritual power I shall I think make your pretence therein appear so weak as that upon that account you will no more assume it. He was sent to a people freeborn, that being called into a nation as friend and their placed, and by the laws of hospitality ought to have had free egress, besides that very nation obliged to the ancestors of this people for

[*page break*]

[206] An ancient dyke or embankment raised up to hold back fen water: *OED*, XII, p. 259.

for their very being, which notwithstanding they were by a tyrant that had no natural right over them kept in vassalage as people taken captive in war and were *not* permitted to the laws and freedoms of natives. To this people and king Moses was sent, yet would not go, though their brother till entrusted with such miracles as were never since done in the world, and such as those spirits that had rule in Egypt and were consulted withal by his priest could neither imitate nor resist. So that Moses brought not forth this people by his prudence nor did their own strength vindicate them from this vassalage, but God appeared, visibly overthrew their enemies with his own hand without any assistance from them. And therefore when he derives his title to govern them, he insists upon his purchase, and their voluntary submission by covenant. Nor was there any plague or punishment of the people (though they murmured, disobeyed and provoked him before), till they had entered that covenant, and the law did not claim any power over them either as from God or just or good but as accepted.

Moses proposeth a condition they accept thereof, and the Lord came down in the sight of all the people. This Lord spoke the law by an outward voice, and the people answered all that the Lord has said we will do, and Moses was called to have the law written in two tables of stone. Now when such a visible appearance as this comes forth, redeems, protecteth, apparently and to the outward eye of man comes forth to any nation that are free to covenant, and they accept that condition proposed, they ought to bow down to no law made by man because of their covenant and voluntary submission, and *a* people thus espoused may in a sense be termed the seed of God.

But the seed of God properly so called is only Christ who was begotten by God on a woman, yet was he subject to his reputative father and true mother most what till toward 30 years of age, and when he disobeyed he gave this reason: that his true father who really begot him commanded him. Otherwise his doctrine had been no better than the Pharisees teaching su*b*straction of obedience and relief to parents under the specious pretext of consecrating their estates to corban,[207] which I suppose was for to repair the temple.

Now that reason why the sober spirited man is so extreme nice and wary in the admission of these powers pretended from the God that made man are many and very weighty, but I shall keep close to the questions.

[207]The treasury of the temple of Jerusalem where monetary offerings were placed: *OED*, III, p. 923.

To the 2nd I answer that it is so clearly contradicted in Scripture that it need little to be said to it. The Pharisees sit in Moses chair, whatever they say unto you that do, and from Moses to Christ all were but successors in the ministration, and still had recourse to the letter of the law and present high priest though he bought his office of the Roman deputy.

To the 3rd the term of waiting upon God only is a fine word but when men make themselves gods, equally, one and the same I see no warrant of Scripture or reason so to unman mankind as to subject them to the dictates of any person; but much exhortation to teach him to subdue his lusts, and improve his noblest faculties. And if towards this improvement anything be offered or revealed by a spirit or man I doubt not but the willing man will give it a fair hearing, but it hath no

[*page break*]

authority over him, either that *it* is revealed in that fashion or by those persons, but as in the self convincingly good to the just ordering of a community, and is so accepted by that community. And certainly all the assumptions of authority or dominion which either the Popish, Protestant clergy or pretenders to new light under pretence of designation from God will prove groundless, without they being that evidence God ever gave when He [*seven words deleted*] Himself appointed the ruler and the law. And as before I said God insists in his title to rule Israel most what upon their Covenant and not upon his general right of creation, which Covenant had not been of force to subject him according to the tenor of it had he not had a right to Covenant.

Of the fourth, it is *hard* to me to make common sense of it, for if it be answered that what laws have not come from God have been contrived by wise Heathen, it makes the laws no whit the worse. As for the name Heathen, it is used in contempt by proud Jew, for which the Prophets and especially our Saviour gives them solid reproof, laying low this their high contempt, seclusion of God's general love to and providence over the whole creation. 'Tis true neither the civil laws nor worship of the Heathen was to be assumed by the Jew because he had covenanted to obey another; as a woman before marriage is equal for every man, but when contracted to one she is under veil, and though there be thousands as good yet she is affianced to live under his law she hath chosen, and her desires to and obedience to another are whorish, be that man to whom she inclines it may be better. And this is the aim throughout Scripture of the notion of Heathen and is very seldom extended further than the nations mixed with them and confiners upon them who were the worst and most foolish of the Heathen, and is neither a condemnation of all the laws of the world as positively bad, but not fit for them to use, that had subjected themselves to another, nor are invective against their persons. Though I confess the nations about Judea were the worst and most foolish of the Heathen. Indeed the proud, haughty Jew did contemn all the world besides himself upon this very notion of the perfection of his law and the manner of receiving of it. Which if good histories may be believed was not proper to their law only. And it is such an outrageous folly to believe that the great God hath but one sort of appearance to his creatures, and limits his whole work in the world to the narrow plot of ground in Judea. Elijah believed nobody worshipped God but himself, and it hath been the fault of many saints to have narrow conceits of God and confine him to themselves. And their words in Scripture are recorded to this effect, being very rash in condemning and judging the whole creation unto perdition unless they submit <to frame> themselves to that apish garb they have framed to be the sole mode of righteous walking and the worsh [*MS damaged*] said one casting our libels and we forbad him because he follo [*MS damaged*]. But ere to be remembered is the wisdom of our Saviour in the Parable of the Samaritan and Publican, and his first sermon in the synagogue that gave so much offence about God's hiding his prophets in heathen countries and not trusting them in Israel.

In that word (to that in the conscience) lies much of the design and I wonder much you use it being both the word and notion is wholly borrowed from the Heathen, Greek and Latin philosophers, and never used by the pen men of Scripture till after our

[*page break*]

our Saviour's time when St Paul and others borrowed it out of the Heathen school as many other notions which Moses and the whole Hebrew philosophy express in far different manner. And truly having with a narrow eye observed your dealings since you came forth, I have found that (in the conscience) to be like a finger watch or clock which seems to tell what time of the day it is by the springs and motions within, but really asks what of the clock it is by you, and moves with your finger to that point. For they, and that you call the light within them, hath as perfect direction from your outward word as though they were only cast of men and had no soul nor motion of their own, and things practised by them as from the light within when by you condemned left of and cried out against <all>. Now for that other expression of laws made in the will of man, I answer as before that whatever man makes laws for others, they seem in their own nature (as so made) not to have any compulsion upon the major part of a community that have not submitted themselves to them. Otherwise if you mean laws made by the will of man, those that are made by the deliberate advice of a community, they are the ordinance of God and cannot be said in an ill sense to be made in the will of man because every man there lays by his own will and interest, and contrives and submits to a rule for the good of the whole body. And certainly he that will not bow down and submit his will to laws thus made sets himself up not only to be his own God, but other men's, and worship himself and his own peculiarity with the destruction of the whole, <and though the pretence be that he will yield to death or [*word illegible from deletion*]> I have read some history and therein have seen ambitious spirit stalking under this tenderness and dissatisfaction of spirit, till by sufferance and feigned humility they had drawn in a party strong enough to set up and maintain their own private conceptions.

The fifth I answer as in the foregoing that they were not obliged to any form of worship or law otherwise than by their Covenant and stipulation with God, and acceptance of the law when proposed. And Moses his either seeing God or talking with him face to face did neither entitle him to any jurisdiction over the people or right of lawmaking, nor oblige them to any obedience to his words, till they had desired it of God that he might speak to them and not God himself. As for the bowing down of Israel to any other law, I affirm they were not so to do, (but as to the Gentiles, it is said in some of the Epistles, submit to every ordinance of man for the Lord's sake) in things wherein their law had provided remedy, but in other affairs their Sanhedrin had power and did make ordinances and those were to be obeyed, and in cases difficult in the law the high priest was to be submitted unto.

And for what you say that Moses was a judge to the corrupt will, it seems to [*MS damaged*] for it was the law that was judge, but for the law I had not known [*MS damaged*]. And that law, and all laws made by a community to the universal interest of the whole are judges to the corrupt will, that is to that wilful man that being a member of a community would live to his own peculiar wisdom or will, and exempt himself from obedience to the just provisions of the body whereof he is a member upon any specious pretext whatever.

As for Israel's respecting of persons, if by that be meant civil reverence, that they both did it and were not prohibited to do it is clear. The reverence of those parts of the East seems to have been laying their hands on their breasts and saying Shalom Lae

[*page break*]

Shalom Lae, that is peace be to you, to which our Saviour alludes in sending out his Apostles saying into whatever house you enter say peace be to that house. Another Evangelist says salute it, that is the men in it, which was the civil ceremony of the time, which he commands them to continue. And truly this irreverence that is practised by most of you was I believe very unworthy taken up and without any just ground from Scripture, example or reason, but to defend it as the garb in which all saints must be, is a notion (in my poor apprehension[)] fetched from the <school of of> cave of supercilious melancholy, and far from being taught in the School of Love. And now having once taken it, it is in stiffness and infallibility endeavoured to be maintained. But far more from reason is it to decry this civil entertainment of each other as the worshipping of the creature. Did Abraham worship the Canaanites when he bowed to them or Jacob Pharaoh? Truly, truly this contriving yourselves into distinction of garbs and frames of words will I fear devour all other parts of your religion. And he that makes himself exact in these will be the man in the light. And the sweet virtues of a Christian conversation will be laid low in respect of this assumed dress and livery you have given your followers. Verily had not on the one side the civil magistrate kept you in, and the eyes and tongues of all people requiring of you a more just and upright life than other men if you would assume to be more religious which you call the light within, did and had further led your followers into vile and unseemly exorbitances.

To the sixth I answer that the natural seed of Abraham is the same and under the same law as formerly, but not the Gentile by any evident reason or Scripture. The Pharisees were of that opinion and taught the Gentiles that they ought to be circumcised and keep the law. But the first council of the Apostles determined otherwise, and declared that it was a burden which neither they nor their forefathers were able to bear, and through the whole second ministration is not the least footsteps of your doctrine in this particular. And truly I do believe that I can make it manifest that the law of Moses is in many parts of it suited to the nature of that people, the place and age wherein they lived, and that it was the law of God to that people, but to us is not the law of God.

As for that expression of yours (according to that in the conscience), there lies hid much in it, for I find that the Mahometan makes much use of that notion, and gives forth that all nations are born with and have inbred in them a disposition to Islam (that [*MS damaged*] doctrine of Mahomet and that they have by nature a seed [*MS damaged*] that would teach it), but being born in several countries and under several disciplines, they are perverted from it. And verily such is the apish nature of man, especially such as live much in the imagination, that let a man of reverence give forth what he will and tell them that there is something within them says the same, they shall certainly believe it doth, as when we were children and the bells rung, place what words we would in our fancy and the bells sounded the same

[*page break*]

the same. As it likewise frequently happeneth to those that study physic and read the symptoms of diseases, they believe presently that they have them all and if the credulous fancy be not checked by reason, their strong imagination shall work the fluid humour to the distemper which as then had no root in his body, especially if they be driven from the cheerful company of men, and converse of their fellow creatures into the dark cave of silence and melancholy.

The seventh is answered in the first to the law if one man he is not by original right to submit except he being free hath so covenanted to do, the King of Israel that broke his covenant to a heathen prince is reproved. But to the law of a communi [*sic*] he is to submit in thing enacted for the ordering of civil communion. The heaven is the Lord's, the earth hath he given to the children of men. For everything lives beautiful in the perfection of its own sphere, and in the limits of its principle. And surely the name of Providence and divine designation hath in times past been the refuge for the usurpations of ambitious men, who by outward flatterers or by the pride of their own spirits have been induced to take upon the right of lawgiving to their fellow creatures.

The eight is before answered for either every man's conscience is the same, which it is evident it is not, and yourselves have often found, for that heathen word of conscience is in the old Scripture called fear, which God hath put in men's heart. The fear of God is the beginning of wisdom. And put them in fear O Lord that they may know themselves to be but men. And it is said among the wise that fear first taught the knowledge of God. Now this fear according to the laws and teaching wherein a man is educated, is pressing upon him to performance according to the terror that the law sets forth, will follow his disobedience in and under which fear each nation that is not grown whorish in their religion do live and will die or suffer, under its impression of a duty. But that fear as it seems to me is not the light, nor was ever given forth to be so by the old or new penmen of Scripture, or our Saviour. For He to the man that would know how to get eternal life, directs to an outward law, keep the commandments.

As for that you term man's lawmaking, man's inventions and his will, and [*MS damaged*] Pharaoh taskmaster, I agree that there are such men as make [*MS damaged*] that way and are tyrants. But as I said before the laws of a community are not such, for lawmaking is but the affirmation of right reason to persons, times, and places with penalties annexed. And though it may be that there have been communities gathered together for lawmaking that have made laws of private designment, either for support of some person's greatness or some sinister end, yet is not the right of a community thereby taken away or their power of lawmaking invalidated? And I can make it clear that where any people have but come near the just aiming of their laws they have

[*page break*]

prospered beyond parallel with evident owning from the righteous God.

To the 9th, I say it is in the former answered. No man can withdraw himself from the common obedience to the just legislative power seated in a loyal authority set up by Covenant. To make contract of obedience to a foreign power without at least as evident demonstration of a divine designment from a great God <ye> as the children of Israel showed unto Pharaoh, who did unjustly detain them without any pretence of human right, nay against it, but much more ought it to be showed to those that have as good right as can be imagined by the just rules of human fellowship.

To the 10th, I answer no, for a law made as in the 9 is a law of God and endures forever, that is hath the eternity of its own sphere and is an ordinance of God. And this right of covenanting for rule and submission was never taken from any people but upon manifest miracle and their own consent. For if a man had not a right to covenant the Scriptures, urging the breach of Covenant were not a fault. I have twice before answered something concerning that frequently reiterated expression that in the conscience. Truly if man by outward means of either hearing that word or of viewing and considering the order and rule of the outward beautiful world, or by the revelation of some spirit, had not the belief there is a God that in the conscience would not teach the same, much less direct a worship. But the mystery will I am afraid come forth that the man described in the eight will be affirmed to be a god, and that he must direct the conscience which will prove a Pope armed with stronger weapons claiming power over kings, princes, laws, fatherhood and setting rules for all.

The 11 is the same with the former.

To the 12, I agree that all laws must be general [*MS damaged*] community generally and equally time, place and other ?circumstances? well considered.

To the 13, I say that right of superiority or lawmaking, right to the participation or distribution of any creature, or other civil or rational enjoyment lies not in the principle you speak on but in what I have showed before.

To the 14, I say that if they know God the more subject they will be to a righteous government, which cannot that I know of be anyways be established than choice, covenant or purchase.

[*page break*]

To the 15, I know not whether the magistrate knows the soul or not nor is it much material to the controversy. The question is of a person joined in soul and body, how he is to be governed. If souls were uncased and placed in the sphere of spirits, they do and must submit to the order God hath set up among spirits.

To the 16, truly those places of St Paul and St Peter commanding obedience to the outward heathen magistrate, and observance and reverence towards him, are so clear (that unless we will deny there is a sun and moon when we evidently see them shine), that there is no evasion from them. And are indeed so contrary to this doctrine of yours that till it be manifested with more evident miracle than was entrusted in the Apostles' hands to persuade, no sensible man that sees the plain contexture and aim of the words can assent to yours. Put them in mind to obey magistrates the 13 of the Romans throughout: 1 Tim: 2:1 and in every Epistle almost he inculcates this obedience to these outward relations, for it seems it was then by some begun to be taught that being a professed Christian, a man was loosed from the subjection to heathen laws, and must solely eye Christ his king. But the Apostle saith if any teach such doctrine, he is proud, knowing nothing. Further he saith submit yourselves to every ordinance of man for the Lord's sake, with many more such like Scriptures. As for those distorted expositions of yours, which are commonly given to those places they are no better than when St Paul forbids women to speak in the church. Some of you say it is meant only the female nature or carnal part and 'tis forsooth in favour of you female preachers. Certainly these unwary notions you put upon the Scripture are of no advantage to you, but will in time lay you low in the esteem of good men.

The 17, 18, 19 are already answered.

To the 20 I say that laws as you call them made in the will of man have lasted many 1,000 of years, but I will not compare them with that you call the law of God.

Finis.

[*On reverse*] Answer to queries.

HHC: Hotham MS, U DDHO/1/50: Petitions of Isabel Hotham on behalf of her son Henry to the House of Commons and to Oliver Cromwell, 1651

2. To the supreme authority of this nation, the Parliament of the Commonwealth of England.

The humble petition of Isabel Hotham, relict of John Hotham, esq., and Henry Hotham, an infant, his son.

Showeth that your petitioner brought her said husband £2,500 portion, and was to have provision for her and hers out of his personal estate. To which end (upon his first engagement for the Parliament), he left with your petitioner at Hull £4,000 in monies and the value of £3,000 in plate, which upon his death were all seized on for the state's use. All which the petitioner, the 12 January 1645 presenting to the House, they were pleased to order that she should have all her said husband's goods and monies undisposed of and all rents in arrear at his death, as by the annexed appears. But the same being then before disposed of, your petitioner had no benefit thereby.

In consideration whereof, may it please your honours to grant your petitioner (in lieu of the loss of her said monies, rents, goods and plate so taken as aforesaid) £7,000 out of the £14,000 which she to that end will discover out of monies, rents and arrearages of rents due to the crown before the year 1645, or else be content to lose the benefit of the said former orders. That so your petitioners may by the favour of this House be preserved (as many others have been) from utter ruin and misery. And your petitioners as in duty bound shall ever pray, etc.,

Isabel Hotham,
Henry Hotham.

1. Monday 12 January 1645.

Upon Sir Phillip Stapleton's report from the Northern Committee of the petition of Mrs Hotham and of Henry Hotham, son of John Hotham, esq., deceased, it is this day ordered upon the question by the Commons assembled in Parliament: that the arrears of rents due to Mr Hotham before his death by order of both Houses of Parliament now in the tenants' hand shall be paid to Mrs Hotham. It is this day also ordered upon the question, that such goods as were the proper goods of John Hotham and secured by order of the Lord Fairfax and are not disposed to public uses shall and may be received and taken by Mrs Hotham and her child for their own uses.

Henry Elsynge, clerk of the House of Commons.

3. Monday 25 August 1651.

Ordered by the Parliament that the petition of Isabel Hotham, relict of John Hotham, esq., and of Henry Hotham, an infant her son, be referred to the Council of State to take such order herein as they shall think fit.

Henry Scobell,[208] clerk of Parliament.

4. Thursday 18 September 1651.

At the Council of State at Whitehall.

Ordered that the Council doth declare that what shall be done by Mr Attorney, Mr Leman and Colonel Fielder by way of promise to Mrs

[208] Scobell replaced Henry Elsynge as clerk of the House of Commons in January 1649: S. Kelsey, 'Henry Scobell (bap. 1610, d. 1660)', *ODNB*.

Hotham upon her tendering of a discovery to them shall be of the same force as if it were the act of the Council, and shall be performed on their part in case she makes good what she propounds.
Gualter Frost.[209]
To his excellency, the Lord General Cromwell.
The most humble petition and address of Henry Hotham, an infant, the only son of John Hotham, esq., deceased by Isabel, his late wife also deceased.
Your excellency being a most ready reliever of the oppressed and a succour and zealous preserver of those that are in distress.
Your poor petitioner, the son of him that once did seasonable good service to the public, whose mother brought to his father a great portion and the same (with the addition intended for your petitioner's provision and livelihood), in all to the value of £7,000, seized on as his father's and employed for the supply of the soldiery and other public uses.
Most humbly beseecheth your excellency to consider his distressed sad condition and to present this his annexed petition to the Parliament for their relief to him, in such way as your excellency shall think most meet, they having already upon proof and report of his case formerly to them by their orders intended the same to him out of the arrears of the late crown, but your petitioner prevented therein by the late general votes that pardon the same.
And your excellency's charity herein will be very great, he being fatherless and motherless and having no other means of livelihood, his father's whole estate being entailed on children by a former wife, and this by contract of marriage intended for your petitioner.
And he shall pray, etc.

HHC: Hotham MS, U DDHO/1/51: Order of the Attorney General concerning Henry Hotham, 17 November 1651

5. Whereby an order of 18 September last, the Council of State did then declare that what should be done by Mr Attorney General, Mr Leamon and Colonel Feilder, or any two of them, in the case of Mrs Hotham and her son, should be of the same force as if it were the act of the Council, in pursuance of which said order, and according to the power therein given us, we do order and allow unto Henry Hotham,

[209] Frost was secretary to the Rump's Council of State: G.E. Aylmer, 'Gualter Frost (bap. 1598, d. 1652)', *ODNB*.

son of the said Mrs Hotham deceased, the moiety or half part of ten thousand pounds, which shall be by him, or others intrusted for him, discovered and brought into the Council of State. As also the moiety or half part of four thousand pounds more, which shall be forthwith discovered to the said Council. And we do hereby order and declare that the said Henry Hotham, his trustees, or assignees shall have the full benefit of this, his discovery, according to the order aforesaid, he the said Henry Hotham bringing in his first discovery of ten thousand pounds before the first day of December next, issuing the date hereof:

Witness our hands,
William Prideaux,
William Leman,
Jo: Feilder.

HHC: Hotham MS, U DDHO/1/52: Petition of William Wyvell, esq., on behalf of Henry Hotham, to the House of Commons, *c.*1651–1652

To the supreme authority of this nation the Parliament of the Commonwealth of England.

The humble petition of Henry Hotham, a poor fatherless and motherless infant, by William Wyvell, esq., his guardian.

Showeth that your petitioner's mother brought with her to his late father, John Hotham, esq., deceased, a very great portion, and in regard that all his lands were settled upon his sons by a former wife, provision was to be made for her, and hers, out of his personal estate.

That upon the apprehending of your petitioner's father at Hull, £7,000 in money, plate and jewels (that was upon his first engagement for the Parliament left with your petitioner's mother for the purpose aforesaid) was then seized upon by the then Committee and by them reported to the Parliament the 12 January 1645. Whereupon the Parliament then ordered your petitioner's mother to have forthwith delivered here all that was undisposed of for the public (they not being then in a condition presently to repay that which was disposed of).

But it was so long time before the said order was obtained and the exigency of the soldiery then so great that the same was all disposed of for provision of the soldiery, and other public uses, and no benefit at all accrued by the said order.

That your petitioner and his mother for divers years together daily attended your honours, therein desiring the moiety of £14,000 which they should discover to be owing and in arrear to the late King. And after a very great expense therein, your honours 25 August last referred their petition to the Council of State, to do therein, as they should think meet. They taking the same into consideration, ordered that your petitioner should have the moiety of the said £14,000 so to be discovered.

But now before any fruit can be made thereof, your honours have pardoned and discharged all the said debts and arrears whereout the same should issue.

Wherefore your petitioner, being thereupon left destitute of all remedy and in a miserable and perishing condition, having no other livelihood (the money so disposed of being the estate intended for provision of your poor petitioner, who is now fatherless and motherless).

He most humbly beseecheth your honours to take him into your further consideration and to appoint such other way for his relief, as in your great wisdoms shall seem most meet, so that your petitioner may by the favour of this honourable House be preserved (as many others have been) from utter ruin and misery.

And he shall be ever bound to pray for your honours.

HHC: Hotham MS, U DDHO/1/53: First petition of Henry Hotham to the Council of State, *c.*1651–1652

To the right honourable the Council of State.

The humble petition of Henry Hotham, an infant.

Showeth, that whereas your petitioner by an order of 17 November last, as by a copy thereof hereunto annexed appeareth, was to have the moiety or half part of ten thousand pounds which should be by him, or some others entrusted for him, discovered and brought to the state before the first of December last past as also the moiety of £4,000 more. And whereas your petitioner and his trustees were not able to perfect their discovery by the time limited, by reason the discoverer was absent and returned but two days before the expiration of the said order.

In consideration whereof, may it please your honours to grant to your petitioner, his trustees, or assignees, such further convenient time to bring in and perfect his said discovery as to your honours shall seem meet. That so your petitioner may by your honours' favour reap the benefit in the said former order intended to him, and may be as many others have been preserved from utter ruin and destruction.

And your petitioner shall ever pray,
Henry Hotham.

HHC: Hotham MS, U DDHO/1/65: Warrant from John Bradshaw[210] to Sir William Strickland, Luke Robinson,[211] John Anlaby,[212] and Durand Hotham, 8 December 1651

Manuscript missing

HHC: Hotham MS, U DDHO/1/54: Order of the Council of State, Whitehall, 17 December 1651

At the Council of State at Whitehall.
Ordered that a month's time more be given unto Henry Hotham to perfect his discovery which he hath to make.
Gualter Frost, secretary.

HHC: Hotham MS, U DDHO/1/55: Second petition of Henry Hotham to the Council of State, *c.*1651–1652

To the right honourable the Council of State.
The humble petition of Henry Hotham, an infant.
Humbly showeth, that by virtue of a reference from the Parliament to your honours, in his case touching his discovery of £14,000, several orders have been granted unto your petitioner and one moiety thereof allotted to the state, the other to your petitioner in recompense of his losses, and your petitioner 17 December last, was ordered by your honours to make his discovery within 6 months.
That your petitioner accordingly made discovery of several sums of money, and is ready to make more, but wants power to give discharges for such monies as shall be received, and to collect and levy the same (from those it is justly due and deny to pay it) to the prejudice of the state and your petitioner. That your petitioner's trustees have made choice of Captain Henry Harris for his agent therein.
And most humbly beseecheth your honours to empower him by himself or with any other your honours shall think fit, to collect, levy, take, and receive the debts and arrears that shall be discovered, from such as it shall be justly due, and to give discharges for such monies as shall be received, in such manner as is used in such cases, and as to your honour's judgments shall seem meet, and that you will

[210] Bradshaw was lord president of the court that tried Charles I and was a member of the Rump's Council of State: S. Kelsey, 'John Bradshaw (bap. 1602, d. 1659)', *ODNB*.
[211] Robinson was recruiter MP for Scarborough from 1645 and a member of the Rump's Council of State: D. Scott, 'Luke Robinson (bap. 1610, d. 1669)', *ODNB*.
[212] For John Anlaby, see Appendix II.

be pleased to expedite the same, and to appoint who shall receive the moiety thereof due to the state.

And he shall be ever bound to pray, etc.,
Henry Hotham.

[*On reverse*] Mr Hotham's 2nd petition.

HHC: Hotham MS, U DDHO/1/56: Order of the Council of State, Whitehall, 5 January 1652

Ordered that Sir William Constable,[213] Colonel Marten,[214] Mr Neville,[215] Mr William Mast*ers*, and Lieutenant-General Fleetwood[216] or two of them be a committee to receive a more particular <relation> information from Mr Hotham of his discovery of £14,000 before a further power be given for the levy of it.
Gualter Frost, secretary.

HHC: Hotham MS, U DDHO/1/85: Printed broadsheet petition to parliament for restoration of civil liberties, 1652[217]

To the supreme authority, the Parliament of the Commonwealth of England
The humble petition of divers constant adherers to this Parliament, and faithful assertors of the fundamental laws and liberties of the Commonwealth.

[*Handwritten on reverse*] Petition of 13 heads

HHC: Hotham MS, U DDHO/1/48: Order of the Committee for Petitions for the Committee at Hull to prepare an inventory of property of Sir John Hotham seized at his arrest, on petition of Lady Hotham, London, 15 September 1653

At the Committee for Petitions.

[213] Constable was brother-in-law to Ferdinando, Lord Fairfax, and elected to the Council of State in February 1649: D. Scott, 'Sir William Constable, baronet (bap. 1590, d. 1655)', *ODNB*.

[214] Marten was an original member of the Rump's Council of State from 1649: S. Barber, 'Henry Marten (1601/2–1680)', *ODNB*.

[215] Neville was elected to the Council of State in November 1651: N. von Maltzahn, 'Henry Neville (1620–1694)', *ODNB*.

[216] After military service in Scotland, Fleetwood was elected to the Council of State by the Rump in February 1651: T. Barnard, 'Charles Fleetwood (*c.*1618–1692)', *ODNB*.

[217] A full copy of this petition can be found at BL, 669.f.16[54].

Upon reading and debate of the petition of the Lady Sarah Hotham, relict of Sir John Hotham, knight and baronet, on the behalf of herself and children, it is ordered that Thomas Raikes, Lancelot Roper, John Barnard, Henry Barnard, Nicholas Denman, William Popple, gentlemen, and Robert Johnson, clerk,[218] who were heretofore of the Committee in Kingston-upon-Hull when the person and goods of Sir John Hotham were seized upon, or any three of them do send unto this Committee *by writing* under their hands, a list or inventory of such money, plate, household stuff, or other goods which were seized *on* upon his apprehension and also a copy of such order or orders as they received from any, or issued out from that committee for the disposal of the said goods etc. And their said certificate with this order is to be returned upon or before 18 November next. Upon which this committee will take the said petition into further consideration.
This is a true copy of the Lady Hotham
Order: Left with Alderman Popple, Alderman Denman and Alderman Barnard on Friday, October 14, 1653, aldermen of Kingston-upon-Hull.
By me, Robert Harbert.

Wednesday 12 October, 1653

	li	s	d
Charges at my landlady, Isabel Keyes}			
Imprimis at Bainton for supper and a quart of ale	0	0	8
It[e]m on Thursday morn for a quart of ale	0	0	2
For my horse grass, hay and oats at Bainton	0	0	9
Charges at my landlord, provisions in Kingston-upon-Hull}			
For my supper on Thursday night and a quart of beer after supper	0	0	10
For my dinner on Friday mu ordinary	0	0	8
For my horse grass, hay, and oats	0	1	0
Charges at my landlady, Keis on Friday night and on Saturday morn, October 15, 1653}			
For my supper on Friday night	0	0	6
For a caun [*sic*] of ale on Saturday morn	0	0	2
For my horse hay and oats	0	0	9
	Sum	5s	6d

[*On reverse*] The order of the Committee of Petitions

[218] Hopper, 'A directory of parliamentarian allegiance in Yorkshire', pp. 90–91.

HHC: Hotham MS, U DDHO/1/86: Copy of a letter from the Council of State concerning raising the Yorkshire militia, Whitehall, 17 April 1660

My lords and gentlemen,
The Council have taken further consideration of the officers recommended to them for the militia of your county and finding by the informations received concerning the state of Yorkshire, that there is good cause to question, whether according to the rules prescribed by the act, that county will bear the four regiments of horse, and the six regiments of foot by you agreed upon. And perceiving in your own letters but a general estimate of the numbers that can be raised there, they have thought it necessary for the present to lessen the number of horse regiments to two and the number of foot regiments to four, and have passed these regiments by name, vizt. the Lord Fairfax and Sir Henry Cholmley's regiments of horse, and Colonel John Dawnay,[219] Colonel Henry Arthington,[220] Colonel Francis Boynton, and Colonel Barrington Bourchier's[221] regiments of foot, each to consist of the number in the established regiments of the army.[222] And have issued commissions for all the officers by you presented for command therein. And whereas you have proposed three hundred in each regiment of horse, the Council leave it to you to enlarge the number to the proportion formerly agreed by the Council, vizt. four hundred apiece if at a general meeting you shall find the country able to bear it according to the rules which the act appoints. And if upon a full view of the whole affair, it shall appear hereafter, that the country will bear a greater number than will be comprehended in the regiments so agreed by the Council, they will upon your returning of fit officers for command of such additional forces take the same into speedy consideration and give all convenient dispatch therein. In the mean time you are desired to proceed with effect, for putting the militia in your county as it is now agreed to the ends proposed by the act. Upon the grounds aforementioned, the commissions formerly

[219]John Dawnay was the grandson of Sir Thomas Dawnay of Sessay, high sheriff of Yorkshire in 1610: Ormrod, *The Lord Lieutenants and High Sheriffs of Yorkshire*, pp. 130–131.

[220]Henry Arthington was son-in-law to Ferdinando, Lord Fairfax, and was recruiter MP for Pontefract from 1646: Hopper, 'A directory of parliamentarian allegiance in Yorkshire', p. 102.

[221]Barrington Bourchier of Beningbrough was high sheriff of Yorkshire in 1658. Son of the regicide, Sir John Bourchier, he supported the Restoration, and was MP for Thirsk in the Convention Parliament of 1660: Ormrod, *The Lord Lieutenants and High Sheriffs of Yorkshire*, pp. 142–143.

[222]For the involvement of these Yorkshire gentry in the Restoration, see A. Woolrych, 'Yorkshire and the Restoration', *YAJ*, 39 (1958), pp. 483–507.

issued to four noble persons in your county for command of the other regiments of horse and foot by you presented, vizt., the Lord Castleton, Sir John Hotham, Sir Christopher Wyvell, and Sir William Cholmley and their officers are suspended for the present, wherein the Council supposes they will rest satisfied they having no other aim herein but the ease of the country, to which they stand related.
Signed in the name and by order of the Council of State appointed by authority of Parliament,

Arthur Annesley,[223] president.

[223]Annesley returned to Westminster when General Monck readmitted the secluded members, and was president of the Council of State from 25 February to 31 May 1660: M. Perceval-Maxwell, 'Arthur Annesley, first earl of Anglesey (1614–1686)', *ODNB*.

UNDATED LETTERS AND PAPERS

HHC: Hotham MS, U DDHO/1/49: William Cobb to Lady Hotham, concerning legal matters, undated

Madam,
I do know your ladyship to be so discreet and honourable that nothing you say (I am very sure of it), but both you and Sir John will perform. And upon that score it will be no matter for producing the deeds of entail, I perceive by yours, Sir John made when he was 21, 3 years after he was married. No doubt these will insist upon it to know what estate was entailed upon. Whatever you name, set the value. Be what it will must be believed and <not doubted> will be owned and confirmed by Sir John when he seals the articles. This or what you may think on to be better may be answered. If they desire to see the deed, which as to your present purpose I cannot think them concerned in, but that Sir John do sign such articles as may be agreed on. The performance of which puts an end to all. Their dilatory scrutinies whether they think me a fit person to consult with or no, I know not, or that the monster hath not strength enough to appear, whether it be born or no, or their brains <stand> stand need of a midwife to bring the brat to light, I am ignorant. I hear no noise and therefore am apt to believe the pains of delivery are not yet come upon them. And I think your son may do well to venture his being brought to the Scotch soul of repentance, rather than stay too long for an English ceremony: to get a maidenhead ?met? fear of God may be religious but the other is an argument of more metal. Madam, pray you pardon this little bright gleam of love that hath warmed me. I am now cold again, and shall return so for to your business before I end. As to desires (for reasons I shall acquaint you with), when I write on you that Mr Ho man go to Sr ?EB? when he comes to town and desire him to be of Mr Ho counsel if there be occasion. My thanks for your venison, my service as being, madam,

your most humble servant,
William Cobb.

[*In margin*] Madam, my service to your fireside.

[*On reverse*] These for the honourable my Lady Hotham at Scorborough.
[*In a different hand*] Lockington, Cranswick, Winthrop land and colt landing.

HHC: Hotham MS, U DDHO/1/82: List of officers nominated in the petition with their rates of monthly pay, undated

A list of the several officers nominated in the petition

William Moyle, Lieutenant-Colonel makes by month	25 - 4 - 0	
Edward Aldridge, Lieutenant-Colonel makes by month	25 - 4 - 0	} 75 - 12 - 0
Robert Hamon, Lieutenant-Colonel makes by month	25 - 4 - 0	
Thomas Sherley, Sergeant-Major makes by month	19 - 12 - 0	
Captains (viz.)	£ s d	
Captain Thomas Middleton, makes by month	11 - 4 - 0	
Captain Robert Burrell, makes by month	11 - 4 - 0	
Captain Leon Lidcot, makes by month	11 - 4 - 0	
Captain William Rolston, makes by month	11 - 4 - 0	
Captain Jo: Fox, makes by month	11 - 4 - 0	
Captain Robert Baker, makes by month	11 - 4 - 0	
Captain Thomas Collins, makes by month	11 - 4 - 0	
Jere: Manhood Captain, makes by month	11 - 4 - 0	
Captain Robert Philipps, makes by month	11 - 4 - 0	
Captain Roger Buggs, makes by month	11 - 4 - 0	
Captain James Barsy, makes by month	11 - 4 - 0	
Captain James Powell, makes by month	11 - 4 - 0	
Captain Hercules Huncks, makes by month	11 - 4 - 0	
Captain Shirley Snelling, makes by month	11 - 4 - 0	
Captain Jo: Middleton, makes by month	11 - 4 - 0	
Captain Richard Hall, makes by month	11 - 4 - 0	
Captain Francis Stradling, makes by month	11 - 4 - 0	
Captain Jo: Bates, makes by month	11 - 4 - 0	
Captain Thomas Pettus, makes by month	11 - 4 - 0	
Captain Stephen Hawkins, makes by month	11 - 4 - 0	
Captain George Leake, makes by month	11 - 4 - 0	
Captain Thomas Gardiner, makes by month	11 - 4 - 0	
Captain George Windam, makes by month	11 - 4 - 0	
Captain Gregory Collins, makes by month	11 - 4 - 0	
Captain Thomas Philipps, makes by month	11 - 4 - 0	
In all to the captains the sum of	280 - 0 - 0	
Lieutenants (viz.)		
Lieutenant Richard Oxeldayle, makes by month	5 - 12 - 0	

Lieutenant Nicholas Freestone, makes by month	5 - 12 - 0
Lieutenant Jo: Bowers, makes by month	5 - 12 - 0
Lieutenant Wingfeild, makes by month	5 - 12 - 0
Lieutenant Ralp Sutton, makes by month	5 - 12 - 0
Lieutenant George Okes, makes by month	5 - 12 - 0
Lieutenant Thomas Rushe, makes by month	5 - 12 - 0
Lieutenant Henry Adkinson, makes by month	5 - 12 - 0
Lieutenant Thomas Bromley, makes by month	5 - 12 - 0
Lieutenant Bartholomew Philipps, makes by month	5 - 12 - 0
Lieutenant Henry Hacker, makes by month	5 - 12 - 0
Lieutenant Philip Dutton, makes by month	5 - 12 - 0
Lieutenant Jo: Grove, makes by month	5 - 12 - 0
Lieutenant Nicholas Deane, makes by month	5 - 12 - 0
Lieutenant Robert Benbrigge, makes by month	5 - 12 - 0
Lieutenant Ed: Allen, makes by month	5 - 12 - 0
Lieutenant Etho: Linch, makes by month	5 - 12 - 0
Lieutenant Ed: Watts, makes by month	5 - 12 - 0
Lieutenant William Batter, makes by month	5 - 12 - 0
Lieutenant William Brooke, makes by month	5 - 12 - 0
Lieutenant Robert Davies, makes by month	5 - 12 - 0
Lieutenant Francis Fitzhugh, makes by month	5 - 12 - 0
Lieutenant Thomas Richardson, makes by month	5 - 12 - 0
Lieutenant Antony Norton, makes by month	5 - 12 - 0
< Lieutenant George Okes, makes by month	5 - 12 - 0>
Lieutenant Nicholas Burnett, makes by month	5 - 12 - 0
Lieutenant Jo: Connocke, makes by month	5 - 12 - 0
Lieutenant Jo: Pawmer, makes by month	5 - 12 - 0
Lieutenant Jo: Clifton, makes by month	5 - 12 - 0
[Total for the lieutenants]	156 - 16 - 0

	£ s d
Jaso: West Quarter Master, makes by month	7 - 0 - 0
Ensigns (viz.)	
Richard Ford, Ensign, by month	3 - 10 - 0
Thomas Coote, Ensign, by month	3 - 10 - 0
Jo: Shipman, Ensign, by month	3 - 10 - 0
Thomas May, Ensign, by month	3 - 10 - 0
William Tomkins, Ensign, by month	3 - 10 - 0
Christopher Elsing, Ensign, by month	3 - 10 - 0
Michael Bland, Ensign, by month	3 - 10 - 0
Thomas Plomer, Ensign, by month	3 - 10 - 0
Ed: Allen, Ensign, by month	3 - 10 - 0
Jo: Watson, Ensign, by month	3 - 10 - 0
George Hartridge, Ensign, by month	3 - 10 - 0

George Burrell, Ensign, by month	3 - 10 - 0
Thomas Bike, Ensign, by month	3 - 10 - 0
Richard Francis, Ensign, by month	3 - 10 - 0
Jo: Elrington, Ensign, by month	3 - 10 - 0
Edward Bray, Ensign, by month	3 - 10 - 0
Robert Lloyd, Ensign, by month	3 - 10 - 0
Robert Rustate, Ensign, by month	3 - 10 - 0
William Gage, Ensign, by month	3 - 10 - 0
Howard Kellet, Ensign, by month	3 - 10 - 0
Michael Doughty, Ensign, by month	3 - 10 - 0
Jo: Vaughan, Ensign, by month	3 - 10 - 0
Poole: Turvile, Ensign, by month	3 - 10 - 0
Hercules Baskervile, Ensign, by month	3 - 10 - 0
Owen Philipps, Ensign, by month	3 - 10 - 0
Thomas Whitney, Ensign, by month	3 - 10 - 0
Isaac Shawbery, Ensign, by month	3 - 10 - 0
Ed: Knightly, Ensign, by month	3 - 10 - 0
William Draper, Ensign, by month	3 - 10 - 0
In all to the ensigns	101 - 10 - 0
	£ s d
The total sum of all amounts unto }	640 10 0

This money should have been ?drawen men <to>? have been paid here in 20 days upon 7 or 8 per cent, now the business is lost.

[*On reverse*] A list of the Protestant officers, etc.

HHC: Hotham MS, U DDHO/1/57: Draft letter probably by Sir John Hotham, intended for William Lenthall, and endorsed by Durand Hotham, undated, but *c.*1642–1643

Sir, I have formerly expressed to you the face of affairs with us. This letter is of another subject. I am a member of your House, and therefore think myself in capacity (though absent) to offer to you my humble advice. He hath not the heart of a Christian nor Englishman who is not moved with the deplorable estate of this late flourishing kingdom, once the subject of envy, now of pity to all nations. Every county, nay, almost every family divided, and ready to sheath their swords in one another's bowels. It is not to be denied, but this commonwealth was <ready> in that declination, as both religion and liberty were almost wounded to death, by the plot of a Jesuitical faction. You have like men of honour, courage, and honesty, appeared to the <receiving> *redeeming* of both, and as I hope, and believe, have so crushed the vigour and strength of their designs, as there will not be much life or success *hereafter*. Nor is it likewise to be denied, but, in discharging these your just duties, which God and man required, you have stirred up a swarm of malignant spirits which leave no stone <unrolled> *unturned*, no way nor means unattempted to defame and destroy you. The question now is, what should be done in these sad extremities? Two great armies and many more are amongst us, exhausting the treasure, violencing the laws, shedding the blood of our nation, and those are actors and fomenters of our divisions who regard more their own business, than their master's honour or safety. And though I am confident there are some, and many of those, yet I am as confident that there are others who have unhappily fallen in and would as cheerfully *come for the* to become instruments of a happy union betwixt His Majesty and the Parliament. While things are in this vast difference, the one party disables the other, by suggesting to His Majesty such intentions of yours (as on my soul your thoughts abhor), and the <other> better are obstructed by the nearness of the worse from all means of doing good offices, if clearly representing to His Majesty your just intentions of settling religion, his honour and your liberties. Sure great reformations are then wholesomest when they are naturally, not too violently ripened. Gain once but this upon His Majesty that your own counsels and those of his good servants may be presented to him upon even terms of advantage, and your work is half done. Then it will appear to him how the other have misled him to their own ends, and there will likewise appear to him the glorious mixture and *temperament* of a just prerogative and a people's liberty. Then will likewise appear to him the wicked practices of those prelates who for promotions had almost sold our religion, and he will then discover the precious happiness of a religious and affectionate people. 'Tis true some of your just and necessary privileges may seem to be endangered by such moderation, but wise men in the hazards of ruin and desolation will choose the least. And I am persuaded you will please both God and all good men, when it shall appear that you have rather seceded from your just rights, than put all their fortunes into such a crazy bottom as the chance of a battle, whose event (beside all advantage of force and number) is always uncertain. And if we conquer, it is true we have more power to settle the affairs of the commonwealth, but if we lose we are under a heavier *power* to *our* desolation. For the cavaliers, by their power with the soldiery, may force and necessitate His Majesty to do clear contrary to his now <royal> intendments. Sir, if you put into the balance the loss and the gain, by winning or losing a battle the odds will soon appear, besides the blood to be spilt on both sides. I write this in thought of a present trial of a battle,[224] which sure if all hopes of composing be taken away, is the best to quit us of a languishing misery. Truly my soul abhors to think of the miseries [which] must follow. Should this war be delayed, the kingdom's treasures will be exhausted by several forces in every county, the privilege of the subject (of which we should be all preservers) necessarily broken, and the wounds of dissension made wider, and strangers brought in by degrees amongst us to possess our inheritances <all stories presenting the lamentable events of foreign forces brought in whose> <Sir may all >. Sir, may all advantages of peace and unity be ever in our eyes and endeavours, and if our honourable attempts cannot reach to make us so happy as we desire, let them at least make us less miserable than we fear.

[*On reverse by Durand Hotham*] Papers concerning my father's trial.

HHC: Hotham MS, U DDHO/1/79: Report recommending that part of Sir John Hotham's estates be discharged from sequestration, undated

May it please this honourable committee.
We have received the order and copy of the petition enclosed, and in obedience to the said order we have perused the several conveyances produced by the petition. And thereby it appears that Sir John Hotham, knight and baronet, deceased, named in the petition and order did by one indenture dated 1 May 17 James I and by fine levied thereupon Pasch 17 James I convey (*inter alia*) certain closes and parcels of ground called Eastfield, Newclose, Southbyclose and Bird Paddock in Risom[225] and a close called Gildcroft, in Skeffling to the use of himself, for life, and after to the use of Charles Hotham,[226] his son, entailed with other remainders over (as thereby appears).

And did by another indenture, dated 15 January, 11 Charles I, in consideration of blood and of love to his wife Dame Sarah Hotham[227] and for her jointure coven[an]t to stand seized of his chief mansion house in Fylingdales, and of all houses, barns, stables, gardens, yards and backsides thereto belonging, and the gill on both sides the beck

[224]Here Sir John Hotham may have been anticipating Edgehill: B. English, 'Sir John Hotham and the English civil war', *Archives*, 20 (1992), pp. 221–222.

[225]Rysome Garth in the parish of Holmpton, Holderness: A.H. Smith, *The Place-names of the East Riding of Yorkshire and York*, English Place-name Society, 14 (1937), p. 22.

[226]Charles Hotham, rector of Hollym, was third son of Sir John Hotham by his second wife, Anne Rokeby.

[227]On 7 May 1635, Sir John Hotham married his fifth wife, Sarah, daughter of Thomas Anlaby of Etton.

as far upon close to seaward called Bownell, and the close called the Fairhall Garth, and all the grounds betwixt the house of John Pates and the mansion house to Lambfield, and the close, with the <hill> *gill* called Bownhill,[228] and the close called Lambfield, and the farm called Pate's Farm in Fyling, to the use of himself and the said Dame Sarah his wife, for their lives, and the life of the longer liver of them, and of the heirs males of their bodies with other remainders over (as thereby appears).

And did by another indenture dated 7 May 1635 in consideration of a marriage betwixt him and Sarah Anlaby, and for a jointure (which marriage afterward took effect), and the said Sarah is now the relict of Sir John Hotham) <covent> *Covenant* to stand seized of the parcel of ground called Ramsday side, one tenement and lands in the occupation of John Biggin, one close called Little moor close and Ramsdale[229] Bank, certain parcels of ground called Swallow Head, Hessell Riggs, Pates Bank and Colcroft Bank and Gill, <and> certain parcels of ground called Horsclose, Highfield Garbutts and Four Nobles Close, the High Park and Park Close, two farms late in the occupation of <John> *Geo* Stephenson and Robert Gilson called Mounckmans Park, Gate Farm, one farm with the appurtenances in the occupation of <John> *Laurence*

[*page break*]

Laurence Gurdon, one cottage and parcel of ground late in the occupation of Joshua Lime, and one cottage with the appurtenances in the occupation of James Woodhouse. All situated within the parish of Fyling to the use of himself and the said Sarah Anlaby (whom he intended to marry during their natural lives and the longer liver of them with other remainders over).

And did by another indenture dated 9 April 15 Charles I, in consideration of blood coven[an]t to stand seized of his manor of Uleeton which he had by deed from Richard Hotham,[230] his son, to the use of him the said Sir John Hotham for life, and after his death to the use of the said Richard Hotham his son for life with other remainders over (as thereby appears).

And did by another indenture dated 9 April 15 Charles I, in consideration of blood covenant to stand seized of the farm in the occupation of George Stevenson or his assignees, and of one little

[228] Bownhill in the parish of Fylingdales: A.H. Smith, *The Place-names of the North Riding of Yorkshire*, English Place-name Society, 5 (1928), p. 116.

[229] Ramsdale in the parish of Fylingdales: *ibid.*, p. 117.

[230] Richard Hotham was second son to Sir John Hotham by his first wife, Katherine Rhodes.

close in the occupation of Robert Stephenson, and one farm in the occupation of Widow Lawnd, and one close in the occupation of John Wilkes, late Marshal's Close, one farm in the occupation of John Gilleson, one farm in the occupation of James Browne. All situated and being in Fyling, to the use of himself for life, and after to the use of his son, Durand Hotham, and his heirs (as thereby appears).

And did by another indenture dated 9 April 15 Charles I, in consideration of blood covenant to stand seized of the farm in the occupation of John Boyes or his assignees, the close called Riggfield, the close without the park called Colcroft, the two Oxcloses and the several closes in the occupation of Thomas Tailor: rented at £33 per annum. All situated in Fyling to the use of himself for life and after his death then to the use of his <selfe> *son*, William Hotham,[231] and his heirs (as thereby appears).

And did by a deed poll dated 29 October 17 Charles I, grant and convey to Charles Hotham, his son, and to his heirs and assignees forever the perpetual donation and the presentation of the church of Hollym[232] (as thereby appears).

And we do further humbly certify that the said several indentures and conveyances being sufficiently attested and proved before us, are by us allowed of accordingly. And we have thereupon by virtue of the said order discharged the said several conveyed premises of and from any sequestration for the delinquency of Sir John Hotham, if this honourable committee think fit to approve of the same.

HHC: Hotham MS, U DDHO/1/60: Draft letter, possibly by Durand Hotham, concerning Captain Hotham and the war in Yorkshire, undated, spring 1643

[*In margin*] I would I had made this my account almanac wise with day and month

Sir, the intercourse twixt you *and me* is not often. You see I bring forth but one a month, (<and then to have labour enough to set the true lustre of our gallant men's actions, so has the babbling mouth of common fame besmirched their actions>) but be confident *that* to my best understanding, I *write* the sincere truth of what the utmost of my endeavours could attain to. And for your satisfaction who feed

[231] William Hotham, fourth son of Sir John Hotham, by his second wife, Anne Rokeby, was a captain in his father's Hull garrison during 1643: see below in Appendix II; TNA, SP 28/7/478, 28/7/525; HHC: C BRS/7/67.

[232] The parish church of Hollym, two miles south of Withernsea in the East Riding of Yorkshire.

only on the quintessence of business, I made a narrow survey of every man's actions *by* <if> what I knew to be his principle and shall accordingly give you an account. My last left Captain Hotham in his full career, who after he had broken of the western treaty, and preserved that chicken which since is grown into an eagle, *or some other bird* had advanced northward and after some metalled, but disadvantageous and disproportioned encounters, retreated with the enemy in his face, possessed again his own quarter <and> at Cawood, and straitened the enemy in his at York. Things came to be framed into a settled course of war and every officer ___ to his particular *a-be or* employment. Then was my Lord Fairfax made generalissimo, his valiant son general of the horse, and Captain Hotham Lieutenant-General, whose soldiers (which he drew <all the> out of Hull at the earnest solicitation of the western gentry) *overawed then by ____ who had us 2 hours before them* were as so many tutors to the inept countrymen whom my Lord Fairfax's honesty and reputation in that country had engaged in the mutual defence of him and themselves. I told you of the unhappy difference twixt men so equally worth and my inmost thoughts and conjectures of it. And what I observed then continued <observation> *experience* has confirmed to me, that were there not some engineer at work whose wit is beyond country bringing up, the b [*sic*] public good had crowded them *(on my so*u*le both their aims)* <both> ere this in to one centre. Well I am grieved at heart about it. But for my account, I then left my Lord of Newcastle in the <west r> York after his flight when nobody pursued him. From whence he has unfortunately broken in upon the East Riding; <which> the occasion was thus. The Queen *purposing* to set herself in the head of this popish, fixt her resolution to land in Yorkshire, her landing at Newcastle being extreme hazardous by sea by reason of our 4 ships there, and by land being a long journey from thence to York, and *Lord of* Newcastle being in no plight to spare so long a convoy as was honourable for such a guest. Now there was but one convenient pass *for my lord to return* in the East Riding *whereof necessity she must ?come? a shore* which is at Stamford Briggs, that Sir John Hotham had so secured that Mars and Pallas; *wit and fortitude* could not have entered, had they not taken a ticket from the supine negligence and cowardice of those that kept it. Which really they did *__ __* and broke through and marched their *horse* straight to Malton where Sir Hugh Cholmley and Colonel Boynton's quarters were, and

[*page break*]

had without ill peradventure surprised them, had not Sir John Hotham's timely notice to son and *his immediate* dispatch saved them in that extremity. For he was *sudden*ly upon them before they were aware, routed them, and joined with the force in the town. Now by this time Newcastle had passed his foot all over Stamford Bridge <and twas not to> and marched towards Hull, which being well perceived by those in Malton, they wisely got twixt Hull and them and enquartered themselves in a town called Beverley and there stayed. Now as soon as the Queen <had notice>, who all this while had laid hovering at sea, had notice of this, she struck in at Bridlington, and all Newcastle's forces roll thitherward into a corner of the county much like the <catch>*brock* of a fisherman's net. And might have been really so in effect had my Lord Fairfax condescended to the solicitations of Sir John Hotham, Captain Hotham and Sir Hugh Cholmley, and all the rest who were violently earnest for the assistance of 1,000 men, only to let Newcastle see in to what a handsome snare *unprovident counsel* engaged himself. But it pleased God otherwise to dispose of it. My lord was positive in his refusal, and they tell us here made a reference of his reasons to the House, which they unsatisfied with, send him order to march, but all too late. For Newcastle march*ed* immediately away and *we* all be plundered over, left to bewail an ill lost opportunity. I must confess I was then present with Sir John, *Captain Hotham, Sir Hugh Cholmley* and the rest and I never saw (?nor I think the sun a greater and forthe traverser then I?) men more resolute, more full of provident counsels, a sense of public suffering, and more regardless of the *dis*advantage of <a numerous> a numerous enemy. <Nay> I remember I heard Sir John Hotham say, gentlemen, 'tis the authority of Parliament has filled our nerves with spirit, 'tis our religion, 'tis our liberty <we aime> *we draw* our swords for, and let the ghost of their courageous ancestors haunt them that draw back their arms from chastising this insolent tyranny. And let the ancient English courage rise from the head that extorted our precious privilege of the Norman Law and the zeal *again wake* of the reformers unchained us from the Romish servitude. <These were his word> This said, which *he spoke with that fervour* that I shall always lay <them> *his words* by me as pledge, that these words were the issue of a spirit that dare not be false to the commonwealth. But I should have told you that as soon as Her Majesty was landed, the commission of array was presently put in execution by Sir Marmaduke Langdale, Sir William Savile and Sir Ralph Hansby, men and their estates confiscated to my Lord of Newcastle, the county driven together and pinfolded like so many stray cattle. His army all this while living at as free cost as pilgrims do when they go to our Lady *to Lorett*. <Thus> in this place they stayed about 14 days, and about their going away they were mustered 7,000. The Queen had her lifeguard all of Walloon and Dutch only, and gentlemen's sons dwelling thereabout, all with pistol and long birding pieces. Now they are all at York, only in their passage have scattered about 2,000 at Malton and Stamford Bridge, making as though they had an *as an ___* intend upon the first advantage to slide back again. Which Sir John Hotham to prevent has proposed to all the east gentry that themselves would appear in arms in a body

[*page break*]

rally into troops and bind themselves in covenant, themselves and estates, to prosecute to ruin this popish army. And the convenience of this will be with a little exercise these troops will be so many treasuries of commander for the count*r*y people, that we may no more trust to those men of fortune whose slow paced endeavours has produced our misery to this length. Well, if <promise> *probably that* the solid consequences of this, but may it happen as well as it is intended. 800 now is the most <not above> *are* now in those parts commanded by Captain Hotham who has lately been very sick, and since that our affairs are like a clock run down. And but I that Sir Hugh Cholmley's do like himself and family they might write over us *fruges consumere nat<y>*i**.[233] Last week he met the choicest troope the enemy had upon equal term, routed them, took 17 prisoners and pulled the prey out of their teeth. Thus far sir you have an exact relation, and because they in the west have of late done nothing, I'll fit them with saying nothing of them. One thing more I'll add. A gentleman came lately from London that astonisheth us all here. It happened very opportunely that I had the honour to be acquainted with him beyond the sea. So we enjoyed one another's observations with a very great freedom. He tells *us* of strange whispers and misdoubtings, fear and jealousies of some in great place, and that first they *were low creeping* crept low and were suddenly trodden down, but now the mouths of the wiser sort are full of questions. I deal truly, I wondered, and run over in my mind all the actions and counsels I was privy to by the favour of a special friend and <never> found none unfraught with <mett> g*a*llant metal, all full of public considerations. <I never heard *never heard* of any complaints> At last I began to consider at what aim these arrows were shot abroad and I immediately remembered myself <that> of some discou*r*se I had with a gentleman I dined with about a fortnight ago at North Cave. The man I had not seen in two years. I met him at Paris, but the last time was at Rome <he little knowing my engagements>. If I mistake not, he is an emissary from that Sea.[234] He little knowing my engagements, was extreme plentiful

[233] They will consume the fruits they have sown.

[234] The Holy See.

<full> in discourse of that nature. <I was very attentive>. And there was not an action, but he had created an ill end for it. I perceived at last he had been at London, and as he had all languages, so he had all religions at his fingers' ends and no farther. And had applied himself to some really honest but simple *and religious*, and others wise enough but not so cautious, *their names he told me*, had dealt very subtly in these and such like discourses, pretended much zeal to the prosperity of the cause and vigilancy that it should no way suffer by the unfitness of the agents. This discourse <and> which then I did not well understand, and what has since happened well laid together, I well remember the principle in that all politique religion, when a man is thoroughly violent in cause gallant and successful there is no way to ruin him but by distrust and jealousy from his own party. Sir, I count myself very happy that I remembered this discourse. I should ?else? have been far to seek for probable grounds for your conceits above, though I well know I might have attributed it to the common principle that no man's fame is so sacred but an itching tongue will rub [*MS damaged*] self upon it. I read lately the <common fatte> Roman story I [*sic*] and found it the [*MS damaged*] fate of the bravest generals that while the their utmost <?gain? *extent* of their wit> strength to the [*MS damaged*] extent of their understanding employed in the public concernment, some pol [*MS damaged*] butcher *at home* cried treason. Some inconsiderable creature could construe this or that [*MS damaged*] but so perisheth the elephant, so the whale.

[*On reverse*] A letter *sub falo nomine* [*There follows a medical recipe in Latin*]

HHC: Hotham MS, U DDHO/1/59: 'Notions' on the laws by Durand Hotham, undated

I shall now in part be as good [as] my word and in that business wherein I am at present most versed, give you an account of my thoughts in which I must <for the same part> *if this straitness of time* because the proof of them would be too large, take some general propositions for granted. As first that it is the interest of a commonwe*a*lth to leave no such thing as an unwritten law as a reserve against them, especially in this, where that called the common law is in its frame and essence a nurse and mother of monarchy and irrational superiority entailed upon a birthright, a family right, and throught [*sic*] it whole body <making> *evoking* an uncontrolled custom into the place and dignity of a law.

2. That there is a necessity of new moulding the statute laws and abrogation of all whatever made before the act for declaring this to

be a Commonwealth that neither old laws, customs nor the reasons of our forefathers become anyway corrival for the civil government. For if anything <of thing> of these be permitted to come in upon the nation except unclothed of its authority and pretence of right to rule and merely set before you in its natural strength and aptitude to the present ?rorag? you are still unfree and in guardianship to those old crooked hags that bewitched this nation and hindered them of their manly growth in successive reformations.

That it being of necessity to frame all the commanding reasons of the nation into acts of Parliament and so put the highest disobligation upon the *corporation* lawyers that can be. And *because* for the honour of his law he will endeavour for many generations to make yours seem irrational, incongruous, and inept, provision for the management of justice or decision of property, it be not much conducing, yea necessary to the peace of the commonwealth to disincorporate them (for that only reason besides many weighty ones), and <forbid> *inhibit* all manner of pleading or fee for pleading, and making the plain letter and vulgar sense which is by easy perceivance the rule of judgment (and which will if the common law be taken away be far more easy).

[*page break*]

Because formerly the common law was on a difference upon a statute made the umpire of the controversy and not the bare literal sense.

4. That if the common lawyer be taken away and <and> the courts freed of that unnecessary <orator> and chargeable oratory it will be of necessity to avoid the wild and partial judgments of magistrates to have in every county a court of censor to which the magistrate shall answer for false judgment, partiality, bribery, etc. In the contrivance of which court is much wisdom necessary. For that appeals are necessary is palpable, but that local appeals (which are always excessively chargeable) are *not* so much as convenient I dare assume upon myself to defend. But all our appeals as hitherto managed are only local as from inferior courts <to superior> *in the county* to London, etc., it if tolerated *then* ought of necessity to make them just to be these <there> things.

That it be after judgment} else the complaint is but a suggestion of injustice to be done and a superiority claimed in that case is irrational.

2. That the matter of false judgment if any be; be always inquired into and punished as if ignorance remove the judges if bribery punish it and the like to the pay.

3. If none of these appear that all the whole charge remove and false clamour be laid upon the plaintiff, which never is nor was there interest to do and great damages to the court.

HHC: Hotham MS, U DDHO/1/66: Sir John Hotham,[235] second baronet, to Durand Hotham, undated (*c.*1645–1653)

Sir, the grounds which you spoke to Mr Bourdenand about at Lockington I am very willing you should have. And when I come at age I shall confirm you a lease of 21 years. So with my service to your lady I remain your affection*ate* nephew to serve you.

John Hotham

[*On reverse*] For his honoured uncle, Durand Hotham, esq., at Cranswick, this Sir John Hotham's letter for my grounds.

HHC: Hotham MS, U DDHO/1/67: Sir John Hotham, second baronet, to Durand Hotham, 9 June (*c.*1650)

Sir,
I am very glad that you are returned safe from London both for your <own> particular and my own, for I have desired my grandfather[236] to write to you and further do myself to entreat your company here, to do me the favour (or rather the happiness) as to treat with Sir John Monson about the settling of some land which is the portion of the gentlewoman I am a servant to, whom I hope may be my wife. Sir, I have made several addresses to her, therefore the sooner you come the better, which I beseech you may be this week if possible, wherein you will ever oblige your most faithful nephew and servant to serve you,

John Hotham.

Sir, my service to my aunt and both my uncles.

[*On reverse*] For his most honoured uncle, Mr Durand Hotham, at his house in Cranswick, Yorkshire. These:

[235] Sir John Hotham, second baronet (1632–1689), the eldest son of Lieutenant-General John Hotham, became heir to the family estates on the execution of his father and grandfather in 1645. He was baptized at Glentworth, Lincolnshire, on 21 March 1632, and buried at South Dalton on 29 September 1689, where a striking memorial remains. He was MP for Beverley in the Cavalier Parliament and became a leading Williamite Whig. He married Elizabeth, daughter of Sapcote, Viscount Beaumont of Swords in Ireland, at Burton near Lincoln on 8 August 1650: Foster, *Pedigrees of the County Families of Yorkshire*, III, unpaginated.

[236] This was his maternal grandfather, Sir John Wray of Glentworth, Lincolnshire: D. Scott, 'Sir John Wray, second baronet (bap. 1586, d. 1655)', *ODNB*.

HHC: Hotham MS, U DDHO/1/75: Notes on the actions, trial, and execution of Sir John Hotham and 'Captain' John Hotham, in an eighteenth-century hand[237]

Anno. 1642. Caro. 18.
The Parliament committed the charge of the town and magazine of Hull to Sir John Hotham. April 23, the King went to Hull. Sir John Hotham denied admittance, as it would be a breach of his trust to the Parliament. The King proclaimed Sir John Hotham a traitor. The King sends to the Parliament to demand justice against Sir John Hotham. The Parliament justify Sir John Hotham and authorize him to raise the trained bands in Yorkshire to march with their arms into Hull. Sir John Hotham disarmed them, and sent them home. Sir John Hotham and Sir John Meldrum, his assistant, sallied out upon the earl of Lindsey's forces near Hull, killed some and took others. This was the first place where blood was drawn in this contest. January 16 the Parliament forces under Sir Matthew Boynton and Sir Hugh Cholmley defeat the enemies at Malton, and Sir Matthew Boynton routs a party at Guisborough of 600, killed many, took 150 prisoners, whereof their commander Slingsby[238] was one, and 200 arms.

Anno 1643 Caro. 19. In the north, some difference had been between Lord Fairfax and Sir John Hotham, who refused to submit to Lord Fairfax, the General to the Parliament in those parts. But Sir John Hotham was as high and morose, as Lord Fairfax was meek and courteous. The Parliament, hearing of this contest, intended to displace Sir John Hotham, which he discovering by letters that he intercepted, began to have other designs. His son, Captain Hotham, being suspected by the Parliament, was imprisoned at Nottingham. From whence escaping, he underhand treated with the earl of Newcastle, and coming to Hull, he and his father stood upon their guard. The Parliament doubting the consequence hereof, sent Sir Matthew Boynton with a commission to seize them both, and to be governor there.[239] Who, not suspected by Sir John Hotham, being his

[237] These notes were copied from the 1682 edition of Bulstrode Whitelock's *Memorials of English Affairs*. The relevant page references from the later, more accessible edition are given here: *Memorials of English Affairs from the Beginning of the Reign of King Charles the First to the Happy Restoration of King Charles the Second*, 4 vols (Oxford, 1853), I, pp. 167–169, 194, 206, 239, 280, 320, 348, 351, 359–361, 497; II, pp. 370, 374.

[238] Colonel Guilford Slingsby was mortally wounded in this engagement: Newman, *Royalist Officers*, pp. 345–346.

[239] Parliament was mindful that Sir Matthew Boynton's religious radicalism made him unlikely to defect to the royalists. Boynton was the parliamentary high sheriff of Yorkshire from 1643 to 1645 and was well acquainted with Hull's defences, having been appointed a commissioner to report on the condition of Hull castle and blockhouses in 1634: J. Broadway,

brother-in-law, had the more opportunity to tamper with the garrison, and gain an interest with the soldiers, so that he gained them and the magazine. Then Sir John Hotham, too late seeing the design against him, fled to Beverley, where his own soldiers set upon him, and forced him back to Hull, where he was taken by Sir Matthew Boynton, his brother, and with his lady, his son, and all his children, sent up prisoners to the Parliament, and Sir Matthew Boynton remained governor of Hull in his place. The Commons allowed five pounds a week to Sir John Hotham and three pounds a week to Captain Hotham for their maintenance in prison.

1644. Caro. 20. Letters were produced under Sir John Hotham's hand, amongst the papers of the earl of Newcastle, taken at Marston Moor, by which Sir John Hotham expresses his affection to the earl, and thereupon the Commons called for the ordinance for martial law, and it being agreed upon, was sent up to the Lords. Sir John Hotham petitioned that he might not be tried by the commissioners for the court martial, and he demanded the judgement of the House thereupon and offered his reasons. But they would not hear them. December 1644. Sr J. Hotham was tried by the court martial.

1. For betraying his trust, and adhering to the enemy. Proved, by his words, letters and actions, his compliance with the Lord Digby, the marquis of Newcastle, and others of that party.
2. His refusal to supply Lord Fairfax with ammunition, to the great prejudice of the Parliament.
3. His scandalous words against the Parliament.
4. His endeavour to betray Hull to the enemy.
5. His correspondence with the Queen, and his seeking to escape.

Thirty witnesses were examined against him, and divers for him in his defence. The court martial adjudged Sir John Hotham to have his head cut off. Captain Hotham was tried before the court martial, for betraying a regiment of horse of the Parliament's to the enemy, and for treachery and betraying his trust in divers particulars. Proved against him by his own words, letters and actions, and many witnesses produced to make good the charge. Captain Hotham made his defence before the court martial and justified treaties with the enemy, as a commander for the service of the Parliament. Other charges he denied, and excepted against some witnesses. The Lords reprieved Sir John Hotham for a few days, until he had better settled his estate. The court martial pronounced sentence of death against Captain Hotham.

R. Cust, and S.K. Roberts (eds), *A Calendar of the Docquets of Lord Keeper Coventry, 1625–1640*, List and Index Society, special series, 34 (2004), p. 40; Ormrod, *The Lord Lieutenants and High Sheriffs of Yorkshire*, p. 135.

The Lords upon the petition of Sir John Hotham, and his son, thought fit to pardon the father, and desired the concurrence of the Commons therein. But upon the question, it was carried in the negative, not to be taken by them into consideration. Sir John Hotham was going to his execution and much company expecting it on Tower Hill, when a messenger came with a reprieve from the Lords. But the Commons sent to the Lieutenant of the Tower, to know the reason of deferring the execution, when they did not consent to any reprieve for him. Upon the debate touching the reprieve of Sir John Hotham by the Lords, the Commons voted that no officer made by ordinance of both Houses should stay the execution of justice by any order of either House, without the concurrence of both Houses. They likewise ordered that the Lieutenant of the Tower do proceed to the execution of Sir John Hotham. Captain Hotham sent a petition to the Lords, and one to the Commons, praying his pardon. But it was denied and the same day his head was cut off. Sir John Hotham in the morning before his execution, procured a motion in the House of Commons for his pardon, occasioned a debate, and Sir John Hotham being brought to the scaffold, expected the news of his pardon, and the time was protracted till two o'clock in the afternoon. But the House of Commons would not grant his desire. He spake shortly to the people, and Mr Hugh Peters[240] prayed with him, and spoke to the people in his name, and told them that Sir John's father said to him when he was going forth to be a soldier, 'son, when the crown of England lies at stake, you will have fighting enough'. He was somewhat fearful of death, and his head was cut off.

Anno. 1645. Caro. 21. Letters informed the surrender of Scarborough castle to Colonel Sir Matthew Boynton, with the articles there was taken 37 pieces of ordnance, 1,000 arms, and great store of ammunition and plunder. A letter from the Committee at York informed that they had chosen Colonel Sir Matthew Boynton to be governor of Scarborough castle. Colonel Poyntz[241] desired the same government and it was referred to a committee to consider of it. It was resolved by the House the 19th August 1645 that the committees in the north had no power to appoint governors of forts there. The House nominated Colonel Sir Matthew Boynton governor of Scarborough.

[240]The appointment of this sectarian preacher was a deliberate offence to Sir John Hotham's religious inclinations: C. Gardina Pestana, 'Hugh Peter (bap. 1598, d. 1660)', *ODNB*.

[241]Poyntz succeeded Ferdinando, Lord Fairfax, as commander of parliament's northern army and was commissioned as colonel-general in the summer of 1645: D.N. Farr, 'Sydenham Poyntz (bap. 1607)', *ODNB*.

Anno. 1648. Caro. 24. In a letter from Charles, Prince of Great Britain, I refer you to T. Hamilton for the west. That in the north is ours already, and Colonel Sir Matthew Boynton shall be sainted: 29 is not ready. Commissioners were sent to treat with Colonel Boynton for the surrender of Scarborough castle to the Parliament from whom he had revolted. But they made no agreement with him. The commissioners shot in a printed order to the soldiers in the castle, promising them one thousand pound, to deliver it up to them.

HHC: Hotham MS, U DDHO/1/81: Articles of enquiry into the behaviour and affairs of the mayor, aldermen, and Charterhouse of Hull

Manuscript missing

HHC: Hotham MS, U DDHO/1/68: Bound manuscript volume, no date

Item 1: 100 pages
Observations, rules and orders collected out of diverse journals of the House of Commons entered in the several reigns of King Edward VI, Queen Mary, Queen Elizabeth and King James. With a declaration of the Commons drawn up by a select committee in the first year of King James concerning their privileges.
Item 2: 25 pages
A protestation of the House of Commons concerning their privileges.
Item 3: 13 pages
A memorial of some matters of fact in England since the year 1628.

HHC: Hotham MS, U DDHO/1/70: Queries and opinions on the liability of subjects for military service, no date[242]

1. Whether any subject of England be bound by law to show arms foot or horse, or to find them appointed with arms and other furniture such as the deputy lieutenants or captains shall appoint?
2. Whether if he refuse any or all of these, and be detained in the hands of a messenger or committed, may he not have his habeas corpus?

[242] It is likely that this document was drafted in 1640 to inform Sir John Hotham's critique of royal policy and county grievances in Yorkshire during the Second Bishops' War.

3. Whether may he refuse to march out of his county, unless the enemy be entered the kingdom?
4. Whether he may refuse to march forth of his county if not paid?
5. How <must> *much* those that have already accepted commissions of captains or colonels are obliged thereby?
6. Whether may not a colonel or captain give over his commission, and if he be committed for it, may he not have his habeas corpus and be freed by law?
7. Whether any subject may refuse to take the King's press money?
8. Whether the trained bands may be compelled to serve against an enemy out of the kingdom?
[*In a different hand*]
The first question consists of 2 parts.
1. Whether by law the subject be bound to show their arms. Secondly whether to find such as the deputy lieutenants or captains shall appoint. For the first I am of opinion that they are bound to show and to go to the musters upon the statute the 4 and 5 Philip and Mary, cap. 3, the statute is in force as I conceive, but extend no further than to appear and show such arms as they have. But for this the commissioners for musters have no power to commit if the person that makes default will pay 40s ?p[ro]vt? by the act. Secondly for finding of arms, the statute of Winchester, which in particular

[*page break*]

appoint what arms each man is to find, was repealed by the statute the 4 and 5 Philip and Mary, cap. 2, which statute is repealed by the statute of 1 James I, cap. 25. Whereupon the statute of Winchester being revived that is repealed by the statute 21 James I, cap. 28, so that there is no statute or authority in ?printa? for arms, but the statute the 5 Henry IV in the parliament roll 10:24 provides that every man <fo> *juxta statu. et facultates* shall find arms. That statute likewise provides in what manner and by what persons men shall be compelled; ?viz? commissioners and the sheriff of the county, the commissioners to the number of 13 persons. This statute is expressed in the negative, that no commissioners in other manners or words than is there expressed shall issue for the arming of the subjects. Whereupon I rather think that the deputy lieutenants and captains cannot compel men to find arms, in respect their authority is not derived to them according to the provision of that statute. For first the deputy lieutenants and captains have no immediate authority under the great seal but are only deputies *viz. no commissioners but deputies of commissioners*. Secondly because the statute of 5 Henry IV intends a competent *number* of country gentlemen as appears by the number, and therein pursues the statute of Winchester, whereby the two constables of the hundred were to certify defects in arms to the 2 justices to be assigned by the ?Lieutenancy?, and those 2 justices were to present such defects to the next Parliament. And now by 5 Henry IV although the same be not so much in favour of the country, yet so far soldiers that a great number, viz. 13 at least besides the sheriff ought to be commissioners. Nor is the sheriff as I conceive to be left out who hath the custody that the county committed to him, and who upon any tumults or rebellions is to take the *posse comitatus* to appease them.

And thirdly, by that statute the commissioners for the array or arms

[*page break*]

are to take care of the ?braluous? with all ?syling? in that commissions to the Lieutenants and the statute being express that no commissions in other ways than are there set down shall issue. I conceive that the deputy lieutenants and or captains have nothing to [*MS damaged*] do with compelling to find arms only upon the statute of <5 Henry IV> *4 and 5 Philip and Mary, cap. 3* they may compel men to come to secure such arms as they have, but I am clear that they cannot issue any ?mysterious? fees, nor coat or conduct money, regarding for that the petition of right, the statute 1 Elizabeth cap 7, 25 Elizabeth cap 8, 4 Henry IV, cap ?15? and by the parliament roll ?20 Elizabeth no: 12 and other authorities *ques nunc ?presulere?* etc.

2. The second question is answered by the first for if they have *no* authority then the practice is legal upon habeas corpus.

3. I conceive they are not otherwise than is expressed in the statute of 1 Elizabeth, cap. 5 and 4 Henry IV, cap. 3. And of sudden coming of strange enemies into the realm, neither is that of 11 Henry VII, cap. 1 against it as I conceive, because that in such case of coming of enemies we be bound and if that preamble were not to both these statutes of 1 Elizabeth and 4 Henry IV, yet it being but a preamble and not in the body of the act, clearly it doth not repeal those statutes.

4. He may refuse. The statutes 25 Elizabeth cap.? and 4 Henry IV 13 are clear in this, for those that soldier by knight service are bound at their own charge for 40 days to be in service upon summons, but these statutes discharge all others or them otherwise than according to their tenures *upon summons legally made*. And 25 Elizabeth doth not alter the law herein for it was so at the common law as appears by the petition whereupon the statute was made, viz: <that it is against> the *encount le droyt de realme*, the precedents are many in

it before the statute: regarding afore the statute the 19 Henry VIII, cap.1.

5, 6. To the fifth and sixth for times of action it may not be. I am doubtful whether it may be done without first giving notice to the Lord Lieutenant or those that placed them, although in times of peace and I conceive they cannot without giving notice, and after notice convenient time must be given for providing others.

7, 8. The seventh and eighth answered ?p[ro]vt? the third.

APPENDIX I: PRINTED MATERIAL RELATING TO THE CIVIL WAR AND INTERREGNUM

The Hotham family's collection of printed material relating to the civil war and interregnum period is now held in the Hull History Centre.[1] Early English Books Online has been used to identify these tracts with Thomason numbers (in bold), which have been given in preference, although Wing numbers have been cited if the tract is not listed in Thomason. The length of each tract in pages is also given. The collection is listed under 82 items but contains over 400 pamphlets and ordinances; the ordering and numbering here retains those of the archive catalogue. Items 80 to 82 were deposited in the East Riding Record Office on 7 April 1972. A great deal of the collection consists of the paper war that preceded and accompanied the outbreak of war in 1642. This was probably gathered and preserved by the Hothams, anxious to justify their defiance of the king, and to monitor their reputations in print. Items 76 to 79 are four bound volumes of acts and ordinances of the interregnum parliaments, between them containing over 250 items. These may have been collected and bound by or for Durand Hotham to inform his employment as an East Riding justice of the peace during the interregnum. A handful of post-Restoration tracts are appended at the end. For a detailed discussion of this collection, see A.L. Capern, 'The Hotham family and its papers', *Archives*, 23 (1998), pp. 102–103.

The tracts

1. *An appeale to the world in these times of extreame danger* (London, 1642), 8pp. **E107(26)**

2. *The coppy of a letter sent from General Leishley, to the Lord Generall the Earle of Holland, and read in the House of Commons, the 7th of July* (London, 1641), 4pp. **E164(18)**

[1] HHC: Hotham MS, U DDHO/2.

3. *The Lord of Hollands letter from Yorke, the 13. of this instant moneth of August; to the honourable Lords of Parliament* (13 August 1641), 6pp. **Wing (2nd ed.), H2421**

4. *The true coppy of a letter sent from Thomas, Earle of Arundell, Lord Marshall, from Middleborough in Zealand, to Mr. Pym. And read before the committee the 18. of September, 1641. Whereunto is added the coppy of another letter sent to Mr. Pym also from the committee in Scotland, Sep. 13. 1641. With the names of the committees that sat there for that day. Printed for John Thomas* (London, 1641), 5pp. **E172(17)**

5. *A continuation of the true diurnall of passages in Parliament from January 17. to January 24. Printed for Humphry Blunden* (London, 1642), 15pp.

6. *A perfect diurnall of the passages in Parliament: from the last of January to the seventh of February* (London, 1642), 8pp.

7. *The declaration of the right honourable Henry Earle of Cumberland Lord Lieutenant Generall of His Majesties forcs [*sic*] in York-shire. And of the nobility, gentry, and others His Majesties subjects now assembled at Yorke for His Majesties service and the defence of this city and county. First printed at Yorke, and now re-printed at London; by speciall command* (London, 1642), 8pp. **E244(18)**

8. *The petition of the knights, gentlemen, freeholders, and others the inhabitants of the county and city of York, presented to the honourable House of Commons now assembled in Parliament wherein (inter alia) they humbly offer to billet and mayntain at their own charge 300 of their horse, and 3000 of their trained bands within their owne shire for three moneths, if the Parliament shall think fit: subscribed by the Lord Major and Aldermen of York, by the high Sheriff and very many knights, esquires, and gentlemen of good quality: with the manner of their taking the protestation, before they subscribed the petition. Printed for John Franke* (London, 1642), 6pp. **Wing, P1807A**

9. *A declaration of the valiant resolution of the famous prentices of London, with their protestation. Who are willing to adventure their lives and fortunes under His Excellencie the Earle of Essex. For the honour of the King, the preservation of the priviledge of Parliament, the libertie of the subject, the good of the kingdome, and especially of the Citie of London. And for the maintenance of the Protestant religion, expelling all poperie, and the subduing of all the enemies of the true Church of England. Printed for Thomas Bankes* (London, 1642), 6pp. **E109(5)**

10. *The resolving of conscience upon this question whether upon such a supposition or case as is now usually made (the King will not discharge his trust, but is bent or*

seduced to subvert religion, laws, and liberties) subjects may take arms and resist, and whether that be the case now? By H. Fern D.D. &c. Printed by Roger Daniel printer to the Universitie (Cambridge, 1642), 51pp. A similar copy with different printers is listed at **Wing, F801**

11. Bound volume of pamphlets, itemized below:

11a. *To the Kings most excellent Majestie, the humble petition of the lords and commons assembled in Parliament* (no place or date), 8pp.

11b. *His Majesties answer to the petition of both houses of Parliament, presented to him at York, on Saturday, the 26. of March, 1642. By the Lord Willoughby, Lord Dungarvan, and Sir Anthony Irby* (no place, 1642), 12pp.

11c. *The humble petition of divers noblemen and gentlemen, estated in Ireland, and now at London, presented to His Majestie at York together with His Majesties answer thereunto, March 28. Printed by Robert Barker* (York, 1642), 5pp. **Wing, H3458**

11d. *The humble petition of the gentry, ministers, and freeholders of the county of York, assembled at the assizes there holden. Presented to His Majestie the 5. of April 1642. Together with His Majesties speech at the presenting thereof. And his gracious answer thereunto. Printed by Robert Barker* (York, 1642), 14pp. **E143(3)**

11e. *His Majesties message sent to the high court of Parliament, April 8. 1642. Concerning his resolution to go into Ireland, for suppressing the rebellion there. Printed by Robert Barker* (York, 1642), 6pp. **Wing (CD-ROM, 1996), C2444**

11f. *The humble petition of the Lords and Commons in Parliament, sent to His Majestie at York. Concerning the removall of His Majesties arms, cannon, and ammunition, in his magazin at Hull. And the taking off the reprive of six condemned priests, prisoners in Newgate. With His Majesties answer thereunto. 14. April. 1642. Printed by Robert Barker* (York, 1642), 10pp. **E144(11)**

11g. *The humble petition of the Lords and Commons in Parliament, presented to His Majestie at York, 18. April. Concerning his message lately sent unto them, touching his resolution of going into Ireland. With His Majesties answer thereunto. Printed by Robert Barker* (York, 1642), 26pp.

11h. *His Majesties message sent from Beverley to both Houses of Parliament, 24. April concerning Sir John Hothams refusall to permit His Majestie to enter into his town of Hull: together with a petition presented unto His Majestie in the name of the gentry and commons of the county of York: with His Majesties letter to the major, aldermen, and burgesses of the town and port of Kingston upon Hull, 25. April 1642. Printed by Robert Barker* (York, 1642), 18pp. **Wing, C2436**

11i. *His Majesties message to both houses of Parliament, 28. April. 1642. Declaring the reasons of his refusal to passe the bill lately sent unto him for setling [*sic*] of the militia. Printed by Robert Barker* (York, 1642), 10pp. **Wing, C2454**

11j. *The declaration and votes of both Houses of Parliament. Concerning the magazine at Hull; and Sir John Hotham. With the order of assistance. And His Majesties answer thereunto. With the statute of II. Hen. 7. Cap. I. Printed by Robert Barker* (York, 1642), 29pp. **Wing (2nd ed.), E1326A**

11k. *The humble petition of 85. gentlemen and freeholders, and 15. ministers of the county palatine of Chester Preferred to His Majestie at York, the seventh of May, 1642. In behalf of themselves and others. Together with His Majesties gracious answer. Printed by Robert Barker* (York, 1642), 9pp. **Wing (2nd ed.), H3463A**

12. *His Majesties answer to the petition of the Lords and Commons assembled in Parliament* (no place, 1642), 18pp.

13. *Another message sent to the Kings Majesty at Yorke, from both Houses of Parliament, March 28. 1642. With His Majesties auswer [*sic*] concerning the same, dated March 31. 1642. Sabbathi, 2. Aprilis, 1642. Ordered by the Lords in Parliament, that this message be published and printed. Jo. Browne Cler. Parliament. Whereunto is added the petition of the citizens of Yorke delivered to His Majesty by the High Sheriffe. Also an order from the House of Commons to the sheriffes of every county for the collection of the foure subsidies. With the new bill for tonnage and poundage passed by both Houses of Parliament. H. Elsynge, Cler. Parl. D. Com. Printed for John Thomas* (London, 1642), 8pp. **E143(2)**

14. *The humble petition of the gentry, ministers, and freeholders of the county of York, assembled at the assizes there holden; Presented to His Majestie the fifth of April. 1642. With His Majesties speech at the presenting thereof. Together with His Majesties gracious answer thereunto, April 7. Printed by Robert Barker* (York, 1642), 6pp.

15. *The humble petition of the gentry, ministers, and freeholders of the county of York, assembled at the assizes there holden. Presented to His Majesty, April 5. 1642. Together with His Majesties speech at the presenting thereof. And his gracious*

answer thereunto. First printed at York, and now reprinted in London, by the same copy, for Charles Greene, MDCXLII (London, 1642), 6pp. **E142(18)**

16. *The petition of the Lords and Commons, presented to His Majestie by the Earle of Stamford, Master Chancellour of the Exchequer, and Master Hungerford, April 18. 1642. Together with His Majesties answer thereunto. Printed by Robert Barker* (London, 1642), 14pp. **E144(19)**

17. *Five remarkable passages, which have very lately happened betweene His Maiestie, and the high court of Parliament. 1. The humble petition of the gentry and commons of York, presented to His Majesty, April 22. 1642. 2. His Majesties message sent to the Parliament April 24. 1642. concerning Sir Iohn Hotham's refusall to give His Majestie entrance into Hull. 3. The Parliaments resolution concerning the said Sir Joh. Hotham. 4. A declaration from both Houses of Parliament concerning the stopping of passages between Hull and the Parliament. 5. The true catalogue of all the names of the divines approved of by both Houses of Parliament, for each severall county in this Kingdome of England and Wales; as fit persons to be consulted with by the Parliament, touching the reformation of church-government, and the liturgie. Together with an order from both Houses to the same effect. 28. of Aprill 1642. Printed for F. Cowles, and T. Bates* (London, 1642), 8pp. **E146(1)**

18. *The declaration and votes of both Houses of Parliament, concerning the magazine at Hull, and Sir John Hotham governour thereof. Printed by Robert Barker* (London, 1642), 8pp. **E144(24)**

19. *The declaration and votes of both Houses of Parliament concerning the magazine at Hull, and Sir John Hotham, governour thereof. Also the order of assistance given to the committees of both Houses, concerning their going to Hull. April 28, 1642. Printed for F. Cowles, and T. Bates* (London, 1642), 8pp. **Wing (2nd ed.), E1326A**

20. *The declaration and votes of both Houses of Parliament, concerning the magazine at Hull, and Sir John Hotham governour thereof. With an order of assistance given to the committees of both Houses, concerning their going to Hull. Printed by Francis Leach* (London, 1642), 6pp. **Wing (2nd ed.), E1325**

21. *The declaration of Lords and Commons in Parliament assembled, concerning His Maiesties severall messages about the militia. Jovis 5. Maii. 1642. Printed for John Wright* (London, 1642), 8pp. **Wing, E1377**

22. *The answer of both Houses of Parliament, presented to His Majestie at York the ninth of May, 1642. To two messages sent to them from His Majestie, concerning*

Sir John Hothams refusall to give His Majestie entrance into his town of Hull. With His Majesties reply thereunto. Published by His Majesties command. Printed by Robert Barker (London, 1642), 5pp. **E147(5)**

23. *A letter from the right honourable Ferdinando Lord Fairfax, Sir Hugh Cholmley, Sir Philip Stapleton, Sir Henry Cholmley, committees of the Commons House of Parliament residing at Yorke. Together with a relation of all the passages at the great meeting at Yorke, on Thursday the 12. of this instant May, with the freeholders protestation inclosed in the letter from the said committee to Master Speaker, and ordered by the said house to be forthwith published in print. Printed by A. Norton for John Franke* (London, 1642), 16pp. **E148(4)**

24. *A remonstrance of the state of the kingdome agreed on by the Lords and Commons assembled in Parliament the 19 of May 1642, and published by order of both houses. Printed for F.C.* (London, 1642), 33pp. **Wing, E2223**

25. *His Majesties answer to a book, entituled, The declaration, or remonstrance of the Lords and Commons, of the 19th of May, 1642. Printed by Robert Barker* (London, 1642), 33pp. **E150(29)**

26. *The votes of both Houses of Parliament, the 20. of May, 1642. With the humble petition of the Lords and Commons in Parliament assembled, to the Kings most Excellent Majesty at Yorke. Die Lunae 23. Maii, 1642. Ordered by the Lords in Parliament, that these votes and this petition, shall be forthwith printed and published. Jo. Brown Cleric. Parliamentorum. Printed for Joseph Hunscot and John Wright, May 24* (London, 1642), 6pp. **E148(16)**

27. *The petition of both Houses of Parliament presented to his Majestie at York, the 23 of May, 1642 concerning the disbanding of his guard, with the three votes of both Houses of the 20, and His Majesties answer thereunto. Printed first at York, and now repninted* [sic] *at London, by A.N. for Edward Husbands* (London, 1642), 8pp. **Wing, E2166**

28. *A remonstrance or the declaration of the Lords and Commons, now assembled in Parliament, 26. of May. 1642. In answer to a declaration under His Majesties name concerning the businesse of Hull, sent in a message to both Houses the 21. of May, 1642. Reprinted by speciall order from the House of Commons, and the faults amended which escaped in the former impressions. H. Elsyng Cler. Par. D. Com. Printed by A.N. for John Franke* (London, 1642), 44pp.

29. *A remonstrance or the declaration of the Lords and Commons, now assembled in Parliament, 26. of May. 1642. In answer to a declaration under His Majesties name concerning the businesse of Hull, sent in a message to both Houses the*

21. of May, 1642. According to an order made in the House of Commons, on Saturday last, I have examined this copie with the originall, and have mended it. H. Elsyng Cler. Parl. D. Com. Printed for Richard Lownds (London, 1642), 21pp. Annotated on reverse cover, 'my honored good Lady Leigh To my worthy friend'.

30. *Votes of both Houses of Parliament: with sundry articles, or acts of Parliament to confirme the same. Taken out of the records of the Tower. Also, two orders of both Houses of Parliament: the one, to all high sheriffes, justices of the peace, and other officers, within 150. miles of the city of Yorke: the other, in particular to the high sheriffs, justices of the peace, and other officers within the county of Lancaster. In generall, to all the counties of England, and Dominion of Wales. Die Sabbathi 28. Maii 1642. Ordered by the Lords in Parliament, that these votes with the articles be forthwith printed and published. Printed by E. Griffin, for Cristopher Latham* (London, 1642), 8pp. **E149(8)**

31. *A declaration of the Lords and Commons in Parliament assembled concerning His Majesties proclamation given at his court at York, May 27th, 1642 with the statute of the 7 of Edward the First. Printed for Joseph Hunscott and John Wright* (London, 1642), 6pp. **Wing, E1372**

32. *A declaration of the Lords and Commons in Parliament concerning His Majesties proclamation given at his court at York, the 27. of May, 1641 with the statute of the 7 of Edw. I. Printed for William Gaye* (London, 1642), 6pp. **Wing (2nd ed.), E1371B**

33. *Five speciall passages viz., two petitions of the countie of Yorke: the one presented to the Kings most excellent Majestie at York the third of Iune, 1642, the other to the Lords and Commons in Parliament assembled: with the additionals thereunto annexed. The petition of the Kingdom of Scotland to the Lords of His Majesties most honourable Privie Councell of that Kingdome: also His Majesties letter to the Lords of his Privie Councell of the Kingdome of Scotland: and a letter from Sir Io. Bourchier to Sir Thomas Barrington, knight and baronet. Printed for Edmund Blackmore, June 8* (London, 1642), 7pp. **Wing, F1122**

34. *The declaration of the Lords and Commons assembled in Parliament concerning His Majesties letter and the petition of diverse noblemen, gentlemen, burgesses, and ministers, to the Privy Councell of Scotland likewise severall passages concerning the Lord Keeper of the Great Seale of England: as also an order for the searching and staying of all armes, ammunition, powder, light-horses, or any other provision that shall be carried towards the north part of England. Printed for Joseph Hunscott and John Wright* (London, 1642), 6pp. **Wing, E1370**

35. *His Majesties declaration to all His loving subjects, occasioned by a false and scandalous imputation laid upon His Majestie, of an intention of raising or leavying war against his Parliament, and of having raised force to that end. Also, His Majesties declaration and profession, together with that of the Lords and others of his councell there present, disavowing any preparations or intentions of leavying war against his two Houses of Parliament. Printed by Robert Barker* (London, 1642), 13pp. **Wing (CD-ROM, 1996), C2237A**

36. *His Majesties answer to the petition of the Lords and Commons in Parliament assembled: presented to His Majestie at York, June 17. Printed by Robert Barker* (London, 1642), 14pp. **E152(2)**

37. *His Majesties resolution concerning the setting up of his standard. Together, with the resolution of certain noblemen, who were present with His Majestie at York. Who when His Majestie resolved to set up his standard at York, did disswade him from it; and rather then they would contenauce [*sic*] His Majestie in that resolution, left His Majestie, and would have come for London. Also, Sir John Bankes his perswasion, for His Majesties return to London. His Majesties consent at the first, but afterwards his refusall. Together with an order from the House of Peers, concerning the stopping of all kinds of ammunition. Joh. Brown Cler. Parl. June 18. Printed for I. Thompson and A. Coe* (London, 1642), 8pp. **E151(10)**

38. *Two proclamations by the King. His Maiesties proclamation for the more free passage of all his loving subjects, and the free carriage and conveyance of their horses, provisions, or other goods from any one place or part to another within his kingdom of England, and the dominions thereof. Printed at York, and re-imprinted at London, by A. N. for Richard Lownds* (London, 1642), 6pp. **E151(28)**

39. *The declaration of the Lords and Commons in Parliament assembled, in answer to his Majesties letter to the Lord Major and the Court of Aldermen of the citie of London, and concerning his declaration to the county of Yorke at Heyworth Moore by his last speciall summonds, Luna 20. day of Junae 1642. Printed for John Wright and Joseph Hunscot* (London, 1642), 8pp. **Wing (CD-ROM, 1996), E1442A**

40. *A new declaration of the Lords and Commons in Parliament, in answer to His Majesties letter dated the fourteenth of June and sent to the lord mayor, aldermen and sheriffs of the city of London as also concerning His Majesties declaration published in Heweth More: together with the vindication of the Parliament from scandals which are cast upon them. Printed by A.N. for Edw. Husbands and John Frank* (London, 1642), 6pp. **Wing, E1666**

41. *His Majesties declaration concerning leavies. Charles R. Our expresse pleasure is, that this our declaration be published in all churches and chappells within the kingdom of England and dominion of Wales, by the parsons, vicars or curates of the same. Printed by Robert Barker* (London, 1642), 13pp. **E153(24)**

42. *His Majesties answer to a printed paper, intituled, A new declaration of the Lords and Commons in Parliament, of the 21. of June, 1642 in answer to His Majesties letter dated the fourteenth of June, and sent to the Lord Major, aldermen, and sheriffs of the city of London. Printed by Robert Barker* (York, 1642), 8pp. **Wing, C2109**

43. *A letter sent by a Yorkshire gentleman* [Sir John Bourchier], *to a friend in London: being a full and true relation of the proceedings betweene His Majesty and the county of York, at Heworth Moore, upon Friday, June 3. Also the most materiall passages of this weeke, from London, Westminster, &c* (no place, 1642), 8pp. **E150(5)**

44. *The speech of Denzell Holles Esquire. Delivered at the Lords Barr, Wednesday the 15th. of Iune. Vpon the impeachment of the Earles of North-hampton, Devonshire, Monmouth, and Dover, and of the Lords Rich, Andever, Grey of Ruthen, Coventry and Capell, for their contempt in departing from the Parliament, and not returning upon summons. Die Mercurij, 22. Iunij, 1642. Printed for Thomas Underhill* (London, 1642), 6pp. **E200(48)**

45. *His Majesties answer to the declaration of both Houses of Parliament, concerning the Commission of Array: of the first of July, 1642. Printed by Roger Daniel* (Cambridge, 1642), 62pp. **E114(20)**

46. *Two declarations of the Lords and Commons assembled in Parliament. One, July 12, for the preservation and safety of the kingdom, and the town of Hull. The other, July 13, concerning the miserable distractions and grievances this kingdom now lieth in, by means of Jesuiticall and wicked councellors now about His Majesty. With an order of both Houses of Parliament to all Lord Lieutenants and Deputy Lieutenants of their severall counties, to raise forces to suppresse all disturbers of the peace. Printed for E. Husbands and I. Franck* (London, 1642), 8pp. **Wing, E2387**

47. *The humble petition of the Lords and Commons in Parliament assembled, to the Kings most Excellent Majesty. For a pacification between His Majesty and both Houses. Veneris Julii 15. 1642. Ordered by the Lords in Parliament, that this petition be forthwith printed and published. Jo. Brown Cler. Parliamentorum. Printed for Christopher Latham, and T. Creake* (London, 1642), 7pp. **E155(3)**

48. *A declaration of the Commons assembled in Parliament; concerning the rise and progresse of the grand rebellion in Ireland. Together with a multitude of examinations of persons of quality, whereby it may easily appear to all the world, who were, and still are the promoters of that cruell and unheard of rebellion. With some letters and papers of great consequence of the Earl of Antrims, which were intercepted. Also some letters of Mart, which were granted by the Lord Mohun, Sir Ralph Hopton, &c. And likewise another from the rebells in Ireland, who term themselves, the supreme councel for the Catholique-cause. Printed for Edw. Husbands, July 25 1643* (London, 1643), 63pp. **E61(23)**

49. *A declaration of the Lords and Commons in Parliament assembled willing that no messenger or officer [. . .] shall arrest, take, or carry away any of His Majesties subjects against their wils [. . .] as also the vindication of both houses of Parliament of the Earle of Stamford, and others, from His Maiesties imputation of treason: with certain instructions from His Majesty to all the judges of the Kingdome of England. Printed for John Wright, July 28 1643* (London, 1642), 8pp. **Wing, E1478**

50. *A replication of the Lords and Commons assembled in Parliament to His Maiesties last answer sent by the Right Honourable the Earle of Holland. Printed for John Wright, July 29* (London, 1642), 8pp. **Wing, E2230**

51. *A replication of the Lords and Commons assembled in Parliament to his Majesties last answer, sent by the right honorable the Earl of Holland. Die Jovis 28. July, 1642. Ordered by the Lords in Parliament, that the petition of the Lords and Commons in Parliament delivered to his Majesty the 16. day of July, together with his Majesties answer thereunto, and a replication of the said Lords and Commons, to the said answer, dated the 26. of July 1642. shall be read in all churches and chappels within the kingdome of England and dominion of Wales, by the parsons, vicars or curates of the same. John Brown Cler. Parliamentorum. July 29. Printed for Nathaniel Allen* (London, 1642), 6pp. **Wing (CD-ROM, 1996), E2230A**

52. *A declaration of the Lords and Commons assembled in Parliament setting forth the grounds and reasons that necessitate them at this time to take up defensive armes for the preservation of His Majesties person, the maintenance of true religion, the lawes and liberties of this kingdom and the power and priviledges of Parliament. Printed at London by Thomas Banks and William Lee, August 3* (London, 1642), 8pp. **Wing, E1451**

53. *A declaration of the Lords and Commons assembled in Parliament, setting forth the grounds and reasons, that necessitate them at this time to take up defensive arms for the preservation of His Majesties person, the maintenance of the true religion,*

the laws and liberties of this kingdom, and the power and priviledge of Parliament. Ordered by the Commons in Parliament, that this declaration be forthwith printed and published. Hen. Elsynge, Cler. Parl. D. Com. August 3 1642. Printed for Edward Husbands, and John Franck (London, 1642), 16pp. **E108(42)**

54. Further copy of item 53 (DDHO/2/53).

55. *His Majesties speech, to the gentlemen of Yorkshire, on Thursday, the fourth of August. 1642. Printed at York by Robert Barker, and re-printed at London, by A. Norton, August 8* (London, 1642), 6pp. **Wing (2nd ed.), C2803**

56. *The presentment and articles proposed by the grand jury of the county of York: and the declaration of the nobility, grand jury, and gentry of the said countie: at the assises assembled in August, 1642. With His Majesties answer thereunto. Printed by Robert Barker, and re-printed at London, August 12* (London, 1642), 6pp. **E116(37)**

57. *A declaration of the Lords and Commons assembled in Parlament [*sic*] whereby the good subjects of this kingdome may better discerne their owne danger, and be stirred up with more earnestnesse to assist the Parliament, in the maintenance of religion, the common justice and liberty of the kindgome, which seemes to be in no lesse hazard, then if we had an army of Irish rebels in the bowels of the land. Also some observations and directions to the knights, gentlemen, and other inhabitants of Yorkshire, and other the Northerne counties. Die Sabbathi August 20. 1642. Ordered by the Lords and Commons assembled in Parliament that this declaration be forthwith printed and published. John Browne Cler. Parliamentor. August 22. Printed at London for John Wright* (London, 1642), 6pp. **E113(9)**

58. *A copy of the commission of array granted from His Majesty, to the Marquesse of Hertford. Printed for E. Husbands and I. Frank, August 24* (London, 1642), 8pp. **Wing, C2168A**

59. *A declaration of the Lords and Commons assembled in Parliament for the disarming of all popish recusants, and that it shall be lawfull for any of His Majesties subjects to seize upon the persons of all such as shall execute the illegall commission of array. Ordered by the Lords and Commons in Parliament, that this declaration thus amended be forth-with reprinted. H. Elsyn. Cler. Parl. Dom. Com. Together with a declaration of the Lords and Commons in Parliament that all persons whatsoever, which shall assist his Majesty in this war with horse, arms, or mony, shall be traytors to his Majesty, the Parliament and kingdom. Printed by A.N. for Ed. Husbands and J. Franke, August 25* (London, 1642), 6pp. **Wing (CD-ROM, 1996), E1414A**

60. *The Kings Majesties intention concerning the setting up of his standard, and levying of warre against both Houses of Parliament; wherein he declares his full resolution therein to both the said houses. Likewise the resolution of the lords that are now resident with His Majesty. Also the parliaments desires to all his Majesties loving subjects, for a meet concurrence with them, to maintain the peace of these kingdoms. Printed for H. Blunon, August 6* (London, 1642), 6pp. **E109(20)**

61. A *true copy of the instructions agreed upon by the Lords and Commons assembled in Parliament, and sent to his Excellency the Earl of Essex, lord general of the army, concerning the advancing of his forces towards his Majesty, &c. Also the last declaration and votes of the Lords and Commons assembled in Parliament, concerning the late treaty of peace in Yorke-shire. Wherin they renounce the sayd agreement as being very prejudiciall and dangerous unto the whole kiugdome* [sic]*, that any one county should stand as newters, and withdrew themselves from the assistance of the rest. Together with the instructions, sent to Mr. Edward Hotham,*[2] *and Sir Edward Rhodes, with power to them to publish it, and withall to pardon all those that shall submit within ten dayes. Die Martis, Octob. 4. Printed for Fr. Coles, Octob. 6.* (London, 1642), 7pp. **E121(16)**

62. *A declaration of the Lords and Commons assembled in Parliament, concerning his Majesties advancing with his army toward London. With direction, that all the trained bands and volunteers be put into a readinesse, that so the kings army may find opposition in every place as they march. Also, how Sir John Hinderson urged one David Alexander a Scotchman, to kill Sir John Hotham, and blow up the Parliaments magazine; to whom his Majesty gave money, and he received it. Printed for J. Wright, Octob. 17* (London, 1642), 8pp. **E122(24)**

63. *The second part of Vox populi. Being the peoples report unto the King, upon the severall appeales declared in his Majesties name. An egge long since hatcht and covered, and now fledg'd, and upon the wing toward the deserts of His Majesties present abode. May it prove a dove with an olive branch to prepare his resting on these his mountaines of Ararat. 28 October* (London, 1642), 20pp. **E124(34)**

64. *A remonstrance of the Lords and Commons assembled in Parliament, or, The reply of both Houses, to a printed book, under His Majesties name, called, His Majesties answer to a printed book, entituled, A remonstrance, or the declaration of the Lords and Commons now assembled in Parliament the 26 of May 1642. in answer to a declaration under His Majesties name, concerning the businesse of*

[2] This newsbook referred to the deeds of 'Captain' John Hotham but misnamed him as 'Edward'.

Hull. November 2. Printed for J. Wright, Novemb. 3 (London, 1642), 65pp. Annotated 'John Lord Hotham 4/6 1876'. **E126(10)**

65. *Two declarations of the Lords and Commons assembled in Parliament. The one, for the raising of all power and force, as well trained bands as other, in the severall counties of this kingdome, to lead against all traitors and their adherents, and all such as shall oppose any of His Majesties loving subjects that shall be imployed in this service by either or both Houses of Parliament. The other, that the good subjects of this kingdome may the better discerne their own danger, and be stirred up with more earnestnesse to assist the Parliament in the maintenance of religion, the common iustice and liberty of the kingdome. Also some observations and directions to the knights, gentlemen, and other the inhabitants of Yorkeshire, and other northerne counties. Decemb. 10. Printed by R. Austin and A. Coe* (London, 1642), 8pp. **E129(26)**

66. *A declaration of the Lords and Commons assembled in Parliament: shewing the imminent danger in which the kingdom now stands, by reason of a malignant party prevailing with His Majesty, putting him upon violent and perilous wayes, and now in arms against them, to the hazarding of His Majesties person, and for the oppression of the true religion, the law and liberties of this kingdom, and the power and priviledges of Parliament; all which every honest man is bound to defend. Wherefore the Lords and Commons do now think fit to give this accompt unto the world, to be a satisfaction unto all men; of the justice of their proceedings. Printed for John Frank, Jan. 26* (London, 1643), 8pp. **E245(23)**

67. *Articles of peace and commerce between the high and mighty kings, Charles by the grace of God King of Great Britain, France, and Ireland, Defender of the Faith, &c. and John the 4th king of Portugal, Algarres, &c. and their subjects concluded at London the nine and twentieth day of January in the yeer of our Lord 1642. Printed by Robert Barker* (London, 1642), 22pp. **Wing, C2147**

68. *A copy of a letter written by Mr. Stephen Marshall to a friend of his in the city, for the necessary vindication of himself and his ministry, against that altogether groundlesse, most unjust, and ungodly aspersion cast upon him by certaine malignants in the city, and lately printed at Oxford, in their Mendacium Aulicum, otherwise called Mercurius Aulicus, and sent abroad into other nations to his perpetuall infamy. In which letter the accusation is fully answered. And together with that, the lawfulnesse of the Parliaments taking up defensive arms is briefly and learnedly asserted and demonstrated, texts of Scripture cleared, all objections to the contrary answered, to the full satisfaction of all those that desire to have their consciences informed in this great controversie. Printed for John Rothwell* (London, 1643), 30pp. **E102(10)**

69. *A learned usefull and seasonable discourse concerning the Church of England, and the Church of Rome. Addressed by way of letter to M. St. Iohn, a Romish priest, by that eminent author and worthy patriot, Dr. John Bastwick, now prisoner under the popish tyranny at Yorke. Printed for John Wright, Junior* (London, 1643), 12pp. **E77(26)**

70. *A vindication of the treatise of monarchy, containing an answer to Dr Fernes reply; also, a more full discovery of three maine points; 1. The ordinance of God in supremacie. 2. The nature and kinds of limitation. 3. The causes and meanes of limitation in governments. Done by the authour of the former treatise. Printed by G. M. for John Bellamy* (London, 1644), 80pp. **E39(12)**

71. *A declaration to all His Majesties loving subjects within the Kingdome of England and dominion of Wales; concerning a King and his representative councell, touching the government of his people, according to the known laws of the realme. With the opinion and proceedings of seven ambassadours concerning the governement of the common-wealth. Imprinted at York by Tho: Broad; And reprinted at London* (London, 1648), 6pp. **E429(13)**

72. *Mercurius Elencticus: Communicating the unparallell'd proceedings at Westminster, the head-quarters, and other places; discovering their designes, reproving their crimes, and advising the kingdome, no. 29, 7–14 June* (London, 1648), 8pp. **E447(11)**

73. *Considerations humbly presented to the high court of Parliament by Captain Francis Swaine, of the City of York* (no place, post 1649), 7pp.[3]

74. *Mercurius Politicus, comprising the sum of foreign intelligence with the affairs now on foot in the three nations of England, Ireland, & Scotland for information of the people, no. 602, 5–12 January* (London, 1660), 16pp. **E773(42)**

75. Bound volume of pamphlets, itemized below:

75a. John Jubbes, *Several proposals for peace & freedom, by an agreement of the people, offered unto Commissary General Ireton for the concurrence of the Army, by the approbation and consent of many worthy persons of the Common Councel and others of the city of London, on the eleventh of this instant December, to be agreed unto, and subscribed by all the inhabitants of England & Wales. Printed for J: Hanes, Decemb. 22* (London, 1648), 11pp. **E477(18)**

[3] This pamphlet called for reforms to the law. For the parliamentarian Captain Francis Swaine, see TNA, SP 16/513/141; SP 19/121/20b; SP 19/126/9; SP 28/249.

75b. Henry Anderson,[4] *A meanes to reconcile the present distempers of these times, as things now are. Set out by a member of the present Parliament* (London, 1648), 8pp. **E458(18)**

75c. William Ashurst, *Reasons against agreement with a late printed paper, intituled, Foundations of freedome: or, The agreement of the people. Whereby it doth appear, that the particulars proposed in the said paper are not foundations of freedome, but of tyrannie and slaverie to the people; being destructive to religion, laws, liberty, and government; against our Covenant and protestations, and very dangerous and unsafe for the kingdom* (London, 1648), 14pp. **E536(4)**

75d. John Lilburne, *Englands new chains discovered; or The serious apprehensions of a part of the people, in behalf of the Commonwealth; (being presenters, promoters, and approvers of the large petition of September 11. 1648.) Presented to the supreme authority of England, the representers of the people in Parliament assembled. 26 February* (London, 1649), 16pp. **E545(27)**

75e. Sir Francis Nethersole, *Problemes necessary to be determined by all that have, or have not taken part on either side in the late unnaturall warre. For the making of their peace with God and disposing them to a hearty peace one with another. By reflecting upon what they have done, before they engage in a new more dangerous and doubtfull warre: dedicated to the Lord Major, aldermen and Common-Councel of the Honorable City of London. By P.D.* (London, 1648), 24pp. **E458(20)**

75f. *True information of the beginning and cause of all our troubles, how they have been hatched and how prevented wherein we may see the manifold contrivances and attempts of forraigne and home-bred enemies against the Parliament, Kingdome, and purity of religion* (London, 1648), 41pp. **Wing, T2705**

75g. John Cook, *King Charls his case: or, An appeal to all rational men, concerning his tryal at the High Court of Iustice. Being for the most part that which was intended to have been delivered at the bar, if the King had pleaded to the charge, and put himself upon a fair tryal. With an additional opinion concerning the death of King James, the loss of Rochel, and, the blood of Ireland. Printed by Peter Cole for Giles Calvert* (London, 1649), 43pp. **E542(3)**

75h. John Dury, *Considerations concerning the present Engagement, whether it may lawfully be entered into; yea or no? Written at the desire of a friend, by J.D.*

[4] This was Sir Henry Anderson of Long Cowton (1583–1659), father of Isabel, third wife of Lieutenant-General John Hotham: M.F. Keeler, *The Long Parliament, 1640–1641: a biographical study of its members* (Philadelphia, 1954), pp. 86–87.

November 27. Printed by John Clowes for Richard Wodenoth (London, 1649), 24pp. **E584(12)**

75i. John Warr, *The corruption and deficiency of the lawes of England soberly discovered: or, Liberty working up to its just height. Printed for Giles Calvert* (London, 1649), 18pp. **E559(10)**

75j. John Streater, *A glympse of that jewel, judicial, just, preserving libertie. By Jo. Streater, a member of the Army of the Commonwealth of England serving in Ireland. Printed for Giles Calvert* (London, 1653), 15pp. **E690(11)**

75k. *A declaration of the Parlament of England, upon the marching of the Armie into Scotland. Die Mercurii Junii 26. 1650. Ordered by the Parlament, that it bee referred to the Council of State, to see this declaration forthwith printed and published. Printed by William Du-gard, by the appointment of the Council of State* (London, 1650), 10pp. **E604(6)**

75l. *A declaration of the Parliament of England concerning their late endeavors, in a peaceable way, to remove all misunderstandings, and differences between the Common-wealth of England, and the kingdome of Scotland. Herewith is printed the last paper of the Scotch Commissioners, with the sense of the Parliament thereupon. Also the letter of the Parliament of England to the Parliament of Scotland, with their answer thereunto, which is answerd by this declaration. Die Sabbathi 14 Julii 1649. Printed for Matthew Simmons* (London, 1649), 30pp. Only pp. 12–28 survive in this copy. **E565(17)**

75m. *A declaration of the Parliament of the Commonwealth of England, relating to the affairs and proceedings between this Commonwealth and the States General of the United Provinces of the Low-Countreys, and the present differences occcasioned [*sic*] on the States part [. . .] Friday the ninth of Iuly, 1652. Printed by John Field* (London, 1652), 70pp. **E669(19)**

75n. *The proceeds of the Protector (so called) and his Councill against Sir Henry Vane, Knight. A late eminent Member of the Councill of State of the Common-wealth of England: as touching his imprisonment in the Isle of Wight. Together with his testimony delivered in writing to the said Protector, by way of a peculiar addresse to himself, and faithfull advice of an old friend and acquaintance. Faithfully transcribed and attested out of the original copy's, and published by a reall well-wisher to Sions prosperity and Englands liberty* (London, 1656), 9pp. **E889(11)**

75o. *The humble petition and addresse of the officers of the Army, to the Parliament of the Common-Wealth of England, &c. Thursday, May 12, 1659. Ordered by the officers of the Army, that this petition and address be forthwith printed and published. Printed by Henry Hills, for him and Francis Tyton* (London, 1659), 13pp. **E983(7)**

75p. *An exact relation of the proceedings and transactions of the late Parliament: their beginning and ending. With a briefe account of their expence of the time of their session, and of the acts that were made by them, who were dissolved the 12. Decemb. 1653. As likewise of foure great votes, viz. I. For abolishing the Court of Chancery. II. For a new modell of the law. III. For taking away the power of patrons to make presentations. IV. That innocent negative vote of not agreeing with the report of the committee for tithes. And an account of some reasons of those votes: with a briefe apology in way of vindication of those gentlemen that appeared for the votes from the great out-cry made against them. By L.D. a Member of the late Parliament. Printed for Livewell Chapman* (London, 1654), 27pp. **E729(6)**

75q. Unidentified pamphlet with title page missing and only pp. 5–34 remaining. It contains a speech of Oliver Cromwell, Lord Protector, concerning the healing and settling of the nation.

75r. *His Highnesse the Lord Protector's speech to the Parliament in the Painted Chamber on Tuesday the 12th of September. 1654. Taken by one who stood very near him, and published to prevent mistakes. Printed by T.R. and E.M. for G. Sawbridge* (London, 1654), 43pp. **E812(11)**

75s. *The Lord General Cromwel's speech delivered in the Council-Chamber, upon the 4 of July, 1653. To the persons then assembled, and intrusted with the supreme authority of the nation. This is a true copie: published for information, and to prevent mistakes* (London, 1654), 26pp. **E813(13)**

75t. *A declaration of the Parliament of England. Written to the high and mighty Lords, the Lords States General of the United Provinces of the Low-Countreys: concerning their last embassie extraordinary into England. Printed for Lawrence Blaiklock* (London, 1645), 35pp. **E297(13)**

75u. *The speech of Their Excellencies the Lords Ambassadours Extraordinary. From the high and mighty States General of the United Provinces of the Netherlands, taking their leave of both the Honourable Houses of Parliament assembled at Westminster. 10. April 1645. Translated out of French into English: and printed by their Excellencies order. Steph. Taylor secr. Together with a moderate answer by a private gentleman. Printed by M.B. for Robert Bostock, 16 April* (London, 1645), 6pp. **E278(9)**

75v. *The humble desires and propositions for a safe and well-grounded peace, agreed upon by the mutuall advice and consent of the Parliamets [*sic*] of both* *kingdoms, united by Solemn league and covenant. Presented unto His Majesty at Oxford the 24 of Novemb. last, by committees from both Houses of Parliament, and commissioners from the kingdom of Scotland. Together with an order, and severall votes of the Commons assembled in Parliament, the 4. and 8. of this present Octob. 1645. for delinquents, to compound according to the said propositions, and to come in to the Parliament before December next ensuing. Printed for Edward Husband, 13 October* (London, 1645), 15pp. **E304(23)**

75w. *His Majesties last declaration, and finall resolution, concerning a speedy accomodation with His high Court of Parliament; as it was lately delivered by himselfe to the Lords of his Privy Councell in Oxford at a conference there for that purpose. Ordered to be printed. First printed at Oxford by Leonard Lichfield, and now reprinted at London for Adam Bell* (London, 1642), 8pp. **E83(4)**

75x. *Three letters intercepted by Sir Tho: Fairfax in Cornwal. The first, from the E: of Glamorgan to His Majesty; the second, from the Lord George Digby to his lady, the third, to his servant Walsingham; concerning their proceedings in Ireland. Sent by Mr. Peters to the Honorable House of Commons, and read in the said House. Printed for Edward Husband, 26 March* (London, 1646), 8pp. **E329(12)**

75y. *The Parliaments answer to His Majesties two letters, concerning His Majesties personall treaty with them. The one dated the 26. and the other the 29. of December last. Printed for Edward Husband, 17 January* (London, 1646), 8pp. **E316(18)**

75z. *The Parliaments severall late victories in the west, obtained by Sir Thomas Fairfax army, as it was certified by several letters sent unto the House of Commons, and read in the said House. Together with a list of the several prisoners taken, and the number of men and horse. Printed for Edw. Husbands, 21 January* (London, 1646), 8pp. **E317(2)**

75aa. *His Majesties message, to the kingdome of Scotland; shewing that he hath given order for disbanding all his forces in both kingdoms, for recalling all commissions to any at sea, and that he is resolved to apply himselfe totally to the councels and advices of his Parliaments, for setling of truth and peace. Together with divers papers presented to His Majesty at Newcastle by a committee of the Estates of the kingdome of Scotland. Printed for L. Chapman, 26 May* (London, 1646), 8pp. **E338(5)**

75ab. *The Kings letter to the Marquesse of Ormond: and the Marquesse of Ormonds letter to Monroe. Relating the Kings whole design, concerning all the three kingdoms. Printed, by I.C. 8 June* (London, 1646), 6pp. **E340(5)**

75ac. *The propositions of the Lords and Commons assembled in Parliament. For a safe and well-grounded peace. Sent to His Majestie at Newcastle, by the Right Honourable the Earle of Pembroke and Montgomery. The earle of Suffolke. Members of the House of Peeres. Printed for John Wright, 17 July* (London, 1646), 29pp. **E344(25)**

75ad. *A particular charge or impeachment, in the name of His Excellency Sir Thomas Fairfax, and the army under his command. Against Denzill Hollis Esq; Sir Philip Stapleton. Sir William Lewis. Sir John Clotworthy. Sir William Waller. Sir John Maynard, Knights. [*double brace*] Major Gen. Massey. John Glynn Esq; Recorder of London. Walter Long Esq; Col. Edward Harley. And Anthony Nicoll Esq; members of the House of Commons. Imprinted at London: for George Whittington* (London, 1647), 29pp. **E397(17)**

75ae. *Three speeches delivered in the Guild-hall, London, on Tuesday the fourth of March, By the Earl of Northumberland, the Lord Lowden, and Sir Henry Vane junior. Concerning the treaty at Uxbridge; wherein is shewed the candor of the Houses of Parliament, and the unreasonablenesse of the Kings Commissioners; in urging that the militia might be put into the hands of such as have taken arms against the Parliament. Justifying the cessation in Ireland, and no promise would be given that there should be no further peace made with them. Our propositions for religion rejected. Also, what course is now to be taken. Licensed, and printed according to order. Printed for Peter Cole, 11 March* (London, 1645), 11pp. **E273(3)**

75af. *The Archbishop of Canterbury's speech: or his funerall sermon, preacht by himself on the scaffold on Tower-Hill, on Friday the 10. of January, 1644. Upon Hebrews 12. 1,2. Also, the prayers which he used at the same time and place before his execution. All faithfully written by John Hinde, whom the Archbishop beseeched that he would not let any wrong be done him by any phrase in false copies. Licensed and entred according to order. Printed by Peter Cole* (London, 1645), 19pp. Annotated 'Speeches in p[ar]liament: 1659'. **E24(15)**

75ag. *A full vindication and answer of the XI. accused members; viz. Denzill Holles, Esq; Sir Philip Stapleton, Sir William Lewis, Sir John Clotworthy, Sir William Waller, Sir Iohn Maynard Kts Major Gen. Massey, Iohn Glynne Esq; Recorder of London. Walter Long Esquire Col. Edward Harley, Anthony Nichols Esq to a late printed pamphlet intituled, A particular charge or impeachment, in the name of Sir Thomas Fairfax and the army under his command; against the said members, by his appointment and the Councel of War* (London, 1647), 42pp. **E398(17)**

75ah. *A declaration of the Lords and Commons assembled in Parliament, concerning the papers of the Scots commissioners, entituled, The answer of the commissioners of the kingdom of Scotland to both Houses of Parliament, upon the new propositions of peace, and the four bills to be sent to His Majesty: and concerning the proceedings of the said commissioners in the Isle of Wight. Printed for Edward Husband, 13 March* (London, 1648), 95pp. **E432(1)**

75ai. W. Wheatly, *A declaration of the Scottish armie concerning their immediate marching towards the borders of England; as also their reasons of their comming, together with their resolution touching the same. Likewise the number of their army, both horse and foot, and their advance, with this motto in their ensignes, For religion, crown, and kingdome. Whereunto is annexed, the resolution of the northern counties, concerning the Scottish army, and their present proceedings therein. Printed for R. V.* (London, 1647), 8pp. **E406(22)**

75aj. *His Maiesties most gracious message, May the 12th. from Holdenby, to the Lords and Commons in the Parliament of England, assembled at Westminster, and the Commissioners of the Parliament of Scotland; with his answer to the propositions. Printed for Rich. Royston* (London, 1647), 8pp. **E388(19)**

75ak. *The votes of the Lords & Commons assembled in Parliament touching no farther address to the King with a declaration thereupon published by the Commons of England in Parliament assembled. Printed for Edward Husband, 18 February* (London, 1648), 32pp. A similar tract is listed as **Wing, E2456**

75al. William Prynne, *A briefe memento to the present un-parliamentary junto touching their present intentions and proceedings, to depose & execute Charles Steward [*sic*], their lawfull King. By William Prynne Esquire, a Member of the House of Commons, and prisoner under the Armies tyranny; who, it seemes, have levyed war against the Houses of Parliament, their quandam-masters whose Members they now forcibly take and detaine captives, during their lawfull pleasures* (London, 1649), 16pp. **Wing (2nd ed.), P3909A**

75am. *A remonstrance of His Excellency Thomas Lord Fairfax, Lord Generall of the Parliaments forces. And of the Generall Councell of officers held at St Albans the 16. of November, 1648. Presented to the Commons assembled in Parliament, the 20. instant, and tendred to the consideration of the whole kingdome. Printed for John Partridge and George Whittington* (London, 1648), 70pp. **E473(11)**

76. Large bound volume of Acts of Parliament, comprising seventy-nine items, predominantly 1649–1650.

77. Large bound volume of Acts and Proclamations of Parliament, comprising ninety-seven items, 1650–1657.

78. Large bound volume of Ordinances of Parliament, comprising fifty-two items, 1653–1654.

79. Large bound volume of Acts of Parliament, comprising twenty-seven items, 1657.

80. Bound volume of pamphlets, itemized below:

80a. *A declaration of the Lords and Commons assembled in Parliament. In answer to His Majesties declaration, intituled His Majesties declaration to all his loving subjects, after his late victory against the rebels, on Sunday the 23 of October, 1642. Together, with a catalogue of the names of divers of the colonels, lievtenant-colonells, serjeant majors, captains, and lieutenants, that are papists and commanders in the army, under the command of the Earle of New-Castle. Printed for Edward Husbands, and John Franke* (London, 1642), 12pp. **E244(23)**

80b. *To the Kings Most Excellent Majestie, the humble petition of vs the inhabitants of Lancashire, whose names are hereunder written, in the behalfe of our selves and divers others, being recusants* (London, 1643), 2pp. **Wing (2nd ed.), T1544**

80c. *A remonstrance shewing the occasion of the arming of the county of Kent* (London, 1648), 1p. **Thomason, 669.f.12(34)**

80d. *Some speciall arguments which warranted for the Scottish subjects lawfully to take up armes in defence of their religion and liberty when they were in danger. Extracted out of the manuscripts of one of their chiefe reformers. Very usefull and necessary for these present times. The times doe require that the points following be pressed upon the people, both by the preachers in publick, and by understanding, and well-affected persons in private conference* (Amsterdam, 1642), 8pp. **Wing (2nd ed.), S4619A**

80e. James I, *The true law of free monarchy, or The reciprocall and mutuall duty betwixt a free king and his naturall subjects. By a well affected subject of the kingdome of Scotland. Printed by T.P.* (London, 1642), 16pp. Title page damaged. **E238(23)**

80f. *His Maiesties declaration to all his loving subjects of August 12. 1642. Printed by His Majesties special command by N.N.* (Cambridge, 1642), 38pp. **Wing, C2242**

80g. *Two declarations of the Lords and Commons assembled in Parliament the former being a full narration of the proceedings of the evill councellors about His Majestie in many parts of the kingdome, with the necessity that lyes upon them speedily to provide for the safety of His Majesty, and the whole realme: the other to assure the inhabitants neare Hull that they shall be fully satisfied by both Houses for what damages may ensue to that county by Sir John Hotham's necessary letting in some tides from Humber, for securing the towne: together with their assurance of protection and full recompence for all necessary provision that shall be sent in by land or sea to the use of the said towne of Hull. Printed for John Burroughes* (London, 1642), 8pp. **Wing, E2389**

80h. *The petition of the Lords and Commons in Parliament, delivered to His Majestie the 16 of July: Together with His Majesties answer thereunto. Whereunto is added the votes Die Martis. 12 Julii. 1642. Printed by F. Leach, for M. Walbancke and R. Lownds* (London, 1642), 8pp.

80i. Ludwig Friedrich Gifftheil, *Two letters directed to the mighty ones of England, Scotland, and Ireland, but especially to the King, concerning these present calamities and commotions of warre: being great and present judgements denounced against these kingdomes, by Lodowick Frederick Gifftheyl. Printed for Rob. Wood* (London, 1643), 6pp. A similar tract is listed at **E247(14)**

80j. William Chillingworth, *The petition of the most substantiall inhabitants of the citie of London, and the liberties thereof, to the Lords and Commonns [*sic*] for peace. Together with the answer to the same. And the reply of the petitioners. Also a letter from a country gentleman to a member of the House of Commons, concerning the taking of Marlborough. Printed by Leonard Lichfield* (Oxford, 1643), 20pp. **E244(39)**

80k. Charles Herle, *A fuller answer to a treatise written by Doctor Ferne, entituled The resolving of conscience upon this question, whether upon this supposition, or case (the King will not defend, but is bent to subvert religion, lawes, and liberties) subjects may with good conscience make resistance. Wherein the originall frame, and fundamentalls of this government of England, together with those two texts of Scripture are sufficiently cleered. Viz. Rom. 13. 1. Let every soule be subject unto the higher powers: for there is no power but of God, the powers that be, are ordained of God. 1. Pet. 2. 13. Submit your selves to every ordinance of man for the Lords sake, whether it be to the King as Supreame. Done by another author. Printed for John Bartlet* (London, 1642), 28pp. **E244(27)**

80l. *A soveraigne antidote to prevent, appease, and determine our unnaturall and destructive civill wars and dissentions wherein divers serious considerations tending to this purpose, are propounded both to the king and subjects [. . .]: with a most serious exhortation both to the king and subjects to embrace and preserve peace, and abandon civill warres, with other matters worthy of consideration; also Vox popvli, or the peoples humble discovery of His Majesties ungrounded iealousies and their own loyaltie. Printed by A.N. for R. Lownds* (London, 1642), 23pp. **Wing (2nd ed.), P4086**

80m. William Prynne, *The soveraigne power of parliaments & kingdomes, or, Second part of the treachery and disloialty of papists to their soveraignes wherein the Parliaments and kingdomes right and interest in, and power over the militia, ports, forts, navy, ammunition of the realme, to dispose of them unto confiding officers hands, in these times of danger, their right and interest to nominate and elect all needful commanders, to exercise the militia for the kingdomes safety and defence: as likewise to recommend and make choice of the lord chancellor, keeper, treasurer, privy seale, privie counsellors, iudges, and sheriffes of the kingdome, when they see full cause: together with the Parliaments late assertion, that the king hath no absolute negative voice in passing publicke bills of right and iustice, for the safety, peace, and common benefit of his people. Printed by J.D. for Michael Sparke, Senior* (London, 1643), 79pp. **Wing, P4089**

80n. William Prynne, *Romes master-peece. Or, the grand conspiracy of the Pope and his Jesuited instruments, to extirpate the Protestant religion, re-establish popery, subvert lawes, liberties, peace, parliaments, by kindling a civill war in Scotland, and all his Majesties realmes, and to poyson the King himselfe in case he comply not with them in these their execrable designes. Revealed out of conscience to Andreas ab Habernfeld, by an agent sent from Rome into England, by Cardinal Barbarino, as an assistant to Con the Popes late nuncio, to prosecute this most execrable plot, (in which he persisted a principall actor severall yeares) who discovered it to Sir William Boswell His Majesties agent at the Hague, 6 Septem. 1640. He, under an oath of secresie, to the Arch-Bishop of Canterbury (among whose papers it was casually found by Master Prynne, May, 31. 1643) who communicated it to the King, as the greatest businesse that ever was put to him. Printed for Michael Sparke, Senior* (London, 1643), 37pp. **E249(32)**

80o. William Prynne, *A moderate, and most proper reply to a declaration printed and published under His Majesties name, December, 8. Intended against an ordinance of Parliament for assessing. But indeed animating and encouraging the malignants, and delinquents, in their violent courses for the maintenance of themselves, and their malignant army* (London, 1643), 8pp. **E244(35)**

80p. William Prynne, *The Popish royall favourite or, a full discovery of His Majesties extraordinary favours to, and protections of notorious papists, priestes, Jesuites, against all prosecutions and penalties of the laws enacted against them; notwithstanding his many royall proclamations, declarations, and protestations to the contrary. As likewise of a most desperate long prosecuted designe to set up popery, and extirpate the Protestant religion by degrees, in this our realme of England, and all His Majesties dominions. Manifested by sundry letters of grace, warrants, and other writings under the Kings owne signe-manuall, privy-signet, his privy-councels, and Secretary Windebanks hands and seals, by divers orders and proceedings in open session at Newgate, in the Kings Bench, and elsewhere. Printed for Michael Spark, Senior* (London, 1643), 76pp. **E251(9)**

81. *A collection of all the publicke orders, ordinances, and declarations of both houses of Parliament from the ninth of March, 1642 untill December, 1646 together with severall of His Majesties proclamations and other papers printed at Oxford: also a convenient table for the finding of the severall date and title of the particulars herein mentioned. Printed by T.W. for Ed. Husband* (London, 1646), 643pp. Bookplate of Sir Charles Hotham, bart, and annotated: 'A booke of the ordinances for the use of the generall sessions of the peace for the East Ridinge of the countie of Yorke bought the xith of Aprill 1648. ?pretium? xxi^{s}. A booke for the generall use of the common welth Jury men all.' Inside back cover: 'For Mr Thomas Milner att the Ladie Gees house in Beverley this deliver'. **Wing (2nd ed.), E878**

82. Bound volume of pamphlets, itemized below:

82a. John White, *The first century of scandalous, malignant priests, made and admitted into benefices by the prelates, in whose hands the ordination of ministers and government of the church hath been. Or, A narration of the causes for which the Parliament hath ordered the sequestration of the benefices of severall ministers complained of before them, for vitiousnesse of life, errors in doctrine, contrary to the articles of our religion, and for practising and pressing superstitious innovations against law, and for malignancy against the Parliament. Printed by George Miller* (London, 1643), 51pp. **E76(21)**

82b. Peter Hausted, *Ad populum: or, A lecture to the people. Printed [by Henry Hall]* (Oxford, 1644), 16pp. **E49(2)**

82c. John Russell, *Sampsons foxes agreed to fire a kingdom: or, The Jesuit, and the Puritan, met in a round, to put a kingdom out of square. Printed by H[enry] H[all]* (Oxford, 1644), 8pp. **E52(6)**

82d. Richard Head, *The floating island, or, A new discovery relating the strange adventure on a late voyage from Lambethana to Villa Franca, alias Ramallia, to the eastward of Terra del Templo, by three ships, viz. the Pay-naught, the Excuse, the Least-in-sight, under the conduct of Captain Robert Owe-much, describing the nature of the inhabitants, their religion, laws and customs. Published by Franck Careless, one of the discoverers* (London, 1673). 39pp. **Wing, H1253**

82e. Richard Orpen, *An exact relation of the persecutions, robberies, and losses, sustained by the Protestants of Killmare, in Ireland with an account of their erecting a fortress to defend themselves against the bloody insolencies of the papists: also, the way and manner of their happy escape into England: together with the reasons why the Protestants there did not regiment themselves, and take the field, or make their flight sooner: as likewise, some natural conclusions that plague and famine will arise forthwith in that kingdom by a principal manager in that action. Printed for Tho. Bennet* (London, 1689), 30pp. **Wing, O466**

82f. *Mad verse, sad verse, glad verse and bad verse. Cut out, and slenderly sticht together, by John Taylor. Who bids the reader either to like or dislike them, to commend them, or come mend them. Printed by Leonard Lichfield* (Oxford, 1644), 8pp. **E46(13)**

82g. *Gazette de Londres, no. XXXI, du Mardi, 18. Mai, 1742*, pp.12 [361–372].

APPENDIX II: THE ACCOUNTS OF THE GARRISON OF HULL, 1642–1643

Garrison warfare was a far more characteristic action of the civil wars than set-piece battles, with more soldiers employed in garrisons than in the field armies. Yet historians have neglected these garrison histories because they appear less dramatic and more mundane than battlefield engagements. This is partly due, as Ian Atherton has recently pointed out in his study of royalist Lichfield, to few garrison accounts having survived, with even fewer in print.[1] Therefore the voluminous accounts for the major garrisons of Hull and Beverley held in The National Archives deliver a rare insight into garrison life. A garrison was planted at Hull in 1639 as the town was the key arsenal for equipping and supplying the royal army during the Bishops' Wars. What became the civil war garrison was established on 23 January 1642, when John Hotham marched several companies of the East Riding trained bands from his father's trained band regiment into Hull. Five days later, he was able to supplement them with companies of Hull's own militia.[2]

The garrison accounts survive from 13 March 1642 to 5 December 1642 in a slim, bound volume of sixty-four folios, along with several additional files scattered among the Commonwealth Exchequer Papers covering 5 December 1642 to 16 January 1643 and 20 March to 5 June 1643.[3] The accounts therefore began the week before Sir John Hotham arrived in Hull and trail off just three weeks before his arrest. Even allowing for the gaps in their coverage from 16 January to 20 March and from 8 to 15 May 1643, they constitute over a year's record for the garrison's pay, business, and expenses. The longest set runs from 13 March 1642 to 5 December 1642 and these were copied for Sir John Hotham during his imprisonment in the Tower of London, the autumn before his trial in December 1644. Upon being asked to swear on oath about his garrison accounts before the Committee for

[1] I. Atherton, 'Royalist finances in the English civil war: the case of Lichfield garrison, 1643–1645', *Midland History*, 33 (2008), pp. 44–45; *idem*, 'The accounts of the royalist garrison of Lichfield Close, 1643–1645', *Staffordshire Studies*, 18 (2007), p. 64.

[2] A.J. Fletcher, *The Outbreak of the English Civil War* (London, 1981), p. 314; I.E. Ryder, 'The seizure of Hull and its magazine, January 1642', *YAJ*, 61 (1989), pp. 139–148.

[3] 'The account of Sir John Hotham as governor of the town of Hull, 1643': TNA, SP 28/138/4. There is further material in SP 28/6/48–49; SP 28/6/371–372; SP 28/6/379–380; SP 28/6/423–424; SP 28/6/440–441; SP 28/7/160; SP 28/7/168; SP 28/7/228; SP 28/7/251; SP 28/7/478; and SP 28/7/525.

Accounts in London on 11 September 1644, Sir John 'answered that he knew not what alterations might be in them, and that his papers are now at Hull in the hands of the Committee, especially his own copies which he desires they may compare with these'. A request was then sent to Hull for his accounts to be delivered to London for examination by a committee to sit at Alderman Freeman's house in Cornhill. The two accounts sent were dated between 13 March 1642 and 16 January 1643 and are partially transcribed in this appendix.[4]

The accounts for each company are formulaic, listing the pay for every officer and under-officer, so a full transcription would be wordy and repetitive. Instead the details of each individual company have simply been summarized in the first section for each week, and are followed in the second section of each week by a full transcription of the more varied irregular and extraordinary expenses. Where there is a discrepancy between the weekly total in the manuscript and the mathematical weekly total, as is sometimes the case, the total presented here remains true to that given in the manuscript. The total number of men mustered in the garrison is given in the column preceding the pay. These totals might be larger than the actual numbers because officers might augment their own earnings by claiming pay for more soldiers than they had mustered. However, Sir John Hotham's long experience of county administration, carefulness with money, and reputation for avarice probably militated against such corruption among his subordinates, so that the figures given are likely to be accurate approximations of actual musters. The garrison consisted entirely of infantry, whose companies usually mustered around 120 but could vary in strength from 26 to 257 men. A foot company retained as its commanding officer a captain or above, then a lieutenant and ensign, plus two or three sergeants, drummers, and corporals. The pay for a company averaged about £40 per week.

The pay has been given in pounds, shillings, and pence throughout the appendices. On 20 August 1642 the House of Commons approved the payment of £35-00-00 per week to Sir John as governor.[5] His lieutenant-colonel and sergeant-majors were paid £6-06-00 per week, his captains £4-04-00, lieutenants £1-08-00, ensigns £1-01-00, sergeants £0-10-6, corporals and drummers £0-07-00, and the rank and file £0-04-08. This amounted to eight pence a day for the common soldiers. Sir John also consistently paid the lieutenant in his own double-strength company of foot more than the other lieutenants, at £1-15-00 per week. The company officers have been identified in footnotes; their names were spelt in a variety of ways, but have been standardized for consistency.

[4] TNA, SP 28/252/9.
[5] *CJ*, II, p. 729.

The financing of the Hull garrison drew upon various funding sources. The national trend of moving from voluntary loans upon the Propositions to compulsory taxation over the winter of 1642 to 1643 was replicated at Hull.[6] The accounts suggest that the garrison was remarkably well paid by parliament throughout 1642, in recognition of Hull's priority status. This enabled Sir John Hotham to refrain from forced billeting at first. In June 1642 John Pym overcame objections in the House of Commons to divert to the Hull garrison £2,000 raised in Lincolnshire by the Act for a Speedy Contribution and Loan for the Distressed Protestants in Ireland.[7] Durand Hotham received £2,000 for the pay of Hull garrison on 26 August 1642[8] and Sir John received a further £4,000 from parliament around 1 January 1643. By then, however, the Hull garrison alone was costing approximately £600 per week. As the war lengthened and money from parliament went into arrears, Sir John was forced upon his own initiatives to pay the soldiers in his garrison network.[9] Unwilling to dip into his vast fortune, he levied a voluntary loan at Beverley in the autumn of 1642.[10] He also raised £1,611 from the inhabitants of Hull 'upon the propositions' in November 1642, and issued receipts for at least a further £3,600 in money and plate lent to the parliamentary cause.[11] With the consent of the aldermen, he further imposed an excise tax on goods within the town of Hull.[12] In addition, the merchant William Sykes furnished the garrison with £1,000 worth of arms and ammunition on 5 November 1642, £500 worth on 23 November, a further £1,000 worth on 20 February 1643, and £300 in money on 12 June 1643. Sir John issued Sykes with receipts for parliament to redeem these sums.[13] John Hotham raised further income in 1642 by imposing arbitrary fines upon royalist gentry vulnerable to his troops. He took £1,000 from Lord Savile in exchange for promising a protection for Savile's estates from parliament.[14] Further arbitrary fines were imposed upon Robert Shaw of Ardsley and William Weddell of Earswick, yielding £500 and £200 respectively.[15]

[6] R. Armstrong, 'The Long Parliament goes to war: the Irish campaigns, 1641–3', *Historical Research*, 80 (2007), p. 93.

[7] J. Cope, *England and the 1641 Irish Rebellion* (Woodbridge, 2009), p. 150.

[8] TNA, SP 28/143/23.

[9] By the spring of 1643 these garrisons included not only Beverley and Hull but also Scorborough House and Cawood and Wressle castles.

[10] TNA, SP 28/202/129–132.

[11] TNA, SP 28/6/473–474.

[12] HHC: Hotham MS, U DDHO/1/35.

[13] TNA, SP 28/250/311, SP 28/298/222, 232, 366, 848.

[14] *CSPD 1645–1647*, pp. 401–403, 423–424.

[15] J. Binns, *Yorkshire in the Civil Wars: origins, impact and outcome* (Pickering, N. Yorks, 2004), p. 156.

From the beginning of 1643, Sir John Hotham allotted the maintenance of his dragoon companies to particular bailiwicks and divisions of wapentakes. Consequently, he was receiving hundreds of pounds in 'dragoon money' as early as January 1643. In the middle and south bailiwicks of Holderness, on 28 February, Sir John ordered constables to deliver their parishes' arrears of 'dragoon money', and to assist one of his sergeants in apprehending those who had refused to pay. A voluntary loan upon the propositions across several East Riding parishes was collected at Beverley on 23 January 1643.[16] A more rigorous assessment upon Beverley ensued, collected by the aldermen on 24 February 1643, with the names of those who refused being handed over to John Hotham.[17] These contributions were followed by regular formal assessments levied across the whole East Riding from March to June 1643 to pay for the Beverley garrison. Extensive returns for these assessments in the wapentakes of Harthill, Holderness, and Howdenshire survive in The National Archives.[18] These 'sesses', as they became known by contemporaries, yielded large sums. The wapentake of Holderness was expected to pay £1,200 on 10 April 1643, of which £1,088 was successfully collected. Officers such as Lieutenant-Colonel Matthew Boynton, Sir Thomas Remington, and Captain William Goodricke were sent with dragoons into Harthill, Holderness, and Howdenshire respectively to collect arrears by force. Lieutenants, ensigns, and even corporals were allotted parishes from which to collect.[19] By the spring of 1643 the Hothams' war effort was geared towards reinforcing their family's power and status by sustaining these garrisons at the expense of the East Riding's inhabitants. Refraining from decisive confrontations with the royalists protected their powerbase and maintained their position. It enabled them to court the earl of Newcastle's good opinion from a position of strength and bide their time in choosing the most advantageous moment to change sides.

The accounts

A just and true account of monies disbursed for pay and other things concerning the garrison in Hull by Sir John Hotham, knight and baronet, and Governor of Hull aforesaid, from 13 March 1641[2] till the <27 September> *5 December* 1642[20]

[16] TNA, SP 28/189.
[17] ERRO, BC II 7/4/1, fo. 73r.
[18] TNA, SP 28/189.
[19] TNA, SP 16/497/93, SP 24/50, SP 28/138/3, SP 28/189.
[20] TNA, SP 28/138/4.

First week: 13–19 March 1642

	Men	Pay
Foot		
Lieutenant-Colonel Legard's company[21]	130	38-13-06
Captain Goodricke's company[22]	130	36-11-06
The Governor's company	211	52-12-04
Captain Appleyard's company[23]	130	36-11-06
Total:	601	
Captain Lowinger[24]	1	4-04-00
Major Jefford[25]	1	6-06-00
My own pay	1	35-00-00
Provost marshal	1	1-01-00
Thomas Coatsworth,[26] cannoneer at 2s 6d per diem	1	0-17-06
James Hunter, cannoneer at 2s 6d per diem	1	0-17-06
To Sergeant-Major which he paid for coals and candles		1-16-06
Week's total:	607	214-11-04

[21]Christopher Legard of Anlaby had been one of Sir John Hotham's captains in his East Riding trained band regiment. His house was plundered by the royalists during the first siege of Hull in July 1642. Francis Bacon served as his lieutenant: J.D. Legard, *The Legards of Anlaby and Ganton* (London, 1926), pp. 27, 45, 84–86; TNA, E121/4/8, no. 29; BL, Add. MS 28,082, fo. 80v.

[22]William Goodricke of Skidby had been one of Sir John Hotham's captains in his East Riding trained band regiment. In early November 1642 he was promoted to sergeant-major. After the arrest of the Hothams, he or more likely his son served as captain of horse in Lord Fairfax's regiment: TNA, E121/4/8, no. 37; BL, Add. MS 28,082, fo. 80v; C.A. Goodricke, *History of the Goodricke Family* (London, 1885), p. 44.

[23]This was most probably one of the sons of Thomas Appleyard of Burstwick Garth and East Halton, who became a professional soldier on the continent. He may have been the Christopher Appleyard who was a captain in Sir Matthew Boynton's trained band regiment in Holderness. His brother Sir Matthew Appleyard became a royalist colonel: BL, Add. MS 28,082, fo. 80v.

[24]Lowinger was a Dutch officer who commanded a company of foot in Beverley and Hull, and a troop of horse that accompanied Captain John Hotham into Lincolnshire in April 1643. He was arrested under suspicion of involvement in the Hothams' conspiracy, but was released and later served as major in Lord Willoughby of Parham's regiment of horse in Lincolnshire: BL, Sloane MS 1,519, fo. 121; TNA, E121/5/7, no. 10; TNA, SP 28/300/441; HHC: C BRS/7/81; *CJ*, III, pp. 158, 192; *LJ*, VI, pp. 412–416; BL, TT E124(14), *Speciall passages*, 18–25 October 1642 (London, 1642), p. 96.

[25]John Gifford was a professional soldier from Darlington who had been given an important command in the Bishops' Wars. He served in the Hull garrison before being appointed sergeant-major general to Lord Fairfax's army in the West Riding. He fought at Adwalton Moor but was arrested for treachery in October 1643. He was to have stood trial alongside the Hothams but was exonerated in 1646 and subsequently served in Ireland as captain of Cromwell's lifeguard. For a discussion of his career, see A. Hopper, *'Black Tom': Sir Thomas Fairfax and the English revolution* (Manchester, 2007), pp. 229, 236.

[26]Thomas Coatesworth later gave evidence against Sir John Hotham after his arrest: J. Tickell, *History of the Town and County of Kingston-upon-Hull* (Hull, 1798), pp. 465–466.

Second week: 19–26 March 1642

Foot		
Lieutenant-Colonel Legard's company	160	48-09-06
Captain Lowinger's company[27]	160	45-00-02
The Governor's company	211	53-16-10
Captain Goodricke's company	130	36-11-06
Captain Anlaby's company[28]	130	38-10-06
Captain Appleyard's company	130	36-11-06
Total	921	
Major Jefford at 18s per diem	1	6-06-00
To him for coals and candles		2-03-10
My own pay	1	35-00-00
To two cannoneers this week	2	1-11-06
Provost	1	1-01-00
Week's total	926	305-02-04

Third week: 26 March–2 April 1642

Foot		
Captain Lowinger's company	160	43-11-06
Lieutenant-Colonel Legard's company	160	45-13-06
The Governor's company	210	52-08-10
Captain Goodricke's company	130	36-11-06
Captain Anlaby's company	130	36-11-06
Captain Appleyard's company	130	36-11-06
Total:	920	

[27]This included £1-04-00 for thirty-six-odd men for one day. William Fugill was Lowinger's lieutenant: TNA, E121/5/5, no. 28.

[28]John Anlaby of Etton was brother-in-law to Sir John Hotham and son-in-law to Sir Matthew Boynton. In 1647 he succeeded the latter as recruiter MP for Scarborough. He was named a commissioner for the trial of Charles I but did not attend: W. Dugdale, *The Visitation of the County of Yorke*, Surtees Society, 36 (1859), p. 334; W.W. Bean, *The Parliamentary Representation of the Six Northern Counties of England* (Hull, 1890), pp. 680, 1045; Greaves and Zaller, I, p. 17; W.L.F. Nuttall, 'The Yorkshire commissioners appointed for the trial of King Charles the first', *YAJ*, 43 (1971), p. 152.

Major Jefford at 18s per diem	1	6-06-00
To him for a door and a lock which he laid out for the South Blockhouse		1-08-00
For candles		0-05-04
Mine own pay	1	35-00-00
To two cannoneers	2	1-11-06
Provost	1	1-01-00
To the surgeon for 3 weeks' unpaid at 2s per diem	1	2-02-00
Paid for boats		8-02-04
Week's total:	926	307-04-06

Fourth week: 2–11 April 1642

This falls out a week of nine days because I found pay day on Saturday made the soldiers drunk upon Sunday, and so I removed it till Monday.

Foot		
Lieutenant-Colonel Legard's company	160	58-14-06
Captain Lowinger's company	160	56-00-06
The Governor's company	211	67-10-00
Captain Goodricke's company	130	47-00-06
Captain Anlaby's company	130	47-00-06
Captain Appleyard's company	130	47-00-06
Total:	921	
Major Jefford for 9 days	1	8-02-00
Mine own pay	1	45-00-00
To two cannoneers	2	2-00-06
Provost	1	1-07-00
Surgeon	1	0-18-00
Week's total:	927	380-11-02[29]

[29] This total is later given as £380-11-06 in the summary of disbursements at the end.

Fifth week: 11–18 April 1642

Foot		
Captain Lowinger's company	160	43-11-06
Lieutenant-Colonel Legard's company	160	45-13-06
Captain Goodricke's company	130	36-11-06
The Governor's company	211	52-08-10
Captain Appleyard's company	130	36-11-06
Captain Anlaby's company	130	36-11-06
Total:	921	
Major Jefford 18s per diem	1	6-06-00
My own pay	1	35-00-00
Provost	1	1-01-00
Surgeon	1	0-14-00
Two cannoneers	2	1-11-06
For coals and candles		1-13-01
For coynes[30] for the ordnance		3-01-00
Week's total:	927	300-14-11

Sixth week: 18–25 April 1642

Foot		
As week 5		
Total:	921	
Major Jefford 18s per diem	1	6-06-00
Mine own pay	1	35-00-00
Provost marshal	1	1-01-00
Surgeon	1	0-14-00
2 cannoneers	2	1-11-06
To two posts		11-00-00
Week's total:	927	307-00-10

[30] Wedges used for raising and lowering artillery pieces: *OED*, III, p. 455.

Seventh week: 25 April–2 May 1642

Foot		
Captain Lowinger's company	160	43-11-06
Lieutenant-Colonel Legard's company	160	47-06-02
Captain Goodricke's company	130	36-11-06
The Governor's company	211	52-08-10
Captain Appleyard's company	130	36-11-04
Captain Anlaby's company	130	36-11-04
Captain Overton's company[31]	110	31-18-02
Total:	1,031	
Major Jefford's 18s per diem	1	6-06-00
For coals and candles		1-05-11
Mine own pay	1	35-00-00
For removing the magazine to London		98-15-00
Provost	1	1-01-00
Surgeon	1	0-14-00
To 6 carbines	6	0-07-00
Given in earnest for a ship to lie in the road		0-10-00
For boat hire for the post		0-15-06
To two cannoneers	2	1-15-00
To a master cannoneer	1	1-00-00
Given amongst the soldiers that day and the next day after the King was at the walls		101-19-00
To the men that came from Cottingham		7-00-00
To 88 men that came out of Hunsley Beacon: at 1s-4d a man	88	5-17-04
These were men that we got from our friends in the county as we could in that sudden exigent of the King's coming.		

[31] This was Robert Overton of Easington, or possibly his father, John Overton, although the latter was captured and imprisoned by the royalists. Robert Overton became a colonel in the New Model Army and was deputy governor of Hull under Sir Thomas Fairfax from 1648: B. Taft, 'Robert Overton (1608/9–1678/9)', *ODNB*; Greaves and Zaller, II, p. 281; TNA, E121/5/5, no. 39; E121/5/7, no. 29; T. Tindall Wildridge (ed.), *The Hull Letters: documents from the Hull Records, 1625–1646* (Hull, 1886), pp. 53, 155, 158–159.

To James Hunter for wad for the ordnance		0-11-00
To Thomas Coatsworth		0-04-06
To two keels[32] for lying in the road		7-00-00
We had then none of our ships here and being every day advised of plots that the King meant to assail us by water, we hired keels to lie in the road and put soldiers in them.		
To a post for the committee		10-00-00
For things about the ordnance		2-14-10
And for bringing Captain Overton's company arms from Paul		1-06-08
Week's total:	1,132	569-11-09

Eighth week: 2–9 May 1642

Foot		
Captain Lowinger's company	160	43-11-06
Lieutenant-Colonel Legard's company	167	47-06-00
Captain Goodricke's company	130	36-11-06
The Governor's company	211	52-11-02
Captain Appleyard's company	130	36-11-06
Captain Anlaby's company	130	36-11-06
Captain Overton's company	120	34-04-10
Total:	1,048	
Major 18s per diem	1	6-06-00
My own pay	1	35-00-00
Provost	1	1-01-00
Surgeon	1	0-14-00
6 carbines		0-07-00
For a keel to lie in the road		3-10-00
To two cannoneers	2	1-15-00
To James Hunter for work about the ordnance		0-09-06

[32]These were flat-bottomed vessels used to load more seaworthy ships in estuaries and docks in eastern England between the River Tyne and Norfolk: *OED*, VIII, p. 367.

To 6 carbines at 4s-8d a man	6	1-08-00
The carbines are six soldiers that had 4d a day more than their pay in regard they went along with me night and day to send messages and execute commands from me.[33]		
To an odd man for 2 days' pay	1	0-01-04
Week's total:	1,061	338-01-00

Ninth week: 9–16 May 1642

Foot		
Captain Lowinger's company	160	44-03-00
Lieutenant-Colonel Legard's company	167	47-06-02
Captain Goodricke's company	130	36-11-06
The Governor's company	211	52-11-02
Captain Appleyard's company	130	36-11-06
Captain Anlaby's company	130	36-11-06
Captain Overton's company	124	35-03-06
Total:	1,052	
Major at 18s per diem	1	6-06-00
For coals and candles		0-09-04
My own pay	1	35-00-00
Provost	1	1-01-00
Surgeon	1	0-14-00
7 carbines at 5s-10d a man	7	2-00-10
To two cannoneers	2	1-15-00
To 6 cannoneers for 3 weeks' pay at 2s a man per diem	6	12-12-00
To 8 cannoneers for a week	8	5-01-06
To a post from London		4-00-00
To a post sent by my Lord Stamford[34] unto London and back		18-00-00

[33]These soldiers sound like bodyguards. They remained with Sir John Hotham until his flight from Hull on 29 June 1643. One tract reporting Sir John's capture reflected that they were clothed in 'the same Red Coates which the Earle of Strafford made for his Life-guard': BL, TT E59(2), *A true relation of the discovery of a most desperate and dangerous plot, for the delivering up, and surprising of the townes of Hull and Beverley*, 4 July 1643 (London, 1643), p. 5.

[34]Stamford was the parliamentarian lord lieutenant of Leicestershire sent to Hull to confer with Sir John Hotham in April 1642: A. Hopper, 'Henry Grey, first earl of Stamford (*c.*1599–1673)', *ODNB*.

For mending the boats		1-06-10
For boom,[35] and defence of the bridge		5-13-10
For bringing money from Beverley		0-15-00
To Thomas Coatsworth and the cannoneers at the blockhouse for 14 days' pay		9-05-06
To James Hunter and the cannoneers in the town		3-00-00
Given for an intelligence		10-00-00
To Cowling the gunner	1	0-14-00
To a man to attend the boom	1	0-02-06
To Lieutenant-Colonel's men at 4d a man		2-10-00
To a foot post		2-00-00
To 4 odd men	4	0-18-08
To two boatmen for 2 weeks' pay	2	1-08-00
To Captain Goodricke for odd men		1-05-04
Week's total:	1,087	404-17-08

In this and some of the weeks following, you will find a most unjust, unheard of proportion of cannoneers, more I believe than was paid at Ostend.[36] But I was forced to do it to give the town content, every seaman almost tendering himself for a cannoneer, and it was no time to argue it for as I have had good proof since, deny but one request though never so unjust, [and] all which is granted is nothing. I paid as you may see more than a good number of those that I allowed of: Yet after a great many that affirmed they served at the walls with the cannon clamoured for pay and remained much discontented, I paid not them as well as the rest.

[35] A boom was a strong chain or line of timber pieces bound together, stretched across the mouth of the harbour to hinder navigation: *OED*, II, p. 399.

[36] Sir John was showcasing his military knowledge by this reference to the famous siege of Ostend in 1602–1604, where English soldiers participated in a determined but ultimately unsuccessful defence of the town from the Spanish.

Tenth week: 16–23 May 1642

Foot		
Captain Lowinger's company	160	43-11-06
Lieutenant-Colonel Legard's company	167	47-06-02
Captain Goodricke's company	130	36-11-06
The Governor's company	221	54-19-00
Captain Appleyard's company	130	36-11-06
Captain Anlaby's company	130	36-11-06
Captain Overton's company	123	34-18-10
Total:	1,061	
Major's at 18s per diem	1	6-06-00
For candles, etc.		0-05-04
Mine own pay	1	35-00-00
Provost	1	1-01-00
Surgeon	1	0-14-00
To 7 carbines at 5s-10d a man	7	2-00-10
To two cannoneers	2	1-15-00
To Thomas Coatsworth for 6 more at 2s per diem	6	4-04-00
To them for work about the ordnance, etc.		0-07-06
To James Hunter for 7 cannoneers	7	4-18-00
To a carpenter for making a platform for the ordnance		0-03-09
To a mason		0-08-09
Given to the seamen		3-00-00
To a foot post		2-00-00
More for seven men	7	0-07-00
To 5 odd men	5	1-03-04
Week's total:	1,099	354-04-06

Eleventh week: 23–30 May 1642

Foot		
Captain Lowinger's company	160	45-10-10
Lieutenant-Colonel Legard's company[37]	167	50-01-02
Captain Goodricke's company	130	36-11-06
The Governor's company	217	54-00-04
Captain Appleyard's company	130	36-11-06
Captain Anlaby's company	130	36-11-06
Captain Overton's company	121	34-19-06
Total:	1,055	
Major at 18s per diem	1	6-06-00
To him for coals and candles		0-14-02
Mine own pay	1	35-00-00
Provost	1	1-01-00
Surgeon	1	0-14-00
To 7 carbines at 5s-10d a man	7	2-00-10
To one odd man	1	0-03-04
To 5 odd men	5	1-03-04
To James Hunter, cannoneer at 2s-6d per diem	1	0-17-06
To him for 7 cannoneers at 14s a man	7	4-18-00
To him for provision for the ordnance		2-17-06
For a man and a horse to York		0-09-00
For a boat for the post		0-04-00
For a man's charges to York		0-03-00
Given to Lieutenant Fowkes[38]		21-00-00
This was the lieutenant that revealed Beckwith's treason for surprising the town.		
To Egglefield the post to London		8-00-00
To Thomas Coatsworth for his week's pay	1	0-17-06
To him for 7 cannoneers more	7	4-18-00
Week's total:	1,088	385-00-00

[37] This included £2-15-00 for odd men and 'the man that kept the boom'.

[38] Fowkes was lieutenant to Captain Lowinger. In May 1642 Fowkes's father-in-law, Thomas Beckwith, met Fowkes at Beverley and offered him £500 in cash and £500 per annum to betray Hull to the King. Fowkes returned to Hull and revealed the plot, and Sir John Hotham ordered him to go along with it. Fowkes was instructed to let the royalists in at the North Gate, and Lowinger to hand over the main guards. The day before this was planned to happen, to avoid bloodshed Hotham wrote to the King, smugly remarking 'he might spare himself the trouble of carrying on the contrivance'. For further details see P. Saltmarshe, *History and Chartulary of the Hothams of Scorborough in the East Riding of Yorkshire, 1100–1700* (York, 1914), p. 124.

Twelfth week: 30 May–6 June 1642

Foot		
Captain Lowinger's company	160	45-10-06
Lieutenant-Colonel Legard's company[39]	167	49-01-10
Captain Goodricke's company	130	36-11-06
The Governor's company	218	54-05-00
Captain Appleyard's company	121	34-11-06
Captain Anlaby's company	130	36-11-06
Captain Overton's company	121	34-09-06
Total:	1,047	
Major at 18s per diem	1	6-06-00
For candles, etc.		0-03-02
Mine own pay	1	35-00-00
Provost	1	1-01-00
Surgeon	1	0-14-00
7 carbines	7	2-00-10
To James Hunter for his pay and 7 cannoneers more	8	5-15-06
To Thomas Coatsworth the same	8	5-15-06
To five odd men	5	1-03-04
To the scouts for 8 nights at 2s per night		0-16-00
To Mrs Drew for wharfage for the magazine		2-00-00
Week's total:	1,079	351-16-10

Thirteenth week: 6–13 June 1642

Foot		
Captain Lowinger's company	160	43-11-06
Lieutenant-Colonel Legard's company[40]	167	49-06-08
Captain Goodricke's company	130	36-11-06
The Governor's company	222	55-08-04
Captain Anlaby's company	130	36-11-06
Captain Appleyard's company	123	34-18-10
Captain Overton's company	116	33-06-02
Total:	1,048	

39 This included £1-15-08 'for work done about the garrison'.
40 This included £2-00-06 for coals.

Major Jefford 18s per diem	1	6-06-00
For coals, etc.		0-05-04
Mine own pay	1	35-00-00
Provost	1	1-01-00
Surgeon	1	0-14-00
7 carbines	7	2-00-10
To James Hunter for 5 cannoneers	5	3-13-06
To Thomas Coatsworth for 8 cannoneers	8	5-15-06
For 6 odd men	6	1-08-00
To the scouts for two nights		0-04-00
To the 4 cannoneers that came from London	4	3-10-00
To a mason for work		0-02-09
Week's total:	1,082	353-07-01

Fourteenth week: 13–20 June 1642

Foot		
Captain Lowinger's company[41]	160	45-15-10
Lieutenant-Colonel Legard's company[42]	167	49-02-02
Captain Goodricke's company	130	36-11-06
The Governor's company	224	55-13-00
Captain Appleyard's company	130	36-11-06
Captain Anlaby's company	130	36-11-06
Captain Overton's company	130	36-11-06
Total:	1,071	
Major Jefford at 18s per diem	1	6-06-00
For candles, etc		0-03-02
Mine own pay	1	35-00-00
Provost	1	1-01-00
Surgeon	1	0-14-00
7 carbines	7	2-00-10
To the cannoneers	c.16	13-12-06

[41] This included £2-04-04 for odd men.
[42] This included £1-15-00 for coals.

To Captain Overton for 4 odd men	4	0-18-00
To the porter	1	0-04-08
To Mr Towry		0-06-00
To 6 odd men	6	1-08-00
For a boat into Lincolnshire		0-09-00
Week's total:	1,109	359-00-01

Fifteenth week: 20–27 June 1642

Foot		
Captain Lowinger's company[43]	160	46-02-06
Lieutenant-Colonel Legard's company[44]	167	48-03-04
Captain Goodricke's company	130	36-11-06
The Governor's company	221	54-19-00
Captain Appleyard's company	130	36-11-06
Captain Overton's company	130	36-11-06
Captain Anlaby's company	130	36-11-06
Total:	1,068	
Major Jefford at 18s per diem	1	6-06-00
For candles, etc.		0-03-00
Mine own pay	1	35-00-00
Provost	1	1-01-00
Surgeon	1	0-14-00
7 carbines	7	2-00-10
Mr Towry		0-06-00
For turf		0-00-06
For a line for the engineers		0-05-00
To the porter	1	0-04-08
To Thomas Coatsworth for 8 cannoneers	8	5-15-06
To James Hunter for 6 cannoneers	6	4-07-06
To Marmaduke Thompson for work about the ordnance		1-04-00
For oak planchers[45]		2-00-00

[43] This included £2-11-00 for odd men.

[44] This included £0-02-06 for turves, £0-04-08 for the boatmen, and £0-03-00 for 'the man that keeps the boom'.

[45] A plancher was a floor or platform of planks or boards: *OED*, XI, p. 960.

For a post		9-00-00
To Captain Appleyard for an odd man	1	1-13-02
For carrying soldiers aboard on the catch[46]		0-01-06
Week's total:	1,095	365-13-06

Sixteenth week: 27 June–4 July 1642

Foot		
Captain Lowinger's company	160	43-11-06
Lieutenant-Colonel Legard's company[47]	167	48-00-10
Captain Goodricke's company	130	36-11-06
The Governor's company	227	56-07-01
Captain Appleyard's company[48]	131	38-11-06
Captain Anlaby's company	130	36-11-06
Captain Overton's company[49]	138	39-02-04
Total	1,083	
Major Jefford at 18s per diem	1	6-06-00
For candles, etc		0-03-00
Mine own pay	1	35-00-00
Provost	1	1-01-00
Surgeon	1	0-14-00
7 carbines	7	2-00-10
To James Hunter for 6 cannoneers	6	4-07-06
To Thomas Coatsworth for 8 cannoneers	8	5-15-06
To 6 odd men	6	1-08-00
To keels that conveyed the soldiers into Paul Road		3-04-00
To two seamen	2	0-10-00
To James Hunter for provision to furnish the keels		2-00-06
To the porter	1	0-04-08
To Captain Billops[50] for 122 men at 4d a man		2-07-04

[46]This was a strongly built vessel, usually with two masts, and of 100–250 tons burden: *OED*, II, p. 973.

[47]This included £0-07-08 'to the boom keeper and the boatman'.

[48]This included £2-00-00 for an odd man.

[49]This included £0-13-06 for messengers to Paul in Holderness, and £1-17-04 for odd men.

[50]Robert Billops of Beverley later commanded a foot company in Lord Fairfax's regiment and was granted the estates of William Langdale, a sequestered recusant: TNA, SP 23/99/299–319; TNA, E121/5/7, no. 26; College of Arms, Curia Militaris 2/147 and 11/9.

To Edward Andrew for ironwork about the garrison		2-07-10
To a skiff[51] for carrying soldiers aboard		0-01-06
To two posts to London		18-00-00
For provision for a boat		0-08-00
To 4 boatmen	4	1-00-00
To the cannoneers that came from London	4	3-10-00
To the engineers for a month's pay	1	15-08-00
To the engineer which he laid out for work about the garrison		1-00-00
To Captain Goodricke for 5 odd men	5	1-03-04
Week's total	1,131	406-06-10

Seventeenth week: 4–11 July 1642

Foot		
Captain Lowinger's company	160	43-11-06
Lieutenant-Colonel Legard's company[52]	167	51-05-04
Captain Goodricke's company	130	36-11-06
The Governor's company	227	56-07-00
Captain Appleyard's company[53]	130	38-13-06
Captain Anlaby's company	130	36-11-06
Captain Overton's company[54]	139	38-13-06
Captain Alured's company[55]	150	41-04-10
Captain Skarfe's company[56]	75	25-04-04
Total:	1,308	

[51] This was a small, light, seaworthy boat, adapted for rowing and sailing, and often attached to a ship and used for purposes of communication and transport: *OED*, XV, p. 601.

[52] This included £0-02-06 for the 'boom keeper' and £3-16-08 for odd men.

[53] From this week, Captain Appleyard was paid £6-06-00, the same as Major Jefford and Lieutenant-Colonel Legard.

[54] This included £2-02-00 for 9 odd men.

[55] John Alured of Sculcoates was MP for Hedon in the Long Parliament and had been a captain in Sir Matthew Boynton's trained band regiment in Holderness. He was also a noted religious radical and later a regicide. He left London for Hull on 20 May 1642, where he fell out with the Hothams the same year, supporting the Fairfax family (who commissioned Alured as a colonel) against them: BL, Add. MS 28,082, fo. 80v; J.T. Cliffe, *The Yorkshire Gentry from the Reformation to the Civil War* (London, 1969), pp. 269, 272, 309; M.F. Keeler, *The Long Parliament, 1640–1641: a biographical study of its members* (Philadelphia, 1954), pp. 85–86; Greaves and Zaller, I, p. 12; Nuttall, 'The Yorkshire commissioners', p. 151; TNA, SP 28/1A/18; D. Scott, 'John Alured (bap. 1607, d. 1651)', *ODNB*.

Major Jefford 18s per diem	1	6-06-00
More to him for candles, etc.		0-16-06
Mine own pay	1	35-00-00
Provost	1	1-01-00
Surgeon	1	0-14-00
6 carbines at 7s a man	7	2-02-00
For odd men	6	1-08-00
To Thomas Coatsworth upon his note		0-12-02
To 3 men for making platforms		0-11-00
To Captain Goodricke for his men		2-16-00
To the wrights		2-02-00
To the cannoneers in the town this week	c.40	29-03-06
A goodly number of cannoneers all townsmen but four sent me from London.		
To Thomas Coatsworth for 33 cannoneers	33	23-05-06
For dressing 120 muskets		3-00-00
To the porter	1	0-04-08
Given to 12 constables		1-04-00
For 58 men which wrought all one night		2-13-00
Week's total:	1,399	482-05-08

Eighteenth week: 11–18 July 1642

Foot		
Captain Lowinger's company	160	43-11-06
Lieutenant-Colonel Legard's company	168	47-13-02
Captain Goodricke's company	130	36-11-06
The Governor's company	228	56-11-08
Captain Appleyard's company	130	38-13-06
Captain Overton's company	139	36-11-06
Captain Anlaby's company[57]	130	39-17-02
Captain Alured's company	203	53-18-04
Captain Skarfe's company	89	27-00-02
Captain Legard's company	26	12-19-04
Total:	1,403	

[56]In spring 1643, Timothy Scarth was entrusted with command of the garrison at Sir John Hotham's seat, at Scorborough House. After the arrest of the Hothams, his company was ordered to reinforce the garrison at Beverley. He was later a captain of horse in Sir William Constable's regiment: BL, Add. MS 21,418, fos 181, 238; HHC: C BRS/7/17; TNA, E121/5/7, no. 55.

[57]This included £3-05-08 due to Anlaby 'for odd pay'.

Major Jefford 18s per diem	1	6-06-00
For coals and candles		1-02-03
Mine own pay	1	35-00-00
Provost	1	1-01-00
Surgeon	1	0-14-00
6 carbines	6	2-02-00
7 odd men	7	1-12-08
To William Gibson for work about the ordnance		0-16-04
To the cannoneers this week	c.60	50-09-00
To the porter	1	0-04-08
To a messenger to York		0-04-00
To Captain Lowinger for odd men	19	4-08-04
To Captain Alured which he paid for fixing the arms for his company		7-01-00
Week's total:	1,500	504-09-02

Nineteenth week: 18–25 July 1642

Foot		
Captain Lowinger's company[58]	160	48-19-06
Lieutenant-Colonel Legard's company[59]	167	48-12-09
Captain Goodricke's company	130	36-11-06
The Governor's company	232	57-10-04
Captain Overton's company	148	40-15-06
Captain Appleyard's company	130	38-13-06
Captain Legard's company	111	32-02-10
Captain Anlaby's company	110	31-18-02
Captain Alured's company[60]	206	54-15-06
Captain Skarfe's company[61]	95	28-14-02
Captain Hammond[62] for 163 men at 2s a man	163	16-06-06
Total:	1,652	

[58]This pay included £5-08-00 for odd men.

[59]This included £1-06-07 'for coals etc'.

[60]This included £0-03-06 'for odd men'.

[61]This included £0-06-00 'for odd pays'.

[62]Among the captains that arrived from the south that week, John Hampden recommended his nephew Robert Hammond to Sir John Hotham on 18 July 1642: HHC: Hotham MS, U DDHO/1/7; Greaves and Zaller, II, p. 44.

To Sir John Meldrum for five weeks' pay which was due to him 7 July at	1	37-16-00
Mine own pay	1	35-00-00
Major Jefford	1	6-06-00
For the scout watch		1-08-00
For candles, etc.		0-04-02
Provost	1	1-01-00
Surgeon	1	0-14-00
To the cannoneers this week	c.110	96-15-06
For ironwork for a bridge		3-08-00
For fixing 244 muskets		6-00-00
To 6 odd men	6	1-08-00
To 6 carbines	6	2-02-00
To the porter	1	0-04-08
Given to the seamen		7-00-00
To Mr Hollis[63] which he laid out for the works about the walls		3-03-00
Week's total:	1,780	637-10-01

This and the week before was when we were besieged. You must needs look we drive away the enemy with these cannoneers, all townsmen but four.

[63] Maccabeus Hollis, a merchant of Hull, later played an important part in the arrest of the Hothams: Tindall Wildridge, *The Hull Letters*, pp. 152, 156, 158; Tickell, *History of Hull*, p. 467.

Twentieth week: 25 July–1 August 1642

Foot		
Captain Lowinger's company	175	47-01-06
Lieutenant-Colonel Legard's company[64]	167	49-05-00
Captain Goodricke's company	130	36-11-06
The Governor's company	229	55-15-04
Captain Appleyard's company	130	38-13-06
Captain Overton's company[65]	149	41-11-10
Captain Anlaby's company[66]	130	40-15-06
Captain Legard's company	76	23-19-06
Captain Alured's company	201	53-08-08
Captain Hammond for 163 men at 8d a man	163	21-14-08
Captain Hammond		8-00-00
Captain Skarfe's company	96	28-12-02
Captain Purefoy's company[67]	216	58-02-04
Captain Mathews's company[68] (1/2 week)	193	23-10-00
Captain Carter's company[69] (1/2 week)	172	21-05-03
Total:	2,227	

[64]This included £1-18-10 'for odd men'.

[65]This included £0-11-08 'for odd men'.

[66]This included £4-04-00 'for odd men'.

[67]Purefoy's company accompanied John Hotham into the West Riding in October 1642 and into Lincolnshire in April 1643, where many reportedly deserted. Purefoy was appointed governor of Lincoln and was arrested along with his brother for plotting to betray the city to the royalists at Newark. They were conveyed to London where, on 11 August 1643, the House of Commons ordered that they should be dealt with by the committee appointed to examine Sir John Hotham. In November 1643 they were delivered to the earl of Essex to be tried by council of war but their fate remains unknown: BL, TT E126(1), *Speciall passages*, 25 October–1 November 1642 (London, 1642), pp. 103–104; BL, TT E97(9), *The kingdomes weekly intelligencer*, 11–18 April 1643 (London, 1643), p. 125; BL, TT E249(2), *A perfect diurnall of the passages in parliament*, 1–8 May 1643 (London, 1643); *CJ*, III, pp. 86, 202, 303, 309; BL, TT E249(24), *A perfect diurnall of the passages in parliament*, 3–10 July 1643 (London, 1643), p. 12; BL, TT E59(12), *The parliament scout*, 29 June–6 July 1643 (London, 1643), p. 14; BL, Harleian MS 165, fo. 107r; J. Vicars, *Jehovah-Jireh: God in the Mount or Englands Parliamentarie Chronicle* (London, 1644), pp. 372–373; Tickell, *History of Hull*, p. 464.

[68]The Welshman Captain Humphrey Mathews commanded this company of London volunteers: R. Slack, *Man at War: John Gell in his troubled time* (Nottingham, 1997), p. 73; TNA, E121/5/7, no. 12.

[69]The companies under Purefoy, Mathews, and Carter were raised by the beat of the drum in London and its suburbs in Middlesex, Essex, Kent, and Surrey during July 1642 for the relief of Hull. Carter's company was subsequently attached to the garrisons at Beverley, Cawood, and Wressle: *LJ*, V. p. 187; TNA, SP 28/189; BL, TT E60(4), *Two letters, the one being intercepted by the parliament's forces which was sent from Sir Hugh Cholmley to Captain Gotherick* (London, 1643).

Major Jefford 18s per diem	1	6-06-00
For the scout watch and candles		1-15-08
Mine own pay	1	35-00-00
To Sir John Meldrum for four weeks and 3 days' pay from Thursday 7 July till Monday 8 August at £7-08-00 per week	1	34-04-00
To the engineers for a month's pay		15-06-00
Provost	1	1-01-00
Surgeon	1	0-14-00
6 carbines	6	2-02-00
6 odd men	6	1-08-00
To the porter	1	0-04-08
For beer for the boats		0-18-00
To the engineers which was laid out for work about the ordnance		3-16-04
To James Hunter upon 2 notes		1-03-02
For fixing 90 muskets		2-05-00
For 4 dozen of musket baskets		1-17-04
For 3 odd pays		0-14-00
To Mr Hotham which he paid for a man to London		5-00-00
To Mr Mather upon his note for the cannoneers this week	c.80	71-01-06
Week's total:	2,325	735-08-05

This week the southern soldiers came.

Twenty-first week: 1–8 August 1642

Foot		
Captain Lowinger's company	175	46-07-10
Lieutenant-Colonel Legard's company[70]	178	49-07-02
Captain Goodricke's company	130	36-11-06
The Governor's company	229	56-16-00
Captain Appleyard's company	131	38-15-06
Captain Anlaby's company	130	36-11-06

[70]This included a minister paid at £0-10-00, a boatman at £0-04-08, and a further £0-03-00 for 'looking to the boom'.

Captain Overton's company	139	38-13-06
Captain Skarfe's company	108	31-08-10
Captain Alured's company	201	53-08-08
Captain Carter's company (2 ½ days)	172	27-06-04
Captain Legard's company	83	25-12-02
Captain Mathews's company (½ week)	194	29-02-02
Captain Hammond's company	177	45-09-08
Captain Purefoy's company	221	58-07-04
Total:	2,268	
Mine own pay	1	35-00-00
Major Jefford 18s per diem	1	6-06-00
To the scouts		1-08-00
For candles, etc.		0-11-03
Provost	1	1-01-00
Surgeon	1	0-14-00
To the engineers for 3 days		1-13-00
To 6 carbines	6	2-02-00
To 6 odd men	6	1-08-00
For work aboard the catches		0-09-02
For making a pump		2-15-00
This was when the enemy had cut off the water from us.		
For web lead for the ordnance		0-02-04
To the porter	1	0-04-08
To a messenger to Beverley		0-05-06
For fixing 226 muskets		5-13-04
To a post which lay at York		6-00-00
To the cannoneers	c.60	57-06-06
To the prisoners		0-06-00
For charges at London about ?refnuneing? money		11-00-00
Week's total:	2,345	716-03-03

Twenty-second week: 8–15 August 1642

Foot		
Captain Lowinger's company	175	47-15-06
Lieutenant-Colonel Legard's company[71]	178	49-05-06

[71]This included a minister paid at £0-10-00, a boatman at £0-04-08, and a further £0-02-06 for the boom keeper.

Captain Goodricke's company	130	36-15-00
The Governor's company	233	57-15-00
Captain Anlaby's company	130	36-15-00
Captain Legard	1	4-04-00
Captain Appleyard's company[72]	130	40-10-04
Captain Overton's company	139	38-17-00
Captain Alured's company	148	41-04-10
Captain Skarfe's company	115	33-05-00
Captain Mathews's company	199	53-10-02
Captain Purefoy's company	215	54-02-00
Captain Hammond's company	181	48-10-02
Captain Carter's company	187	50-09-02
Total:	2,161	
Mine own pay	1	35-00-00
Major Jefford 18s per diem	1	6-06-00
For coals and candles, etc		0-19-04
To Sir John Meldrum	1	10-00-00
To the engineer at 6s per diem	1	2-02-00
To his assistant at 3s per diem	1	1-01-00
To the conductor at 2s per diem	1	0-14-00
To an odd man	1	0-05-08
To Captain Billops for 4 odd men	4	0-10-08
Provost	1	1-01-00
Surgeon	1	0-14-00
To the prisoners		0-05-06
To the scouts		1-08-00
To the cannoneers this week	c.50	42-16-00
This week I somewhat abated the unreasonable number of town cannoneers		
To the smith for fixing muskets	1	12-12-06
To the porter	1	0-04-08
To six odd men	6	1-08-00
To six carbines	6	2-02-00
For making a cabin in the catch		3-03-10
For three odd pays		0-14-00
Week's total:	2,233	716-03-02

[72] Appleyard was also paid £1-13-04 for 'beer and tobacco for Captain Owen's soldiers'.

Twenty-third week: 15–22 August 1642

Foot		
Captain Lowinger's company	175	47-15-06
Lieutenant-Colonel Legard's company[73]	174	49-05-06
Captain Goodricke's company	130	36-15-00
The Governor's company	230	57-01-00
Captain Appleyard's company	130	40-07-08
Captain Anlaby's company	130	36-11-06
Captain Legard	1	4-04-00
Captain Skarfe's company	101	29-15-00
Captain Alured's company	116	35-03-06
Captain Purefoy's company	218	57-13-04
Captain Mathews's company	201	53-14-06
Captain Carter's company	190	51-03-02
Captain Overton's company	124	35-07-00
Captain Hammond's company	178	48-07-02
Total:	2,098	
Mine own pay	1	35-00-00
Major Jefford 18s per diem	1	6-06-00
For candles, etc		0-08-08
Provost	1	1-01-00
Surgeon	1	0-14-00
To the engineer	1	2-02-00
To his assistant	1	1-01-00
To the conductor	1	0-14-00
To six carbines	6	2-02-00
To six odd men	6	1-08-00
To the porter	1	0-04-08
To the prisoners		0-04-00
To the cannoneers	c.50	42-19-00
To five odd men	5	1-03-04
For tarring and making fit a rope for the chain		0-17-00
To Edward Andrew for ironwork		1-09-06
Week's total:	2,173	681-00-10

[73]This included a minister paid at £0-10-00, a boatman at £0-04-08, and a further £0-02-06 for the boom keeper.

Twenty-fourth week: 22–29 August 1642

Foot		
Captain Lowinger's company	175	48-02-02
Lieutenant-Colonel Legard's company[74]	178	54-05-01
Captain Goodricke's company	130	36-15-00
The Governor's company	231	57-05-02
Captain Appleyard's company	133	39-11-00
Captain Legard	1	4-04-00
Captain Anlaby's company	130	36-15-00
Captain Overton's company[75]	135	37-18-04
Captain Skarfe's company	107	31-17-08
Captain Alured's company	111	32-12-02
Captain Purefoy's company	218	57-14-02
Captain Hammond's company	178	48-07-02
Captain Carter's company	190	51-03-02
Captain Mathews's company	201	53-14-06
Total:	2,098	
Mine own pay	1	35-00-00
Major Jefford 18s per diem	1	6-06-00
For turves and candles, etc.		0-12-06
To the engineer	1	2-02-00
To his assistant	1	1-01-00
To the conductor	1	0-14-00
Provost	1	1-01-00
Surgeon	1	0-14-00
To the cannoneers	10	8-01-00
To the prisoners		0-04-00
To the porter	1	0-04-08
To six carbines	6	2-02-00
To six odd men	6	1-08-00
To seven odd men more	7	1-12-08
For ten chalder of coals		12-16-06
Week's total:	2,135	663-14-05

[74] This included a minister paid £0-10-00, a boom keeper paid £0-07-08, and £3-15-09 spent on '2 chalder of coals'.

[75] This included £1-03-04 for 5 'odd men'.

Twenty-fifth week: 29 August–5 September 1642

Foot		
Captain Lowinger's company	160	43-15-06
Lieutenant-Colonel Legard's company[76]	178	50-19-04
Captain Goodricke's company	126	35-16-04
The Governor's company[77]	223	55-08-04
Captain Overton's company	124	35-07-00
Captain Appleyard's company[78]	132	37-04-04
Captain Anlaby's company	113	32-15-08
Captain Skarfe's company	100	29-15-00
Captain Alured's company	111	32-12-02
Captain Carter's company	187	50-09-02
Captain Hammond's company	178	48-07-02
Captain Mathews's company	201	53-14-06
Captain Purefoy's company	218	57-14-02
Captain Legard	1	4-04-00
Total:	2,052	
Mine own pay	1	35-00-00
Major Jefford	1	6-06-00
For candles, etc.		0-05-05
To the engineer	1	2-02-00
To the conductors	1	0-14-00
Provost	1	1-01-00
Surgeon	1	0-14-00
For mending a drum		0-02-04
For six odd men	6	1-08-00
For six carbines	6	2-02-00
To Thomas Cart for deals[79] for making platforms and the catch		16-00-00
To the prisoners		0-04-00
To William Chambers for deals and joists for the platforms		10-00-00
To Christopher Gray for joists		0-18-00

[76] This included a minister paid £0-10-00, £0-07-08 for boatmen and the boom keeper, and £0-15-04 spent on turves.

[77] This included £1-17-04 in pay 'for 8 odd men'.

[78] This week Captain Appleyard's pay was reduced to £4-04-00, the same as the other captains.

[79] Deals were planks sawn from timber: *OED*, IV, pp. 295–296.

To Henry Hardy for conducting the expedition to the Downs[80]		7-00-00
To Edward Nisgill for going with the catch		2-00-00
To ten cannoneers	10	8-01-00
To the porter	1	0-04-08
To two odd men	2	0-09-04
For carrying the tents aboard to Mr Blaides[81] his ship		0-05-00
For paper royal for the cannoneers		0-01-04
To Thomas Dwarris for going with the catch to the Downs		4-00-00
To William Dickinson for victualling the said catch		5-17-04
Week's total:	2,083	672-16-11

You will find many charges of this kind, which though justly I might have referred them to their payments from the navy. Yet knowing it just, that the townsmen taken for that service should be paid, to give them content I paid them here. Here you will find the pay for cannoneers well abated, which gave some discontent. But I could not to please others throw away your money.

Twenty-sixth week: 5–12 September 1642

Foot		
Captain Lowinger's company	160	43-15-00
Lieutenant-Colonel Legard's company	183	50-15-00
Captain Goodricke's company	128	36-05-08
The Governor's company	224	55-12-06
Captain Appleyard's company	133	37-09-00
Captain Anlaby's company	116	33-09-08
Captain Overton's company	130	36-15-00
Captain Legard	1	4-04-00
Captain Alured's company	110	32-01-08
Captain Skarfe's company	100	29-15-00
Captain Purefoy's company	218	57-13-10
Captain Carter's company	190	51-01-02

[80] The Downs were an area of sea off the east coast of Kent between the North and South Foreland. They were a favoured anchorage in heavy weather and a gathering place for merchant ships en route to London.

[81] Joseph Blaides, an alderman of Hull: TNA, SP 28/189; Tindall Wildridge, *The Hull Letters*, pp. 151, 156.

Captain Hammond's company	178	48-07-02
Captain Mathews's company	201	53-14-06
Total	2,072	
Mine own pay	1	35-00-00
Major Jefford	1	6-06-00
For candles, etc.		0-07-00
Provost	1	1-01-00
Surgeon	1	0-14-00
To the engineer	1	2-02-00
To the conductor	1	1-14-00
To his assistant for two weeks	1	2-02-00
To six odd men	6	1-08-00
To 7 carbines	7	2-02-00
To 2 sick men	2	0-09-04
To the porter	1	0-04-08
To the cannoneers this week	11	8-04-06
For fixing 72 muskets		1-16-00
For nails		0-04-06
For 5 odd men	5	1-03-04
To Lieutenant-Colonel for the boatmen		0-04-08
To him which he gave to a prisoner		0-04-00
For 2 dozen of candles		0-10-00
For deals		0-07-06
To the minister	1	0-10-00
To the boom keeper	1	0-03-00
For five odd men	5	1-03-04
Week's total:	2,118	637-01-01

Twenty-seventh week: 12–19 September 1642

Foot		
Lieutenant-Colonel Legard's company	189	50-05-08
Captain Lowinger's company	154	42-07-00
Captain Goodricke's company	130	36-15-00
The Governor's company	233	57-15-00
Captain Anlaby's company	116	33-09-08
Captain Overton's company	130	36-15-00
Captain Appleyard's company	130	36-15-00
Captain Alured's company	110	32-01-08
Captain Legard	1	4-04-00

Captain Skarfe's company	110	32-01-08
Captain Purefoy's company	218	57-13-10
Captain Hammond's company	170	46-09-10
Captain Carter's company	188	50-13-10
Captain Mathews's company	201	53-14-06
Total:	1,980	
Mine own pay	1	35-00-00
Major Jefford	1	6-06-00
Provost	1	1-01-00
Surgeon	1	0-14-00
To the engineer	1	2-02-00
To his assistant	1	1-01-00
To the conductor	1	0-14-00
To 7 odd men	7	1-12-08
To 6 carbines	6	2-02-00
To a post		10-00-00
To Lieutenant-Colonel for coals and candles and for the repairing the castle, burnt by casualty		3-13-02
For 14 odd men	14	3-00-08
To the cannoneers	11	8-04-06
For a horse hire		0-05-00
For 12 odd men	12	2-16-00
To the porter	1	0-04-08
For candles		0-06-02
Week's total:	2,038	650-04-00

Twenty-eighth week: 19–26 September 1642

Foot		
Lieutenant-Colonel Legard's company[82]	188	52-12-08
Captain Carter's company	188	50-13-10
Captain Anlaby's company	116	33-09-08
Captain Goodricke's company	130	36-15-00
Captain Hammond's company	174	47-18-06

[82] The pay for this company included £0-10-00 for a minister, £0-06-00 for the boatman and provost, and £0-03-00 for the boom keeper.

Captain Purefoy's company	218	57-13-10
Captain Overton's company	130	36-15-00
Captain Skarfe's company	117	33-14-04
The Governor's company	239	58-18-04
Captain Lowinger's company	154	42-07-00
Captain Mathews's company	171	46-12-02
Captain Appleyard's company	128	36-05-08
Total:	1,953	
Mine own pay	1	35-00-00
Major Jefford	1	6-06-00
To him for coals and candles		0-05-08
Captain Alured his pay	1	4-04-00
To him which was given at the disbanding of his company[83]		1-14-08
For fixing of his arms		2-01-06
Captain Legard his pay	1	4-04-00
For his man	1	0-04-08
Paid upon a note for deals		3-00-00
Provost	1	1-01-00
Surgeon	1	0-14-00
To 3 odd men	3	1-13-00
To 6 carbines	6	2-02-00
To the porter	1	0-04-08
To an odd man	1	0-04-08
To the engineer	1	2-02-00
To his assistant	1	1-01-00
To the conductor	1	0-14-00
To the cannoneers	9	0-07-07
For bringing deals from Cottingham		3-01-00
To a skinner upon his note		0-12-10
Week's total:	1,983	610-12-10

[83]Captain Alured probably disbanded his company to take command of a troop of horse. On 10 August 1642 Durand Hotham had signed for over £700 to furnish troops of horse for Captain John Hotham and Captain John Alured. The troops were established by the following month, with Alured's brother Matthew serving as his lieutenant: TNA, SP 28/1A/17–18; SP 28/261/246–248; SP 28/252/178.

Twenty-ninth week: 26 September–3 October 1642

Foot		
Captain Overton's company	130	36-15-00
Captain Goodricke's company	130	36-15-00
Lieutenant-Colonel Legard's company[84]	190	53-02-00
The Governor's company	243	60-01-08
Captain Hammond's company	136	38-11-02
Captain Anlaby's company	116	33-09-08
Captain Skarfe's company	115	33-05-00
Captain Purefoy's company	215	57-06-00
Captain Appleyard's company	120	41-15-00
Captain Lowinger's company	154	51-19-00
Captain Mathews's company[85]	192	63-12-06
Captain Carter's company	165	45-06-00
Total:	1,906	
My own pay	1	35-00-00
Sergeant-Major	1	6-06-00
Captain Legard his pay	1	4-04-00
His man	1	0-04-08
To Captain Alured	1	3-00-00
Provost	1	1-01-00
Surgeon	1	0-14-00
To 6 carbines	6	2-02-00
To 7 odd men	7	1-12-08
Engineer	1	2-02-00
His assistant	1	1-01-00
His conductor	1	0-14-00
To Captain Hammond for 12 sick men	12	2-16-00
To Captain Billops for 3 odd men	3	0-14-00
For 4 odd men more	4	0-18-08
To Lieutenant-Colonel for candles		0-04-06
For turves		0-07-06
To him for 2 men	2	0-09-00
For 10 chalder of coals		12-00-00
For horse hire to carry the wagons		0-16-00
For one odd pay more		0-04-08

[84]The pay for this company included £0-10-00 for a minister, and £0-09-00 between the boatmen, provost, and boom keeper.

[85]The pay for the companies of Appleyard, Lowinger, and Mathews was raised to 6s per man this week, probably because they were drawn out of the garrison for field service under Captain John Hotham.

To James Hunter	1	0-17-06
To Thomas Coatsworth	1	0-17-06
To two Londoners		1-15-00
To John Skoley		0-14-00
To 2 cannoneers more at the blockhouses	2	1-08-00
To Major for coals and candles		0-09-08
To a man for writing		0-07-06
To the ship carpenters upon their notes		8-13-00
To Captain Hammond for 6 odd men	6	1-08-00
For 2 sick men	2	0-09-04
To 6 odd men	6	1-08-00
To 4 cannoneers at Cawood[86]	4	3-10-00
Week's total:	1,972	649-17-00

Thirtieth week: 3–10 October 1642

Foot		
Lieutenant-Colonel Legard's company	194	53-15-08
Captain Overton's company	130	36-15-00
Captain Anlaby's company	130	36-15-00
The Governor's company	251	61-19-00
Captain Goodricke's company	130	36-15-00
Captain Skarfe's company	120	34-08-04
Captain Mathews's company	182	49-05-10
Captain Hammond's company	156	43-04-06
Captain Appleyard's company at 3s-4d per man	70	18-15-00
Captain Lowinger's company	154	42-06-00
Captain Purefoy's company	215	57-06-00
Captain Carter's company	165	45-06-06
Total:	1,897	

[86]Forces under Captain John Hotham captured Cawood castle on 4 October 1642, from where Hotham signed a declaration against Lord Fairfax's treaty of neutrality: BL, TT E121(21), *A true relation of the taking of a great ship at Yarmouth [. . .] Likewise the manner of Master Hothams taking of Keywood castle in Yorkshire* (London, 1642); BL, TT E121(32), *The declaration of Captain Hotham sent to the parliament* (London, 1642); BL, TT E240(36), *A perfect diurnall of the passages in parliament*, 3–10 October 1642 (London, 1642), p. 8.

My own pay	1	35-00-00
Major Jefford	1	6-06-00
Captain Alured	1	3-00-00
Captain Legard	1	4-04-00
His man	1	0-04-08
Provost	1	1-01-00
Surgeon	1	0-14-00
To 6 carbines	6	2-02-00
To 7 odd men	7	1-12-08
For a horse 2 times to Selby[87]		0-10-00
To Captain Anlaby for 11 odd men	11	2-11-04
For horses to trail the drakes[88] to Beverley		0-06-08
For beer for the soldiers at Beverley		1-09-00
To Lieutenant-Colonel upon his note		4-06-00
For 2 sick men	2	0-09-04
For 2 odd pays	2	0-09-04
To the conductor of the work	1	0-14-00
To the porter	1	0-04-08
To James Hunter	1	0-17-06
To 2 London cannoneers	2	1-15-00
To Thomas Coatsworth	1	0-17-06
To John Skoley	1	0-14-00
To two cannoneers more	2	1-08-00
To the men that brought the money		0-02-06
To two wrights for 9 days		0-09-00
To two more for 7 days		0-07-00
To a man that came from London with the catch		3-00-00
To a drummer	1	0-10-00
To 2 prisoners		0-04-00
To a surgeon to buy his necessaries		2-00-00
To Captain Alured		1-04-00
To the engineer	1	3-03-00
To boatmen		1-08-00
To 4 cannoneers at Cawood	4	3-10-00
Week's total:	1,949	600-01-04

[87] Forces under John Hotham, accompanied by Sir Edward Rodes and Major John Gifford, captured Selby on 1 October 1642, tightening the stranglehold on York: *Sutherland MS*, HMC, 5th Report, Appendix (London, 1876), p. 191; BL, TT E119(24), *Speciall passages*, 27 September–4 October 1642 (London, 1642), pp. 61–62.

[88] Drakes were medium-sized pieces of field artillery.

Thirty-first week: 10–17 October 1642

Foot		
Lieutenant-Colonel Legard's company	204	56-02-04
Captain Hammond's company	181	49-01-02
Captain Goodricke's company	127	36-01-04
The Governor's company	257	63-02-04
Captain Overton's company	130	36-15-00
Captain Appleyard's company	121	34-12-08
Captain Skarfe's company	127	36-01-04
Captain Anlaby's company	130	36-15-00
Captain Lowinger's company	154	42-06-00
Captain Purefoy's company	171	46-17-06
Captain Carter's company	160	44-05-04
Total:	1,762	
My own pay	1	35-00-00
Major Jefford	1	6-06-00
Captain Legard	1	4-04-00
His man	1	0-04-08
To Captain Appleyard for 52 odd men the last week at 3s-4d a man	52	8-13-00
To a sergeant	1	0-10-06
For carrying soldiers to Selby		2-00-00
For candles		0-11-00
To two London cannoneers	2	1-15-00
To John Skoley	1	0-14-00
To the porter	1	0-04-08
To 6 carbines	6	2-02-00
To 10 odd men	10	2-06-00
To a pilot for going to Cawood		1-00-00
For making sentry houses		0-06-00
To Thomas Coatsworth for himself and 2 more	3	2-05-00
To 2 surgeons	2	1-08-00
Provost	1	1-01-00
To prisoners		0-04-00
To James Hunter	1	0-17-06
To the men that carried money to Cawood		1-00-00

To the workmen at Cawood[89]		3-11-06
To Captain Alured	1	1-04-00
To the engineer	1	3-03-00
To 4 cannoneers	4	3-10-00
To three odd men	3	0-14-00
To Captain Mathews[90]	1	30-00-00
Week's total:	1,856	596-13-10

Thirty-second week: 17–24 October 1642

Foot		
Captain Overton's company	130	36-15-00
Lieutenant-Colonel Legard's company	178	50-03-04
Captain Goodricke's company	130	38-17-00
The Governor's company	229	56-16-04
Captain Appleyard's company	203	29-02-00
Captain Anlaby's company	127	36-06-00
Captain Skarfe's company	130	36-15-00
Captain Hammond's company	147	41-02-06
Major Jefford's company	110	34-03-08
Captain Lowinger's company	154	42-06-00
Captain Purefoy's company	171	46-14-00
Captain Carter's company	160	44-01-10
Total:	1,769	
My own pay	1	35-00-00
Captain Legard	1	4-04-00
His man	1	0-04-08
Provost	1	1-01-00
Surgeon	1	0-14-00
To 4 cannoneers at 17s 6d a man	4	3-10-00

[89] Well connected by river to Hull, Cawood castle was fortified as an operational headquarters in the West Riding for Captain John Hotham's forces from October 1642 to March 1643. On 31 January 1643, the earl of Essex ordered Lord Fairfax to allow Captain Hotham to remain as governor of Cawood with full command of all the forces that he had brought there from Hull: BL, Add. MS 18,979, fo. 131.

[90] This final payment was made to Captain Mathews as he departed with his company to aid Sir John Gell in Derbyshire. Mathews was recalled to Hull for questioning on 25 November 1642: Slack, *Man at War*, p. 73.

To 3 cannoneers at 14s a man	3	2-02-00
To 6 carbines	6	2-02-00
To Lieutenant-Colonel for 3 men vizt boatmen at provost	3	1-00-00
For the minister	1	0-10-00
For the prisoners		0-02-00
For 9 odd men	9	2-02-00
To Captain Hammond for 5 odd men	5	1-00-00
To Lieutenant-Colonel for work		1-16-00
To the prisoners		0-04-00
To Egglefield the post for London		5-00-00
To 6 workmen for making sentry houses for a week at 3s a man		0-18-00
To Thomas Smart for carrying some to Wilton		1-00-00
To Henry Hopper for serving in the catch		2-00-00
To 3 odd men	3	0-14-00
To some seamen being prisoners at York		2-00-00
To the engineer	1	3-03-00
To 4 cannoneers	4	3-10-00
To 6 odd men	6	1-08-00
To Robert Story for being pilot to the Mayflower[91]		4-10-00
To a surgeon	1	0-14-00
To the porter	1	0-04-08
Week's total:	1,821	573-15-00

Thirty-third week: 24–31 October 1642

Foot		
Lieutenant-Colonel Legard's company	181	50-12-08
Captain Goodricke's company[92]	130	38-17-00
The Governor's company	230	56-16-04
Captain Skarfe's company	112	33-04-00

[91] The *Mayflower* was a twenty-eight-gun ship sent to Hull in April 1642 under the command of Captain Joseph Piggott. It saw active service during the first siege of Hull in July 1642: J.R. Powell, *The Navy in the English Civil War* (London, 1962), pp. 16, 22.

[92] This week Captain Goodricke's pay was increased to £6-06-00, the same pay as Lieutenant-Colonel Legard and Major Jefford.

Captain Appleyard's company	122	33-09-08
Captain Overton's company	133	37-09-00
Captain Anlaby's company	129	36-04-00
Captain Hammond's company	159	43-12-08
Captain Lowinger's company	145	40-10-04
Major Jefford's company	136	35-11-08
Captain Carter's company	157	43-09-06
Captain Purefoy's company	171	46-13-06
Total:	1,805	
My own pay	1	35-00-00
Captain Legard	1	4-04-00
His man	1	0-04-08
For fitting the Providence[93]		23-11-06
For fitting a keel from the river		10-00-00
Given away to the mariners at their going away		10-00-00
Provost	1	1-01-00
To the prisoners		0-04-00
To two London cannoneers	2	1-15-00
To Mr Crompton's man for a week's pay for himself and his horse	1	0-14-00
To 6 carbines	6	2-02-00
To 7 odd men	7	2-02-00
To Lieutenant-Colonel upon his note for coals, etc.		10-03-6
To Major Goodrick which he paid for making the guard houses		0-15-06
To 2 surgeons	2	1-08-00
To a messenger into Holderness		0-02-00
To Captain Hammond which he paid for beer for the soldiers		0-19-06
To a prisoner		0-02-00
To James Hunter	1	0-17-06
To Thomas Coatsworth	1	0-17-06
To the porter	1	0-04-08

[93]The *Providence* was a royalist ship that ran aground near Paul in Holderness in July 1642. It was later captured for parliament by Captain Joseph Piggott: J.R. Powell and E.K. Timings (eds), *Documents Relating to the Civil War, 1642–1648*, Navy Records Society, 105 (1963), pp. 19–20; Powell, *The Navy in the English Civil War*, p. 18.

To 2 cannoneers more at blockhouse	2	1-08-06
To the workmen with Captain Hotham		15-00-00
For 12 odd pays	12	2-16-00
Paid Antonio		3-03-00
Paid the cannoneers	4	3-10-00
Week's total:	1,848	627-00-02

Thirty-fourth week: 31 October–7 November 1642

Foot		
Lieutenant-Colonel Legard's company[94]	156	45-15-08
Captain Goodrick's company	125	37-14-08
Captain Overton's company	134	37-13-08
Captain Appleyard's company	129	35-02-04
The Governor's company[95]	201	52-10-04
Captain Owram's company[96]	90	27-08-04
Captain Anlaby's company	129	34-08-04
Captain Skarfe's company	125	35-11-08
Captain Lowinger's company	146	40-09-08
Major Jefford's company	115	35-07-06
Captain Carter's company	160	43-16-04
Captain Purefoy's company	167	45-16-00
Captain Hammond's company	142	39-19-02
Captain Bethell's company[97]	70	22-15-00
Total:	1,889	
My own pay	1	35-00-00
Captain Legard	1	4-04-00
Provost	1	1-01-00
2 surgeons	2	1-08-00
To James Hunter	1	0-17-04

[94] This included £0-19-00 between the minister and provost, and £0-10-00 for turves.

[95] This included an advance of nine weeks' pay at £0-05-00 per week for the lieutenant.

[96] Robert Owram was commissioned a captain of foot under the earl of Essex and was sent to Hull in October 1642. His company was transferred to Beverley in April 1643 and became part of Lord Fairfax's regiment following the arrest of the Hothams: TNA, E121/3/4, no. 69; E121/4/1, no. 63.

[97] Hugh Bethell of Rise was a captain of foot under Sir John Hotham before becoming captain-lieutenant to Colonel Francis Boynton's troop of horse. He lost an eye at Marston Moor and finished the war as colonel of a regiment of horse: TNA, E121/5/7, no. 26; West Yorkshire Archive Service, Wakefield, C469/1; A. Hopper, 'A directory of parliamentarian allegiance in Yorkshire during the civil wars', *YAJ*, 73 (2001), p. 101; B.D. Henning (ed.), *The House of Commons, 1660–1690*, 3 vols (London, 1983), I, p. 648.

To Thomas Coatsworth	1	0-17-06
One Londoner	1	0-17-06
John Skoley	1	0-14-00
To 6 carbines	6	2-02-00
8 odd men	8	1-17-04
To the prisoners		0-08-00
For fixing of 30 firelocks		1-15-04
To Captain Legard upon his note for beer and other things for the soldiers at Beverley, etc.		2-14-06
To Antonio		3-03-00
To Captain Owram for himself and officers and some soldiers for the last week		10-00-00
To Mr Raikes[98] for deals for the Providence		3-02-06
Week's total:	1,913	621-14-02

Thirty-fifthweek: 7–14 November 1642

Foot		
Captain Hammond's company	142	39-15-08
Lieutenant-Colonel Legard's company[99]	144	41-16-04
Captain Appleyard's company	128	34-17-08
Captain Bethell's company for 5 days	130	26-05-00
Captain Carlill's company for 5 days[100]	130	26-05-00
Captain Skarfe's company[101]	128	40-00-04
The Governor's company	192	47-19-00
Sergeant Major Goodrick's company	125	38-17-00
Captain Anlaby's company	127	35-10-06

[98] The Raikes family were a prominent family of Hull aldermen, and Thomas Raikes was mayor in 1643: HHC: C BRS/7/19, BRS/7/67; TNA, SP 28/189; J. Rushworth, *Historical Collections* (London, 1691), Part III, II, pp. 276–80; Tindall Wildridge, *The Hull Letters*, pp. 35–41, 44, 62, 77–78, 84, 151–152, 154–155, 159.

[99] This included £0-19-00 between the minister, boatmen, boom keeper, and provost.

[100] This may have been William Carlile, a gentleman of Brandesburton and Beverley: HHC: C BRS/7/30; College of Arms, Curia Militaris, Acta (4), fos 55–56.

[101] This included £13-04-08 for sixteen men who were with Captain Goodricke at Beverley the previous week.

Captain Overton's company	133	37-09-00
Captain Lowinger's company	147	40-16-08
Captain Carter's company	158	43-13-10
Captain Purefoy's company	166	45-16-03
Major Jefford's company	118	36-06-02
Total:	1,968	
My own pay	1	35-00-00
Captain Legard	1	4-04-00
Provost	1	1-01-00
2 surgeons	2	1-08-00
6 carbines	6	2-02-00
8 odd men	8	1-17-04
To 4 cannoneers at 17s-6d per week	4	3-10-00
To Skoley	1	0-14-00
To 2 more at the blockhouses	2	1-08-00
To a man for serving aboard the keel		2-00-00
For bringing arms from Rowley		0-04-00
For purses and paper		0-03-00
To 4 cannoneers	4	3-10-00
The workmen with Captain Hotham		9-16-00
For 6 odd pays	6	1-08-00
To Antonio		3-03-00
Week's total:	2,004	606-19-09[102]

Thirty-sixth week: 14–21 November 1642

Foot		
Captain Overton's company	133	37-09-00
Captain Legard's company[103]	207	51-16-00
Lieutenant-Colonel Legard's company[104]	157	47-17-00
Captain Owram's company	118	33-19-00
Captain Skarfe's company	131	36-19-08
Major Goodricke's company	128	38-07-04
Captain Appleyard's company	128	36-05-04

[102]This total is later given as £606-19-01 in the summary of disbursements at the end.

[103]Captain Legard appears to have taken over command of the governor's own company for this week.

[104]This included £1-01-00 between the 'preacher' and 'provost'.

Captain Anlaby's company	124	35-07-00
Captain Lowinger's company	146	40-12-00
Major Jefford's company	115	35-07-06
Captain Carter's company	164	44-03-10
Captain Purefoy's company	167	45-15-10
Captain Hammond's company	142	39-19-02
Captain Bethell's company	110	32-01-08
Total:	1,970	
My own pay	1	35-00-00
Two surgeons	2	1-08-00
Provost	1	1-01-00
8 odd men	8	1-17-04
6 carbines	6	2-02-00
Prisoners		0-05-00
To 3 cannoneers at 17s-6d per man	3	2-13-06
To John Skoley	1	0-14-00
More to the prisoners		0-07-00
To the engineer	1	3-03-00
To 4 cannoneers	4	4-07-06
The workmen with Captain Hotham		9-13-00
For 6 odd pays	6	1-08-00
For wagon horses		4-15-00
To the dragoons		1-12-00
Week's total:	2,003	628-11-02

Thirty-seventh week: 21–28 November 1642

Foot		
Lieutenant-Colonel Legard's company[105]	171	49-18-06
Captain Appleyard's company	130	36-15-00
Captain Anlaby's company	120	34-08-00
Major Goodricke's company	129	38-06-06
Captain Overton's company	101	29-19-08
Captain Skarfe's company	130	36-15-00
The Governor's company	215	53-11-04

[105] This included money for the minister, provost, boatmen, and boom keeper, plus twenty-four candles, three locks, and a messenger sent into Lincolnshire.

Captain Lowinger's company	146	40-09-08
Major Jefford's company	115	35-07-06
Captain Carter's company	158	43-13-10
Captain Purefoy's company	167	45-16-00
Captain Hammond's company	142	39-19-02
Captain Bethell's company	70	22-15-00
Total:	1,794	
My own pay	1	35-00-00
To the carpenters		0-15-00
Engineer	1	3-03-00
To James Hunter	1	0-17-06
To a messenger for 3 times to Northallerton[106]		0-17-00
For a messenger to Boston		0-05-00
To Thomas Coatsworth	1	0-17-06
To John Skoley	1	0-14-00
To Hunniburd	1	0-17-06
For fixing 5 case of pistols		0-10-00
Captain Legard his pay	1	4-04-00
For a man for carrying ammunition to Cawood		1-00-00
Paid the workmen with Captain Hotham		7-08-08
For 6 odd men	6	1-08-00
To the cannoneers	4	3-10-00
For wagon horses		4-10-00
To Captain Carter's dragoons		1-10-00
Week's total:	1,811	579-09-00

Thirty-eighth week: 28 November–5 December 1642

Foot		
Lieutenant-Colonel Legard's company[107]	171	48-17-08
Major Goodricke's company	130	38-17-00
The Governor's company	215	53-16-00
Captain Appleyard's company	124	36-07-00
Captain Overton's company	110	32-01-08

[106] Captain John Hotham was campaigning with some of the Hull forces in Durham and the North Riding of Yorkshire from 9 November to 1 December 1642.

[107] This included money for the minister, boatmen, and boom keeper.

Captain Anlaby's company	120	34-08-04
Captain Skarfe's company	128	36-08-08
Captain Lowinger's company	147	40-16-08
Major Jefford's company	116	35-07-06
Captain Purefoy's company	151	42-05-02
Captain Carter's company	164	45-02-00
Captain Hammond's company	142	39-19-08
Lieutenant Bethell's company	59	16-04-04
Total:	1,777	
My own pay	1	35-00-00
Captain Legard his pay	1	4-04-00
To James Hunter	1	0-17-06
For fitting the carriages for the 2 pieces that went to my Lord Fairfax[108]		0-04-06
To Thomas Coatsworth	1	0-17-06
To Antony		3-03-00
To 6 carbines	6	2-02-00
To 8 odd men	8	1-17-08
To a post		10-00-00
For 3 odd men	3	0-14-00
To John Skoley	1	0-14-00
Provost	1	1-01-00
Porter	1	0-04-08
Surgeon	1	0-14-00
To a man for going to London		2-00-00
To a foot post		0-10-00
To a man for serving aboard the catch		1-00-00
To a man for carrying the ordnance to Cawood		1-00-00
To 4 cannoneers	4	4-07-06
To the workmen with Captain Hotham		9-13-00
For 6 odd men	6	1-08-00
To the dragoons		1-12-00
Week's total:	1,812	583-11-00

[108] These pieces were to aid Lord Fairfax and Captain John Hotham in their defence of Tadcaster from the earl of Newcastle's army on 6 December 1642.

Disbursements

1 week	From the 13th of March 1642 to the 19th of the same	214-11-04
2 week	From the 19th of March to the 26th of the same	305-02-04
3 week	From the 26th of March to the 2d April	307-04-06
4 week	From the 2 of April to the 11th of the same	380-11-06
5 week	From the 11th of April to the 18th of the same	300-14-11
6 week	From the 18th of April to the 25th of the same	307-00-10
7 week	From the 25th of April to the 2d of May	569-11-09
8 week	From the 2d of May to the 9th of the same	338-01-00
9 week	From the 9th of May to the 16th of the same	404-17-08
10 week	From the 16th of May to the 23d of the same	354-04-06
11 week	From the 23d of May to the 30th of the same	385-00-00
12 week	From the 30th of May to the 6th of June	351-16-10
13 week	From the 6th of June to the 13th of the same	353-07-01
14 week	From the 13th of June to the 20th of the same	359-00-01
15 week	From the 20th of June to the 27th of the same	365-13-06
16 week	From the 27th of June to the 4th of July	406-06-10
17 week	From the 4th of July to the 11th of the same	482-05-08
18 week	From the 11th of July to the 18th of the same	504-09-02
19 week	From the 18th of July to the 25th of the same	637-10-01
20 week	From the 25th of July to the 1 of August	735-08-05
21 week	From the 1 of August to the 8th of the same	716-03-03
22 week	From the 8th of August to the 15th of the same	716-03-02
23 week	From the 15th of August to the 22th of the same	681-00-10
24 week	From the 22th of August to the 29th of the same	663-14-05
25 week	From the 29th of August to the 5th of September	672-16-11
26 week	From the 5th of September to the 12th of the same	637-01-01
27 week	From the 12th of September to the 19th of the same	650-04-00
28 week	From the 19th of September to the 26th of the same	610-12-10
29 week	From the 26th of September to the 3d of October	649-17-00
30 week	From the 3d of October to the 10th of the same	600-01-04
31 week	From the 10th of October to the 17th of the same	596-13-10
32 week	From the 17th of October to the 24th of the same	573-15-00
33 week	From the 24th of October to the 31th of the same	627-00-02
34 week	From the 31th of October to the 7th of November	621-14-02
35 week	From the 7th of November to the 14th of the same	606-19-01
36 week	From the 14th of November to the 21th of the same	628-11-02
37 week	From the 21th of November to the 28th of the same	579-09-00
38 week	From the 28th of November to the 5th of December *inclusively*	583-11-00

The total sum of the disbursements for thirty-eight weeks from the 13th of March 1642 till the 5th of December 1642, is}	19,479-06-09
More for a catch	00155-00-00
For the outworks about the garrison	00362-14-07
Paid by my son Durand at London for advance of Sir John Meldrum}	00150-00-00
More since for the outworks, which are now finished	00162-00-00
Disbursed for soldiers' apparel by order from the House	01,000-00-00
Total:	01,829-14-07
Sum total, *disbursed* is	21,309-01-06
Received in total:	19,437-19-00
Disbursed more than received:	01,871-02-06

John Hotham.

In the disbursement of these monies, I have disbursed them to the best of my judgement with the best frugality I could possibly, regard had to the nature of the service for time, place, and persons I had to deal with. I speak it with confidence that all those that were upon the place think I was too good a husband of your monies. If any think otherwise, I have the worse fortune.

John Hotham.

11 September 1644
The account of Sir John Hotham whereunto his hand is subscribed was this day showed unto him, and his oath was required thereto. To which he answered, that to the best of his knowledge it is the same account which he sent up to Mr Pym, and that that account was a true account, but whether it be the same *without any alteration* or no in regard that his papers are now at Hull in the hands of the committee there, he cannot positively set down, unless he had his own copy to compare it withal, which he is verily assured remains in the hands of the said committee.

John Hotham

Subscribed in the presence of
Henry Hunter, Thomas Andrews, Edmund Casson.

A just and true account of monies disbursed by Sir John Hotham, knight and baronet, Governor of Hull, for pay and other things for the garrison since 5 December 1642 till 16 January 1643.[109]

Thirty-ninth week: 5–12 December 1642

Foot		
The Governor's company[110]	206	48-14-00
Captain Anlaby's company	120	34-08-04
Captain Appleyard's company	126	35-16-04
Captain Owram's company	113	32-18-08
Captain Skarfe's company	130	36-15-00
Major Goodricke's company	128	37-19-06
Lieutenant-Colonel Legard's company[111]	177	50-08-08
Captain Overton's company[112]	130	41-15-00
Major Jefford's company	115	35-07-06
Captain Carter's company	155	42-05-10
Captain Purefoy's company	165	45-06-06
Captain Hammond's company	137	38-15-10
Captain Lowinger's company	145	40-05-04
Lieutenant Bethell's company	56	15-01-00
Total:	1,903	
My own pay	1	35-00-00
Captain Legard	1	4-04-00
For 6 carbines	6	2-02-00
For 8 odd men	8	1-17-06
Provost	1	1-01-00
Prisoners		0-04-00
Surgeon	1	0-14-00
To 2 cannoneers at 17s-6d each man	2	1-15-00
To the workfolk		3-19-00
To Mr Anthony	1	3-03-00
To William Spinck upon his note for horse hire		2-12-00

[109] TNA, SP 28/189.
[110] This included £1-17-04 for eight sick men and £3-00-08 for '13 men at worke'.
[111] This included £1-01-00 for a minister and the boatmen, with £1-08-00 for '6 odd pays'.
[112] This included £5-00-00 given to his men at Beverley.

To 5 cannoneers with Captain Hotham at 17s-6d a man	5	4-07-06
To 6 odd men	6	1-08-00
For chain shot and other work about the cannon		2-02-00
To the carpenters		3-10-00
Bricklayers		1-12-04
To labourers		1-10-00
Week's total:	1,935	608-08-11

Fortieth week: 12–19 December 1642

Foot		
Lieutenant-Colonel Legard's company[113]	171	48-17-00
Captain Anlaby's company	120	34-08-04
Captain Skarfe's company	127	36-01-00
Major Goodricke's company	124	37-09-00
Captain Appleyard's company	126	35-16-04
Captain Owram's company	124	35-07-00
The Governor's company	206	49-14-00
Major Jefford's company	111	35-02-04
Captain Carter's company	148	40-17-10
Captain Purefoy's company	165	45-06-00
Captain Hammond's company	137	38-15-10
Captain Lowinger's company	144	40-01-04
Lieutenant Bethell's company	54	15-01-04
Total:	1,757	
My own pay	1	35-00-00
Captain Legard his pay	1	4-04-00
Provost	1	1-01-00
Surgeon	1	0-14-00
Work		4-00-00
6 carbines	6	2-02-00
To 8 odd men	8	1-17-00
Prisoners		0-04-00
To the men for bringing in beasts		5-00-00
To 8 cannoneers	8	7-00-00

[113] This included £1-01-00 for 'minister, boatmen, and boom' and £0-01-08 for 'odd pays'.

For work with Captain Hotham		17-14-08
To the bricklayers		2-15-00
6 odd men	6	1-08-00
To Captain Hotham which he wanted for the last week		6-02-10
Week's total:	1,789	581-19-10

Forty-first week: 19–26 December 1642

Foot		
Captain Overton's company	119	34-03-08
Captain Anlaby's company	120	34-08-04
Captain Owram's company	121	34-13-00
Captain Appleyard's company	120	33-14-04
The Governor's company	185	44-15-04
Lieutenant-Colonel Legard's company[114]	166	49-04-00
Major Goodricke's company	123	36-19-04
Captain Skarfe's company	118	33-11-08
Major Jefford's company	111	35-02-04
Captain Carter's company	148	40-17-10
Captain Purefoy's company	165	45-06-06
Captain Hammond's company	185	52-08-10
Captain Lowinger's company	144	40-01-04
Total:	1,825	
My own pay	1	35-00-00
Captain Legard his pay	1	4-04-00
For work		3-19-00
Provost	1	1-01-00
Surgeon	1	0-14-00
6 carbines	6	2-02-00
8 odd men	8	1-17-00
Prisoners		0-04-00
To 8 odd men which went to be dragoons in Captain Beckwith's troop[115]	8	4-12-06

[114]This included £1-01-00 for 'minister etc', with another £1-00-00 for turves.

[115]This was either Captain Arthur Beckwith of Aldborough or his brother Captain Matthew Beckwith of Tanfield: Hopper, 'A directory of parliamentarian allegiance in Yorkshire', pp. 96, 102.

Paid 5 cannoneers with Captain Hotham	5	4-07-06
Paid the workmen		14-19-00
Bricklayers		1-12-06
6 odd men	6	1-08-00
For journeying prisoners		2-08-00
Week's total:	1,862	593-14-10

Forty-second week: 26 December 1642–2 January 1643

Foot		
Lieutenant-Colonel Legard's company[116]	176	50-03-04
Captain Anlaby's company	120	35-08-04
Major Goodricke's company	124	38-09-00
Captain Overton's company	124	33-17-00
Captain Appleyard's company	118	34-12-00
The Governor's company	201	50-04-10
Captain Skarfe's company	118	33-19-00
Captain Owram's company	128	36-05-08
Major Jefford's company	111	35-02-04
Captain Carter's company	148	40-17-10
Captain Purefoy's company	165	45-06-06
Captain Hammond's company	188	51-13-10
Captain Lowinger's company	147	40-14-04
Total:	1,868	
My own pay	1	35-00-00
Captain Legard his pay	1	4-04-00
8 odd men	8	1-17-00
6 carbines	6	2-02-00
To men that went into Captain Hearne's troop to be dragoons, for their week's pay	11	6-06-06
To Mr Thompson for the horse charges that was taken at sea		8-00-00
To James Hunter for his pay	1	0-17-06
To Thomas Coatsworth	1	0-17-06

[116]This included £1-01-00 for the minister, boatmen, and provost, with another £0-05-04 for 'odd pays'.

To John Skoley	1	0-14-00
To the conductor	1	0-14-00
Provost	1	1-01-00
Surgeon	1	0-14-00
To 5 cannoneers with Captain Hotham	5	4-07-06
For 6 odd pays	6	1-08-00
To him for odd pays more		0-11-10
Week's total:	1,912	594-18-02

Forty-third week: 2–9 January 1643

Foot		
Lieutenant-Colonel Legard's company[117]	178	53-19-04
Captain Anlaby's company	120	34-08-04
Major Goodricke's company	126	37-18-04
Captain Overton's company	124	35-07-08
Captain Appleyard's company	126	35-16-04
The Governor's company	203	50-14-02
Captain Skarfe's company	127	36-01-00
Captain Owram's company	128	36-05-08
Major Jefford's company	111	35-06-08
Captain Carter's company	148	41-16-04
Captain Purefoy's company	171	46-14-06
Captain Hammond's company	188	51-13-10
Captain Lowinger's company	144	40-00-04
Total:	1,868	
My own pay	1	35-00-00
Captain Legard	1	4-04-00
Provost	1	1-01-00
Surgeon	1	0-14-00
Workfolks		3-19-00
2 cannoneers at 17s-6d per diem	2	1-15-00
To the joiner for 5 weeks' pay		15-15-00
To a post to London		2-16-08
7 carbines	7	2-09-00
6 odd men	6	1-08-00
To a pilot to Cawood		0-12-00

[117] This included £1-01-00 for the minister, boatmen, and provost.

Porter	1	0-04-08
For fitting the catches to sea		10-00-00
To Captain Hotham's surgeon for 3 weeks' pay	1	1-10-00
To 5 cannoneers	5	4-07-06
6 odd men	6	1-08-00
Week's total:	1,900	623-17-00

Forty-fourth week: 9–16 January 1643

Foot		
Captain Overton's company	124	35-07-08
Lieutenant-Colonel Legard's company[118]	178	53-19-04
Captain Appleyard's company	126	35-16-04
Major Goodricke's company	126	37-18-04
Captain Anlaby's company	120	34-08-04
Captain Skarfe's company	127	36-01-00
The Governor's company	204	51-04-08
Captain Owram's company	128	36-05-08
Major Jefford's company	111	35-06-08
Captain Carter's company	148	41-16-06
Captain Purefoy's company	171	46-14-04
Captain Hammond's company[119]	188	51-13-10
Captain Lowinger's company	144	40-00-04
Total:	1,895	
My own pay	1	35-00-00
Captain Legard his pay	1	4-04-00
Provost	1	1-01-00
Surgeon	1	0-14-00
Workfolks		3-19-00
2 cannoneers at 17s-6d per diem	2	1-15-00
To the engineer for a week's pay	1	3-03-00
7 carbines	7	2-09-00
6 odd men	6	1-08-00

[118]This included £1-01-00 for 'minister, provost etc'.

[119]Captain Robert Hammond disappears from the accounts after this week. By May 1643 he was receiving pay as captain of the earl of Essex's lifeguard: TNA, SP 28/7/121; TNA, E121/5/7, no. 44.

Porter	1	0-04-08
To a surgeon with Captain Hotham for one week's pay	1	0-10-00
To 5 cannoneers	5	4-07-06
6 odd men	6	1-08-00
Week's total:	1,929	597-01-02

Disbursements

From the 5th of December 1642 to the 12th of the same	0608-08-11
From the 12th of December 1642 to the 19th	0581-19-10
From the 19th of December 1642 to the 26th	0593-14-10
From the 26th of December 1642 to the 2nd of January 1643	0594-18-02
From the 2nd of January to the 9th	0623-17-00
From the 9th to the 16th of January	0597-01-02
Sum total of the disbursements from the 5th of December 1642 till the 16th of January 1643	3,599-19-11
And disbursed upon my last reckoning more than received	1,871-02-06
See disbursed in total	5,471-02-05
Received	4,000-00-00
Disbursed more than received	1,471-02-05
There is upon Monday next *being 30 January instant* a fortnight's pay more which is about	1,200-00-00
So as that day we have spent more than received	2,671-02-05

[Fifty-third week]: 13–20 March 1643[120]

Foot		
Lieutenant-Colonel Legard's company[121]	212	59-00-00
Captain Overton's company	146	40-09-08
Major Goodricke's company	145	42-07-00
The Governor's company	226	56-07-04
Captain Anlaby's company	133	37-09-00
Captain Skarfe's company	140	39-01-08
Captain Owram's company	118	33-15-00
Total:	1,120	
My own pay	1	35-00-00
Captain Legard his pay	1	4-04-00
For work		2-07-08
To the conductor for 2 weeks	1	1-08-00
One cannoneer	1	0-14-00
To the prisoners at work		3-02-06
Provost	1	1-01-00
To the engineer for 6 weeks' pay	1	18-18-00
For 5 carbines	5	1-15-00
To 8 odd men	8	1-17-04
More for work		0-15-00
For a house to lie coals in		0-18-00
Week's total:	1,139	380-10-02

[Fifty-fourth week]: 20–27 March 1643[122]

Foot		
Captain Overton's company	139	38-17-00
Lieutenant-Colonel Legard's company[123]	213	58-02-00
The Governor's company	236	58-09-04
Captain Anlaby's company	106	31-03-06

[120] TNA, SP 28/6/42–43.

[121] This included £0-10-00 for a minister, £0-01-04 for a provost, £0-04-08 for a boatman, £0-03-00 for a boom keeper, and £0-02-00 for a prisoner.

[122] TNA, SP 28/6/48–49.

[123] This included £0-10-00 for a minister, £0-01-04 for a provost, £0-04-08 for a boatman, £0-03-00 for a boom keeper, and £0-02-00 for a sick man.

Major Goodricke's company	132	39-06-04
Captain Skarfe's company	126	35-16-04
Captain Owram's company	103	30-09-04
Captain Purefoy's company (3 days)	122	15-02-06
Captain Hotham's company (3 days)	115	12-12-06
Total:	1,292	
My own pay	1	35-00-00
Captain Legard his pay	1	4-04-00
Provost	1	1-01-00
Surgeon	1	0-14-00
For work		3-18-00
To the engineer	1	3-03-00
Conductor	1	0-14-00
To 3 cannoneers	3	2-09-00
Porter	1	0-04-08
To 5 carbines	5	1-15-00
To 8 odd men	8	1-17-04
To 7 odd men more	7	1-12-08
To 44 men that went to Scarborough[124]	44	10-05-04
More for work		7-10-08
More to the conductor		0-07-00
Week's total:	1,366	384-14-08

[Fifty-fifth week]: 27 March–3 April 1643[125]

Foot		
Captain John Legard's company[126]	156	42-16-04
Captain Overton's company	142	39-11-00
Captain Anlaby's company	128	36-05-08
Captain Skarfe's company	130	36-15-00

[124]These were the seamen that Sir John Hotham despatched with Browne Bushell to recapture Scarborough castle for parliament: J. Binns, 'Captain Browne Bushell: North Sea adventurer and pirate', *Northern History*, 27 (1991), pp. 94–96.

[125]TNA, SP 28/6/371–372.

[126]John Legard had been a captain in Sir Henry Griffith's East Riding trained band. He was part of the garrison of Scarborough when Sir Hugh Cholmley changed sides. Refusing to countenance this defection, he withdrew to Hull, where his kinsman Sir John Hotham immediately found a command for him: BL, Add. MS 28,082, fo. 80v; Legard, *The Legards of Anlaby and Ganton*, pp. 83–85; BL TT E95(9), *A true and exact relation of all the proceedings of Sir Hugh Cholmleys revolt*, 7 April 1643 (London, 1643); Dugdale, *The Visitation of the County of Yorke*, p. 111.

Lieutenant-Colonel Legard's company[127]	209	62-08-11
Major Goodricke's company	137	40-09-08
The Governor's company	251	62-03-00
Total:	1,153	
My own pay	1	35-00-00
Captain Robert Legard's pay[128]	1	4-04-00
To the conductor	1	0-14-00
For work		9-10-02
For victualling the catches with bread and beer when they went to Scarborough		1-07-00
To 5 carbines	5	1-15-00
To 8 odd men	8	1-17-04
To 2 odd men of Captain Goodricke's	2	0-09-04
To 6 men which lies sick in the tower of Captain Purefoy's	6	1-08-00
To the prisoners at work		2-15-06
Provost	1	1-01-00
Surgeon	1	0-14-00
To 4 cannoneers	4	3-06-06
For getting the bullets ashore and the guns that came from Scarborough		0-06-00
For mending the carriages for the ordnance		1-02-02
For mending the boat		0-06-07
Week's total:	1,183	386-05-02

[Fifty-sixth week]: 3–10 April 1643[129]

Foot		
Captain Skarfe's company	132	37-04-04
Captain Overton's company	147	40-14-04
Major Goodricke's company	140	41-03-08
Captain Anlaby's company	125	35-11-08

[127] This included £0-10-00 for a minister, £0-01-04 for a provost, £0-04-08 for a boatman, £0-03-00 for a boom keeper, £1-04-09 for candles since 28 November 1642, £2-14-08 for repairs to Hull castle, and £1-03-06 for nails and iron work.

[128] Robert Legard of Anlaby was a younger brother of Lieutenant-Colonel Christopher Legard. He served as a reformado captain and scoutmaster in the Hull garrison before commanding a troop in Lord Fairfax's regiment: HHC: C BRS/7/2, BRS/7/10; TNA, E121/4/7, no. 48; Legard, *The Legards of Anlaby and Ganton*, pp. 83–86.

[129] TNA, SP 28/6/379–380.

Lieutenant-Colonel Legard's company[130]	212	58-00-00
Captain John Legard's company	146	40-09-08
The Governor's company	257	63-07-04
Total:	1,159	
My own pay	1	35-00-00
Captain Robert Legard's pay	1	4-04-00
Provost	1	1-01-00
Surgeon	1	0-14-00
Engineer for 2 weeks	1	6-06-00
For work		10-10-04
To the prisoners at work		2-17-06
To the conductor	1	0-14-00
To 10 men which was not mustered	10	2-06-08
To 3 men that came from Scarborough	3	0-14-00
To 3 cannoneers	3	2-09-00
To 8 odd men	8	1-17-04
To 6 carbines	6	2-02-00
To the boatmen for taking <the> four troops of horse into Lincolnshire[131]		3-08-00
To a cannoneer for a month's pay	1	3-10-00
For a lame man	1	0-04-08
Week's total:	1,198	394-19-06

[Fifty-seventh week]: 10–17 April 1643[132]

Foot		
Lieutenant-Colonel Legard's company[133]	205	56-04-00
Captain Skarfe's company	131	36-19-08
Captain Overton's company	144	40-00-00
Major Goodricke's company	136	40-05-00

[130] This included the usual £0-10-00 for a minister, £0-01-04 for a provost, £0-04-08 for a boatman, and £0-03-00 for a boom keeper.

[131] This was a force led by Lieutenant-General John Hotham, invited into Lincolnshire by his parliamentarian relatives there. The horse comprised the troops of John Hotham, Sir John Hotham (commanded by Major Lowinger), Sir Edward Rodes, Sir Matthew Boynton, and, later, Captain Bethell. They were joined by Hull greycoat infantry under Captain Purefoy: TNA, SP 28/300/441; C. Holmes, *Seventeenth-century Lincolnshire* (Lincoln, 1980), p. 163.

[132] TNA, SP 28/6/423–424.

[133] This included the usual £0-10-00 for a minister, £0-01-04 for a provost, £0-04-08 for a boatman, and £0-03-00 for a boom keeper.

Captain Anlaby's company	120	34-08-04
Captain John Legard's company	149	41-03-08
The Governor's company	246	61-00-08
Total:	1,131	
To the prisoners at work		2-18-06
Provost	1	1-01-00
For fixing arms for Captain Bethell's troop		0-17-00
To 4 cannoneers	4	3-06-06
For work		9-02-02
To the engineer	1	3-03-00
To 8 carbines	8	3-04-00
To the conductor	1	0-14-00
Surgeon	1	0-14-00
Porter	1	0-04-08
My own pay	1	35-00-00
Captain Robert Legard's pay	1	4-04-00
To 5 poor ministers		2-10-00
To 9 odd men	9	2-02-00
Week's total:	1,159	379-12-02

[Fifty-eighth week]: 17–24 April 1643[134]

Foot		
Captain Overton's company	146	40-09-08
The Governor's company	242	60-02-00
Major Goodricke's company	136	40-05-00
Captain Skarfe's company	143	39-15-08
Captain Anlaby's company	122	34-17-08
Lieutenant-Colonel Legard's company[135]	190	52-08-00
Captain John Legard's company	165	44-18-04
Total:	1,144	

[134] TNA, SP 28/6/440–441.

[135] This included the usual £0-10-00 for a minister, £0-01-04 for a provost, £0-04-08 for a boatman, and £0-03-00 for a boom keeper.

My own pay	1	35-00-00
To one odd sergeant	1	0-10-00
To the engineer	1	3-03-00
Provost	1	1-01-00
Surgeon	1	0-14-00
To the prisoners at work		2-18-06
To 5 poor ministers		2-10-00
To 7 men that was not mustered	7	1-12-08
To 8 men more of Captain Anlaby's	8	1-17-04
To the porter	1	0-04-08
To 4 cannoneers	4	3-06-06
To 5 carbines	5	1-15-00
To 10 odd men	10	2-06-08
To 7 Paul boats for taking the dragoons to Boston[136]		1-01-00
To another boat		0-02-06
To the smith for fixing arms for Captain Bethell's troop		0-16-03
For work		9-10-00
To the conductor	1	0-14-00
To the great boat for 4 voyages to Boston		2-00-00
To a little boat		0-05-00
To a man for bringing £1,300 from London		1-00-00
Captain Legard's pay	1	4-04-04
Week's total:	1,186	389-15-05

[Fifty-ninth week]: 24 April–1 May 1643[137]

Foot		
Lieutenant-Colonel Legard's company[138]	204	55-18-08
Captain Anlaby's company	125	35-11-08
The Governor's company	224	55-18-00
Captain Overton's company	151	41-13-00
Captain John Legard's company	165	44-18-04
Major Goodricke's company	141	41-08-04
Captain Skarfe's company	142	39-12-00
Total:	1,152	

[136]This looks like an attempt to reinforce John Hotham's troops in Lincolnshire after their defeat at Ancaster Heath on 11 April 1643.

[137]TNA, SP 28/7/160–161.

[138]This included the usual £0-10-00 for a minister, £0-01-04 for a provost, £0-04-08 for a boatman, and £0-03-00 for a boom keeper.

My own pay	1	35-00-00
Captain Legard's pay	1	4-04-00
To the prisoners at work		2-18-00
To the engineer	1	3-03-00
To the conductor	1	0-14-00
To 4 cannoneers	4	3-06-06
Surgeon	1	0-14-00
Provost	1	1-01-00
Work		3-06-00
Porter	1	0-04-08
To 9 odd men	9	2-02-00
To 5 carbines	5	1-15-00
For binding the carriage for the ordnance		7-19-00
To the porters and boatmen for taking them up		0-14-00
To 18 men that was at work and not mustered	18	4-04-00
To 5 poor ministers		2-10-00
To one poor minister that was banished from his living		5-00-00
To a boat for going to Barton with 4 horses of Captain Bethell's troop		0-03-00
To four men that went into Lincolnshire	4	1-10-00
To 4 cannoneers that went thither	4	0-08-00
To the boatman for taking them and some others over		0-04-00
To a post		10-00-00
For mending a drum		0-04-06
To an overseer of the works	1	0-10-00
Week's total:	1,204	406-13-08

[Sixtieth week]: 1–8 May 1643[139]

Foot		
Captain Overton's company	153	42-02-04
Captain John Legard's company	167	45-07-08
The Governor's company	229	57-01-04

[139] TNA, SP 28/7/168–169.

Lieutenant-Colonel Legard's company[140]	202	55-13-04
Captain Anlaby's company	129	36-10-04
Major Goodricke's company	132	39-06-04
Captain Skarfe's company	139	38-17-00
Total:	1,151	
My own pay	1	35-00-00
Captain Legard's pay	1	4-04-00
Provost	1	1-01-00
Surgeon	1	0-14-00
Porter	1	0-04-08
To 6 carbines	6	2-02-00
To 6 odd men	6	1-08-00
To 15 men that was at work and not mustered	15	3-10-00
For work this week		12-16-03
To ye prisoners at work		2-18-00
To 5 poor ministers		2-10-00
To 6 cannoneers	6	5-01-06
To an overseer of the works	1	0-10-00
To the engineer	1	3-03-00
To the conductor	1	1-01-00
For carrying a foot company over to Barton		0-10-00
Week's total:	1,192	392-11-01

[Sixty-first week missing]

[Sixty-second week] 15–22 May 1643[141]

Foot		
Lieutenant-Colonel Legard's company[142]	198	54-14-08
Major Goodricke's company	141	40-08-04
The Governor's company	216	54-00-02
Captain Overton's company	154	42-07-00
Captain Lowinger's company	129	36-10-04
Captain Hotham's company	130	35-16-04

[140] This included the usual £0-10-00 for a minister, £0-01-04 for a provost, £0-04-08 for a boatman, and £0-03-00 for a boom keeper.

[141] TNA, SP 28/7/228–229.

[142] This included the usual £0-10-00 for a minister, £0-01-04 for a provost, £0-04-08 for a boatman, and £0-03-00 for a boom keeper.

Captain Skarfe's company	150	41-08-04
Captain Anlaby's company	140	38-15-08
Total:	1,258	
Captain Robert Legard's pay	1	4-04-00
My own pay	1	35-00-00
To the engineer	1	3-03-00
Conductor	1	1-01-00
To 5 poor ministers		2-10-00
To the surgeon	1	0-14-00
To 6 carbines	6	2-02-00
To 6 odd men	6	1-08-00
To 66 men that came from Brigg which wanted their pay from the last week		15-08-00
To one cannoneer	1	0-14-00
To 4 cannoneers more	4	3-10-00
Porter	1	0-04-08
Provost	1	1-01-00
To the prisoner		2-06-06
To two men for overseeing the work	2	1-00-00
For work this week		24-00-00
To 4 men that was wounded at Brigg[143]	4	0-18-08
To 15 men of Captain William Hotham's[144] company	15	3-10-00
Week's total:	1,303	447-15-08

Examined these accounts, 5 June 1643, and allowed by my master,

John Bourdenand.[145]

[143] Captain John Legard was killed in an engagement with the royalists at Brigg in 1643: J. Binns (ed.), *The Memoirs and Memorials of Sir Hugh Cholmley of Whitby, 1600–1657*, YASRS, 153 (2000), p. 143n.

[144] A younger son of Sir John Hotham, William was commissioned a captain in the Hull garrison in 1643: HHC: C BRS/7/67.

[145] John Bourdenand was a gentleman of Scorborough and secretary to Sir John Hotham. His house was ransacked when the Hothams were arrested: TNA, SP 28/299/754; HHC: C BRS/7/29; *CSPD, 1641–1643*, p. 465.

[Sixty-third week]: 22–29 May 1643[146]

Foot		
Lieutenant-Colonel Legard's company[147]	216	58-10-08
Captain Anlaby's company	135	37-18-04
Captain Hotham's company	154	41-19-04
Captain Overton's company	151	41-13-00
Major Goodricke's company	130	38-17-04
Captain Lowinger's company	142	39-11-00
The Governor's company	212	53-02-00
Captain Skarfe's company	148	40-19-00
Total:	1,288	
My own pay	1	35-00-00
Captain Robert Legard's pay	1	4-04-00
To Lieutenant-Colonel for turves and coals		4-14-09
To 8 men that was upon a party	8	1-17-04
To 33 men that was at work and not mustered	33	7-14-00
For work this week		12-15-10
To the engineer	1	3-03-00
To the conductor	1	1-01-00
To an overseer	1	0-10-00
To 5 poor ministers		2-10-00
To 6 cannoneers	6	5-01-06
To a Norfolk gentleman that was driven out of his country		1-00-00
For victualling the keel to go up the river		4-18-03
For seamen's wages aboard of the pink[148] and victualling her		17-00-00
Porter	1	0-04-08
To 6 carbines	6	2-02-00
To 6 odd men	6	1-08-00
Provost	1	1-01-00
Surgeon	1	0-14-00
Week's total:	1,355	459-09-08

[146]TNA, SP 28/7/251–252.

[147]This included the usual £0-10-00 for a minister, £0-01-04 for a provost, £0-04-08 for a boatman, and £0-03-00 for a boom keeper, as well as £0-15-04 for 5 men for 23 days and £3-00-08 for 13 odd men.

[148]A small sailing vessel, usually having a narrow stern, or a boat with a flat bottom and bulging sides, used for coasting and fishing: *OED*, XI, p. 869.

[Sixty-fourth week]: 29 May–5 June 1643[149]

Foot		
Lieutenant-Colonel Legard's company[150]	211	57-04-04
Captain Anlaby's company	125	35-11-08
The Governor's company	192	48-08-08
Major Goodricke's company	124	37-09-00
Captain William Legard's company	71	22-16-02
Captain William Hotham's company	94	28-07-00
Captain Lowinger's company	125	35-11-08
Captain Overton's company	139	38-17-00
Captain Skarfe's company	138	36-15-00
Total:	1,219	
My own pay	1	35-00-00
Captain Robert Legard's pay	1	4-04-00
Provost	1	1-01-00
Surgeon	1	0-14-00
To 6 carbines	6	2-02-00
To 6 odd men	6	1-08-00
Porter	1	0-04-08
To 7 Dutchmen	7	0-15-00
To 86 men that was at work and not mustered	86	20-01-04
For work this week		7-03-06
To the engineer	1	3-03-00
To the conductor	1	1-01-00
To an overseer	1	0-10-00
To 5 poor ministers		2-10-00
To 5 cannoneers	5	4-04-00
For mending the chain that goes over the haven		0-06-06
For crossing a piece of ordnance up to Wressle		0-10-00
For seamen's wages and victualling the pink		21-02-00
For victualling the keel		3-05-00
To the prisoners at Gainsborough		5-05-00
To the boatmen for bringing up Hessle great boat, etc.		1-17-00
For fixing of 50 muskets		2-18-08
Week's total:	1,337	460-09-02

[149] TNA, SP 28/7/478–479.

[150] This included the usual £0-10-00 for a minister, £0-01-04 for a provost, £0-04-08 for boatmen, and £0-03-00 for a boom keeper, as well as £0-16-04 for 6 men for 24 days.

[Sixty-fifth week?] From the [blank left in MS] of [blank] to the [blank] 1643[151] (probably 5–12 June 1643)

Foot		
Captain Skarfe's company	130	36-15-00
Lieutenant-Colonel Legard's company[152]	221	60-03-06
Captain Overton's company	158	43-05-08
The Governor's company	169	43-01-04
Major Goodricke's company	126	37-18-04
Captain Lowinger's company	125	35-11-08
Captain William Hotham's company	116	33-17-00
Captain William Legard's company	86	26-09-00
Captain Anlaby's company	128	36-05-04
Total:	1,259	

[151] TNA, SP 28/7/525.

[152] This included the usual £0-10-00 for a minister, £0-01-04 for a provost, £0-04-08 for a boatman, and £0-03-00 for a boom keeper, as well as £0-17-06 for a cannoneer.

APPENDIX III: THE ACCOUNTS OF THE GARRISON OF BEVERLEY, 1643

After the King's failed siege of Hull in July 1642 he left a small garrison in Beverley, but this was soon ejected by forces under Colonel Francis Boynton.[1] Thereafter Beverley remained in parliamentarian hands until August 1643. It became an important fundraising centre for the East Riding parliamentarians and a large garrison was established there in March 1643. The garrison accounts begin on 20 March and this date is corroborated by records from the Committee of Indemnity that demonstrate the garrison's inception as between Lady Day and Easter. This committee's records also show that Sir Edward Rodes of Great Houghton was appointed the garrison's commander-in-chief.[2] According to Sir John Hotham, the corporation of Beverley had agreed to quarter the garrison provided the town was reimbursed by an assessment collected across the East Riding.[3] The accounts cease a week before the arrest of Sir Edward Rodes and the unsuccessful attack on Beverley by royalist forces sent by Sir Hugh Cholmley on 29 June 1643.

Unlike Hull, whose garrison was entirely composed of infantry, Beverley's garrison was a composite force of cavalry, dragoons, and infantry. This made it more expensive to maintain. The accounts from 20 March to 22 June 1643 survive in a slim bound volume of forty-two folios in The National Archives.[4] Like the Hull garrison accounts, the lists of the individual troops and companies are repetitive and formulaic, so the same practice of summary and transcription has been employed as in Appendix II. The strength of infantry companies varied more widely and had larger numbers of under-officers. Their structure and pay were the same as their counterparts in the Hull garrison, but the companies in Beverley ranged in size from 70 to 200 men and their wage bills from £26 to £66.

[1] B.N. Reckitt, *Charles the First and Hull, 1639–1645* (2nd edn, Howden, 1988), p. 61.

[2] TNA, SP 24/7/13; SP 24/1/189; SP 24/3/35; SP 24/71.

[3] Bodl. MS Nalson II, no. 173.

[4] 'Disbursements to the garrison at Beverley, 1642 and 1643': TNA, SP 28/138/3.

The usual establishment for a troop of horse in these accounts included a captain, lieutenant, cornet, quartermaster, three corporals, and two trumpeters, with around sixty to seventy troopers. Captains were allowed six horses and received £13-13-00, lieutenants four horses and £6-06-00, cornets three horses and £4-14-06, quartermasters two horses and £3-03-00. The corporals and trumpeters were paid £1-01-00 each, and the troopers £0-17-06 each. The Governor's and Captain Hotham's troops retained a surgeon each paid at £1-08-00, along with a gunsmith and saddler at £1-15-00 between them. The usual weekly wage bill for a troop therefore ranged from £80 to £100.

The establishment for a company of dragoons included a captain, lieutenant, cornet, quartermaster, two or three corporals, and one or two drummers, with around fifty to sixty men. Dragoons were essentially mounted musketeers, whose principal function in the East Riding in 1643 appears to have been collecting assessments. Dragoon officers were paid considerably less than their counterparts among the cavalry, but the under-officers and men were allowed a higher rate than infantry, presumably to maintain their horses. Captains received £4-04-00 per week, lieutenants £1-15-00, cornets £1-08-00, quartermasters £1-01-00, corporals and drummers £0-14-00, with the rank and file receiving £0-10-06. The weekly pay bill for such a company was around £40.

For further notes on the presentation of the accounts, see the introduction to Appendix II.

Accounts

First week: disbursed for a week's pay on 20 March 1643

	Men	Pay
Horse		
The Governor's troop[5]	71	88-14-06
Captain Hotham's troop[6]	72	88-14-06

[5] This referred to Sir John Hotham as governor of Hull. With Sir John in Hull, in practice this troop would have been commanded by the lieutenant.

[6] Captain Hotham's lieutenant in this troop was the Dutchman Captain Lowinger.

Colonel Boynton's troop[7]	81	96-15-06
Sir Edward Rodes's troop[8]	69	89-18-00
Total:	293	364-01-18
Dragoons		
Captain Remington's company	69	42-14-00
Captain Crompton's company[9]	59	37-16-00
Captain Goodricke's company[10]	63	40-01-06
Total:	191	120-11-06

7 After the Hothams, the Boyntons were the next most prominent parliamentarian family in the East Riding, headed by the radical puritan baronet Sir Matthew Boynton of Barmston. His eldest son, Francis, married Constance Fiennes, daughter of Viscount Saye and Sele, and became a parliamentarian colonel. On 10 December 1642, Lord Fairfax complained to the Committee of Safety that Colonel Francis Boynton's regiment of foot had retired towards Hull, but on 29 December he acknowledged that Boynton had reinforced him at Selby with 40 horse and 500 foot. It was probably Colonel Francis Boynton, rather than his younger brother, Lieutenant-Colonel Matthew Boynton, who arrested Sir John Hotham at Beverley on 28 June 1643: C.V. Collier, *An Account of the Boynton Family and the Family Seat at Burton Agnes* (Middlesbrough, 1914); W. Dugdale, *The Visitation of the County of Yorke*, Surtees Society, 36 (1859), p. 126; BL, Add. MS 18,979, fos 129r–130v; *LJ*, V, p. 527; BL TT E59(2), *A true relation of the discovery of a most desperate and dangerous plot, for the delivering up, and surprising of the townes of Hull and Beverley*, 4 July 1643 (London, 1643), p. 5.

8 Sir Edward Rodes was arrested with the Hothams on 29 June 1643. Never brought to trial, he was later released and remained loyal to parliament during the second civil war: J. Rushworth, *Historical Collections* (London, 1691), Part III, II, pp. 276–80; Dugdale, *The Visitation of the County of Yorke*, p. 266; J.T. Cliffe, *The Yorkshire Gentry from the Reformation to the Civil War* (London, 1969), pp. 343, 359; C.W. Hatfield, *Historical Notices of Doncaster* (Doncaster, 1870), pp. 204–205; J. Wilkinson, *Worthies, Families and Celebrities of Barnsley and the District* (London, 1883), pp. 137–152.

9 Captain Crompton's dragoons were involved in the raid on Sherburn-in-Elmet by Sir Thomas Fairfax and John Hotham on 13 December 1642. Lord Fairfax complained on 29 December that many of Crompton's dragoons had deserted, requiring him to grant Crompton a commission to raise more: BL, TT E83(15), *A true relation of the fight at Sherburn, in the county of Yorke* (London, 1642), pp. 3–4; *LJ*, V, p. 527.

10 This Captain William Goodricke was the son of Major William Goodricke of Skidby in the Hull garrison. He first served as his father's lieutenant before being commissioned captain of a company of dragoons and serving in the Wressle castle garrison, where he succeeded Captain Carter as governor in 1643: TNA, SP 16/497/93, SP 24/50, SP 28/189; E121/4/8, no. 37; *CSPD 1641–1643*, p. 465; BL, TT E60(4), *Two letters, the one being intercepted by the parliament's forces which was sent from Sir Hugh Cholmley to Captain Gotherick* (London, 1643).

Foot		
Colonel Boynton's company	105	38-02-00
Lieutenant-Colonel Boynton's company[11]	124	38-05-06
Sergeant-Major Vickerman's company[12]	104	32-15-08
Captain Willies's company[13]	76	24-17-00
Captain Hotham's company[14]	147	40-17-10
Captain Lowinger's company at Cawood	150	41-08-04
Captain Carter's company[15]	122	39-18-02
Captain Appleyard's company	115	33-05-00
Captain Purefoy's company	132	38-01-10
Total:	1,075	327-11-04
Quartermaster to Colonel Boynton	1	1-08-00
Cannoneer at 2s 6d per diem	1	0-17-06
Wagoner at 4s per diem	1	1-08-06
Clark, 12d per diem	1	0-07-00
For 4 odd men	4	0-18-04
	8	4-19-04

[11] Matthew Boynton was Francis Boynton's younger brother and lieutenant-colonel. He later became governor of Scarborough castle, changing sides in 1648 only to be killed when the royalists were defeated at Wigan in August 1651: J. Binns, *'A Place of Great Importance': Scarborough in the civil wars, 1640–1660* (Preston, 1996), pp. 193–217, 287n.

[12] Henry Vickerman of Fraisthorpe resided in the neighbouring parish to the Boyntons and served as their sergeant-major. He was mentioned in Sir Matthew Boynton's settlement of 22 July 1641 to provide for his wife and family. He was killed during the siege of Scarborough castle in 1645: HHC: Wickham-Boynton MS, U DDWB/24/5; TNA, SP 23/188/336; Dugdale, *The Visitation of the County of Yorke*, p. 115; J. Binns, *Yorkshire in the Civil Wars: origins, impact and outcome* (Pickering, N. Yorks, 2004), p. 118.

[13] This was most probably Captain John Wittie of Beverley. From 1644, a Captain John Witty served in Sir Thomas Norcliffe's regiment of horse. Charges of horse stealing against him, while formerly a lieutenant to Captain Walter Bethell, were suspended by the Committee of Indemnity and handed over to several East Riding justices in 1650: TNA SP 28/266/97; SP 28/202/129; SP 24/5/89; SP 24/86; E121/4/8, no. 29; E121/5/7, no. 109; Dugdale, *The Visitation of the County of Yorke*, p. 221.

[14] This company was previously commanded by Captain Robert Hammond in the Hull garrison.

[15] Carter's company included a surgeon paid £1-00-00 for two weeks, six 'odd men' paid £1-08-00, and six cannoneers (of which five were at Cawood and one at Beverley) paid £0-17-06 each.

Paid to Captain Hansurion, paid by order from Captain Hotham from 13 February to 20 March being for five weeks' pay as Lieutenant to the Horse and his own allowance for 4 horses at £6-06-00 per week	1	31-10-00
For 2 odd men	2	0-09-04
Prisoners		1-01-01
	3	33-00-05
Week's total:	1,570	850-05-0

Second week: disbursed for a week's pay on 29 March 1643

Horse		
The Governor's troop	71	88-14-06
Captain Hotham's troop	72	88-14-06
Colonel Boynton's troop	79	95-01-06
Sir Edward Rodes's troop[16]	69	89-18-00
Total:	291	362-07-18
Dragoons		
Captain Remington's company	69	43-04-06
Captain Goodricke's company	64	40-01-06
Total:	133	83-06-00
Foot		
Colonel Boynton's company	106	39-00-04
Lieutenant-Colonel Boynton's company	121	37-16-00
Sergeant-Major Vickerman's company	125	37-18-04
Captain Willies's company	76	24-17-00
Captain Hotham's company[17]	138	39-13-10

[16] John Boynton of the Inner Temple, esq., was cornet to Sir Edward Rodes's troop. In May 1643 he was appointed lieutenant to Lieutenant-Colonel Matthew Boynton: TNA, SP 24/71; E121/4/8, no. 5.

[17] The pay of this company's lieutenant was advanced by Captain Hotham.

Captain Appleyard's company	117	33-14-04
Captain Purefoy's company	138	38-19-10
Captain Lowinger's company	150	41-08-04
Captain Carter's company[18]	126	52-11-11
Total:	1,107	345-19-11
Quartermaster of the foot	1	1-08-00
The colonel's wagoner	1	1-08-00
The cannoneer	1	0-17-06
The clerk's pay	1	0-07-00
To Lieutenant Sterman's wife		5-00-00
To a trooper who is lame and not fit for service	1	2-00-00
Remaining unpaid since the last pay day		0-05-00
And for 5 odd men	5	1-03-04
	10	12-09-10
This was passed by order from Captain Hotham:		
To Captain Froom[19]	1	6-06-00
Trumpet	1	1-01-00
Corporal	1	1-01-00
23 troopers at 2s 6d a man per diem	23	15-15-00
To Captain Vanderhurst for a fortnight[20]	1	6-01-04
To 5 troopers that came on foot	5	1-15-00
	32	31-19-04
Paid to Captain Hansueron at his going away from Beverley into Lincolnshire for 9 days' pay	1	7-04-00
For 2 odd men for 1 week	2	0-09-04
	3	10-14-10

[18]Carter's men were quartered separately at Cawood castle and there were several additional payments to his company. Six cannoneers were paid £10-10-00 for a fortnight's pay; Mr Watson, the surgeon, received £1-00-00 for a fortnight's pay and £2-00-00 to buy medicines; two sick men were paid £1-17-00 for the month; scouts and messengers received a total of £1-00-00; and £1-17-09 was allotted to the prisoners for a week.

[19]The Dutchman Matthias Froom had been part of the garrison at Scarborough but, refusing to concur in Sir Hugh Cholmley's defection, he offered his services to the Hothams and became captain-lieutenant to Lieutenant-General John Hotham's troop. He was briefly imprisoned at the Hothams' arrest, but served afterwards as a reformado captain under Lord Willoughby of Parham. He was mortally wounded at Gainsborough and died on 31 July 1643: TNA, SP 28/265/171–176.

[20]Another Dutchman, Cornelius Vanderhurst, also deserted Sir Hugh Cholmley at his defection. By 1644 he was a captain in Colonel John Alured's regiment of horse: TNA, SP 28/267/part iv/66–70.

April 5, 1643

This paid at Hull by Robert Stockton[21] and given in account to me		
To Sir Thomas Norcliffe's for his own pay: his officers and 60 men and horses[22]	66	42-14-00
Given to them at their coming from Scarborough		5-00-00
	66	47-14-00
This paid by order from Captain Hotham:		
To the company which was Captain Appleyard's at their coming back from Hull to be entered to Sir Edward Rodes	109	28-03-08
This company paid 5 April		
Week's total:	1,751	922-19-05

Third week: disbursed for a week's pay on 11 April 1643

Horse		
Colonel Boynton's troop	78	93-19-06
The Governor's troop[23]	71	88-14-06
Total:	149	182-14-00
Dragoons		
Captain Remington's company	68	42-14-00
Captain Goodricke's company	68	42-14-00
Total:	136	85-08-00
Foot		
Colonel Boynton's company	76	31-19-04
Lieutenant-Colonel Boynton's company	123	37-18-04
Sergeant-Major Vickerman's company[24]	103	33-16-08
Captain Owram's company[25]	108	31-12-04

[21] This was probably Robert Stockdale, secretary to Sir John Hotham: HHC: C BRS/7/74, BRS/7/79, BRS/7/81; J. Tickell, *History of the Town and County of Kingston-upon-Hull* (Hull, 1798), p. 382.

[22] Sir John Hotham's son-in-law Sir Thomas Norcliffe also abandoned Sir Hugh Cholmley after Cholmley defected: TNA, SP 28/253a/part i/42; SP 28/299/768; Cliffe, *The Yorkshire Gentry*, p. 266; Dugdale, *The Visitation of the County of Yorke*, p. 341; BL, TT E86(40), *The kingdom's weekly intelligencer* (London, 1643); BL, TT E95(9), *A true and exact relation of all the proceedings of Sir Hugh Cholmleys revolt*, 7 April 1643 (London, 1643).

[23] Note in margin: 'This makes 3 weeks that I paid my master's troop as accounted to Robert Stockton.'

[24] This included pay for four sick men of Captain Purefoy's company.

[25] This was probably Robert Orme of South Newbald: Dugdale, *The Visitation of the County of Yorke*, p. 154.

Captain Lowinger's company	139	39-02-10
Captain Willies's company	80	25-01-08
Sir Edward Rodes's company[26]	106	31-03-00
Total:	735	230-14-02
More paid to Sir Thomas Remington[27] which he paid to Captain Crompton's men, which came to him when their captain was taken.		5-01-06
He had before of the country's money of the old assessment £36		
More to Sir Thomas Remington to make up a week's pay at his going into Holderness to collect money		6-14-00
		11-15-06
[Colonel Boynton]		
For his wagoner	1	1-08-00
Quartermaster	1	1-08-00
Cannoneer	1	0-17-06
Clerk	1	0-07-00
	4	4-06-00
This was paid by Robert Stockton but given me in account:		
To Captain Carter		30-00-00
Sir Thomas Norcliffe for a week's pay	66	42-04-00
To his troop when they went to Lincoln		34-08-00
	66	106-12-00
To 4 cannoneers at 17s 6d a man	4	3-09-00
To the prisoners		0-07-06
To a man of Captain Hotham's troop by order from Sir Edward Rodes	1	1-04-00
To two odd men	2	0-09-04
To several messengers for scouts to discover the enemy		1-01-06
	7	6-11-04
Week's total:	1,097	627-15-06

[26] This company was formerly under Captain Appleyard.

[27] Sir Thomas Remington, son of Richard Remington of Lund, captained a troop of horse in the Beverley garrison: TNA, SP 23/113/582–593, SP 28/189, SP 28/202/129, SP 28/299/753; Cliffe, *The Yorkshire Gentry*, p. 359.

Fourth week: disbursed for a week's pay on 18 April 1643

Dragoons		
Captain Remington's company	68	43-04-06
Captain Goodricke's company	68	42-14-00
Total:	136	85-18-06
Foot		
Captain Lowinger's company	137	38-13-06
Sergeant-Major Vickerman's company	124	35-08-08
Colonel Boynton's company[28]	83	43-17-02
Lieutenant-Colonel Boynton's company	135	39-05-08
Captain Owram's company	112	32-11-00
Sir Edward Rodes's company	110	37-06-08
Captain Willies's company	84	25-19-08
Total:	785	253-02-04
To 4 cannoneers at 17s 6d a man	4	03-10-00
To the prisoners this week		0-07-06
To 2 prisoners for a day		0-00-06
To scouts into several places to discover the enemy		1-00-00
For 2 odd men	2	0-09-04
For my pay for 7 weeks till 18 April	1	14-00-00
	7	19-07-04
Week's total:	928	358-08-02

Fifth week: disbursed for a week's pay on 25 April 1643

Dragoons		
Captain Remington's company	69	43-04-06
Captain Goodricke's company	68	44-05-06
Total:	136	87-10-00
Foot		
Colonel Boynton's company	105	47-13-06
Lieutenant-Colonel Boynton's company	152	44-18-00
Captain Lowinger's company	141	39-13-04

[28]Paid as part of Colonel Boynton's company from this week was a drum major at £0-08-02, a wagoner at £1-12-08, a cannoneer at £0-17-06, a quartermaster at £1-08-00, and a clerk at £0-10-00.

Sergeant-Major Vickerman's company	183	51-08-04
Sir Edward Rodes's company	107	37-02-08
Captain Willies's company	86	26-19-08
Captain Owram's company	113	32-15-00
Total:	887	280-10-06
To 4 cannoneers at 17s 6d a man per week	4	3-10-00
Prisoners		0-11-00
For mending the carriages		0-15-00
For bringing arms and ammunition from Hull and removing the magazine		0-05-00
To the provost marshal for 7 weeks ended this day		7-00-00
To scouts this week		0-12-00
For 5 odd men	5	1-03-04
More for my pay for this week	1	2-00-00
	10	15-16-04
Week's total:	1,033	383-16-10

Sixth week: disbursed for a week's pay on 5 May 1643

Dragoons		
Captain Remington's company	72	44-16-00
Captain Goodricke's company listed but sums not entered		
Foot		
Colonel Boynton's company[29]	84	49-08-06
Lieutenant-Colonel Boynton's company	153	45-03-00
Captain Lowinger's company	142	39-16-04
Sergeant-Major Vickerman's company	191	53-06-04
Captain Willies's company	88	26-19-04
Sir Edward Rodes's company	112	37-16-00
Captain Owram's company	113	32-15-08
Total:	883	285-05-02
To 4 cannoneers at 17s 6d a man per week	4	3-10-00
To the prisoners		0-11-00

[29]A separate account for the colonel and lieutenant-colonel's companies, signed by Francis Boynton himself, survives for 5 May, listing the colonel's company at 108 men: TNA, SP 28/7/164.

To Richard Ribles upon his petition by order from Sir Edward Rodes		0-14-00
For salt sent to Cawood castle		1-10-06
For 5 odd men	5	1-03-04
To the provost marshal for a week's pay	1	1-01-00
For several men to go out scouts		0-12-00
My pay this week	1	2-00-00
	11	11-01-10
Week's total:	966	341-03-00

Seventh week: disbursed for a week's pay on 9 May 1643

Horse		
Lieutenant-Colonel Boynton's troop	64	68-15-06
Dragoons		
Captain Remington's company	72	44-16-00
Captain Goodricke's company listed but sums not entered		
Foot		
Colonel Boynton's company[30]	170	62-13-07
Lieutenant-Colonel Boynton's company	159	46-06-04
Captain Lowinger's company	149	41-07-02
Sergeant-Major Vickerman's company	193	52-17-00
Captain Willies's company	91	28-07-00
Sir Edward Rodes's company	108	37-16-00
Captain Owram's company	105	31-17-00
Total:	975	301-04-01
To 3 cannoneers at 17s 6d a man per week	3	2-12-06
To the prisoners		0-08-00
To the provost marshal	1	1-01-00
To several scouts to discover the enemy		0-06-00
To two odd men	2	0-09-04
To one sick man of Captain Purefoy's company	1	0-04-08
For my pay	1	2-00-00
To Major Vickerman for several men which Sir Edward Rodes sent abroad		2-02-06
	8	9-04-00
Week's total:	1,119	423-19-07

[30] An identical separate account for the colonel and lieutenant-colonel's companies, signed by Francis Boynton himself, survives for 9 May. It included £0-05-09 for 'charges about the brass piece': TNA, SP 28/7/172.

Eighth week: disbursed for a week's pay on 19 May 1643

Horse		
Lieutenant-Colonel Boynton's troop	69	74-18-00
Sir Thomas Remington's troop	72	76-13-06
Total:	141	151-11-06
Dragoons		
Captain Remington's company	61	39-00-06
Foot		
Colonel Boynton's company	182	65-03-10
Lieutenant-Colonel Boynton's company	159	46-06-04
Captain Lowinger's company	143	39-19-02
Sergeant-Major Vickerman's company[31]	185	53-11-08
Captain Willies's company	94	28-07-00
Sir Edward Rodes's company	134	42-19-00
Captain Owram's company	109	31-17-00
Total:	1,006	308-04-00
To 5 cannoneers	5	4-07-06
Provost marshal	1	1-01-00
Prisoners		0-08-00
To several scouts to discover the enemy		1-04-00
To a sick man of Captain Purefoy's company	1	0-04-08
To 3 odd men	3	0-14-00
For medicines for the goods in the parks		0-06-08
For my pay	1	2-00-00
For bugg barrels and other things about the ordnance		0-05-00
	11	10-10-07
Week's total:	1,219	509-06-07

[31] This included £0-10-00 for a physician.

Ninth week: disbursed for a week's pay on 3 June 1643

Foot		
Colonel Boynton's company[32]	187	66-12-06
Lieutenant-Colonel Boynton's company[33]	185	52-07-08
Sergeant-Major Vickerman's company	187	53-06-08
Sir Edward Rodes's company	153	45-14-08
Captain Owram's company	111	33-05-04
Total:	823	251-06-10
To 4 cannoneers at 17s 6d a man per week	4	3-10-00
To several scouts for a fortnight, some day ten, some day twenty		4-13-00
To Mr Johnson	1	0-10-00
To the prisoners		0-09-06
For sacks that went with salt to Wressle castle and came not back again		0-04-06
To 2 odd men	2	0-09-04
To one for keeping the goods in the parks for two weeks	1	0-09-04
For my pay for a fortnight	1	4-00-00
To a sick man of Captain Purefoy's company	1	0-04-08
To Sir Edward Rodes for fixing of arms		0-06-08
To Sergeant-Major Vickerman upon his note for bringing arms from Hull and fixing them		0-16-00
To the provost marshal for a week	1	1-01-00
To Sir Thomas Remington the night before he was taken in part of a week's pay. This paid by Robert Stockton in Hull and given me in account		23-02-00
For 8 men which was of Sir Thomas Remington's troop and now paid as foot, by order from Sir Edward Rodes	8	1-17-04
	19	41-13-04
Week's total:	842	302-15-02

32 An identical account for this company, signed by Colonel Francis Boynton, survives for 3 June: TNA, SP 28/7/473.

33 An account for this company, signed by Lieutenant-Colonel Matthew Boynton, survives for 3 June but does not mention that twenty-three of this company had previously been in Lieutenant-Colonel Boynton's troop but were now being paid as foot: TNA, SP 28/7/474.

Paid out of Holderness assessment, and the Governor is to pay yet nothing allowed him for these 4 weeks.

9 June 1643: paid to Captain Legard for a month's pay for his troop, for himself at £2-02-00 per week, and for the rest of his officers and 68 troopers, the sum of	75	286-06-00
And more to him which he paid to Cornet Hotham at his going from the troop for a fortnight's pay		7-00-00
		293-06-00

[Signed by] Robert Legard

Tenth week: disbursed for a week's pay on 12 June 1643

Foot		
Colonel Boynton's company[34]	186	66-09-06
Lieutenant-Colonel Boynton's company[35]	170	48-17-08
Sir Edward Rodes's company	142	46-14-08
Sergeant-Major Vickerman's company	190	53-16-10
Captain Owram's company	111	33-05-04
Total:	794	249-04-00
The cannoneers being 4	4	3-10-00
To the scouts		1-05-00
To Mr Johnson, the minister[36]	1	0-10-00
To the prisoners		0-04-06
In the parks		0-04-08
Mine own pay	1	2-00-00
To 21 men that were of Sir Thomas Remington's troop and a corporal and a trumpet	23	6-10-00
To a sick man of Captain Purefoy's company	1	0-04-08
Provost marshal	1	1-01-00
For 2 odd men	2	0-09-04

[34] A similar account for this company, signed by Colonel Francis Boynton, survives for 12 June, listing 186 men but £65-18-06 in pay: TNA, SP28/7/491.

[35] An identical account for this company, signed by Lieutenant-Colonel Matthew Boynton, survives for 12 June: TNA, SP28/7/492.

[36] This was probably the minister Robert Johnson who replaced the sequestered royalist Richard Faucon in the rectory of Bainton in 1643: TNA, SP 24/57; Rushworth, *Historical Collections*, Part III, II, pp. 276–280.

To 26 troopers which were of Sir Thomas Remington's troop, and now gone to Newland. Paid them 10 June	26	25-01-06
	60	41-00-08
Week's total:	854	290-04-04
More to one of Sir Thomas Remington's men for a fortnight's pay	1	0-09-04

[*Inserted on separate paper*]

Disbursed for prisoner's diet since 27 May till 12 June 1643:

For one prisoner, 2 weeks	0-03-00
For one prisoner, 1 week	0-01-06
	0-04-06

Eleventh week: disbursed for a week's pay on 20 and 22 June 1643

Foot		
Captain Owram's company[37]	118	34-18-00
Colonel Boynton's company[38]	180	65-08-06
Lieutenant-Colonel Boynton's company	158	56-17-08
Sir Edward Rodes's company	146	47-18-06
Sergeant-Major Vickerman's company	192	53-17-02
Total:	794	258-19-10
To John Grant for his week's pay at his going to Hull	1	[*Nothing entered*]
To cannoneers		[*Nothing entered*]
For scouts this week		7-04-00
To Mr Johnson	1	0-10-00
In the parks		0-04-08
For my pay	1	2-00-00
For 2 odd men	2	0-09-04
To a sick man of Captain Purefoy's	1	0-04-08
Provost marshal	1	1-01-00

[37] Note in margin: 'This paid 20 June at his going to Winestead.'

[38] A similar account for this company, signed by Colonel Francis Boynton, survives for 22 June, listing 182 men and £65-03-10 in pay: TNA, SP 28/7/512.

To Lieutenant-Colonel Boynton for 27 men of his troop which came out of Lincolnshire, and now entertained in his company by order from Sir Edward Rodes	27	6-06-00
To two soldiers more of Sir Edward Rodes's company, one a corporal, another a sergeant	2	0-17-06
To one odd man more	1	0-04-08
Prisoners		0-09-06
	37	19-11-04
Week's total:[39]	831	278-11-02

39 The total pay for this week was not given, so it was calculated by the editor.

BIBLIOGRAPHY

Primary Sources

Manuscript sources

Beinecke Rare Book and Manuscript Library, Yale University

Osborn Shelves, b101: The commonplace book of Ralph Assheton of Kirkby Grange

Osborn Shelves, fb87: Memoirs of Sir Philip Warwick

Bodleian Library

MS Carte VI

MS Clarendon XXI, XXIII, XXIV

MS Fairfax XXXVI

MS Tanner LXI, LXII, LXIV, LXVI

MS Nalson II, III, XI, XIII, XXII

British Library

Add. MS 11,692: Manuscripts presented by the Hon. P.P. Bouverie

Add. MS 18,979: Fairfax correspondence, 1625–1688

Add. MS 28,082: Establishments, muster rolls, accounts, and army papers, 1640–1702

Add. MS 31,116: Parliamentary journal of Lawrence Whitacre, 1642–1647

Add. MS 32,096: State papers, historical documents, and official and private letters, 1086–1760, vol. 6

Add. MS 44,848: Historical letters and papers of the sixteenth and seventeenth centuries

Harleian MS 164: Parliamentary journal of Sir Simonds D'Ewes

Sloane MS 1,519: Original letters, 1574–1667

East Riding Record Office, Treasure House, Beverley

BC II 7/4/1: Beverley minute book 1597–1660

PE1/2: St Mary's, Beverley, parish registers, 1637–1665

PE1/53: Churchwardens' accounts of St Mary's, Beverley, 1642–1643

Hull History Centre

C BRB/3: Bench book of the mayor and aldermen of Hull, 1609–1650

C BRF/6: Receipts for money paid by the corporation of Hull, 1541–1910

C BRL: Letters and correspondence of the corporation of Hull

C BRS/7: Documents relating to the civil wars

U DDCY: Cholmley MSS

U DDHO: Hotham MSS

U DDWB: Wickham-Boynton MSS

College of Arms, London

Curia Militaris: Records of the High Court of Chivalry, 1634–1640

The National Archives

E121: Certificates for the sale of crown lands

SP 16: State papers of the reign of Charles I

SP 19: Papers of the Committee for Advance of Money

SP 22: Papers of the Committee for Plundered Ministers

SP 24: Papers of the Committee for Indemnity

SP 28: Commonwealth Exchequer Papers

Printed primary sources

Bell, R. (ed.), *The Fairfax Correspondence: memorials of the civil war*, 2 vols (London, 1849)

Bickley, F. (ed.), *A Report on the Manuscripts of the Late Reginald Rawdon Hastings, esq.*, HMC, 78, 4 vols (London, 1928–1947)

Binns, J. (ed.), *The Memoirs and Memorials of Sir Hugh Cholmley of Whitby 1600–1657*, YASRS, 153 (2000)

Boyle, J.R. *Memoirs of Master John Shawe* (Hull, 1882)

Calendar of State Papers Domestic

Civil War Tracts, York Minster Library

Clay, J.W. (ed.), *Abstracts of Yorkshire Wills*, YASRS, 9 (1890)

Cust, R.P. and A.J. Hopper (eds), *Cases in the High Court of Chivalry, 1634–1640*, Publications of the Harleian Society, new series, 18 (2006)

Dugdale, W. *The Visitation of the County of Yorke*, Surtees Society, 36 (1859)

Green, M.A.E. (ed.), *Calendar of the Committee for Compounding (Domestic), 1643–1660*, 5 vols (London, 1889)

——— (ed.), *Calendar of the Committee for the Advance of Money (Domestic), 1642–1656*, 3 vols (London, 1888)

Hackett, J. *Scrinia Reserata: a memorial offered to the great deservings of John Williams* (London, 1693)

Hope, E. (ed.), *A Puritan Parish Clerk: a commentary on current events made in the registers of St Mary's church, Beverley, by Nicholas Pearson, parish clerk, 1636–1653* (Beverley, n.d.)

Johnson, G.W. (ed.), *The Fairfax Correspondence: memorials of the Reign of Charles I*, 2 vols (London, 1848)

Journals of the House of Commons (*CJ*)

Journals of the House of Lords (*LJ*)

Keeble, N.H. (ed.), *Memoirs of the Life of Colonel Hutchinson* (London, 1995)

Macray, W.D. (ed.), *History of the Rebellion and Civil Wars in England Begun in the Year 1641 by Edward, Earl of Clarendon*, 6 vols (Oxford, 1888)

Parsons, D. (ed.), *The Diary of Sir Henry Slingsby of Scriven, Bart* (London, 1836)

Portland MS, HMC, 29, 13th Report, Appendix, Part I (London, 1891), vol. I

Powell, J.R. and E.K. Timings (eds), *Documents Relating to the Civil War, 1642–1648*, Navy Records Society, 105 (1963)

Rushworth, J. *Historical Collections* (London, 1691), Parts I–IV

Shaw, J. 'The life of Master John Shaw', in C. Jackson (ed.), *Yorkshire Diaries and Autobiographies in the Seventeenth and Eighteenth Centuries*, Surtees Society, 65 (1877), pp. 119–162, 358–444

Sutherland MS, HMC, 5th Report, Appendix (London, 1876)

Thomason Tracts, British Library

Tindall Wildridge, T. (ed.), *The Hull Letters: documents from the Hull Records, 1625–1646* (Hull, 1886)

Trevelyan, W.C. and C.E. Trevelyan (eds), *Trevelyan Papers, Part III*, Camden Society, first series, 105 (1872)

Vicars, J. *Jehovah-Jireh: God in the Mount or Englands Parliamentarie Chronicle* (London, 1644)

Whitelocke, B. *Memorials of English Affairs from the Beginning of the Reign of King Charles the First to the Happy Restoration of King Charles the Second*, 4 vols (Oxford, 1853)

Secondary sources

Books

Allison, K.J. (ed.), *The Victoria History of the County of York, East Riding. Vol. VI: the borough and liberties of Beverley* (Oxford, 1989)

Bean, W.W. *The Parliamentary Representation of the Six Northern Counties of England* (Hull, 1890)

Binns, J. *'A Place of Great Importance': Scarborough in the civil wars* (Preston, 1996)

——— *Yorkshire in the Civil Wars: origins, impact and outcome* (Pickering, N. Yorks, 2004)

Cliffe, J.T. *Puritans in Conflict: the puritan gentry during and after the civil wars* (London, 1988)

——— *The Yorkshire Gentry from the Reformation to the Civil War* (London, 1969)

Collier, C.V. *An Account of the Boynton Family and the Family Seat at Burton Agnes* (Middlesborough, 1914)

Cross, C. *Urban Magistrates and Ministers: religion in Hull and Leeds from the Reformation to the civil war*, University of York: Borthwick Papers, 67 (1985)

Dalton, C. *History of the Wrays of Glentworth, 1523–1852*, 2 vols (London, 1880)

Davis, R. *The Trade and Shipping of Hull, 1500–1700*, East Yorkshire Local History Society, 17 (1964)

English, B. *Beverley North Bar* (Beverley, 2009)

——— *The Great Landowners of East Yorkshire, 1530–1910* (Hemel Hempstead, 1990)

Fissel, M.C. *The Bishops' Wars* (Cambridge, 1994)

——— (ed.), *War and Government in Britain, 1598–1650* (Manchester, 1991)

Fletcher, A.J. *The Outbreak of the English Civil War* (London, 1981)

Forster, G.C.F. *The East Riding Justices of the Peace in the Seventeenth Century*, East Yorkshire Local History Society, 30 (1973)

Gent, T. *Gent's History of Hull, Reprinted in Fac-simile of the Original of 1735* (Hull, 1869)

Gillet, E. and K.A. MacMahon, *A History of Hull* (Oxford, 1980)

Goodricke, C.A. *History of the Goodricke Family* (London, 1885)

Greaves, R.L. and R. Zaller (eds), *A Biographical Dictionary of British Radicals in the Seventeenth Century*, 3 vols (Brighton, 1982–1984)

Hatfield, C.W. *Historical Notices of Doncaster* (Doncaster, 1870)

Heal, F. and C. Holmes, *The Gentry in England and Wales, 1500–1700* (Basingstoke, 1994)

Holmes, C. *Seventeenth-century Lincolnshire* (Lincoln, 1980)

Hopper, A. *'Black Tom': Sir Thomas Fairfax and the English Revolution* (Manchester, 2007)

——— *'The Readiness of the People': the formation and emergence of the army of the Fairfaxes, 1642–1643*, University of York: Borthwick Papers, 92 (1997)

Howes, A. and M. Foreman, *Town and Gun: the 17th-century defences of Hull* (Hull, 1999)

Johnson, D. *Adwalton Moor, 1643: the battle that changed a war* (Pickering, N. Yorks, 2003)

Keeler, M.F. *The Long Parliament, 1640–1641: a biographical study of its members* (Philadelphia, 1954)

Kyle, C.R. (ed.), *Parliament, Politics and Elections 1604–1648*, Camden Society, fifth series, 17 (Cambridge, 2001)

Legard, J.D. *The Legards of Anlaby and Ganton* (London, 1926)

Matthew, H.C.G. and Brian Harrison (eds), *The Oxford Dictionary of National Biography*, 60 vols (Oxford, 2004)

Newman, P.R. *The Old Service: royalist regimental colonels and the civil war, 1642–1646* (Manchester, 1993)

——— *Royalist Officers in England and Wales, 1642–1660: a biographical dictionary* (London, 1981)

Oliver, G. *The History and Antiquities of the Town and Minster of Beverley* (Beverley, 1829)

Ormrod, W.M. (ed.), *The Lord Lieutenants and High Sheriffs of Yorkshire, 1066–2000* (Barnsley, 2000)

Poulson, G. *History and Antiquities of the Seigniory of Holderness*, 2 vols (London, 1840)

Powell, J.R. *The Navy in the English Civil War* (London, 1962)

Pugh, R.B. (ed.), *The Victoria History of the County of York, East Riding*, 6 vols (London, 1969)

Purdy, J.D. *Yorkshire Hearth Tax Returns*, Studies in Regional and Local History, 7 (University of Hull, 1991)

Reckitt, B.N. *Charles the First and Hull, 1639–1645* (2nd edn, Howden, 1988)

Roebuck, P. *Yorkshire Baronets, 1640–1760: families, estates and fortunes* (Oxford, 1980)

Saltmarshe, P. *History and Chartulary of the Hothams of Scorborough in the East Riding of Yorkshire, 1100–1700* (York, 1914)

Sheahan, J.J. *History of the Town and Port of Kingston-upon-Hull* (2nd edn, Beverley, 1866)

Simpson, J.A. and E.S.C. Weiner (eds), *The Oxford English Dictionary*, 20 vols (2nd edn, Oxford, 1989)

Stirling, A.M.W. *The Hothams: being the chronicles of the Hothams of Scorborough and South Dalton from their hitherto unpublished family papers*, 2 vols (London, 1918)

Sunderland, F.H. *Marmaduke, Lord Langdale* (London, 1926)

Tickell, J. *History of the Town and County of Kingston-upon-Hull* (Hull, 1798)

Wheater, W. *History of Sherburn and Cawood* (London, 1882)

Wilkinson, J. *Worthies, Families and Celebrities of Barnsley and the District* (London, 1883)

Articles

Atherton, I. 'The accounts of the royalist garrison of Lichfield Close, 1643–1645', *Staffordshire Studies*, 18 (2007), pp. 63–96

——— 'Royalist finances in the English civil war: the case of Lichfield garrison, 1643–1645', *Midland History*, 33 (2008), pp. 43–67

Binns, J. 'Captain Browne Bushell: North Sea adventurer and pirate', *Northern History*, 27 (1991), pp. 90–105

——— 'Scarborough and the civil wars, 1642–1651', *Northern History*, 22 (1986), pp. 95–122

——— 'Sir Hugh Cholmley: Whitby's benefactor or beneficary', *Northern History*, 30 (1994), pp. 86–104

Broxap, E. 'The sieges of Hull during the great civil war', *English Historical Review*, 20 (1905), pp. 457–473

Capern, A.L. 'The Hotham family and its papers', *Archives*, 23 (1998), pp. 100–117

Cox, J.C. 'The parliamentary survey of the benefices of the East Riding', *TERAS*, 2 (1894), pp. 24–67

——— 'The parliamentary survey of the benefices of the East Riding', *TERAS*, 4 (1896), pp. 50–65

English, B. 'Sir John Hotham and the English civil war', *Archives*, 20 (1992), pp. 217–224

Firth, C.H. 'Sir Hugh Cholmley's memoirs touching Scarborough', *English Historical Review*, 32 (1917), pp. 568–587

Forster, G.C.F. 'County government in Yorkshire during the interregnum', *Northern History*, 12 (1976), pp. 84–104

——— 'Faction and county government in early Stuart Yorkshire', *Northern History*, 11 (1975–1976), pp. 70–86

Hirst, J.H. 'The castle of Kingston-upon-Hull', *TERAS*, 3 (1895), pp. 24–39

Holmes, C. 'Colonel King and Lincolnshire politics, 1642–1646', *Historical Journal*, 16 (1973), pp. 451–484

Hopper, A. 'A directory of parliamentarian allegiance in Yorkshire during the civil wars', *YAJ*, 73 (2001), pp. 85–122

——— '"Fitted for desperation": honour and treachery in Parliament's Yorkshire command, 1642–1643', *History*, 86 (2001), pp. 138–154

——— '"The popish army of the north": anti-catholicism and parliamentary allegiance in Yorkshire, 1642–1646', *Recusant History*, 25 (2000), pp. 12–28

——— 'The self-fashioning of gentry turncoats during the English civil wars', *Journal of British Studies*, 49 (2010), pp. 236–257

Morrill, J. 'The northern gentry and the great rebellion', *Northern History*, 15 (1979), pp. 66–87

Newman, P.R. 'Catholic royalist activists in the north, 1642–1646', *Recusant History*, 14 (1977), pp. 26–38

——— 'Catholic royalists of northern England, 1642–1645', *Northern History*, 15 (1979), pp. 88–95

——— 'The royalist north: a rejoinder', *Northern History*, 17 (1981), pp. 253–255

Nuttall, W.L.F. 'The Yorkshire commissioners appointed for the trial of King Charles the first', *YAJ*, 43 (1971), pp. 147–157

Ryder, I.E. 'The seizure of Hull and its magazine, January 1642', *YAJ*, 61 (189), pp. 139–148

Scott, D. '"Hannibal at our gates": loyalists and fifth-columnists during the Bishops' Wars – the case of Yorkshire', *Historical Research*, 70 (1997), pp. 269–293

——— 'The "Northern Gentlemen", the Parliamentary Independents and Anglo-Scottish relations in the Long Parliament', *Historical Journal*, 42 (1999), pp. 347–375

Woolrych, A. 'Yorkshire's treaty of neutrality', *History Today*, 6 (1956), pp. 696–704

Theses

Bennett, R.A.H. 'Enforcing the law in revolutionary England: Yorkshire, 1640–1660' (unpublished PhD thesis, University of London, 1988)

Hopper, A.J. 'The extent of support for parliament in Yorkshire during the early stages of the first civil war' (unpublished DPhil thesis, University of York, 1999)

Jones, J. 'The war in the north: the northern parliamentarian army in the English civil war, 1642–1645' (unpublished PhD thesis, York University, Toronto, 1991)

Newman, P.R. 'The royalist army in the north of England, 1642–1645' (unpublished DPhil thesis, University of York, 1978)

INDEX

The names of ships and newsbooks are given in italics.